153

COGNITIVE
PSYCHOLOGY

Richard Gross and Rob McIlveen

Hodder & Stoughton

A MEMBER OF THE HODDER HEADLINE GROUP

DEDICATION

To Jan, Tanya and Jo, with even more love.   R.G.
To William. For the benefit of Mr. Kite.   R.M.

ACKNOWLEDGEMENTS

We would like to thank Tim Gregson-Williams and Liz Lowther at Hodder & Stoughton for their continuing patience, help and guidance, and good humour. Liz, we shall be sorry to see you go.

Order queries: Please contact Bookpoint Ltd, 130 Milton Park, Abingdon, Oxon OX14 4SB. Telephone: (44) 01235 400414. Fax: (44) 01235 400454. Lines are open from 9 am - 6 pm Monday to Saturday, with a 24-hour message answering service. You can also order through our website: www.hodderheadline.co.uk

British Library Cataloguing in Publication Data
A catalogue record for this title is available from The British Library

ISBN 0 340 69100 X

First published 1997
Impression number   10 9 8 7 6 5
Year   2004 2003

Typeset by Wearset, Boldon, Tyne and Wear.
Printed in Great Britain for Hodder & Stoughton Educational, a division of Hodder Headline Plc, 338, Euston Road, London NW1 3BH by J. W. Arrowsmith Ltd., Bristol.

CONTENTS

Part 2: Memory

Part 3: Language and thought

PREFACE

Our aim in this book is to provide an introduction to the area of cognitive psychology. In order to do this, we have divided the book into three parts. The first, *Perception and Attention*, comprises six chapters. In Chapter 1, we consider visual perception and perceptual organisation. Chapter 2 deals with some of the most influential theories of visual perception. Chapter 3 looks at the development of visual perceptual abilities in human neonates and infants, while Chapter 4 discusses other approaches to studying perceptual development. Chapter 5 considers focused (or selective) attention, and Chapter 6 deals with divided attention.

Part 2, *Memory*, consists of five chapters. Chapter 7 discusses the nature of memory and introduces the Multi-Store model of memory, while Chapter 8 looks at some alternatives to the Multi-Store model. Chapter 9 deals with the organisation of information in memory, and Chapter 10 is concerned with theories of forgetting. In Chapter 11, we consider some practical applications of memory research.

Part 3, *Language and Thought*, comprises six chapters.

Chapter 12 is concerned with describing language development, while Chapter 13 discusses theories of how that development takes place. Chapter 14 considers attempts to teach human language to non-human animals, especially non-human primates. Chapter 15 looks at some aspects of reading and writing, and Chapter 16 discusses research into problem-solving and decision-making. The final chapter, Chapter 17, considers the relationship between language and thought.

We believe that this book covers the major aspects of cognitive psychology as it would be taught on most courses, including A level and undergraduate courses. While the sequence of chapters and much of the content is based on the revised AEB A level syllabus, the general issues and major theories that are discussed represent the core of this central and influential area of psychology. For the purposes of revision, we have included detailed summaries of the material that is presented in each chapter. Although we have not included a separate glossary, the Index contains page numbers in **bold** which refer to definitions and main explanations of particular concepts for easy reference.

PART 1
Perception and attention

VISUAL PERCEPTION AND PERCEPTUAL ORGANISATION

Introduction and overview

When a person walks away from us, we do not believe that he or she is 'shrinking before our very eyes', and a pint glass of beer remains a pint glass of beer no matter what angle we look at it from. Our experience of the visual world may seem to be mundane and obvious, but when we compare what we experience (a world in which objects remain stable and constant) with what our sense organs receive in the form of physical stimulation (a state of near continuous flux), it is almost as if there are two entirely different 'worlds' involved. Psychologists use the terms *sensation* and *perception* to distinguish between these two 'worlds'. Sensation refers to the experiences that physical stimuli (such as light or sound) elicit in our various sense organs (such as the eye and ear). Perception refers to the ways in which incoming sensory information is organised and interpreted in order to enable us to form inner representations of the external world.

Our aim in this chapter is to look at some basic visual perceptual phenomena and the ways in which visual perception is organised (other visual perceptual phenomena will be discussed in relation to various theories of visual perception presented in Chapter 2). We are concentrating on vision, to the near exclusion of the other senses, because vision is the dominant sense modality in humans and, as a result, much more is known about perception in that sense modality than in any other (Eysenck, 1993). Many of the principles that govern human visual perception were first uncovered

by a German 'school' of psychological thought whose 'students' called themselves *Gestalt psychologists*. We begin this chapter by examining their contribution to our knowledge about visual perception.

Gestalt psychology and visual perception

As long ago as 1890, a German philosopher called Ehrenfels claimed that many groups of stimuli acquire a pattern quality which is over and above the sum of their parts. A square, for example, is more than a simple assembly of lines – it has 'squareness'. Ehrenfels called this 'emergent property' *Gestalt qualität* (or form quality). In the early part of this century, Gestalt psychologists (the best known of whom were Max Wertheimer, Kurt Koffka and Wolfgang Köhler) attempted to discover the principles through which sensory information is interpreted. Gestalt psychologists argued that as well as creating a coherent perceptual experience that is more than the sum of its parts, the brain does this in regular and predictable ways, and that these organisational principles are largely innately determined. We will consider the claim about innateness in Chapters 3 and 4.

Form perception

If we are going to structure incoming sensory information, then we must perceive objects as being separate from other stimuli and as having a meaningful form.

FIGURE AND GROUND

The first perceptual task we have to undertake when confronted with an object (or *figure*) is to recognise it. To do this, we must perceive the figure as being distinct from the surroundings (or *ground*) against which it appears. The *familiarity* of a figure is one 'role' that determines whether it is perceived as figure or ground. However, unfamiliar and even meaningless forms are also seen as figures, as shown in Figure 1.1.

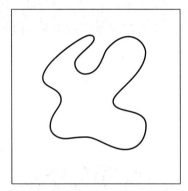

Figure 1.1 Even unfamiliar objects are immediately perceived when the outline is closed.

What this illustrates is that whilst familiarity is important for the perception of form, it is not necessary. If it was, we would have difficulty perceiving objects we had never seen before (Carlson, 1987). One of the strongest determinants of figure and ground is *surroundedness*. Areas enclosed by a *contour* are generally seen as figures, whereas the surrounding area is generally seen as ground. Research indicates that *size*, *orientation* and *symmetry* also play a role in figure-ground separation.

In some cases, though, there may not be enough information in a pattern to allow us to easily distinguish between figure and ground. A good example of this is shown in Figure 1.2.

The dalmatian (the figure) is difficult to distinguish from the ground because it has few visible contours of its own and, as a result, appears to have no more form than its background (and this, of course, is the principle underlying *camouflage*).

In other cases, a figure may have clear contours, but is capable of being perceived in two very different ways

Figure 1.2 In the absence of sufficient cues, figure and ground are difficult to distinguish.

because it is not clear which part of the stimulus is the figure and which the ground. This is known as *figure-ground reversal*. A famous example of this is Rubin's vase (Rubin, 1915), shown in Figure 1.3 (see opposite).

In Rubin's vase, the figure-ground relationship continually reverses, so that it is perceived as either a white vase with a black background or two black profiles on a white background. However, the stimulus is *always* organised into a figure seen against a ground, and the reversal indicates that the same stimulus can trigger more than one perception (and we shall return to this later in this chapter, see page 10).

Figure 1.4 (a) and (b) shows two examples of the ways in which figure-ground reversal has been used by artists (see opposite).

GROUPING

Once we have discriminated figure from ground, the figure can be organised into a meaningful form. Gestalt psychologists believed that objects are perceived as *gestalten* (which has been variously translated as 'organised wholes', 'configurations' or 'patterns') rather than combinations of isolated sensations. When we bring

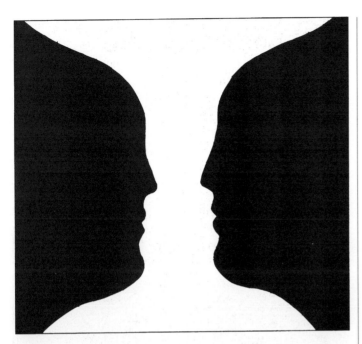

(a)

Figure 1.3   A white vase on a black background or two faces in silhouette?

order to our sensations and try to give them form, we use certain 'laws' for grouping stimuli together. Gestalt psychologists identified a number of 'laws' of perceptual organisation which illustrate their view that the perceived whole of an object is more than the sum of its parts.

These laws can be summarised under one heading, *the law of prägnanz,* according to which: 'psychological organisation will always be as good as the prevailing conditions allow. In this definition, "good" is undefined' (Koffka, 1935). According to Attneave (1954), 'good' can be defined as possessing a high degree of internal redundancy, that is, the structure of an unseen part is highly predictable from the visible parts. Similarly, according to Hochberg's (1978) *minimum principle,* if there is more than one way of organising a given visual stimulus, the one most likely to be perceived is the one requiring the least amount of information to perceive it.

In practice, the 'best' way of perceiving is to see things as symmetrical, uniform and stable, and this is achieved by following the laws of prägnanz. These are shown in Box 1.1, along with some auditory examples of them.

(b)

**Figure 1.4 (a) and (b)   Figure 1.4 (a) shows the use of reversible ground by a potter. The vase, a commemoration of the Queen's Silver Jubilee (1977), can also be perceived as the profiles of the Duke of Edinburgh (left) and the Queen (right).
Figure 1.4 (b) is a woodcut by the artist M.C. Escher. Either black devils or white angels can be seen in the ring.**

Box 1.1   Gestalt laws of perception

Proximity

Elements which appear close together – in space or time – tend to be perceived together, so that different spacings of dots produce four vertical lines or four horizontal lines:

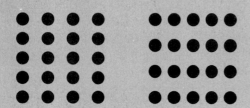

An auditory example of proximity would be the perception of a series of musical notes as a melody because they occur soon after one another in time.

Similarity

If figures are similar to each other, we tend to group them together. So the triangles and circles below are seen as columns of similar shapes rather than rows of dissimilar shapes.

When we hear all the separate voices in a choir as an entity, the principle of similarity is operating.

Good continuation

We tend to perceive smooth, continuous patterns rather than discontinuous ones. The pattern below could be seen as a series of alternating semi-circles, but tends to be perceived as a wavy line and a straight line.

Music and speech are perceived as continuous rather than a series of separate sounds.

Closure

The law of closure says that we often supply missing information to close a figure and separate it from its background. By filling in the gaps, the illustrations below are seen as a triangle and a whole seashell.

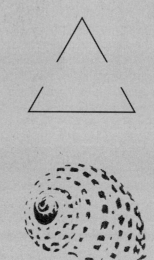

Part-whole relationship

As well as illustrating continuity and proximity, the three figures below illustrate the principle that 'the whole is greater than the sum of its parts'. Each pattern is composed of 12 crosses, but the gestalten are different, despite the similarity of the parts.

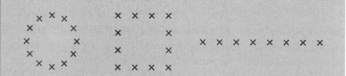

The notes on a musical scale played up the scale produce a very different sound compared with the same notes played down the scale, and the same melody can be recognised when hummed, whistled or played with different instruments and in different keys.

Simplicity

According to this law, a stimulus pattern will be organised into its simplest components. The figure below is usually perceived as a rectangle with an overlapping triangle rather than as a complex and nameless geometric shape.

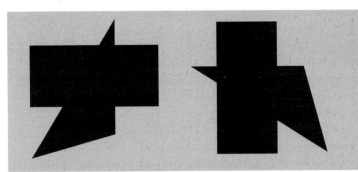

Common fate
Elements seen moving together are perceived as belonging together. This is why a group of people running in the same direction appear to be unified in their purpose.

An evaluation of the Gestalt contribution

At least one major philosophical influence on Gestalt psychology was *phenomenology*. As far as perception is concerned, phenomenology sees the stability and coherence of the world (that is, the world as we ordinarily experience it) as being of central concern. Koffka, for example, believed that the most important question for perceptual psychologists to answer was 'Why do things look as they do?', and for Köhler:

'there seems to be a single starting point for psychology, exactly as for all the other sciences: the world as we find it, naïvely and uncritically'.

For many psychologists, Gestalt psychology has had a major impact on our understanding of perceptual processes. According to Roth (1986), the most comprehensive account of perceptual grouping is still that provided by the Gestaltists, and in Gordon's (1989) view, the discoveries of Gestalt psychology 'are now part of our permanent knowledge of perception', and most psychologists would agree that the Gestaltists were correct about many things.

Many contemporary researchers, however, have argued that, as originally expressed, the various 'laws' proposed by Gestaltists are at best only descriptive and at worst extremely vague, imprecise and difficult to measure (what, for example, makes a circle or square a 'good' figure? (Greene, 1990)). Several studies (e.g. Pomerantz and Garner, 1973; Navon, 1977) have attempted to address the various criticisms made of the Gestalt laws. Navon's study is described in Box 1.2.

Box 1.2   Navon's (1977) experimental test of Gestalt laws

According to Gestalt psychologists, 'the whole is greater than the sum of its parts'. Navon attempted to test the idea that the whole is perceived before the parts that make it up by presenting participants with various stimuli as shown below.

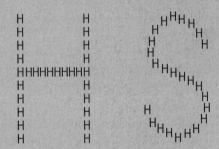

Navon distinguished between the *global* (or 'whole-like' features of a stimulus) and the *local* (or more specific and 'part-like' features). Each stimulus consisted of a large (global) letter made up of many small (local) letters. In some cases, the global and local letters matched (as shown in the stimulus on the left) and in some cases they did not match (as shown in the stimulus on the right).

Participants had to identify either the large letter or the small letter as quickly as they could. Navon found that the time taken to identify the large letter was unaffected by whether the small letters matched or did not match. However, the time taken to identify the small letters *was* affected by whether the large letter matched or did not match, such that when the large letter was different, response times were longer. This suggests that it is difficult to avoid processing the whole and that global processing necessarily occurs before any more detailed perceptual analysis (adapted from Eysenck and Keane, 1995).

The data reported by Navon and the findings of several other studies lend support to the claims made by Gestaltists. However, the Gestalt laws are difficult to apply to the perception of solid objects (as opposed to two-dimensional drawings). Our eyes evolved to see 3-D objects, and when 3-D arrays have been studied, Gestalt laws have not been consistently upheld (Eysenck, 1993). Additionally, Gestalt psychologists place great emphasis on *single* objects; yet in the world around us we are faced with 'whole' scenes in which single objects are but 'parts' (Humphreys and Riddoch, 1987). As a result, many of the Gestalt displays have very low *ecological validity* in that they are not representative of what Gordon (1989) calls 'the objects and events which organisms must deal with in order to survive'.

Depth perception

From the two-dimensional (2-D) images that fall on our retinas, we manage to organise three-dimensional (3-D) perceptions. The ability to see objects in three dimensions is called *depth perception*, and it allows us to estimate their distance from us. Some of the cues that are used to transform 2-D retinal images into 3-D perceptions involve both eyes and rely on their working together. These are called *binocular cues*. Other cues are available to each eye separately, and are called *monocular cues*.

BINOCULAR CUES

Most animals that are preyed upon (such as rabbits) have their eyes on the side of the head. This allows them to see danger approaching over a wide area. Most predators (such as lions) have their eyes set close together on the front of the head. This allows them to have binocular vision, which helps in hunting prey. Like non-human predators, human beings have predatory vision, and this influences the way in which we perceive the world. Four important binocular cues are *retinal disparity, stereopsis, accommodation* and *convergence*.

The fact that our eyes are nearly three inches apart means that each retina receives a slightly different image of the world. The amount of *retinal disparity* (the difference between the two images) detected by the brain gives us an important cue to distance. For example, if you hold your finger directly in front of your nose, the difference between the two retinal images is large (and this can be shown by looking at your finger first with the left eye closed and then with the right eye closed). When the finger is held at arm's length, retinal disparity is much smaller.

Ordinarily, we do not see double images. This is because the two images are combined by the brain in a process called *stereopsis*. This enables the brain to put the two images together and allows us to experience one 3-D sensation rather than two different images. In *accommodation*, which is a muscular cue, the lenses of the eyes change shape when we are focusing on an object. The lenses thicken for objects that are nearby and flatten for objects that are in the distance. Another muscular cue to distance is *convergence*. This refers to the process by which the eyes point more and more inward as an object gets closer. By noting the angle of convergence, the brain is able to provide us with depth information over distances from about six to 20 feet (Hochberg, 1971).

MONOCULAR CUES

Binocular cues are important in judging the distance of relatively near objects. With objects that are at greater distances than this, each eye receives a very similar retinal image whilst looking ahead. At greater distances, we depend on monocular cues, that is, cues suggestive of depth that can be perceived with only one eye. Some monocular cues to depth are described in Box 1.3.

Box 1.3   Some monocular cues to depth

Relative size: The larger an image of an object is on the retina, the larger it is judged to be. Objects that are larger than other objects are judged to be closer.

Overlap (or **Superimposition**): If one object is partially covered by another, it is perceived as being further away. When a smaller object partially obscures a larger object, they seem closer

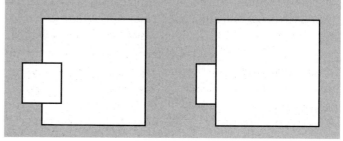

together than if the position of the two objects is reversed (a combination of overlap and relative size).

Relative height: Objects *below* the horizon and *lower down* in our field of vision are perceived as being closer. Objects *above* the horizon and *higher up* in our field of vision are perceived as being further away.

Texture gradient: This refers to the fact that textured surfaces nearby appear rougher than distant surfaces. Thus, at increasing distances the details of the surface blend together and the texture appears increasingly smooth.

Linear perspective: The apparent convergence of parallel lines is interpreted as a distance cue. The greater the convergence, the greater the perceived distance.

Shadowing: Opaque objects block light and produce shadows. Shadows and highlights give us information about the 3-D shape of an object. In the illustration below, the object on the left is perceived as a 2-D circle. The object on the right is perceived as a 3-D sphere because of the highlight on the surface and the shadow underneath.

Relative brightness: Objects that are close to us reflect more light to the eyes. The dimmer of two identical objects appears to be further away from us.

Aerial haze: Objects that are hazy are perceived to be further away than objects more in focus.

Aerial perspective: Objects at a greater distance appear to have a different colour (such as the bluish tint of a distant mountain).

Motion parallax: If we move, objects near to us appear to move more than objects far away from us. When we move past objects located at different distances from us, they appear to move across the visual field at different speeds, with those nearest us moving most rapidly. Such differences in speed help us to judge both distance and depth.

Perceptual constancy

Once we have perceived an object as a coherent form and located it in space, we must next recognise the object without being 'fooled' by changes in its size, shape, location, brightness and colour. The ability to perceive an object as unchanging despite changes in the sensory information that reaches our eyes is called perceptual constancy, and several visual perceptual constancies have been identified.

SIZE CONSTANCY

As people move away from us, the size of image they project on the retina decreases. However, rather than seeing those people as 'growing smaller', we perceive them as people of a fixed height moving away from us. Our tendency to perceive an object as being of a constant size despite changes in the sensory stimulation they produce is called *size constancy*. Size constancy occurs because the perceptual system takes into account the distance of the object from the person perceiving it. So, perceived size is equal to retinal image size taking into account distance. When people move away from us, then, their image on our retina decreases in size as their distance increases. Our perceptual system interprets these changes as resulting from the change in location of an object of constant size.

The perception of an *afterimage* provides an example of a situation in which distance can be varied *without* changing the size of the retinal image. If you stare at a bright light for a few seconds and then look away, you will experience an afterimage. This afterimage has a fixed size, shape and position on the retina. However, if you quickly look at a nearby object and then an object further away, the afterimage appears to shrink and swell, appearing to be largest when you look at a more distant object. As we have seen, real objects cast a smaller image the further away they are and to maintain perceptual constancy, the brain 'scales-up' the image (*constancy scaling*). The same constancy scaling is applied to an afterimage, producing changes in its apparent size.

SHAPE CONSTANCY

We often view objects from angles at which their 'true' shape is not reflected in the retinal image they project. For example, rectangular doors often project trapezoid shapes and round cups often project elliptical-shaped images. In the same way that the perceptual system compensates for changes in the retinal image to produce size constancy, so it maintains constancy in terms of shape. Figure 1.5 illustrates shape constancy.

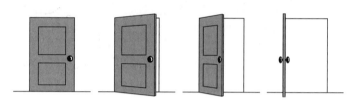

Figure 1.5   No matter what angle a door is viewed from, it remains a door.

There are, however, occasions on which shape and size constancy do not work. When we look down at people from the top of a very tall building, they do *look* more like ants to us, even though we know they are people. So perception can be more powerful than *conception*, although this is an exception to the rule.

LOCATION CONSTANCY

As we move our heads around, a constantly changing pattern of retinal images is produced. However, we do not perceive the world as spinning around. This is because *kinaesthetic feedback* from the muscles and balance organs in the ear are integrated with the changing retinal stimulation in the brain in order to inhibit perception of movement. To keep the world from moving crazily every time we move our eyes, the brain subtracts the eye-movement commands from the resulting changes on the retina and this helps to keep objects in a constant location.

BRIGHTNESS CONSTANCY

We see objects as having a more or less constant brightness even though the amount of light they reflect changes according to the level of illumination. For example, white paper reflects 90 per cent of light falling on it, whereas black paper reflects only 10 per cent. In bright sunlight, however, black paper still looks black even though it may reflect 100 times more light than does white paper indoors (McBurney and Collins, 1984). Perceived brightness depends on *relative luminance* or how much light an object reflects relative to its surroundings. If sunlit black paper is viewed through a narrow tube such that nothing else is visible, it will appear greyish because in bright sunlight it reflects a fair amount of light. When viewed without the tube it is again black, because it reflects much less light than the colourful objects around it.

COLOUR CONSTANCY

In colour constancy, familiar objects retain their colour (or, more correctly, their *hue*) under a variety of lighting conditions (including night light), provided there is sufficient contrast and shadow. Colour constancy is particularly good when we look at familiar objects. However, when we do not already know an object's colour, colour constancy is less effective (Delk and Fillenbaum, 1965). If you have purchased new clothes under fluorescent light without viewing them in ordinary lighting conditions, you will no doubt agree with Delk and Fillenbaum!

Illusions

Mostly, perception is a reliable process. On some occasions, however, our perceptions misrepresent the world. When our perception of an object does not agree with the true physical characteristics of the object, we have experienced an *illusion*. Some illusions are due to the *physical distortion* of stimuli whereas others are due to our *misperception* of stimuli (Coren and Girgus, 1978). An example of a *physical illusion* is the bent appearance of a stick when placed in water. This can be explained by the fact that water acts like a prism, bending the light waves before they reach the eyes. In general, such illusions do not surprise us because they are commonly experienced and easily understood.

Perceptual illusions occur when a stimulus contains misleading cues that cause us to create perceptions that are inaccurate or impossible. Gregory (1983) identifies four types of illusion. These are *distortions* (or *geometric illusions*), *ambiguous* (or *reversible figures*), *paradoxical figures* (or *improbable and impossible objects*) and *fictions*. Figure 1.6 (a–i) shows several examples of distortions.

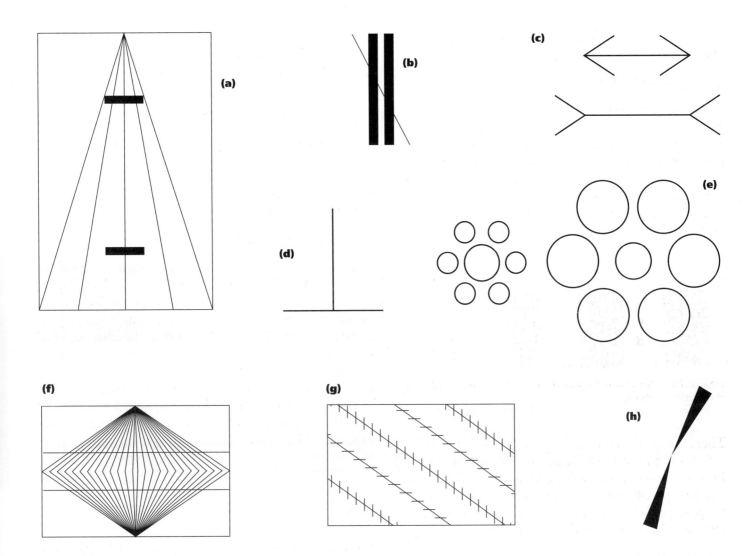

Figure 1.6 In the Ponzo illusion (a), the horizontal bar at the top is seen as being longer than the horizontal line at the bottom, even though they are both the same length. The Poggendorf illusion (b) suggests that the segments of the diagonal line are offset, even though they are not. The line with the outgoing fins in the Müller-Lyer illusion (c) appears to be longer than the line with the ingoing fins, but in fact they are the same length. In the horizontal-vertical illusion (d), the vertical line is seen as being longer, although it is the same as the horizontal line. In Titchener's circles (e), the central circle in the left-hand group is seen as being larger than the central circle of the right-hand group, but they are both the same size. Wundt's illusion (f) suggests that the horizontal lines are bent in the middle. The lines are, in fact, parallel. The short lines in Zollner's illusion (g) cause the diagonal lines to appear to converge and diverge, although they are parallel. In the Bourdon illusion (h), the left edge of the figure is straight, but appears bent. Finally, in the twisted card illusion (i), the twisted cards appear to be a spiral pattern, but the circles are, in fact, concentric.

The Poggendorf illusion (Figure 1.6b) has been shown to be exaggerated when the diagonal line is more steeply slanted and when the parallel bars are more separated. As the line is brought closer to the horizontal, the illusion disappears (MacKay and Newbigging, 1977). In 1965, two American aircraft collided over New York City killing four people and injuring 49. Both of the planes emerged from a sloping cloudbank and, although holding altitudes of 10,000 and 11,000 feet, each pilot saw the other plane emerge from the clouds on an angle and thought they were headed for a crash. As they manoeuvred to avoid a crash, they actually did crash, an accident that could be attributed to a complex version of the Poggendorf illusion (Coren and Girgus, 1978).

Less dramatically, we can explain people's surprise when the tall tree they chopped down actually turns out to be smaller than they believed. As the horizontal-vertical illusion (Figure 1.6d) illustrates, we have a tendency to overestimate the size of vertical objects. So, a tree *does* look shorter when it is cut down than it does when it is standing (Coren and Girgus, 1978).

We encountered one type of ambiguous or reversible figure (Rubin's vase) earlier on in this chapter (see page 3). Three other well-known reversible figures are shown in Figure 1.7 (a–c). The Necker cube (Figure 1.7a) was first described by L.A. Necker (1832). In this illusion, the figure undergoes a *depth reversal*. The cube can be perceived with the crosses being drawn either on the back side of the cube or on the top side looking down. Although our perceptual system interprets this 2-D line drawing as a 3-D object, it seems undecided as to which of the two orientations should be perceived, and hence the cube spontaneously reverses in depth orientation if looked at for about 30 seconds.

Figure 1.7b shows E.G. Boring's 'Old/Young woman'. This (and Figure 1.7c) are examples of reversible figures in which the change in perception illustrates *object reversal*. The figure can be perceived as the profile of a young woman's face with the tip of her nose just visible. However, the young woman's chin can also be perceived as the nose of the face of a much older woman. In Jastrow's reversible duck/rabbit head (Figure 1.7c), the object can be perceived either as the head of a duck with its beak pointing to the left or as a rabbit (the duck's beak becomes the rabbit's ears).

Whilst paradoxical figures look ordinary enough on first inspection, on closer inspection we realise that

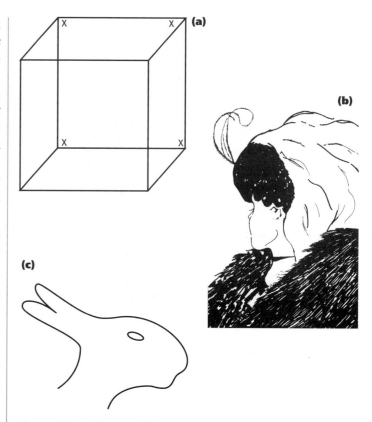

Figure 1.7   Three ambiguous/reversible figures: (a) the Necker cube; (b) Boring's 'Old/Young Woman'; and (c) Jastrow's duck/rabbit head.

they cannot exist in reality (hence 'paradoxical'). Figure 1.8 (a–d) illustrates four such paradoxical figures.

Hochberg (1970) has proposed that it takes us a few seconds to realise that a figure is impossible because we need time to fully examine or scan the figure and organise its parts into a meaningful whole. When we look at a figure, our eyes move from place to place at the rate of about three changes per second (Yarbus, 1967). So when we look at an impossible figure, it takes time (and the more complex the figure, the longer the time) to scan it and perceive its form. It is only after this scanning that the impossible nature of the figure can be appreciated. The painting by M.C. Escher (Figure 1.8d) uses perceptual cues in such a way as to encourage us to perceive a 3-D figure even though the artist is working only in two dimensions. Because it is also complicated, it takes us longer to scan and realise that it is impossible.

Fictions are useful in helping to answer the question of how we perceive that objects possess a specific shape. The idea that shape is determined by the *physical contours* of an object (which cause edge-detectors in the

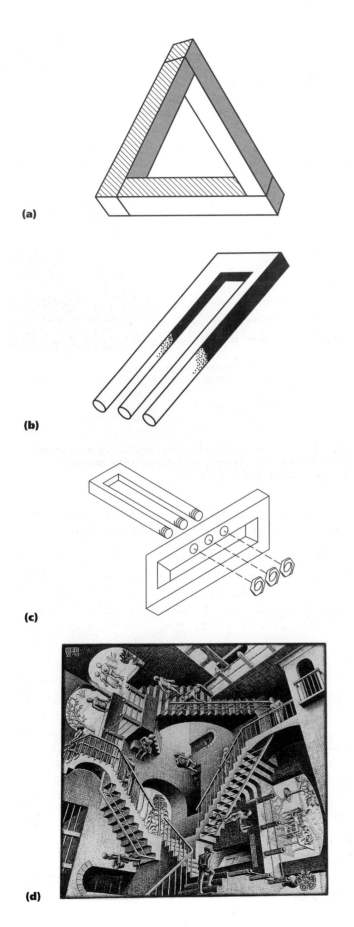

(a)

(b)

(c)

(d)

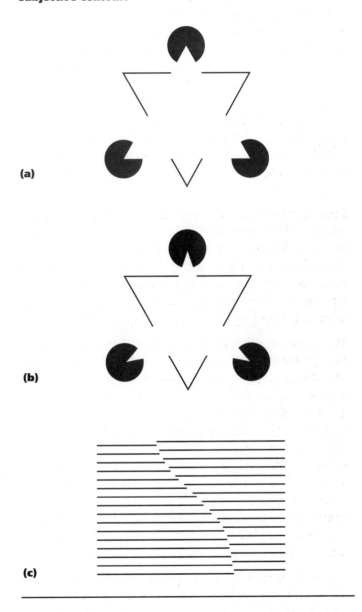

Figure 1.9 (below) Three fictions. In (a), the 'white triangle' is banded by a subjective contour rather than a continuous physical one. In (b), the subjective contours are curved. In (c), lines of different orientation produce a subjective contour.

(a)

(b)

(c)

Figure 1.8 (left) Four impossible objects. (a) is the Penrose impossible triangle and (b) is variously known as 'Trident' and 'The devil's pitchfork'. In (c), Trident has been combined with another impossible object. (d) is M.C. Escher's *Relativity*. Although working in two dimensions, Escher has used perceptual cues in such a way as to encourage the viewer to perceive a three-dimensional figure (see Chapter 2).

cells of the visual system to fire) has been challenged by the existence of *subjective contours*. Kanizsa (1976) defines a subjective contour as the boundaries of a shape perceived in the absence of physical contours. Figure 1.9 (a–c) shows three fictions.

Consider, for example, Figure 1.9a. Although no white triangular contour is physically present, we perceive the shape of a white triangle. Note also that the triangle appears to be opaque and lighter than the background. There are *some* contours that are physically present (the overlap of the triangle and the disc) and these *might* cause enough edge-detector cells to fire to account for our perception of a complete triangle. However, this explanation cannot account for the fact that in Figure 1.9b, the partial and straight physical contours give rise to a *curved* triangle. Nor can it explain the subjective contour in Figure 1.9c which is marked by lines in a totally different orientation (Krebs and Blackman, 1988).

In Rock's (1984) view, it is the relationship between its parts that is the defining characteristic of a shape rather than its physical contours. Physical contours are, of course, usually indicative of the location of an object's parts. For Rock, though, the location of the parts can also be determined by subjective contours. As a result, the perception of shape must involve more than simply detecting the elements of a pattern (Krebs and Blackman, 1988).

The illusions we have considered so far have all been deliberately created. However, we are surrounded by illusions in our everyday life. The use of perspective cues by artists leads us to infer depth and distance, that is, we add something to a picture which is not physically present. We also add something to the images projected on our television screens. Television employs another kind of illusion, namely that of *movement*.

The perception of movement

As we turn our heads and look around a room, the light from various objects stimulates successive and different parts of the retina. Despite this, we perceive the objects to be stationary. At a soccer match, we move our heads so that the light reflected by the players and ball is directed at the same area of the retina. We know, however, that the players and the ball are moving. In order to perceive movement, we use a number of

different cues some, but not all, of the time. Such cues include the movement of our head and eyes, and our knowledge about certain objects (if we are standing on a railway platform, then we know that neither we nor the platform are moving!). Unfortunately, there is no single (and simple) way in which movement is perceived, and our conclusions about movement using environmental cues depend on how such cues are interpreted (Poggio and Koch, 1987).

Just as it is possible for changes in patterns of stimulation on the retina not to be accompanied by the perception of movement, so it is possible to perceive movement without a successive pattern of retinal stimulation (Ramachandron and Anstis, 1986). This is called *apparent movement*, and several types of these illusions of movement have been studied. Some of them are described in Box 1.4.

Box 1.4   Some examples of apparent movement

The autokinetic effect

If you look at a spot of light in an otherwise completely dark room, the stationary light will appear to move. According to Gregory (1973), this illusion of apparent movement is produced by small and uncontrollable eye movements. Another explanation suggests that the illusion is caused by the absence of a stimulating background. A background functions as a frame of reference by which movement is gauged. This explanation is supported by the fact that the autokinetic effect disappears if other lights (which act as frames of reference) are introduced.

Stroboscopic motion

In stroboscopic motion, the illusion of movement is created by the rapid succession of slightly different stationary images. If these are presented sufficiently quickly (around 16 to 22 frames per second), an illusory impression of continuous movement is produced, and this is the mechanism by which moving pictures operate. With fewer than 16 frames per second, the moving picture looks jumpy and unnatural. Smooth *slow motion* is achieved by filming at a rate of 100 or more frames per second and then playing back at about 20 frames per second.

The phi phenomenon

This is a simpler form of stroboscopic motion. In the phi phenomenon, a number of separate lights are turned on and off in quick succession. This gives the

---

impression of a single light moving from one position to another. Both stroboscopic motion and the phi phenomenon can be explained by the law of continuity (see page 4). Because a series of lights (or frames of film) is perceived as having unity, apparent movement is perceived.

Induced movement

This occurs when we perceive an object to be moving, although in reality it is stationary and its surroundings are moving. Movie stars, for example, are often filmed in a stationary car with a projection of a moving background behind them. Similarly, when the moon is seen through a thin cover of moving clouds, we sometimes perceive it to be moving very quickly. This induced movement occurs because of the moon's change in position relative to the clouds that surround it. The experience of sitting in a car at traffic lights and noticing that we are 'moving backwards', when in fact the car at our side is moving forwards, is another example of induced movement.

Motion after-effects

People who work on inspection belts in factories experience movement after-effects when the belt suddenly stops but is perceived as now moving backwards (an effect which has been known to result in inspectors falling off their seats!). Similarly, if you stare at a waterfall and then switch your gaze to the ground surrounding it, the ground appears to be moving in the opposite direction.

Such after-effects are generally accepted as being due to the overstimulation of particular movement-detector cells in the visual system. Because cells sensitive to, say, downward movement have been overstimulated, they are momentarily insensitive when the stimulation ceases. However, the cells sensitive to, say, upward movement are relatively more active, resulting in a motion after-effect.

According to Rock (1983), at least some of the examples of apparent movement can be termed *intelligent errors*, because they result from perceptual strategies that work most of the time. Motion after-effects, however, seem to be much more amenable to explanation in terms of physiological mechanisms.

Pattern recognition

As Eysenck (1993) has observed: 'one of the most crucial functions of visual perception is to assign meaning to the objects in the visual field by recognising or identifying them'. The ease with which we are able to recognise the letter 'T', say, whether it is printed on paper, handwritten or spoken 'is so ingrained in our experience that we rarely even notice that we do it' (Houston et al., 1991). As Figure 1.10 shows, the letter 'T' can be presented in many different ways. So what makes a 'T' a 'T'?

T T TT͡ T T⁊T T⌇T⌐ T͡T͡T⌐T͡T͡TT T͡TT

Figure 1.10   Anyone for t?

TEMPLATE-MATCHING HYPOTHESIS

According to the template-matching hypothesis (TMH), incoming sensory information is matched against miniature copies (or templates) of previously presented patterns or objects which are stored in long-term memory. Template-matching is used by computerised cash registers, which identify a product and its cost by matching a bar code with some stored representation of that code. As most of us know, bar codes occasionally 'fail to scan', causing impatient sighs from others in a queue as the cashier tries to find an alternative way of charging us for the product.

Given that the environment offers us more than a supermarket ever could, we would need to possess an incredibly large number of templates, each corresponding to a specific visual input. Even if we were able to use a wheelbarrow to carry around the cerebrum that would be needed for this, the time needed to search for a specific template would be inordinately long (Solso, 1995), and we would never recognise unfamiliar patterns (just as a computerised supermarket till fails to recognise our purchase of a product that has been reduced).

In an attempt to overcome the limitations of the TMH, Biederman (1987) has advanced a *geon theory of pattern recognition* ('geon' stands for 'geometrical icons'). According to Biederman, we use a limited number of simple geometric 'primitives' that may be applied to all complex shapes (an idea which is similar to the theory of perception advanced by Marr which we will consider in Chapter 2). As shown in Figure 1.11, a number of geons can be combined to produce more complex ones (in much the same way as more complex words can be produced by combining more letters). Biederman's theory proposes that the identification of any visual object is determined by whichever stored representation provides the best fit with the component- or geon-based information obtained from the visual object. In order to establish the number of parts or components making up an object, Biederman believes that the *concave* parts of the contour are of particular importance (Solso, 1995).

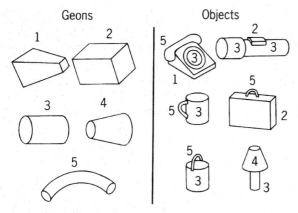

Figure 1.11   Biederman's geons (left) and some of the objects they can combine to make (right).

PROTOTYPE THEORIES OF PATTERN RECOGNITION

An alternative to TMH proposes that instead of storing templates, we store a smaller number of *prototypes* which are 'abstract forms representing the basic elements of a set of stimuli' (Eysenck, 1993). Whereas TMH treats each stimulus as a separate entity, prototype theories maintain that similarities between related stimuli play an important part in pattern recognition. So, each stimulus is a member of a category of stimuli, and shares basic properties with other members of the category.

The main weakness of prototype theories is their inability to explain how pattern recognition is affected by the context as well as by the stimulus itself (Eysenck, 1993). Knowing just what properties are shared by a category of stimuli is important, but not specified by the theories. What, for example, is an 'idealised' letter 'T' and what is the 'best' representation of the pattern? This question has been addressed by *feature detection theories*.

FEATURE DETECTION THEORIES

The most influential approach to pattern recognition maintains that each stimulus pattern can be thought of as a configuration of elementary features. Gibson et al. (1968) argue that the letters of the alphabet, for example, are composed of combinations of 12 basic features (such as vertical lines, horizontal lines and closed curves).

Visual scanning tasks lend some support to feature detection theories. In these, participants search lists of letters as quickly as possible to find a randomly placed target letter. Since finding a target letter entails detecting its elementary features, the task should be more difficult when the target and non-target letters have more features in common. This is exactly what researchers have found (e.g. Rabbit, 1967). Additional support comes from *studies of eye movements and fixation*. Presumably, the more a feature in a pattern is looked at, the more information is being extracted from it. According to Yarbus (1967), the perception of features within complex patterns depends on higher cognitive processes (such as attention and purpose) as well as the nature of the physical stimuli being looked at.

It is also well established that the visual systems of a number of vertebrates contain both peripheral (retinal) and central (cortical) cells that respond only to particular features of visual stimuli. In their pioneering research, Hubel and Wiesel (1968) identified three kinds of cortical cell (which they called 'simple', 'complex' and 'hypercomplex' to refer to the stimuli the cells respond to). In more recent research, it has been claimed that there are face-specific cells in the inferotemporal cortex of the monkey (Ono et al., 1993).

In humans, David Perrett and his colleagues at the University of St. Andrews have uncovered the existence of cells that respond to specific aspects of a face or to a set of features. Their research also indicates that there are cells which respond to many different views of a face, and that such cells may 'sum' inputs from a variety of sources (Messer, 1995).

Whether such cells constitute the feature detectors postulated by feature detection theories is not entirely clear. It is possible that these neurological detectors are a necessary pre-condition for higher-level (or cognitive) pattern task analysis. However, feature detection theories typically assume a *serial* form of processing, with feature extraction being followed by feature combination which itself is then followed by pattern recognition (Eysenck, 1993). It is generally accepted that *parallel* (or non-serial) processing takes place in the visual cortex and that the relationship between different kinds of cortical cell is more complex than originally believed. An early example of a non-serial processing computer program is the *Pandemonium*

model devised by Selfridge (1959). This is described in Box 1.5.

Like prototype theories, feature detection theories have also been criticised for failing to take sufficient account of the role played by context and certain perceiver characteristics (such as expectations: see Chapter 2, page 22). If a feature is ambiguous, then it can produce different patterns, and different features can produce the same pattern depending on the context. This can tell us what patterns are likely to be present and hence what to expect (indeed, we may fail to notice the absence of

---

Box 1.5   Selfridge's (1959) Pandemonium model

Selfridge's computer program was designed to recognise Morse code and a small set of handwritten letters. The components of the model are known as *demons* and there are four kinds of them. *Image demons* simply copy the pattern presented (and these are analogous to the retina). *Feature demons* analyse the information from the

image demons in terms of combinations of features. *Cognitive demons* are specialised for particular letters and 'scream' according to how much the input from the feature demons matches their special letter. Finally, a *decision demon* chooses the 'loudest scream' and identifies the letter as shown below.

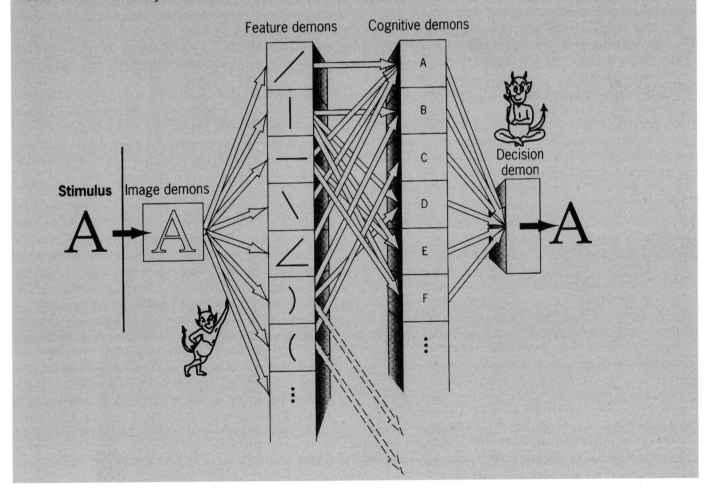

something or a distorted form of a stimulus (such as a typing error) because of its high predictability). One effect of context on pattern recognition may be to allow a partial and selective analysis of the stimulus to be recognised. In other words, pattern recognition involves selectively attending to some aspects of the presented stimuli but not to others. Pattern recognition and *selective attention* are therefore closely related (Solso, 1995). Attentional processes are discussed in Chapters 5 and 6 of this book.

Conclusions

In this chapter, we have looked at some aspects of visual perception and perceptual organisation that have captured and maintained the interest of cognitive psychologists. As we have seen, attempts have been made to account for various aspects of visual perception, some of which have been more successful than others. In the following chapter, we will look at attempts to explain the processes by which perception itself takes place.

SUMMARY

- **Sensation** involves an almost continuous state of flux, produced by physical stimulation of the sense organs, while **perception** refers to our experience of stable, constant objects and involves an **organisation** and **interpretation** of incoming sensory information.
- Vision is the dominant sense modality in humans and this explains why more is known about visual perception than other kinds.
- Influenced by Ehrenfels's claim that objects have a **Gestalt qualität**/form quality, the **Gestalt psychologists** (Wertheimer, Koffka and Köhler) identified innately determined **principles** through which sensory information is interpreted and organised.
- The most basic principle of **form perception** is to organise incoming sensory information into **figure and ground**. While **familiarity** is important for form perception, it is not necessary. More important is **surroundedness, size, orientation** and **symmetry**.
- Underlying **camouflage** is the principle that the figure appears to have no more form than its background. In **figure-ground reversal**, a figure can also be perceived as ground and vice-versa.
- Objects are perceived as **gestalten**: laws for **grouping** stimuli together all rest on the belief that 'the whole is greater than the sum of its parts'. These laws can be summarised under Koffka's **law of prägnanz**, which has been interpreted in terms of internal redundancy (Attneave) and Hochberg's **minimum principle**.

- Major Gestalt laws of perception include **proximity, similarity, good continuation, closure, part-whole relationship, simplicity** and **common fate**.
- A major philosophical influence on Gestalt psychology was **phenomenology**, according to which the world as we commonly experience it is of central concern.
- While Gestalt psychology has had a major impact on our understanding of perceptual experience, providing the most comprehensive account of perceptual grouping, the various 'laws' are seen as merely descriptive and often imprecise and difficult to measure.
- Navon's study involving **global** and **local** features of letter stimuli supports the Gestalt claim that the whole is perceived before the parts that make it up. Despite other empirical support, the Gestalt laws are seen as difficult to apply to 3-D perception and to perception of whole scenes, and therefore as lacking **ecological validity**.
- **Depth perception** allows us to estimate the distance of objects from us. Like non-human predators such as lions, human beings' eyes are set apart but close together on the front of the head, providing **binocular vision**. Major **binocular cues** include **retinal disparity** and **stereopsis** (which relate to the different retinal images of each eye) and **accommodation** and **convergence** (which are both **muscular cues**).
- **Monocular cues** are important for judging

objects at greater distances. They include **relative size, overlap/superimposition, relative height, texture gradient, linear perspective, shadowing, relative brightness, aerial haze, aerial perspective** and **motion parallax**.

- **Perceptual constancy** refers to the ability to recognise an object as unchanging despite changes in its **size, shape, location, brightness** and **colour**. Changes in the apparent size of an afterimage occur due to **constancy scaling**, but size and shape constancy do not always work, since perception can prove more powerful than **conception** under certain conditions.
- **Location constancy** is achieved through the brain's integration of **kinaesthetic feedback** from the muscles and balance organs in the ear with the changing pattern of retinal stimulation produced as we move our heads around.
- **Brightness constancy** involves seeing objects as having a more or less constant brightness despite changes in the amount of light they reflect: perceived brightness depends on **relative luminance**.
- **Colour constancy** is most effective in relation to **familiar** objects and, strictly speaking, refers to the object's **hue**.
- **Physical illusions** are caused by some physical distortion of the stimulus itself, while **perceptual illusions** occur when a stimulus contains misleading perceptual cues.
- The Ponzo, Poggendorf, Müller-Lyer, horizontal-vertical, Wundt's and Zollner's and Bourdon illusions and Titchener's circles are all examples of **distortions/geometric illusions**.
- Rubin's vase, the Necker cube, Boring's 'Old/Young woman' and Jastrow's duck/rabbit are all examples of **ambiguous/reversible figures**, all illustrating **object reversal**.
- The Penrose triangle, the 'trident'/devil's pitchfork and paintings by Escher are all examples of **paradoxical figures/improbable/impossible objects**. It takes a few seconds of scanning these figures to realise that they could not exist in reality: the more complex the figure, the more scanning is needed.
- **Fictions**, such as the Kanizsa triangles, suggest that **subjective contours** are at least as important as **physical contours** in determining the perceived shape of objects. Shape perception is defined by the relationship between the elements of a pattern, not simply by detection of the elements.
- Not all illusions are deliberately created but include **perception of depth** in paintings/drawings and the **perception of movement** in television pictures.
- Movement perception involves use of a number of cues, including the movement of our head and eyes and knowledge about objects. **Apparent movement** refers to the perception of movement in the absence of changes in patterns of retinal stimulation; examples include **the autokinetic effect, stroboscopic motion, the phi phenomenon, induced movement** and **motion after-effects**.
- While some types of apparent movement can be termed **intelligent errors**, arising from **perceptual strategies** that work most of the time, others, such as motion after-effects, are better explained in terms of physiological mechanisms.
- **Pattern recognition** is one of the most crucial functions of perception. According to the **template matching hypothesis (TMH)**, incoming sensory information is matched against miniature copies/templates of previously encountered patterns/objects stored in long-term memory. This is the basis of computerised **bar coding**.
- The major objection to TMH is that it cannot explain our ability to recognise unfamiliar patterns. Biederman's **geon theory** attempts to overcome this limitation by claiming that we use a limited number of simple geometric 'primitives' that can be applied to all complex shapes. Object recognition is determined by the particular stored representation that provides the best match with the geon-based information provided by the object. The **concave** parts of the contour are especially important.
- According to **prototype theories**, we store **prototypes** rather than templates, such that individual stimuli belong to a category and share basic properties with other members of the category.
- Specifying the properties shared by members of a stimulus category has been attempted by **feature detection theories** which represent the most influential approach to pattern recognition. Support comes from **visual scanning tasks** and **studies of eye movements and fixation**.
- The simple, complex and hypercomplex cells in the cortex, identified by Hubel and Wiesel, and the claimed existence of face-specific cells in the cortex of monkeys, may constitute the necessary neurological pre-condition for higher-level/cognitive pattern task analysis.
- While feature detection theories typically assume a **serial** form of processing, it is generally agreed that the kind of processing that takes place in the

visual cortex is **parallel/non-serial**, as represented by Selfridge's **Pandemonium model**.

• Both prototype and feature detection theories have been criticised for failing to take sufficient account of the context and certain perceiver characteristics, such as expectations. They also fail to take account of the close relationship between pattern recognition and **selective attention**.

2

SOME THEORIES OF VISUAL PERCEPTION

Introduction and overview

As we mentioned in the introduction to the previous chapter, sensation and perception are closely related, though different, processes which we often take for granted in everyday life. Actually explaining visual perception is, however, no straightforward task. Some psychologists have addressed the question of whether the way we perceive the world is the result of learning and experience or essentially an inbuilt ability which requires little, if any, learning. We shall consider the findings with respect to this question in Chapters 3 and 4. Others have concerned themselves with explaining the processes by which *physical energy* received by the sense organs forms the basis of *perceptual experience* (and this, of course, is the sensation/perception distinction we made in Chapter 1).

As Dodwell (1995) has observed:

'to perceive seems effortless. To understand perception is nevertheless a great challenge'.

According to some who have responded to this challenge, our perception of the world is the end result of a process which also involves making *inferences* about what things are like. Those who subscribe to this 'end result' view are called *top-down (or conceptually-driven) perceptual processing theorists* and for them, making inferences about what things are like means that we perceive them *indirectly*, drawing on our knowledge and expectations of the world. Such theorists include Bruner (1957), Neisser (1967) and Gregory (1972, 1980). Others who have responded to the challenge argue that our perception of the world is essentially determined by the information presented to the sensory receptors, so that things are perceived in a fairly *direct* way. Supporters of this view are called *bottom-up (or data-driven) perceptual processing theorists* and the most influential of them has been Gibson (1966, 1979).

Our first aim in this chapter is to consider the evidence for and against bottom-up and top-down accounts of perception. Although these theories have received much research attention, they are not, however, the only theories of perception that have been advanced. One alternative is the *computational theory of vision* proposed by Marr (1982), and our second aim in this chapter is to consider Marr's proposals.

Richard Gregory's 'constructivist' theory of perception

According to Gregory (1966):

'perception is not determined simply by stimulus patterns. Rather, it is a dynamic searching for the best interpretation of the available data ... (which) involves going beyond the immediately given evidence of the senses'.

In order to avoid *sensory overload*, we need to select from all the sensory stimulation which surrounds us. Often, we also need to supplement sensory information because the total information that we might need could be missing (not directly available to the senses). This is what Gregory means when he says that perception involves 'going beyond the immediately given evidence of the senses' and it is why his theory is known as *constructivist*. For Gregory, we make *inferences* about the information the senses receive, an idea that was first advanced by Hermann von Helmholtz, a nineteenth-century German physiologist who saw perception as *unconscious inferences*.

GREGORY'S THEORY AND PERCEPTUAL CONSTANCIES

In Chapter 1 (see pages 7–8), we described some perceptual constancies. What these constancies tell us is that visual information from the retinal image is sketchy and incomplete and that the visual system has to 'go beyond' the retinal image in order to 'test hypotheses which fill in the "gaps" ' (Greene, 1990). To make sense of the various sensory inputs to the retina, the visual system must draw on all kinds of evidence, including distance cues, information from other senses, and expectations based on past experience. For all these reasons, Gregory argues that perception must be an indirect process involving a *construction* based on physical sources of energy.

GREGORY'S THEORY AND ILLUSIONS

Gregory argues that visual illusions (see pages 8–13) are another example of how we go beyond the information so that what we perceive may not be physically present in the stimulus (and hence not present in the retinal image). Essentially, the experience of an illusion can be explained in terms of a *perceptual hypothesis* which is not confirmed by the data, so that our attempt to interpret the stimulus figure turns out to be misplaced or inappropriate. An illusion, then, occurs when we attempt to construe the stimulus in keeping with how we normally construe the world and are misled by this (an example being the reading of depth and distance cues into 2-D drawings).

When perceptual cues conflict, the visual system must 'bet' on which interpretation is correct. In the Ponzo illusion, for example (see Figure 1.6a on page 9), our system can accept the equal lengths of the two central bars as drawn on a flat 2-D surface (which would involve assuming that the bars are equidistant from us) or it can 'read' the whole figure as a railway track converging into the distance (so that the two horizontal bars represent sleepers, the top one of which would be further away from an observer but which appears longer since it 'must' be longer in order to produce the same length image on the retina).

The second interpretation is clearly inappropriate, since the figure is drawn on a flat piece of paper and there are no actual distance differences. As a result, an illusion is experienced. This case of mistaken perception illustrates (as do all illusions) how the perceptual system normally operates by forming a 'best guess' which is then tested against sensory inputs. For Gregory, illusions illustrate that perception is an active process of using information to suggest and test hypotheses. What we perceive are not the data but the interpretation of them so that 'a perceived object is a hypothesis, suggested and tested by sensory data' (Gregory, 1966). As

Gregory (1996) has noted, '. . . this makes the basis of knowledge indirect and inherently doubtful . . .'

In the case of reversible figures, Gregory argues that when we view a 3-D scene with many distance cues, the perceptual system can quickly select the hypothesis that best interprets the sensory data. However, reversible figures supply few distance cues to guide the system. For example, the Necker cube (see page 000) provides sensory evidence which fits the hypothesis of either orientation *equally* well. The spontaneous reversal of the cube occurs, says Gregory, because the perceptual system continually tests two equally plausible hypotheses as to the nature of the object represented in the drawing.

Additional evidence that the perceptual system generates hypotheses comes from improbable/impossible objects (see Chapter 1, page 10). One striking illusion is the *rotating hollow mask* (Gregory, 1970) which is shown in Figure 2.1 (see opposite page).

There is sufficient information for us to see the mask as hollow, but it is impossible not to see it as a normal face. When the mask is rotated, it does what Gregory (1970/1996) describes as:

'wonderful things . . . It will swing round to follow the observer . . . The effect may have been the basis of temple miracles: statues moving as though alive, following each devotee with the hollow heads as he moves in the gloom of the sacred place'.

Gregory (1970) explains the illusion in terms of the perceptual system dismissing the hypothesis that the mask is an inside-out face because it is so improbable (and note that in this case, the hypothesis we select is strongly influenced by our *past experiences* of faces). In the case of the impossible triangles (see Figure 1.8a on page 11), our perceptual system makes reasonable, but actually incorrect, judgements about the distance of different parts of the triangle.

Although appealing, Gregory's explanations of illusions have been questioned. According to his *misplaced size constancy theory*, the Müller-Lyer illusion (see Figure 1.6c on page 9) can be explained in terms of the arrow with the ingoing fins providing linear perspective cues which suggest that the arrow could be the outside corner of a building and the ingoing fins the walls receding from us. This would make the arrow appear to be 'close'. In the case of the arrow with the outgoing fins,

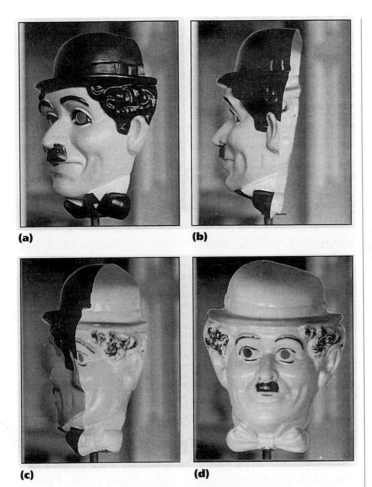

(a)   **(b)**

(c)   **(d)**

Figure 2.1   The rotating hollow mask. (a) shows the normal face which is rotated to (d), which is a hollow face. However, (d) appears like a normal face rotating in the opposite direction.

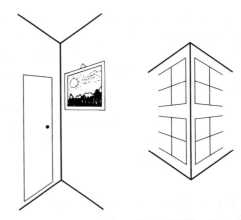

Figure 2.2   A representation of the Müller-Lyer illusion as suggested by Gregory's misplaced size constancy theory.

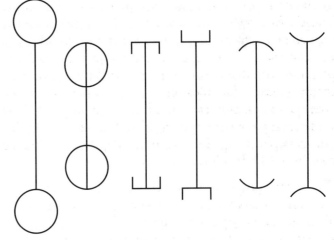

Figure 2.3   The Müller-Lyer illusion with the depth cues removed (after Delbœuf, 1892)

the cues suggest that the arrow could be the inside corner of a room and the outgoing fins as walls approaching us. This would make the shaft appear to be 'far' from us (see Figure 2.2).

However, the retinal images produced by the arrows are equal and, according to size constancy, if equally sized images are produced by two lines, one of which is further away from us than the other, then the line which is furthest from us must be longer! Because this interpretation is taking place unconsciously and quickly, we immediately perceive the illusion. The evidence suggests, though, that if the perspective cues are removed (as shown in Figure 2.3), the illusion remains. This suggests that the misapplied size constancy theory is itself misapplied. Additionally, it could also be that the apparent distance of the arrow is caused *by* the apparent size of the arrows rather than, as Gregory claims, the other way around (Robinson, 1972).

In a variation of the original Müller-Lyer illusion, Morgan (1969) placed a dot mid-way along the arrow as shown in Figure 2.4.

Figure 2.4   Morgan's (1969) modified Müller-Lyer illusion.

The dot appears to be nearer the left-hand end, and the only way this can be explained by Gregory is to claim that the fins make the arrow appear to slope away from us, providing a rather odd perspective interpretation of the figure. According to Gregory (1972), such a slope can be demonstrated, although this claim has been disputed by other researchers (e.g. Eysenck and Keane, 1995). An additional problem for Gregory concerns the relationship between knowledge and perceptions. In the Müller-Lyer, for example, we *know* that the arrows are the same length, yet we still experience the illusion. Our knowledge *should* enable us to modify (however we do this) our hypotheses (whatever these are) in an adaptive way. Whilst some illusions can be explained in terms of the same unconscious processes occurring (an example being size constancy), it is generally believed that not all illusions are amenable to explanation in the way Gregory proposes (Robinson, 1972).

GREGORY'S THEORY AND 'PERCEPTUAL SET'

The concept of *perceptual set* is also directly relevant to Gregory's view that perception is an active process involving selection, inference and interpretation. Perceptual set is 'a perceptual bias or predisposition or readiness to perceive particular features of a stimulus' (Allport, 1955). Put another way, 'perceptual set' refers to our tendency to perceive or notice some aspects of the available sense data and ignore others. According to Vernon (1955) set acts as a *selector*, whereby the perceiver has certain expectations which help focus attention on particular aspects of the incoming sensory information. Set also acts as an *interpreter*, whereby the perceiver knows how to deal with the selected data, how to classify, understand and name it, and what inferences to draw from it.

Several factors can influence or induce set. Most of these are to do with *perceiver* (or *organismic*) *variables*, but some are to do with the nature of the stimulus or the conditions under which it is being perceived (*stimulus* or *situational variables*). Both perceiver and stimulus variables influence perception only indirectly, through directly influencing set which, as such, is a perceiver variable or characteristic. Some of the findings relating to perceptual set are summarised in Box 2.1.

Box 2.1   Some findings relating to perceptual set

Motivation: Several studies (e.g. Sanford, 1937; McClelland and Atkinson, 1948) have shown that people with some particular need to be satisfied (such as hunger) are more likely to perceive vague or ambiguous pictures as relating to that need.

Values: Lambert et al. (1949) found that when children were taught to value something more highly than they had previously done, they perceived the valued thing as being larger, a phe-

---

nomenon which has been termed *perceptual accentuation*.

Status: According to Kassajarjian (1963), 'bigger is better' in that people with more status are judged to be taller. Although the American politician J.F. Kennedy was half an inch taller than his political rival Richard Nixon, Nixon's supporters perceived the two as being the same height whilst Kennedy's supporters saw their politician as being much taller.

Beliefs: The beliefs we hold about the world can affect our interpretation of ambiguous sensory signals. A person who believes in UFOs is likely to perceive an ambiguous object in the sky differently to a person who does not share that belief (Wade and Tavris, 1993).

Emotions: The perception of pain seems to be affected by emotion in that depression can make pain worse than it otherwise would be (Fields, 1991).

Cognitive style: The way in which we deal with our environment appears to affect our perception of it. Some people tend to perceive the environment as a whole and do not clearly differentiate the shape, colour and so on of individual items. Others tend to perceive the elements of the environment as separate and distinct from one another (Witkin et al., 1962).

Cultural background: Turnbull (1961) found that the Mbuti pygmies of Zaire, who seldom leave their forest environment and rarely encounter objects that are more than a few feet away, use perceptual cues differently to people from different cultural backgrounds (see also Chapter 4, pages 48–51).

Context and expectations: The interaction between context and expectations has been demonstrated in numerous studies (e.g. Bruner and Postman, 1949; Bruner et al., 1952). When participants are asked to copy a briefly presented stimulus such as:

PARIS IN THE
THE SPRING

it is typically copied as PARIS IN THE SPRING (Lachman, 1984). According to Loftus (1980), one reason why eyewitness testimony (see Chapter 11) is so unreliable is that our general expectation of people is that they will be of 'average height and weight' and this is what almost all eyewitness accounts describe people as being. The role of context and expectations can also influence what we hear. Reason and Mycielska (1982), for example, describe an incident in which the pilot of an airliner looked over to his apparently depressed co-pilot and said 'cheer up'. The co-pilot promptly raised the wheels of the aircraft, which was still on the ground, because he perceived his captain to have said 'gear up'.

An evaluation of Gregory's theory of perception

According to Gregory (1996), even a minimal amount of 'bottom-up' data (sensory signals) can produce detailed hypotheses. In support of this claim, Gregory cites a study conducted by Johansson (1975) who showed that in darkness, just a few lights attached to a moving person evoke clear perceptions of, for example, people walking or dancing. Gregory has also drawn on research which indicates that vision 'works' by many physiologically distinct 'channels' which are produced by their own 'modules'. A rotating spiral, for example, does not actually change size but appears to expand or contract. Because size and motion are signalled by different 'channels', disagreement between the channels leads to a *physiological paradox* being experienced.

Gregory's theory raises a number of important questions which have yet to be answered satisfactorily (Gordon, 1989). For example, if perception is essentially constructive, then we need to know how it gets started and why there is such commonality among the perceptions of different people, all of whom have had to construct their own idiosyncratic worlds (although a potential answer to this may be suggested by *probabilistic functionalism*: see Brunswick, 1956). Also, given that perception is typically accurate (and our hypotheses are usually correct), it seems unlikely that our retinal images are really as impoverished (in the sense of being ambiguous and lacking detailed information) as Gregory suggests.

According to Eysenck and Keane (1995), Gregory has been successful in explaining at least some types of illusion but much less than successful in explaining perception as a whole. Since illusions occur infre-

quently in everyday life, and since there are very few real-world instances of retinal images containing projections of single, isolated objects, Gregory's theory may be more relevant to explaining perception in artificial situations than perception as it takes place in the ordinary world. In Gordon's (1989) view, the richness of sensory evidence in the real world (the numerous objects, their background, movement and so on) has been underestimated by constructivist theories. For Gordon:

'it is possible that we perceive constructively only at certain times and in certain situations. Whenever we move under our own power on the surface of the natural world and in good light, the necessary perceptions of size, texture, distance, continuity, motion and so on, may all occur directly and reflexively'.

Gibson's theory of 'direct perception'

Constructivists use the retinal image as their starting point for explaining perception. According to Gibson (1966), the constructivist approach makes the mistake of describing the input for a perceiver in the same terms as that for a single *photoreceptor*, namely a stream of photons. In Gibson's view, it is better to begin by considering the input as a pattern of light extended over time and space which can be thought of as an *optical array* containing all the visual information from the environment striking the eye. The optical array provides unambiguous, invariant information about the layout of objects in space and this information takes three main forms: *optic flow patterns*, *texture gradient* and *affordances*. According to Gibson, perception essentially involves 'picking up' the rich information provided by the optic array in a direct way which involves little or no (unconscious) information processing, computations or internal representations.

OPTIC FLOW PATTERNS

During World War II, Gibson was asked to prepare training films describing the problems pilots experience when taking off and landing. Gibson called the information available to pilots *optic flow patterns* (OFPs). As shown in Figure 2.5, the point to which a pilot moves appears motionless, with the rest of the visual environment apparently moving away from that point. Thus, all around the point there is an apparent radial expansion of textures flowing around the pilot's head.

Figure 2.5   The optic flow patterns as a pilot approaches the landing strip (from Gibson, 1950).

The lack of apparent movement of the point towards which the pilot moves is an invariant, unchanging feature of the optic array. Such OFPs provide unambiguous information about direction, speed and altitude. Gibson was so impressed by the wealth of sensory information available to pilots in OFPs that he subsequently devoted himself to analysing other kinds of information available in sensory data under other conditions (Eysenck and Keane, 1995).

TEXTURE GRADIENTS

One such set of conditions are texture gradients (or *gradients of texture density*). Textures expand as we approach them and contract as they pass beyond our head. This happens whenever we move toward something, so that over and above the behaviour of each texture element, there is a 'higher-order' pattern or structure available as a source of information about the environment (and so the flow of the texture is *invariant*). As we saw in the previous chapter (see page 000), texture gradients are an important cue to depth and they are perceived directly without the need for any inferences. The examples of depth cues we identified in Chapter 1 (Box 1.3) are all examples of directly perceived, invariant, higher-order features of the optic array. For Gibson, then, the third dimension (depth) is

available to the senses as directly as the other two dimensions, automatically processed by the sense receptors, and automatically produces the perceptual experience of depth.

AFFORDANCES

Affordances are directly perceivable, potential uses of objects (a ladder, for example, 'affords' climbing) and they are closely linked with what Gibson calls *ecological optics*. To understand an animal's perceptual system, we need to consider the environment in which the animal has evolved, particularly the patterns of light (the optical array) which reaches the eye (ecological optics). As we know from Chapter 1 (see Box 1.3), when an object moves further away from the eye, its image gets smaller (relative size). We also saw that most objects are bounded by texture surfaces and that texture gradient gets finer as an object recedes. The point being made here is that objects are not judged in complete isolation, and the optic array commonly contains far more information than that associated with a single stimulus array (something which has tended to be overlooked by the use of classical optics and laboratory experiments (Gordon, 1989)).

An evaluation of Gibson's theory

According to Marr (1982), whose theory we will consider next, Gibson's concern with the problem of how we obtain constant perception in everyday life on the basis of continually changing sensations indicated that he correctly regarded the problem of perception as that of recovering from sensory information 'valid properties of the external world'. However, Marr argues that Gibson failed to recognise two equally critical things:

'First, the detection of physical invariants, like image surfaces, is exactly and precisely an information-processing problem, in modern terminology. Second, he vastly underrated the sheer difficulty of such detection'.

Gibson's concept of affordances is part of his attempt to show that all the information needed to make sense of the visual environment is directly available in the visual input (which is a purely 'bottom-up' approach to perception: see page 19). Bruce and Green (1990) argue that this concept is at its most powerful and useful in the context of *visually guided behaviour,* such as that of insects. Here, it makes sense to speak of an organism detecting information available in the light needed to organise its activities, and the idea of it needing to have a conceptual representation of its environment seems redundant.

Yet whilst affordance might apply to the detection of distance and other variables involved in the guidance of locomotion, humans act in a *cultural* as well as physical environment. It seems unlikely that no *knowledge* of writing or the postal system is needed in order to detect that a pen affords writing or a postbox affords posting a letter, and that these are directly perceived invariants.

'SEEING' AND 'SEEING AS'

Fodor and Pylyshyn (1981) distinguish between 'seeing' and 'seeing as'. For them:

> 'What you see when you see a thing depends upon what the thing you see is. But what you see the thing as depends upon what you know about what you are seeing'.

This view of perception as 'seeing as' is the fundamental principle of *transactionalism.* Transactionalists (such as Ames, cited in Ittelson, 1952) argue that because the sensory input is always ambiguous, the interpretation selected is the one most likely to be true given what has been perceived in the past.

In the Ames *distorted room* (which is shown in Figure 2.6), the perceiver is put in the situation of having to choose between two different beliefs about the world built up through past experience. The first is that rooms are rectangular, consist of right angles, and so on. The second is that people are usually of 'average' height. Most observers choose the first and so judge the people to be of an odd size (although a woman who saw her husband in the room and judged the room to be odd shows that particularly salient past experiences can override more generalised beliefs about the world).

Because most human activity takes place within a culturally defined environment, in which people see objects and events as what they are in terms of a culturally given conceptual representation of the world, Gibson's theory says much more about 'seeing' than about 'seeing as'.

The Ames room is another example of a visual illusion, and the inability of Gibson's theory to explain mistaken perception is perhaps its greatest single weakness. In his defence, Gibson argues that most 'mistaken perceptions' occur in situations very different from those which prevail in the natural environment. However, to suggest that illusions are nothing but perceptual tricks designed to baffle ordinary people is mistaken, since at least some produce effects that are similar to those found in normal perception (a striking example being the 'hollow mask' illusion described on page 20). As Bruce and Green (1990) have observed:

 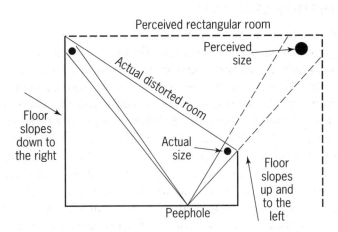

Figure 2.6   The Ames room (left) and a schematic representation of its 'secret' (right). The room is constructed in such a way that, when viewed with one eye through a peephole, a person at one end may appear very small and the person at the other end very tall. When they cross the room, they appear to change size. The room itself appears perfectly normal and regular to an observer.

'The hollow (mask) ... is a difficult one for even the most ardent Gibsonian to discuss as a laboratory trick. We must invoke a memory of some sort (with the illusion) to explain why we see what we are used to seeing despite useful information to the contrary'.

A possible synthesis of Gregory's and Gibson's theories

Clearly, Gibson's and Gregory's theories have important differences. There are, however, some points of agreement between them. Box 2.2 summarises the main points of agreement and disagreement between the two theoretical perspectives.

Box 2.2   The four main similarities and two main differences between Gibson and Gregory

Similarities

- Visual perception is mediated by light reflected from surfaces and objects.
- Some kind of physiological system is needed to perceive.
- Perception is an active process. (In Gibson's (1966) view, 'a perceiving organism is more like a map-reader than a camera'.)
- Perceptual experience can be influenced by learning.

Differences

- Gregory believes that meaningless sensory cues must be supplemented by memory, habit, experience and so on in order to construct a meaningful world. Gibson argues that the environment (initially the optic array) supplies us with a much richer and more usable source of information (indeed, it provides us with *all* the information we need for living in the world). In Gibson's view, perceptual learning consists not in 'gluing' together sensory 'atoms', but in coming to differentiate and discriminate between the features of the environment as presented in the optic array.
- To the extent that Gibson acknowledges the role of learning (albeit a different kind of learning from Gregory), he may be considered

an *empirist* (see Chapter 3), together with his emphasis on what is provided by the physical world. In other respects, though, Gibson can be considered a *nativist* (see Chapter 3). He was very much influenced by the Gestalt psychologists (see Chapter 1, pages 1–6) and like them, he stressed the organised quality of perception (although not in quite the same way: the organised quality of perception for Gibson is part of the physical structure of the light impinging on the observer's eye, whereas for Gestaltists it is a function of how the brain is organised).

Eysenck and Keane (1995) argue that the relative importance of bottom-up and top-down processes is affected by a number of factors. When viewing conditions are good, bottom-up processing may be crucial. However, if a stimulus is presented very briefly and/or is ambiguous, top-down processing becomes increasingly important. Gibson seems to have been more concerned with *optimal* viewing conditions whilst Gregory and other constructivists have tended to concentrate on *sub-optimal* conditions (Eysenck, 1993).

It seems reasonable to propose that, in most circumstances, both bottom-up and top-down processes are needed, and the most clearly constructed model which takes this into account is that described by Neisser (1976) whose *analysis-by-synthesis model* is shown in Figure 2.7.

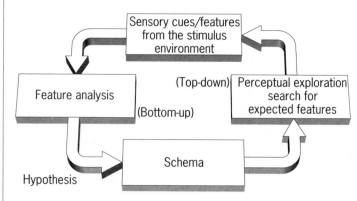

Figure 2.7   Neisser's analysis-by-synthesis model of perception.

Neisser assumes the existence of a *perceptual cycle* involving *schemata*, *perceptual exploration* and *stimulus environment*. Schemata contain collections of knowledge based on past experience (see Chapter 9), and these function to direct perceptual exploration towards relevant environmental stimulation. Such exploration often involves moving around the environment and leads the perceiver to actively sample the available stimulus information. If the sampled information fails to match that in the relevant schema, then the hypothesis is modified accordingly.

An initial *analysis* of the sensory cues/features (a bottom-up process) might suggest the hypothesis that the object being viewed is, say, a chair. This initiates a search for the expected features (such as four legs and a back), which is based on our schema of a chair (and this *synthesis* is a top-down process). However, if the environmental features disconfirm the original hypothesis (the 'chair' has only three legs and no back) then a new hypothesis must be generated and tested (it might be a stool) and the appropriate schema activated.

Neisser argues that perception never occurs in a vacuum, since our sampling of sensory features of the environment is always guided by our knowledge and past experience. In this approach, then, perception is an *interactive process*, involving both bottom-up feature analysis and top-down expectations.

Marr's computational theory of vision

According to Marr (1982), the central 'problem' of perception is identifying the precise *mechanisms* and *computations* by which useful information about a scene is extracted from that scene ('useful information' being that which will guide the thoughts or actions of the total system of which the visual system is but a part). Marr's computational theory of vision begins by asking the question 'what is the visual system for?', because only by answering this question can we understand how it works.

Marr believes that there are three levels at which any process must be understood. The *computational theory level* is a theoretical analysis of the tasks performed by a system (in this case, the visual system) and the methods needed to perform them. At the *algorithmic level*, the concern is with identifying the actual operations by which perceptual tasks (processes and representations) are achieved. Finally, the *hardware* or *implementation level* is concerned with the mechanisms underlying the operation of the system. In the case of a biological visual system, these are neuronal or nervous system structures.

Marr argues that the main 'job' of vision is deriving a representation of shape, and that the first question to answer is how the visual system is able to derive reliable information regarding the shapes of objects in the real world from information contained in the retinal image. His answer was that visual representation is organised as an information processing system consisting of a series of four successive stages which represent individual visual *modules* of progressive complexity (Eysenck, 1993).

Each stage or module takes as its input the information it receives from the previous stage and makes it into a more complex description or representation of the input. By taking the image as the starting point (that is, the result of light rays from objects or scenes in the real world being focused onto a light-sensitive surface, either a screen or the retina), Marr's approach is strictly bottom-up (Roth, 1995). However, and as we will see when we look at 3-D object recognition, there are also top-down aspects to his theory. The four stages or modules are described in Box 2.3.

3-D MODEL REPRESENTATION AND OBJECT RECOGNITION

Since the 3-D model representation involves top-down processes (drawing on stored knowledge of what objects look like), Marr argued that in many cases 3-D structures can be derived from the $2\frac{1}{2}$-D sketch using only general principles of the kind used in the earlier stages. This view rests on the observation that stick-figure representations (especially of animals and plants) are easy to recognise (Garnham, 1991). The brain automatically transposes the contours derived from the $2\frac{1}{2}$-D sketch onto axes of symmetry which resemble stick figures composed of pipe cleaners. The 3-D model consists of a unique description of any object a person can distinguish – the same object should always produce the same unique description no matter what the angle of viewing.

Marr and Nishihara (1978) argued that the parts of the body can be represented as jointed cylinders or

Box 2.3   The four stages or modules of Marr's computational theory of vision

The image (or grey-level description)

This represents the intensity of light at each point in the retinal image, so as to discover regions in the image and their boundaries. Regions and boundaries are parts of images, not parts of things in the world, so this represents the starting point of seeing.

The primal sketch

Useful attributes of a 3-D scene (such as surface markings, object boundaries and shadows) can be recovered from the image by locating and describing the places where the intensity of the image changes relatively abruptly from place to place. The function of the *raw primal sketch* is to describe potentially significant regions, that is, those which may correspond in the real world to the boundaries between overlapping objects, their edges and texture. The *full primal sketch* provides information about how these regions 'go together' to form structures, that is, it provides a functional explanation for the Gestalt grouping principles (see pages 2–5). Grouping is necessary, since in complex scenes, for example, the images of different objects may occlude each other. Overall, it provides a more useful and less cluttered description of the image, hence the term 'sketch'.

2½-D sketch

The primal sketch helps the formation of the 2½-D sketch. The function of the 2½-D sketch is to make explicit the orientation and depth of visible structures, as if a 'picture' of the world is beginning to emerge. It is no longer an image because it contains information about things in the world which provide the image. However, it describes only the visible part of the scene and so is not fully three-dimensional. Object recognition requires that the input representation of the object is mapped against a representation stored in memory, so that non-visible parts are taken into account (and this is essentially what perceptual constancy (see pages 7–8) involves). Also, the sketch changes with the observer's viewpoint (it is *viewpoint dependent*) and so descriptions at this stage are not invariant.

3-D model representation

The function of the 3-D sketch is to make shapes and their spatial organisation explicit as belonging to particular 3-D objects, independently of any particular position or orientation on the retina (they are *viewpoint independent*). The observer now has a model of the external world and knowledge about the nature and construction of the object is utilised (top-down processing). The 3-D model representation corresponds to object recognition.

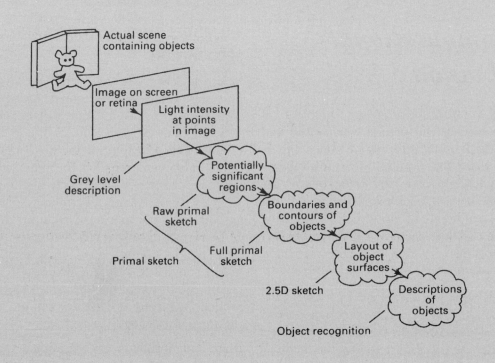

generalised cylinders which change their size along their length as shown in Figure 2.8. They then showed that the cylinders which compose an object can be computed from the 2½-D sketch (the lines running down the centre of these cylinders – important in the recognition process – make up the stick figures). Once

a generalised cylinder representation of objects in a scene has been computed, it can be compared with stored representations of objects in a catalogue of 3-D models where objects are represented in 'standard' orientations (Garnham, 1991).

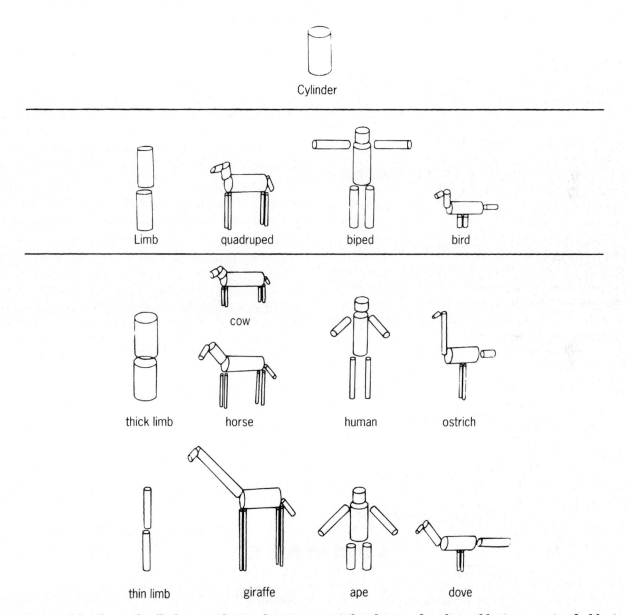

Figure 2.8   Combinations of cylinders can be used to represent the shapes of various objects or parts of objects.

An evaluation of Marr's theory

According to Harris and Humphreys (1995), Marr's theory is an important contribution to perception, and his framework remains the widest-ranging computational account of visual object recognition. Marr and Hildreth (1980) have presented evidence indicating that Marr's model does generate a symbolic representation which corresponds to the significant components of the input. But as Roth (1995) has observed, this does not mean that biological systems necessarily work in the same way, although the research conducted by Hubel and Wiesel (see Chapter 1, page 14) is relevant to Marr's theory (as are other findings from neurophysiology, even if the link has not been explicitly made by those, such as Ono et al. (1993), working in the area).

The least well-supported stage in Marr's theory is the 3-D model, although this is not surprising since the problems are more formidable. As we have seen, the early stages make only very general assumptions about the structure of the external world and do not require knowledge of specific objects. Although a bottom-up approach is not an inevitable consequence of the computational approach, it has dominated recent research. In part, this is because it is easier to derive computational theories from the early stages of perception, where the relationships between the stimulus and the world are much easier to specify (Harris and Humphreys, 1995).

Gardner (1985), too, has argued that most of Marr's theory focuses on the steps prior to the recognition of real objects in the real world ('the most central part of perception') and that:

> 'the procedures (Marr) outlined for object recognition may prove applicable chiefly to the perception of figures of a certain sort, for example, the mammalian body, which lends itself to decomposition in terms of generalised cylindrical forms'.

As Harris and Humphreys (1995) have noted, researchers are beginning to reconsider whether top-down, domain-specific knowledge might be used. This has been encouraged by *connectionist models of visual perception* and Biederman's (1987) *recognition-by-components theory* which, as we saw in Chapter 1 (see pages 13–14), proposes that stored knowledge about objects may be contacted directly from 2-D information in the image, without the elaboration of 2½-D and 3-D descriptions. Nevertheless, Marr's general approach to perception and his particular argument for computational theories is, in Harris and Humphreys' (1995) terms:

> 'likely to remain as one of the most important contributions of research in artificial intelligence to psychological theory. Such theories are able to guide empirical and theoretical research, even if the detailed models specified at any one time later turn out to be wrong'.

Conclusions

All of the various theories of visual perception we have considered are supported to some degree by experimental evidence. At present, however, no one theory seems to be sufficiently well-supported by evidence as to be accepted as a 'best' explanation of visual perception.

SUMMARY

- Some psychologists trying to explain visual perception have asked whether the way we perceive is the result of learning/experience or basically an inbuilt ability. Others are concerned with how **physical energy** received by the sense organs (sensation) forms the basis of **perceptual experience**.
- According to **top-down (conceptually-driven) perceptual processing theorists**, such as Gregory, Bruner and Neisser, perception is the end result of a process that involves making **inferences** about the world, based on our knowledge and expectations, making perception an **indirect** process.
- By contrast, **bottom-up (data-driven) perceptual processing theorists**, such as Gibson, argue that our perception of the world is basically determined by the information presented to the sensory receptors, making perception a **direct** process.

- According to Gregory's **constructivist theory**, perception sometimes involves selecting from all the available sensory stimulation (so as to avoid **sensory overload**), but often we go beyond the immediately given evidence of the senses by supplementing it in the form of **unconscious inferences**.
- Examples of the constructivist nature of perception are **perceptual constancies** and **illusions**. The experience of an illusion involves making a **perceptual hypothesis** which is not confirmed by the data: our normal ways of construing the world turn out to be inappropriate when applied to particular stimulus figures, as when we interpret the Ponzo illusion as a railway track converging into the distance.
- Reversible figures provide few distance cues, and the sensory evidence they do provide fits equally well two different hypotheses as to the nature of the object represented in the drawing. The spontaneous reversal occurs because the perceptual system continually tests the two equally plausible hypotheses.
- Gregory's **misplaced size constancy theory** account of the Müller-Lyer illusion claims that we interpret the ingoing and outgoing fins of the arrows as providing perspective cues to distance. However, removal of the perspective cues does not get rid of the illusion, suggesting that Gregory's theory is mistaken. Also, *knowing* that the arrows are the same length should, but does not, prevent us from experiencing the illusion.
- **Perceptual set** is another demonstration of Gregory's view that perception is an active process involving selection, inference and interpretation. Set acts as a **selector** and as an **interpreter** and can be induced by **perceiver/organismic variables** and **stimulus/situational variables**.
- Perceiver variables that have been shown to influence set include **motivation**, **values** (which are related to **perceptual accentuation**), **beliefs**, **emotion**, **cognitive style**, **cultural background** and **expectations** (which often interact with **context**).
- In support of his theory, Gregory cites Johansson's study in which lights attached to a moving person are sufficient for perception of walking/dancing and research indicating the existence of physiologically distinct visual channels, which can produce a **physiological paradox**, as in a rotating spiral.
- Gregory's theory poses its own questions, such as how perception gets started and why there is such agreement among the perceptual experience of people who are all having to construct their own worlds. Also, the typical accuracy of our perception implies that our retinal images may be richer than Gregory suggests.
- Gregory's theory may be more capable of explaining (at least certain) illusions than perception as a whole, and, hence, more relevant to perception in artificial situations than in everyday life, where it may happen much more directly and reflexively.
- According to Gibson, constructivists are wrong to take the retinal image as the starting point for explaining perception. The correct starting point is the **optical array**, which provides unambiguous/invariant information about the layout of objects in space in the form of **optic flow patterns**, **texture gradient** and **affordances**. Little or no (unconscious) information processing, computations or internal representations are needed.
- Gibson first identified **optic flow patterns (OFPs)** when preparing training films for pilots during World War II. The point towards which the pilot moves appears not to move, while there is an apparent radial expansion of textures flowing around the pilot's head. This provides unambiguous information about direction, speed and altitude.
- Like OFPs, **texture gradients/gradients of texture density** represent an **invariant**, unchanging and 'higher-order' feature of the optic array. They are an important cue to depth, which is directly available to the senses and automatically processed by the sense receptors.
- **Affordances** are directly perceivable, potential uses of objects, closely linked with **ecological optics**; objects are not judged in isolation, and the optic array usually contains far more information than is provided by any single stimulus.
- The concept of affordances is most useful in the context of **visually guided behaviour**, as when insects need to detect distance to guide their locomotion. But humans act in a **cultural** as well as a physical environment, and Gibson seems to have overlooked the role of **knowledge** in perception.
- Gibson failed to draw the distinction between **seeing** and **seeing as**, the latter being largely culturally defined and the fundamental principle of **transactionalism** as demonstrated by the Ames **distorted room** illusion.
- Gibson's theory seems incapable of explaining mistaken perception. Not all illusions are mere perceptual tricks and some, like the hollow-mask illusion, produce effects similar to those found in normal perception.
- Both Gibson and Gregory agree that perception is

mediated by light reflected from surfaces and objects, and requires some kind of physiological system. They also both regard perception as an active process that can be influenced by learning (making them **empirists**), although different kinds of learning are proposed in the two theories. Gibson is also a **nativist** in certain respects and was influenced by the Gestalt psychologists.

- Bottom-up processing (Gibson) may be crucial under **optimal** viewing conditions, but under **sub-optimal** conditions, top-down processing (Gregory) becomes increasingly important.
- According to Neisser's **analysis-by-synthesis model**, perception normally involves **both** types of processing, appearing at different stages of a **perceptual cycle** that comprises **schemata, perceptual exploration** and **stimulus environment**. Perception is an **interactive process** involving both bottom-up feature analysis and top-down expectations.
- Marr's **computational theory of vision** represents one of three levels at which any process must be understood, the others being the **algorithmic** and **hardware/implementation** levels. The computational theory level is concerned with what the visual system is for, i.e. the tasks it performs. For Marr, its main task is to derive a representation of shape.
- We need to know how the visual system is able to derive reliable information regarding the shapes of objects in the real world from information contained in the retinal image. This is achieved by a series of four increasingly complex stages or **mod-**

ules, each taking as its input the information received from the previous stage/module: **the image/grey-level description, the primal sketch (raw primal sketch** and **full primal sketch), the 2½-D sketch** (which is **viewpoint dependent**) and the **3-D model representation/object recognition** (which is **viewpoint independent**).

- By taking the image as the starting point, Marr's approach is bottom-up, but the 3-D model representation involves top-down processes (drawing on stored representations of what objects look like, as in a catalogue of 3-D models). Often, 3-D structures are derived from the 2½-D sketch using stick-figure representations which are composed of the lines running down the centre of jointed or generalised cylinders.
- Despite some supporting evidence for Marr's theory, this does not necessarily imply that biological systems work in the same way, although neurophysiological research (including that of Hubel and Wiesel) is relevant. Not surprisingly, the 3-D model representation is the least well-supported stage in the theory: it is easier to derive computational theories from the early (bottom-up) stages of perception.
- **Connectionist models** of visual perception and Biederman's **recognition-by-components theory** have encouraged a reconsideration of the possible role of top-down, domain-specific knowledge. Nevertheless, Marr's computational approach remains a major influence on research, even if the specific details prove to be mistaken.

STUDYING THE DEVELOPMENT OF VISUAL PERCEPTUAL ABILITIES 1: HUMAN NEONATE AND INFANT STUDIES

Introduction and overview

As we saw in Chapter 1, visual perception is a complex set of interconnected and overlapping abilities, such as the perception of shape, depth and form. Whether these abilities are present at birth or develop through experience has been one of psychology's most enduring concerns. Our aim in this, and the following, chapter is to examine the evidence concerning the development of visual perception.

In this chapter, we will concentrate on studies involving human neonates (or new-born babies) and infants. At least in theory, the study of neonates is the most direct way of assessing which perceptual abilities are present at birth and which develop through experience. Unfortunately, neonates cannot *tell* us about their visual experiences, and so researchers have had to devise ingenious ways to allow them to *infer* what the new-born baby can perceive (and note that we can never be certain that such inferences are correct!). In addition to looking at the findings concerning neonate and infant visual perception, we will also consider some of the methods that have been used in this area of research.

The 'nature' and 'nurture' of visual perception

According to Mehler and Dupoux (1994):

'In certain cultures different from our own, the baby was thought of as a repository of a soul that had already lived before, and therefore possessed of all faculties utilised by adults. Closer to us, gen-erations of parents believed, on the contrary, that their children were born deaf and blind and that they remained in this condition for weeks, even months. The notion that the new-born was about as competent as a potted plant and that it had to learn to see, hear, memorise and cate-gorise, was extremely influential in Western thought'.

The issue of whether visual perceptual abilities (and other abilities for that matter: see Chapter 13) are *innate* (or *inborn*) or the product of *experience and learning* has long been the subject of philosophical and psychological interest. *Nativists* (or *innate theorists*) argue that we are born with certain capacities and capa-bilities to perceive the world in particular ways. Whilst such abilities might be immature or incomplete at birth, nativists argue that they develop gradually there-after, proceeding through a genetically determined process of maturation in which experience is held to play only a minor (if any) role. The Gestalt psycholo-gists (whose views on visual perception were described in Chapter 1) can be considered a good illustration of such a perspective.

Those who believe that our capacities and capabilities develop through experience are called *empirists* (and can be distinguished from *empiricists*, who follow a methodological prescription which says that we should rely on observation, experience and measure-ment to obtain reliable knowledge: Wertheimer, 1970). For the English philosopher John Locke (1690), the mind at birth is a *blank slate* (or *tabula rasa*) on which experience 'writes' and that, in the case of visual perception, the world can only be understood through learning and experience. Locke's belief was supported by the eminent American philosopher and psychologist William James (1890), according to whom:

'the baby, assailed by eyes, ears, nose, skin and entrails at once, feels it all as one great booming, buzzing confusion'.

Studying neonate and infant visual perception

If visual perception is innate, then it ought to be possible to demonstrate perceptual abilities in human neonates. If visual perception is dependent on experience, then such attempts should be doomed to failure. Before we look at the perceptual world of the human neonate, we need to be familiar with some of the methods that have been used in this area of research. Some of these are summarised in Box 3.1.

Box 3.1   Some methods used in studying neonate and infant perception

Spontaneous visual preference technique (or *preferential looking*)
Two stimuli are presented simultaneously to the neonate. If more time is spent looking at one, it can reasonably be assumed that (a) the difference between the stimuli can be perceived, and (b) the stimulus that is looked at longer is preferred.

Sucking rate
In this, a dummy or pacifier is used and the rate at which it is sucked in response to different stimuli is measured. First, a *baseline sucking rate* is established and then a stimulus introduced. The stimulus may produce an increase or decrease in sucking rate but, eventually, *habituation* will occur, and the baby will stop responding to the stimulus. If the stimulus is changed and another increase or decrease in sucking rate occurs, it can be inferred that the baby has responded to the change as a novel stimulus and hence can tell the difference between the two stimuli.

Habituation
As well as being used in the way described above, habituation has been used as a method in its own right. If an external stimulus and a baby's representation of it match, then the baby presumably knows the stimulus. This will be reflected by the baby ignoring it. Mismatches will maintain the baby's attention, so that a novel (and discrim-

---

inable) stimulus presented after habituation to a familiar stimulus re-excites attention.

Conditioned head rotation
In this, the infant is operantly conditioned to turn its head in response to a stimulus. The stimulus can then be presented in, for example, a different orientation, and the presence or absence of the conditioned response noted. This method has been used to test for shape constancy (see page 8) and in auditory perception to study basic abilities such as frequency, localisation and complexity (Bornstein, 1988).

Physiological measures
Two of the most important physiological measures are heart rate and breathing rate. If a physiological change occurs when a new stimulus is presented, it can be inferred that the infant can discriminate between the old and new stimuli.

Measures of electrical activity in the brain
By using electrodes attached to the brain, researchers can look for *visually evoked potentials* (*VEPs*) occurring in response to particular stimuli. If different stimuli produce different VEPs, the infant can presumably distinguish between those stimuli.

The perceptual equipment of babies

At birth, the nervous system as a whole is still immature. The optic nerve is thinner and shorter than in adults and is only partially myelinated (i.e. the myelin sheath, a white, fatty material which encases some nerve fibres, is not fully developed; it will not be fully myelinated until about four months). As a result, visual information is transmitted less effectively to the cortex, which itself has yet to mature. Also, at birth the human eye is about half the size and weight of an adult's, and the eyeball is shorter. This reduces the distance between the retina and lens which makes vision less efficient. So, although the new-born's eyeball is anatomically identical to an adult's, the relationship of the parts to each other is different, and they do not develop at the same rate. Some findings concerning the visual abilities of babies are described in Box 3.2.

Box 3.2   What can babies see?

Colour perception

The retina and its rods and cones are reasonably well developed at birth, being differentiated by the seventh month of pregnancy at the latest. Using the habituation technique, Bornstein (1976) found that in the absence of brightness cues, three-month-olds could discriminate blue-green from white, and yellow from green (tests which are typically failed by those who are red-green colour blind). Bornstein (1988) has argued that babies possess largely normal colour vision by the age of two months and in some as early as one month.

Brightness

The fovea (a small pit in the retina which focuses images) is structurally differentiated by the fourth month of pregnancy, and is fairly well developed at birth. The developing foetus reacts to bright light, and the *pupillary reflex* is present even in premature babies, with the *blink reflex* present at birth. These findings suggest that a baby's sensitivity to brightness is reasonably similar to an adult's. According to Adams and Maurer (1984), the ability to discriminate between lights of varying intensity improves with time and has reached adult levels within one year.

Movement

The *optokinetic reflex* (or *optic nystagmus*), which enables us to follow a moving object, is present within two days of birth. Whilst it is less efficient than that of an adult's, it improves rapidly in the first three months of life. Horizontal movement is better tracked than vertical movement, but is still 'jerky'. This may be because *convergence* (which is essential for fixation and depth perception: see Chapter 1, page 6) is absent at birth, although fully developed by two to three months. *Accommodation* to the distance of objects is equivalent to that of an adult by about four months and, like at least some of the above, is probably due to maturation.

Visual acuity

Gwiazda et al. (1980) used the preference method to show that the *threshold of visual acuity* (the ability to discriminate fine detail) is about 30 times poorer than that of an adult and, at birth, everything beyond 20 centimetres is seen as a blur. However, babies aged one to three months will learn to suck on a nipple connected to the

focus on a projector to bring a blurred picture into focus (Kalnins and Bruner, 1973). Research also indicates that when electrodes are attached to a baby's scalp above its visual cortex, VEPs occur in response to visual stimuli, suggesting that some degree of acuity is present at birth. Between six and 12 months, visual acuity comes within adult ranges, although it may not reach 20/20 vision until the age of ten or 11 (Adams, 1987).

The perceptual abilities of babies

PATTERN OR FORM PERCEPTION

Using the 'preferential looking' technique, Fantz (1961) presented one- to 15-week-old babies with pairs of stimuli (as shown in Figure 3.1). The stimuli were presented at weekly intervals, and Fantz measured the amount of time the babies spent looking at each. As Figure 3.1 shows, there was a distinct preference for more *complex stimuli*, that is, stimuli which contain more information and in which there is more 'going on'. Thus, the most popular stimulus was the checkerboard pattern and the least popular a triangle. According to Fantz:

'the relative attractiveness of the two members of a pair depended on the presence of a pattern difference. There were strong preferences between stripes and bull's-eyes and between checkerboard and square. Neither the cross and circle nor the two triangles aroused a significant differential interest. The differential response to pattern was shown at all ages tested, indicating that it was not the result of a learning process'.

Fantz also found that the preference for complexity appears to be a function of age (reflecting the fact that the eye, the visual nerve pathways and the visual cortex are poorly developed at birth). As we noted, the babies were tested at weekly intervals, and Fantz found that they could discriminate between stimuli with progressively narrower stripes (cf. visual acuity in Box 3.2). In a subsequent experiment, Fantz showed that two- to four-month-old babies prefer patterns to colour or

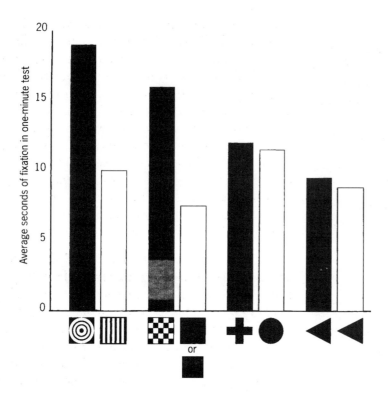

Figure 3.1   Average time spent looking at various pairs of stimulus patterns in babies aged one to 15 weeks (from Fantz, 1961).

brightness. In that experiment, six test objects were used. These were flat discs six inches in diameter. Three of these were patterned (a face, a bull's-eye and a patch of printed matter). The other three were plain (a red disc, a fluorescent yellow disc and a white disc). The discs were presented one at a time against a blue background, and the time spent looking at each was recorded. As Figure 3.2 shows, there was a preference for the face over both the printed matter and the bull's-eye, and all of these were preferred to the plain discs.

The preference for increasing complexity seems to suggest that the baby's capacity for differentiation steadily improves. One possible reason for this is that its ability to scan becomes more efficient and thorough. Support for this possibility comes from studies conducted by Salapatek (1975), who showed that very young infants confine their scanning to one corner of a triangle, suggesting a preference for areas of greatest contrast. It is only later on that the baby begins to explore all around the stimulus and inside it, and attends to the whole pattern and not just specific parts. Slater and Morison (1985) have also shown that before two months of age, neonates probably discriminate between shapes on the basis of lower-order variables such as orientation and contrast. After two months, however, what Slater

(1989) calls 'true form perception' begins, and higher-order variables (such as configurational invariance and form categories) are responded to.

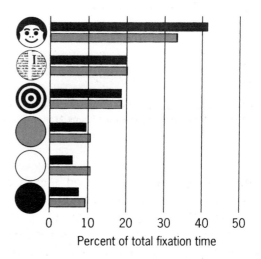

Figure 3.2   Preference for complex stimuli over simple stimuli as demonstrated by Fantz (1961). The black bars show the percentage of fixation time for two- to three-month-olds. The grey bars show the percentage of fixation time for four-month-olds (from Fantz, 1961).

THE PERCEPTION OF HUMAN FACES

The most interesting and attractive stimulus experienced by a baby is the human face. The human face is three-dimensional, contains high contrast information (especially the eyes, mouth and hairline), is constantly moving (the eyes, mouth and head), is a source of auditory information (the voice) and regulates its behaviour according to the baby's own activities. Thus, the human face combines complexity, pattern and movement, all of which babies appear innately to prefer. Whether or not this preference occurs because of this combination of factors or whether there is an innate perceptual knowledge of a face *as a face* was also addressed by Fantz (1961).

Fantz presented babies aged between four days and six months with all possible pairs of the three stimuli shown in Figure 3.3. The stimuli were coloured black, presented against a pink background, and of the approximate shape and size of an adult's head.

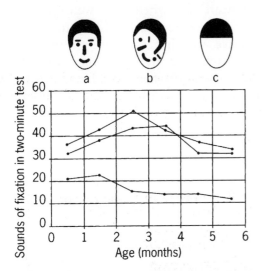

Figure 3.3   Looking times for each of the stimuli used in Fantz's study of the perception of faces (from Fantz, 1961).

Irrespective of age, the data showed that babies preferred to look at the schematic representation of a face (a) more than the 'scrambled' face (b). The control stimulus (c) was largely ignored. Even though the difference between (a) and (b) was small, Fantz concluded that 'there is an unlearned, primitive meaning in the form perception of infants', by which he meant that babies have an innate preference for 'facedness'.

Hershenson et al. (1965) pointed out that (a) and (b)

were more *complex* than (c) and that this might account for Fantz's findings rather than a preference for looking at human faces. In their experiment, complexity was controlled for, and neonates were presented with all possible pairs of three equally complex stimuli. These were: (1) a real female face, (2) a distorted picture which retained the outline of head and hair but altered the position of the other features, and (3) a scrambled face (stimulus (b) in Fantz's experiment). They found *no* preference for any of the three stimuli and, on the basis of this, concluded that a preference for real faces is not innate. In their view, such a preference does not appear until about four months of age.

A number of researchers have argued that rather than babies innately preferring the human face, they actually develop a selective responsiveness to it and things that resemble it. According to Rheingold (1961), the reason for this is that the human face embodies all the stimulus dimensions which neonates do seem innately to prefer, and these are 'packaged' in an attractive and stimulating form. For Rheingold, the human face is a *supernormal stimulus.*

There is now a large body of findings concerning the perception of 'facedness'. Some researchers (e.g. Melhuish, 1982; Kleiner, 1987) have obtained findings which are inconsistent with Fantz's claims, whilst others (e.g. Bushnell and Sai, 1987) have shown that babies as young as two days and five hours old display a clear preference for their mother's face over the face of a female stranger when variables such as the overall brightness of the face and hair colour are controlled for.

According to Slater (1995), given the complexity of the human face, it is hardly surprising to find that babies fail to make subtle distinctions about faces (such as distinguishing male from female) until mid- to late-infancy. Meltzoff and Moore (1992) have found that babies will, only minutes after birth, imitate a range of facial expressions they see an adult produce. For Slater (1995), such a finding indicates that neonates can match what they see to some inbuilt knowledge of their own face, and can use this to produce some facial gesture which, in the case of furrowing the forehead, for example, they cannot see. In Slater's view, the evidence indicates that:

'some knowledge about faces is present at birth, suggesting that babies come into the world with some innate, genetically determined knowledge about faces'.

Depth perception in babies

The question of whether or not neonates can perceive depth has been addressed in a number of different ways. Perhaps the most famous of these is Gibson and Walk's (1960) use of the *visual cliff apparatus*, which is shown in Figure 3.4. It consists of a central platform on one side of which (the *shallow* side) is a sheet of plexiglass. Immediately below this is a black and white checkerboard pattern. On the other side is another sheet of plexiglass, this time with the checkerboard pattern placed on the floor, at a distance of about four feet which gives the appearance of a 'drop' or 'cliff' (and this is called the *deep* side). The baby is placed on the central platform and its mother calls and beckons to it, first from one side and then the other.

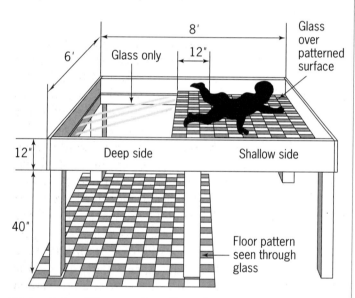

Figure 3.4   Gibson and Walk's 'visual cliff' apparatus.

Gibson and Walk found that most babies aged between six and 14 months would not crawl onto the 'deep' side when called by their mothers. This finding was interpreted as indicating that neonates have the innate ability to perceive depth. Those babies who did venture onto the deep side did so 'accidentally', either by backing onto it or resting on it. It is likely that their poor motor control was responsible for this rather than their inability to perceive depth.

The very nature of the visual cliff apparatus, however, required the researchers to use babies who could *crawl* and, as we mentioned above, the youngest was six

months old. An alternative explanation of Gibson and Walk's findings would be that the babies had *learned* to perceive depth during their first six months. Gibson and Walk subsequently tested a number of members of *precocial species* (who are capable of moving about independently at or shortly after birth). Chicks less than one day old never crossed onto the deep side, nor did goat kids and lambs. Rats would, if they could feel the glass with their very sensitive whiskers. However, when their whiskers were removed and they had to rely on vision, they too did not venture onto the deep side. If forcibly placed on the deep side, the various non-human animals would 'freeze'.

In an ingenious way of assessing human babies younger than six months, Campos et al. (1970) used heart rate as an index of depth perception. Infants of various ages had their heart rates monitored whilst they were on the visual cliff. Older children (nine months) showed an increase in heart rate, a response presumably indicating fear. The youngest babies (two months) showed a *decrease* in heart rate when they were placed on the 'deep' side. They were also less likely to cry and were more attentive to what was underneath them, and clearly not frightened by what they saw. No such changes were observed when the infants were placed on the 'shallow' side. It seems that even two-month-old babies can perceive depth and that avoidance behaviour is probably learnt (perhaps after having a few experiences of falling).

Depth perception has also been studied by looking at how neonates react when an object approaches their face from a distance. For example, if a large box is moved towards a 20-day-old neonate's face, it shows what Bower et al. (1970) have termed an *integrated avoidance response*, that is, it throws back its head, shields its face with its hands, and even cries. This suggests that the baby understands that the box is getting closer and, because it is potentially harmful, some sort of protective reaction is needed. It is interesting to note that the integrated avoidance response occurs even with one eye closed, but does not occur when equivalent pictures are shown on a screen. This indicates that *motion parallax* (see Chapter 1, page 7) is the critical cue for distance.

In his review of the literature on depth perception in neonates, Bornstein (1988) suggests that the roles of innate and experiential factors are both important and inseparable. For Bornstein:

'no matter how early in life depth perception can be demonstrated, no matter how late its emergence, it can never be proved that only experience has mattered'.

The perception of 3-D objects

Bower et al.'s (1970) discovery of the integrated avoidance response (see above) suggests that as well as perceiving depth, neonates see boxes as solid, 3-D objects. In order to consider this suggestion further, Bower (1979) devised a piece of apparatus that creates illusions of 3-D objects. Babies aged 16 to 24 weeks were put in front of a screen. A plastic, translucent object was suspended between lights and the screen so that it cast a double shadow on the back. When the screen is viewed from the front and the neonate wears polarizing goggles, the double shadows merge to form the image of a solid 3-D object. The apparatus is shown in Figure 3.5.

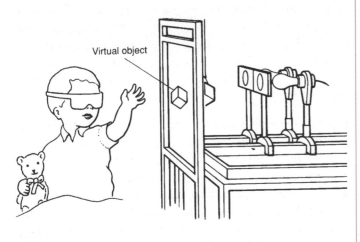

Figure 3.5   Trying to grasp a 'virtual object' produces surprise in a 4–6-month-old baby.

Bower found that none of the babies showed any surprise when they grasped a real and solid object, but when they reached for the apparent object and discovered there was nothing solid to get hold of, they all expressed surprise and some were even distressed. Such a finding indicates that they expected to be able to touch what they could 'see', an ability which Bower believes to be innate.

Perceptual organisation: constancies and Gestalt principles

SIZE CONSTANCY

Perceptual constancy is a major form of perceptual organisation and seems to be a prerequisite for many other types of organisation (see Chapter 1). According to empirists, constancy is learned, and so neonates are likely to be 'tricked' by the appearance of things. For example, if something looks smaller (it projects a smaller retinal image), then it *is* smaller. Nativists, however, would argue that neonates are innately able to judge the size of an object regardless of the retinal image it produces.

In an attempt to assess nativist and empirist claims, Bower (1966) initially conditioned two-month-olds to turn their heads whenever they saw a 30-centimetre cube at a distance of one metre (an adult popping up in front of the neonate whenever it performed the desired behaviour served as a very powerful reinforcer). Once the response had been conditioned, the cube was replaced by one of three different cubes. The first was a 30-centimetre cube presented at a distance of three metres. This stimulus produced a retinal image which was one-third the size of the original. The second was a 90-centimetre cube presented at a distance of one metre. This produced a retinal image that was three times the size of the original. The third was a 90-centimetre cube presented at a distance of three metres. This produced exactly the same-sized retinal image as the conditioned stimulus. Bower's experimental set-up is illustrated in Figure 3.6.

Bower recorded the number of times each stimulus produced the conditioned response, and used this as a measure of how similar the neonate considered the stimulus to be to the original. Compared with the original stimulus, which produced a total of 98 conditioned responses, the first stimulus produced 58, the second produced 54, and the third produced 22. The finding that most conditioned responses occurred in response to the first stimulus indicates that the baby was responding to the actual size of the cube irrespective of its distance, which suggests the presence of size

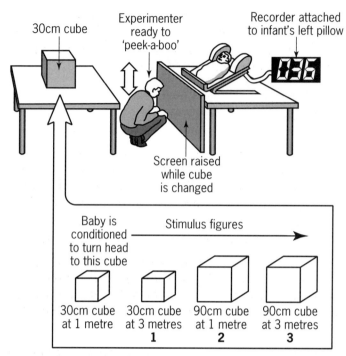

Figure 3.6 The experimental set-up in Bower's study of size constancy.

Labels in figure:
- 30cm cube
- Experimenter ready to 'peek-a-boo'
- Recorder attached to infant's left pillow
- Screen raised while cube is changed
- Baby is conditioned to turn head to this cube
- Stimulus figures
- 30cm cube at 1 metre — **1**
- 30cm cube at 3 metres — **2**
- 90cm cube at 1 metre — **3**
- 90cm cube at 3 metres

constancy and supports the nativist view that this constancy is inbuilt.

The nativist position is further strengthened by the finding that fewest conditioned responses occurred in response to the third stimulus. If size constancy was absent, as predicted by empirists, neonates would 'compare' retinal images and base their perception of similarity on these regardless of distance. Empirists, then, would have expected the third stimulus to produce the most conditioned responses. Other research has used recovery from habituation as an index of size constancy. Such research has indicated that the ability to perceive the true size of an object is present by 18 weeks (Slater, 1989).

SHAPE CONSTANCY

According to Slater (1989), several studies have shown that new-borns are able to extract the constant real shape of an object that is rotated in the third dimension, that is, new-borns are capable of recognising an object form independently of (transformations in) its orientation in space. For example, using a similar procedure to that employed to study size constancy, Bower (1966) found that if a two-month-old infant was con-

ditioned to turn its head to look at a rectangle, it would continue to make the conditioned response when the rectangle was turned slightly to produce a trapezoid retinal image. For Bornstein (1988), the evidence concerning shape constancy indicates that 'babies still only in their first year of life can perceive form *qua* form'.

FEATURE, IDENTITY AND EXISTENCE CONSTANCY

Feature constancy is the ability to recognise the invariant features of a stimulus despite some detectable but irrelevant transformation. If a new-born has been habituated to a moving stimulus, it will show a *novelty preference* when shown the same stimulus paired with a novel shape, both of which are stationary. The fact that the new shape is responded to indicates that the new-born perceives the familiar stationary stimulus as the same stimulus when it was moving, and that feature constancy is present at birth.

Feature constancy is a prerequisite for identity constancy, which is the ability to recognise a particular object as being exactly the same object despite some transformation made to it. Distinguishing feature and identity constancy is extremely difficult, but a study which went some way towards doing this was reported by Bower (1971). In the study, babies younger or older than 20 weeks old were seated in front of mirrors which could produce several images of the mother. The babies younger than 20 weeks smiled, cooed and waved their arms to *each* of the 'multiple mothers', whereas the older babies became upset at seeing more than one mother. What this suggests is that it is only the older babies, who are aware that they only have one mother, that have identity constancy.

Existence constancy refers to the belief that objects continue to exist even when they are no longer available to the senses (a belief which Piaget terms *object permanence*: see, for example, McIlveen and Gross, 1997). Together, existence and identity constancy comprise the *object concept*, which typically appears around the middle of the first year of life. Both existence and identity constancy are more sophisticated than shape, size and feature constancies, and it is possible that the object concept arises from the less sophisticated constancies.

GESTALT PRINCIPLES

Bower has also looked at how neonate perception is organised in terms of certain Gestalt principles (see

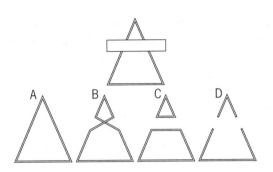

Figure 3.7   The stimulus figures used in Bower's study of closure.

Chapter 1). Bower wanted to discover if *closure* (or *occlusion*) is, as Gestalt psychologists claim, an inborn characteristic. Two-month-olds were conditioned to respond to a black wire triangle with a black iron bar across it, as shown in Figure 3.7 (top). Then, various stimuli, as shown in Figure 3.7 (bottom), were presented. Bower found that the conditioned response was generalised to the complete triangle, suggesting that the neonates perceived an unbroken triangle to lie behind

the black iron bar. Given that the neonates were unlikely to have encountered many triangles, Bower concluded that closure is almost certainly an inborn feature of neonate perceptual ability.

Conclusions

The earlier a perceptual ability is present, the less opportunity there has been for learning to have occurred, and the more likely it is that the ability has a biological basis. According to Slater (1995), the findings of many research studies into human neonate visual perception suggest that the new-born infant:

'comes into the world with a remarkable range of visual abilities... Some rudimentary knowledge and understanding of important stimuli such as objects and faces is present at birth, and experience builds on this'.

The next chapter looks at other evidence bearing on the development of visual perception.

SUMMARY

- The study of neonates represents the most direct way of assessing which perceptual abilities are **innate/inborn** and which develop through **experience** and **learning**. But their inability to **speak** means that researchers must rely on making **inferences** about their visual experiences.
- **Nativists/innate theorists** (such as the Gestalt psychologists) argue that we are born with certain capacities and capabilities to perceive the world in particular ways. If not present at birth, these abilities develop through a genetically determined process of maturation which involves little or no learning.
- **Empirists** (as distinct from **empiricists**), including John Locke, who saw the mind at birth as a **blank slate** or **tabula rasa**, and William James, argue that our perceptual abilities develop through learning and experience.
- Methods used to study neonate perception include **spontaneous visual preference/preferential looking, sucking rate, habituation, conditioned head rotation, physiological measures** (in particular heart rate and breathing

rate) and **measures of electrical brain activity** (such as **visually evoked potentials (VEPs))**.
- The new-born's optic nerve is thinner and shorter than an adult's and does not become fully myelinated until about four months, making transmission of visual information to the still immature cortex less efficient. Although the eyeball is anatomically identical to an adult's, the shorter distance between the retina and the lens makes vision less efficient.
- All babies possess largely normal **colour vision** by about two months. The **pupillary reflex** is present even in premature babies, and the **blink reflex** is present at birth, both suggesting that a baby's sensitivity to **brightness** is quite similar to an adult's.
- The **optokinetic reflex/optic nystagmus** appears soon after birth and quickly improves. But **convergence** is absent at birth, becoming fully developed by about three months, and **accommodation** reaches adult levels by about four months.
- The new-born's **threshold of visual acuity** is

about 30 times poorer than an adult's, but improves during the first six to 12 months. One- to three-month-olds will learn to suck on a nipple in order to bring a blurred picture into focus, and VEPs can be produced in new-borns.

- Fantz found a differential response to pattern among one- to 15-week-old babies, i.e. at all ages they preferred more **complex stimuli**, suggesting that this was not the result of learning. But he also found that this preference is a function of age, reflecting the maturation of the visual system. They also prefer patterns to colour or brightness.

- The preference for increasing complexity may be related to the increasingly efficient and thorough ability to scan the whole stimulus. Before two months, babies discriminate between shapes on the basis of lower-order variables (such as orientation and contrast); after this, higher-order variables (such as configurational invariance and form categories) are responded to.

- The **human face** combines complexity, pattern and movement, all of which babies innately prefer, in an attractive and stimulating form (a **supernormal stimulus**). Fantz claimed that there is also an unlearned, innate preference for facedness, i.e. babies innately know a face **as a face**. But Fantz failed to control adequately for complexity of the face-stimuli presented: when this is done, the preference for 'real' faces over 'scrambled' faces disappears.

- Babies fail to make subtle distinctions about faces (such as male from female) until mid- to late-infancy, but they are capable of imitating a range of facial expressions minutes after birth. This suggests that neonates can match what they see to some inbuilt knowledge of their own face.

- Using the **visual cliff apparatus**, Gibson and Walk concluded that neonates have the innate ability to perceive **depth**. However, the youngest babies studied were six months old, time enough for them to have **learned** depth perception. Members of **precocial species** avoid the deep side of the cliff shortly after birth/hatching.

- Two-month-olds show a **decrease** in heart rate when placed on the deep side of the cliff, indicating interest, but not when placed on the shallow side. Nine-month-olds show an **increase** in heart rate, suggesting fear. Depth perception is probably innate, while avoidance behaviour is probably learnt.

- An **integrated avoidance response** to an approaching object is another indicator of depth perception and is displayed by 20-day-old babies. The response is shown even with one eye closed, but not when equivalent pictures are shown on a screen, indicating that **motion parallax** is the critical cue for distance.

- The integrated avoidance response suggests that neonates possess **3-D perception**, which is also demonstrated by Bower's apparatus that creates the illusion of solid 3-D objects using a translucent object and polarizing goggles. Babies' expectations that they can touch what they can see seems to be an innate ability.

- According to empiricists, **perceptual constancy** is learned, making it likely that neonates will be tricked into believing that if something looks smaller, then it **is** smaller. Nativists argue that constancy is innate, so that neonates are able to judge the size of an object regardless of the retinal image it produces. Bower's experiment using cubes of different sizes presented from various distances provides support for the nativist view, at least as regards **size constancy**.

- Bower also found evidence of **shape constancy** in two-month-olds. Several studies have shown that new-borns are capable of recognising an object form independently of (transformations in) its orientation in space.

- **Feature constancy** also seems to be innate and is a prerequisite for **identity constancy**, which is displayed by babies over 20 weeks old who become upset when shown 'multiple mothers'. Identity constancy, together with **existence constancy** (what Piaget calls **object permanence**), comprise the **object concept**, which normally appears at about six months.

- Bower has shown, using triangle stimuli, that two-month-olds display the Gestalt principle of **closure**. Given that they were unlikely to have had much experience of triangles, the evidence strongly suggests that closure is an inborn ability.

4

STUDYING THE DEVELOPMENT OF VISUAL PERCEPTUAL ABILITIES 2: OTHER APPROACHES

Introduction and overview

In the previous chapter, we looked at what research using human neonates and infants has told us about the development of visual perception. Four other approaches to the study of visual perceptual development can be identified. One of these involves studying people who, through a physical defect occurring early in life, have been deprived of normal visual experiences, but have later had their sight restored. A second approach looks at the effects of sensory restriction early in life on the development of visual perception. This approach, which is an experimental counterpart to the first, has used non-human animals to try to determine how much and what kinds of early experience are necessary for visual perceptual development.

Studying the ability of non-humans and humans to adapt to gross distortions in their visual world is a third approach that has been used. The rationale of this approach is that the greater the degree of adaptation an organism can make, the greater the scope learning can have in the development of visual perception. Finally, a fourth approach looks at the visual perceptual abilities of members of different cultures. The argument here is that if consistent differences between cultural groups are found, then, unless we have good independent reasons for believing that those differences are biologically based, they must be attributable to environmental factors.

Our aim in this chapter is to examine the bearing these approaches have on our understanding of visual perceptual development.

Studies of human cataract patients

Writing to his good friend John Locke in 1688, William Molyneux asked whether:

'a man *born* blind, and now adult, *taught* by touch to distinguish between a cube and sphere could, if his sight was restored, distinguish between those objects without touching them' (Locke, 1690).

Locke's reply, as we would expect given his views about perception considered in the previous chapter, was 'no' because the man would never have *learned* to see.

In 1932, Marius von Senden summarised the data from 65 cases of people who had undergone cataract removal surgery, the earliest taking place in 1700 and the most recent in 1928. A cataract is a film over the eyes which allows only diffuse light to be perceived. It can be present at birth or develop any time afterwards. Surgical removal of the cataract 'restores' vision and enables *Molyneux's question* (see above) to at least be addressed.

Initially, patients who have undergone surgery are typically bewildered by the visual world (in the way William James believed new-born babies to be: see page 34). Hebb (1949) analysed von Senden's 65 cases in terms of *figural unity* (the ability to detect the presence of a figure or stimulus, and which includes things like scanning objects, distinguishing figure from ground, and following moving objects with the eyes) and *figural identity* (being able to name or in some other way identify an already familiar stimulus without touching it or, in the case of geometric figures, counting the corners).

Hebb's analysis showed that the more simple ability of figural unity seemed to be available shortly after surgery and so may not depend on prior visual experience. However, the more complex ability of figural identity appeared to depend on learning. For Hebb, this is how these two aspects of perception *normally* develop. The evidence also indicated the absence of *perceptual constancy* (see Chapter 1, pages 7–8) in the patients. For example, when an object such as a lump of sugar could be identified by sight alone in one situation (such as being seen at a close distance in a person's hand), it often could not be recognised when seen suspended from a piece of string at a distance. This is interesting because, as we saw in the previous chapter (see pages 39–40), evidence from research into human neonates suggests that size and shape constancy *are* innate.

In one of the most widely cited studies in this area, Gregory and Wallace (1963) described the case of S.B., a man who had been blind since the age of six months and whose sight was restored by means of a corneal graft at the age of 52. S.B. showed good judgement of size and distance provided he was familiar with the object in question. Also, he could recognise objects visually *if* he was already familiar with them through touch when he was blind (that is, he showed good *cross-modal transfer*). However, S.B. found it impossible to judge distances by sight alone, and when he looked out of a window 40 feet above the ground (a view he had never experienced), he believed he would 'be able to touch the ground below the window with his feet if he lowered himself by his hands'. S.B. also never learned to interpret facial expressions of emotion, although he could interpret emotional states from the sound of a person's voice.

Although it is tempting to conclude that Locke's response to Molyneux was correct, the data from all of the cases investigated should be treated with some caution. Box 4.1 identifies some of the reasons why.

> **Box 4.1   Some cautions concerning the interpretation of data from human cataract patients**
>
> - Apart from vision, the sense modalities of adults are better developed than those of neonates, so adult cataract patients are *not* the same as neonates. The other adult sense modalities may hinder visual learning because the patient might have to 'unlearn' previous experience in order to use vision. S.B., for example, preferred to use a sense modality he was *familiar* with (touch), and it is possible that figural identity is poorer for this reason rather than for any reason proposed by Hebb (1949).
> - A large number of cataract patients are confused and distressed by their new 'visual world'. Indeed, in some cases (including S.B.) they commit suicide. It could be suggested that their severe emotional distress distorts the findings concerning their perceptual abilities that are obtained from them.
> - The absence of figural identity might, as suggested by Hebb, be due to the lack of visual stimulation and learning. However, it could also be due to some sort of physical damage or deterioration of the visual system over the years of blindness.
> - From a methodological perspective, it is doubtful if all of the cases reported by von Senden were studied as rigorously as S.B. Also, there was great variability in the ages of the patients when they underwent surgery and, importantly, when their cataracts first appeared. As a result, the patients differed in terms of the visual experiences they had *prior* to the cataract developing.

Studies of sensory restriction using non-humans

Because of the limitations concerning the interpretation of data from human cataract patients, researchers have sought other ways of addressing Molyneux's question. From a methodological perspective, research using non-humans is useful because researchers are able (following strict regulations) to manipulate environments in ways that are not permissible with humans. Although studied in a variety of ways, most investigations have typically *deprived* non-human animals of normal sensory and perceptual stimulation and recorded the effects of this deprivation on their sensory and perceptual abilities.

In one of the earliest such experiments, Riesen (1947) reared chimpanzees in total darkness (except for several 45-second periods of exposure to light while they were being fed) for the first 16 months of life. Compared with normally reared chimpanzees, they showed marked perceptual deficits, such as failing to blink in response to threatening movements made towards their faces, and only noticing objects if they were touched or bumped into. On first reading, Riesen's data seem to suggest that perceptual abilities depend on visual experiences.

Riesen (1965) conducted further experiments on three chimpanzees following criticism of his 1947 study by Weiskrantz (1956). Weiskrantz argued that the visual deficiencies observed by Riesen were the result of the chimpanzees' retinas failing to develop normally in the absence of light stimulation, and the likely degeneration of the visual cortex. To overcome Weiskrantz's claim that all the 1947 study showed was that a certain amount of light is necessary to maintain the visual system and allow it to mature normally, Riesen used three chimpanzees. One (Lad) was reared under normal lighting conditions. A second (Debi) was reared in complete darkness. The third (Kova) spent an hour and a half per day wearing special goggles which allowed her to see *diffuse or unpatterned light* of different colours and brightnesses. The rest of her time was spent in darkness.

At seven months, Kova had not suffered retinal damage, but she was noticeably retarded in terms of her perceptual development as compared with Lad, the chimpanzee raised in normal conditions. However, Kova's *receptive fields* (roughly circular regions of the retina whose stimulation affects the firing rate of ganglion cells or cells on the visual cortex to which they are related; Hubel and Wiesel, 1962) failed to develop normally. Debi, the chimpanzee raised in complete darkness, suffered the same retinal damage as Riesen's (1947) chimpanzees. In other studies, Riesen fitted translucent goggles to chimpanzees, monkeys and kittens for the first three months of their lives. He found that simple perceptual abilities (such as differentiating colour, size and brightness) remained intact, but more

complex abilities (such as following a moving object) did not.

Taken as a whole, Riesen's findings suggest at least two things. First, it would appear that light is necessary for normal physical development of the visual system (at least in the species studied by Riesen). Second, patterned light is also necessary for the development of some complex visual abilities (in those species). Early experience, in the form of certain kinds of visual stimulation, then, appears to be essential for normal perceptual development. If perceptual abilities are wholly innate, then environmental factors (over and above those which can either harm the organism or prevent maturation) should have no effects on perceptual development. Riesen's studies dispute this.

Other researchers have looked at the extent to which exposure to visual stimulation *and* motor activity affects the ability of non-humans to guide their movements. For example, Held and Hein (1963) kept kittens in darkness for the first eight weeks after birth. The kittens were then allowed three hours per day in a *kitten carousel* (as shown in Figure 4.1), the remainder of the time being spent in darkness.

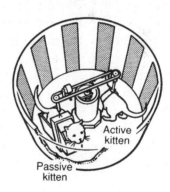

Figure 4.1   The 'kitten carousel' apparatus used by Held and Hein (1963).

The 'active' kitten could move itself around and, via a series of pulleys, its movement caused the 'passive' kitten (whose legs were not free to move) to move in the same direction and at the same speed. Since the visual environment was constant, both kittens had identical visual experiences. When *paw-eye co-ordination* was tested several weeks after these experiences, the 'passive' kittens were markedly inferior to the 'active' kittens, and they showed no evidence of depth perception. However, after normal visual experiences, the 'passive' kittens did display depth perception, which suggests that rather than having failed to learn this ability, they had failed to learn the correct motor responses associated with it. This suggests that it is necessary to distinguish between perception and *sensory-motor co-ordination* (see the section on perceptual distortion and readjustment studies which follows).

Blakemore and Cooper (1970) raised kittens in chambers (see Figure 4.2) which had either vertical or horizontal stripes painted on the inside, and a glass floor so as not to interrupt the pattern of stripes. The kittens wore special collars to prevent them from seeing their own bodies so that the vertical or horizontal stripes were the only visual stimuli they saw. After five months, the kittens' vision was tested. Those raised in the 'vertical world' were insensitive to horizontal lines. For example, when a rod was shaken in front of them in the horizontal plane, they made no attempt to reach for it. However, they would reach for it when it was shaken vertically. The kittens raised in the 'horizontal world' responded when the rod was shaken horizontally but not when it was shaken vertically.

Figure 4.2   The 'vertical world' used in Blakemore and Cooper's (1970) experiment.

The researchers also showed that the kittens, as well as being 'behaviourally blind', were 'physiologically blind'

to horizontal (or vertical) stimuli. So, when the neural activity from the kittens' visual cortex was recorded using micro-electrodes, cells were sensitive to the types of stimuli which corresponded to the visual environment in which they were raised, but insensitive to other stimuli. Similarly, Wiesel (1982) gave infant kittens and monkeys simulated cataracts by sewing their eyelids closed. After infancy, when the eyelids were unstitched, the kittens and monkeys displayed perceptual limitations much like those of human cataract patients. When only the left (or right) eyelid was surgically closed from birth until 18 months, the *ocular dominance columns* (groups of cells in the cortex that respond to visual input from the eyes) were expanded for the seeing eye and dramatically shrunk for the non-seeing eye.

The study conducted by Blakemore and Cooper does not demonstrate conclusively that the environment determines the perception of lines in different orientations. It could be that cells receptive to *all* kinds of stimuli are present at birth, and they functionally reorganise themselves in the absence of relevant stimuli. However, it seems that the environment does play a role in the development of perception in at least some non-human species, although we must acknowledge the fact that, like babies, non-humans cannot tell researchers about their perceptual abilities. So, we don't *know* that particular stimuli cannot be perceived. We only know that non-humans do not *behave* as if particular stimuli can be perceived.

Of course, caution must be exercised in generalising the findings from non-humans to humans. However, the effects of early visual experience on *humans* has been investigated by studying people with an *astigmatism* early in life. Due to a distortion in the shape of the eye, the astigmatism produces an image which is out of focus in either the horizontal or vertical dimension. Even when the astigmatism is corrected, people still see horizontal (or vertical) lines as blurs. This suggests that, like kittens reared in horizontal (or vertical) environments, early visual experience has a permanent effect on the brain and the ability to perceive (Mitchell and Wilkinson, 1974).

Perceptual distortion and readjustment studies

Another way of looking at the effects of experience on perception is to see how well an organism can adjust to new perceptual situations. The greater the degree of adaptation that occurs, the greater the role learning is taken to play. Neither salamanders (Sperry, 1943) nor chickens (Hess, 1956; Rossi, 1968) show any evidence of being able to readjust to distortions in their perceptual world, and so it is likely that for these species, genetic factors exert considerable control over their perceptual abilities.

As far as humans are concerned, Stratton (1896, 1897) was the first to experiment with special lenses that distort the visual world. Stratton constructed a special lens which he wore over one eye whilst keeping his other eye covered. The lens reversed his visual world so that objects in the top of the visual field appeared to be at the bottom and objects on the right appeared to be on the left. For the first three days, Stratton was extremely disoriented and he found even simple behaviours, such as eating and drinking, difficult. After just one day, he reported that he felt nauseous, depressed and tired, and he avoided activity as much as he could.

After three days, however, he began to adapt and imagined unseen parts of his visual field as also being inverted. By the fifth day, Stratton found that he could walk around without bumping into things and that the simple behaviours he initially had difficulty with were easy to accomplish. By the eighth and final day, everything seemed 'harmonious' to Stratton, although his adaptation was not, as he reported, complete:

'I often hesitated which hand was the appropriate one for grasping some object in view, began the movement with the wrong hand and then corrected the mistake'.

When the lens was removed, Stratton immediately recognised his visual environment as the one that existed before he began wearing the lens. He found it surprisingly bewildering, although definitely not inverted. This absence of an inverted after-image or after-effect is important, and shows that Stratton had not actually learnt to see the world as being inverted. If he had, removal of the lens would have caused the now 'normal' world to appear inverted! Instead, Stratton's adaptation took the form of learning the appropriate

motor responses in an inverted world (cf. Held and Hein's kittens described on page 45). However, Stratton did experience an after-effect which caused things before him to 'swing and sweep' as he moved his eyes, which indicates that location constancy had been disrupted by his experiences.

In another experiment, Stratton made goggles which visually displaced his body so that he always appeared horizontally in front of himself. Wherever he walked, he 'followed' his own body image, which was suspended at right angles to his actual body. When he lay down, his body would appear above him, vertically and at right angles to him. After three days, Stratton found that he could adapt to this grossly distorted visual world, and was even able to go out for a walk on his own!

A number of other studies of perceptual adaptation in humans have produced similar findings to those of Stratton. Box 4.2 summarises some of these findings.

Box 4.2   The results of some studies of perceptual adaptation in humans

- Snyder and Pronko (1952) reported adaptation to reversal and inversion of the visual world in participants who wore special lenses for 30 days. Interestingly, when participants were retested two years later, they took less time to adapt than first-time participants, indicating that motor adaptations are resistant to forgetting.
- Held and Bossom (1961) showed that the opportunity for activity is an important factor in perceptual adaptation. In their study, participants who were allowed to walk about freely adjusted quickly and showed after-effects. Those taken about the same environment in wheelchairs adjusted, but showed no evidence of after-effects.
- Kohler (1962) found that inversion of the visual world produced an inverted after-effect in *some* of his participants when the apparatus was removed. However, this lasted for only a few minutes, suggesting that any purely perceptual learning was not substantial.
- Gilling and Brightwell (1982) studied a single participant, Susannah Fienues, who wore an inverting lens for several days. She gradually adapted and reverted to normal vision within a few minutes following removal of her special goggles.

What these (and Stratton's) studies show is that experience does influence our perception of the world, and that our visual system is flexible enough to adjust to distorted conditions. A system which was innate would not allow adaptation to take place (and, as we noted earlier on, such a system appears to be possessed by salamanders and chickens at least). However, it is unlikely that *perceptual adaptation* takes place. Instead, *motor adaptation*, in which we learn to successfully negotiate a different-looking environment, occurs. The fact that humans are capable of learning a new set of body movements does not allow us to conclude that perceptual 'habits' are learned in the first place.

Finally, we should note that all of the participants in perceptual adjustment studies are *adults*, who have already undergone a great deal of learning and in whom maturation has occurred. It is difficult to generalise from adults to babies, and so we cannot conclude that babies *have* to learn to perceive the world just because adults *can* learn to perceive the world differently.

Cross-cultural studies of perceptual abilities

Cross-cultural studies involve a comparison of the ways in which people from one culture perceive things with the ways in which people from other, very different, cultures perceive those things. If we find consistent differences between different cultural groups, then unless we have good independent reasons for believing that those differences are biologically based, we must attribute them to environmental factors (such as social, ecological, linguistic, or some combination of these). In theory, then, cross-cultural studies enable us to discover the extent to which perception is structured by the nervous system (and so common to all humans) and by experience.

STUDIES USING VISUAL ILLUSIONS

Some researchers have used *visual illusions* as their experimental tool, whilst others have used the various perceptual phenomena we described in Chapter 1. There is a long history of cross-cultural research into the development of perception which has used visual illusions. Box 4.3 describes the findings from some of the early research.

Box 4.3   The findings from some early research into cross-cultural differences using visual illusions

- Rivers (1901) compared English adults and children with adult and child Murray Islanders (people from a group of islands between New Guinea and Australia) using the Müller-Lyer illusion and the horizontal-vertical illusion. The results showed that the Murray Islanders were *less* susceptible to the Müller-Lyer illusion than their English counterparts, but *more* susceptible to the horizontal-vertical illusion.

- Allport and Pettigrew (1957) used the *rotating trapezoid* as their visual illusion. As shown below, this is a trapezoid which has horizontal and vertical bars attached to it.

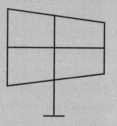

When attached to a motor and revolved in a circle, the trapezoid gives those from Western cultures the impression of being a window, and when rotated through 360°, most Western observers report seeing a rectangle that oscillates to and fro rather than a trapezoid rotating through 360° (which is actually what it is). Allport and Pettigrew reasoned that for people unfamiliar with windows (at least as people from Western cultures know them), expectations of rectangularity would be absent and the illusion not perceived. Using Zulus, who live in a rather 'circular environment', the researchers found that when the trapezoid was viewed with both eyes and from a short distance, the Zulus were less likely than either urban Zulus or Europeans to perceive an oscillating rectangle and more likely to perceive a rotating trapezoid.

- Segall et al. (1963) used the Müller-Lyer illusion with members of African and Filipino cultures. As compared with South Africans of European descent and Americans from Illinois, the Africans and Filipinos were much less susceptible to the illusion. However, on the horizontal-vertical illusion, members of two African

---

cultures (the Batoro and the Bayankole) were most susceptible. People of these cultures live in high, open country where visibility without 'interference' is possible. In such an environment, vertical objects are important focal points and are used to estimate distances. The Bete, who live in a dense jungle environment, were least likely of all groups tested to see the illusion. The South Africans of European descent and Americans tended to fall between the extremes of the three African cultures.

- Stewart (1973) used the Ames distorted room (see page 25) with rural and urban Tongan children. The rural children were less likely to see the illusion than those living in urban environments and European children. The same was true for other illusions, including the Müller-Lyer.

AN ATTEMPT TO ACCOUNT FOR DIFFERENTIAL SUSCEPTIBILITY TO VISUAL ILLUSIONS

According to Segall et al.'s (1963) *carpentered world hypothesis*, people in Western cultures:

'live in a culture in which straight lines abound and in which perhaps 90 per cent of the acute and obtuse angles formed on (the) retina by the straight lines of (the) visual field are realistically interpretable as right angles extended in space'.

In other words, Segall and his colleagues believe that we tend to interpret illusions, which are 2-D drawings, in terms of our past experiences. In the 'carpentered world' of Western societies, we add a third dimension (depth) which is not actually present in the drawing, and this leads to the experience of the illusion (and note the similarity of this to Gregory's account of visual illusions: see Chapter 2, pages 20–22).

Research conducted by Annis and Frost (1973) has lent support to such a hypothesis. These researchers looked at the perceptual acuity of a number of Canadian Cree Indians who live in a non-carpentered environment consisting of summer tents and winter lodges with lines of all orientations. The task involved judging whether two lines were parallel or not, and pairs of lines in different orientations were used. The Crees had no difficulty in judging the lines no matter what angle they were presented at. However, whilst a comparison group

of Crees who had moved away from their original environment were good at judging lines that were horizontal or vertical, they were less good with lines at an angle.

Whilst Annis and Frost's data are consistent with Segall et al.'s hypothesis, a number of other studies are inconsistent with it (e.g. Gregor and McPherson, 1965; Jahoda, 1966; Mundy-Castle and Nelson, 1962). For example, Mundy-Castle and Nelson studied the Knysma forest dwellers, a group of isolated, white, illiterate South Africans. Despite the rectangularity of their environment, they were unable to give appropriate 3-D responses to 2-D symbols on a standard test and, on the Müller-Lyer figure, their responses were not significantly different from non-Europeans, although they were significantly different from literate white adults.

STUDIES USING OTHER PERCEPTUAL PHENOMENA

Research conducted by Hudson (1960), Turnbull (1961) and Deregowski (1972) has shown that in various African cultures, both children and adults find it difficult to perceive depth in both pictorial material *and* the real world. Turnbull (1961), for example, studied the Bambuti pygmies who live in the dense rainforests of the Congo, a closed-in world without open spaces. When a Bambuti was taken to a vast plain and shown a herd of buffalo grazing in the distance, he claimed he had never seen such *insects* before. When informed that the 'insects' were buffalo, the pygmy was offended. Turnbull and the pygmy then rode in a jeep towards the buffalo. The sight of the buffalo in the distance was so far removed from the pygmy's experience that he was convinced Turnbull was using magic to deceive him. What this study shows is that the pygmy lacked *size constancy* (see Chapter 1, page 7), which is an important cue in 'reading' pictures.

In Hudson's studies, people from various African cultures were shown a series of pictures depicting hunting scenes. Two of these are shown in Figure 4.3. The participants saw each picture on its own and were asked to name all the objects in the scene in order to determine whether or not the elements were correctly recognised. Then they were asked about the *relationship* between the objects, such as 'Which is closer to the man?' If the 'correct' interpretation was made, and depth cues were taken into account, respondents were

Figure 4.3   Hudson (1960) found that when shown the picture on the left and asked which animal the hunter is trying to spear, members of some cultures reply 'the elephant'. This shows that some cultures do not use cues to depth (such as overlap and known size of objects). The picture on the right shows the hunter, elephant and antelope in true size ratios when all are the same distance from the observer.

classified as having 3-D vision. If such cues were ignored, they were classified as having 2-D vision. Hudson showed that both children and adults found it difficult to perceive depth in the pictorial material, and whilst this difficulty varied in extent, it appeared to persist through most educational and social levels (Deregowski, 1972).

Deregowski (1972) refers to a description given by a Mrs Fraser (who taught health care to Africans in the 1920s) of an African woman slowly discovering that a picture she was looking at portrayed a human head in profile:

> 'She discovered in turn the nose, the mouth, the eye, but where was the other eye? I tried turning my profile to explain why she could see only one eye, but she hopped round to my other side to point out that I possessed a second eye which the other lacked'.

The woman treated the picture as an object rather than a 2-D representation of an object, that is, she did not 'infer' depth in the picture. What she believed to be an 'object' turned out to have only two dimensions, and this is what the woman found bewildering.

There are, however, reasons to question the various claims that have been made regarding the perceptual abilities of people from different cultures. According to Serpell (1976), when pictorial stimulus material is used which people from a particular culture are familiar with, recognition tends to be better. Thus, some (but not all) of the Me'en of Ethiopia found it much easier to recognise material when it was presented in the form of pictures painted on cloth (which is both familiar to them and free of distracting cues such as a border) than line drawings on paper (Deregowski, 1972).

There is also evidence to indicate that the drawings in some of the studies emphasise certain depth cues whilst ignoring others, and that this puts non-Western observers at a 'double disadvantage'. For example, in Hudson's (1960) pictures (see Figure 4.3), two depth cues were used (namely relative size and overlap or superimposition). However, cues like texture gradient, binocular disparity and motion parallax were absent from all of the pictures used by Hudson. When the pictures were redrawn so as to show texture gradients (by, for example, adding grass to open terrain), more Zambian children gave 3-D answers than had been the case in Hudson's original study (Kingsley et al., cited in Serpell, 1976). Research summarised by Berry et al. (1992) indicates that the absence of certain depth cues in pictorial material makes the perception of depth difficult for non-Western peoples.

Finally, it seems that much of the research in this area implies that the Western style of pictorial art represents the real world in an *objectively* correct way. As

Gombrich (1960) has remarked, 'artistic excellence' is not identical with 'photographic accuracy' and so it might be that people of non-Western cultures 'reject' Western art forms simply on *aesthetic grounds*. As a result, Serpell (1976) suggests that research may have mistakenly described *stylistic preference* as a difference in perception.

Certainly, unfolded 'split', 'developed' or 'chain-type' drawings as shown in Figure 4.4 (left) were originally preferred by African children and adults to the 'orthogonal' or perspective drawings as shown in Figure 4.4 (right), often because the drawing lacked important features (legs in the case of Figure 4.4).

Also, Duncan et al. (1973) have found that the small lines used by cartoonists to imply motion were the least understood of all the pictorial conventions shown to rural African children. When these children were shown a picture in which the artist had drawn a head in three different positions above the same trunk to indicate that the head was turning round, half the children thought the character depicted was deformed (see Figure 4.5 left). Likewise Western observers require guidance from an anthropologist to understand the art forms of American Indians (see Figure 4.5 right).

Our review of cross-cultural studies of visual perception indicates that some psychologists believe that the physi-

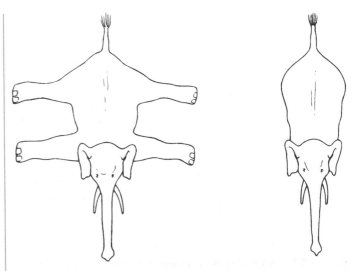

Figure 4.4   Members of certain African cultures generally prefer the 'split elephant' drawing shown on the left to the top-view perspective drawing shown on the right (from J. Deregowski, 'Pictorial perception and culture'. Copyright © (1972) by Scientific American, Inc. All rights reserved).

cal environment (or ecology) is closely linked with perceptual experiences, whilst others believe that ecology actually *determines* perceptual experience. However, since researchers cannot agree about the key features of such cultural experiences, neither of the beliefs can be strongly supported.

Figure 4.5   Is the work of an artist from one particular culture always understandable to a viewer from a different culture?

Conclusions

Whilst the evidence from studies of human neonates that was presented in Chapter 3 suggests that some visual perceptual abilities are probably innate, the evidence from the four approaches considered in this chapter suggests that experience plays a vital role.

Rather than seeing themselves as nativists or empirists, most psychologists see a *transactional perspective* as being the most profitable one to adopt as far as visual perception is concerned. According to this perspective, we may be born with capacities to perceive the world in certain ways, but stimulation and environmental influences in general are crucial in determining how, and even whether, these capacities actually develop.

SUMMARY

- Hebb analysed the 65 cases of people who had undergone **cataract removal** surgery, reported originally by von Senden, in terms of **figural unity** (the ability to detect the presence of a figure or stimulus) and **figural identity** (the ability to identify a stimulus). This represents an attempt to answer **Molyneux's question**.

- Hebb concluded that figural unity seems to be available soon after surgery (and so is not dependent on visual experience), while figural identity and **perceptual constancy** seem to depend on learning. According to Hebb, this is how these two aspects of perception **normally** develop.

- S.B., whose sight was restored when he was 52, showed good **cross-modal transfer**. But he found it impossible to judge distances by sight alone and never learned to interpret facial expressions of emotion.

- Unlike neonates, adults who undergo cataract surgery may have to unlearn previous perceptual experience involving their other sense modalities. The acquisition of vision can be emotionally very upsetting, even to the point of committing suicide, and there may also have been physical deterioration of the visual system during the years of blindness. Also, the cases reported by von Senden lack reliability and adequate detail.

- Another way of trying to answer Molyneux's question involves deliberately manipulating the environment of non-human animals, usually through **depriving** them of normal sensory and perceptual stimulation in order to see its effects on their sensory and perceptual abilities.

- Riesen's early experiment with chimpanzees suggested that perceptual abilities depend on visual experience. But the study was flawed because of the possibility that the animals reared in total darkness may have suffered retinal damage due to lack of light stimulation, which is necessary for normal maturation of the visual system.

- Riesen later exposed one chimp to **diffuse/ unpatterned light** which, while preventing retinal damage, produced retarded perceptual development compared with a chimp raised in normal conditions. Although simple perceptual abilities were unaffected, more complex abilities failed to develop, implying that patterned light is necessary for the latter's development.

- Other deprivation studies have looked at the relationship between exposure to visual stimulation and motor activity. Held and Hein's **kitten carousel** experiment showed that the passive kittens were inferior on tests of **paw–eye co-ordination** and appeared to also lack depth perception. However, what they had failed to learn were the correct motor responses, implying a distinction between perception and **sensory-motor co-ordination**.

- Kittens raised by Blakemore and Cooper in either a vertical or horizontal 'world' became 'behaviourally blind' to the other kind of stimulus. They also became 'physiologically blind', as measured by neural activity in their visual cortex. Studies of humans with **astigmatism** support these findings.

- Similarly, Wiesel's kittens and monkeys whose left or right eyelids were sewn closed, had expanded or dramatically shrunken **ocular dominance columns** for the seeing eye/closed eye respectively.

- Although Blakemore and Cooper's findings suggest that the environment determines the perception of horizontal and vertical lines, it is possible that cells receptive to **all** kinds of stimuli are present at birth but functionally reorganise themselves if relevant stimuli are absent. Whatever the role of environmental stimulation might be, all we can be sure of is that non-human animals sometimes fail to behave as if particular stimuli can be perceived.

- **Perceptual distortion and readjustment studies** assume that the greater the degree of adaptation that an organism displays in distorted perceptual situations, the greater the role of learning. While for salamanders and chickens, genetic factors seem to be all-important, humans seem capable of considerable adjustment.

- Stratton's pioneering studies involved wearing a lens over one eye that turned the visual world upside down. By the eighth day of the experiment, he was able to do most things fairly normally. When he removed the lens, despite initially feeling bewildered, he immediately recognised things as they had looked before the experiment. There was no inverted after-image or after-effect, indicating that adaptation had taken the form of learning appropriate **motor responses**, but location constancy had been disrupted.

- Like Stratton, Susannah Fienues very quickly reverted to normal vision after several days of wearing an inverting lens. Snyder and Pronko found evidence that motor adaptations are remembered two years following the experiment. Also, the opportunity for activity has been found to be an important factor in perceptual adaptation.

- What readjustment studies demonstrate is **motor adaptation** (rather than **perceptual** adaptation), which by itself does not allow us to conclude that perception is originally learned. The adult participants have already undergone extensive learning and maturation, and it is difficult to generalise from what they **can** learn to what babies **must** learn.

- **Cross-cultural studies** compare the perceptions of members of very different cultural groups. Consistent differences between different groups must be attributed to social, ecological or linguistic factors, unless there is good independent reason to attribute them to biological factors.

- Many studies have used **visual illusions**, such as the Müller-Lyer and horizontal-vertical illusions used in the pioneering study of Rivers with the Murray Islanders and the large-scale study by Segall et al. with Africans, Filipinos and Americans. Allport and Pettigrew used the **rotating trapezoid** with Zulus living in both rural and urban environments. Stewart used the Ames distorted room with rural and urban Tongan children.

- A major account of differential susceptibility to visual illusions is Segall et al.'s **carpentered world hypothesis**, according to which members of Western cultures tend to interpret illusion figures by adding depth that is not actually in the figures themselves.

- While Annis and Frost's study of Canadian Cree Indians supports the carpentered world hypothesis, several other studies are inconsistent with it, including Mundy-Castle and Nelson's study of the Knysma forest dwellers in South Africa.

- Turnbull's study, involving the Bambuti pygmies living in dense rainforests of the Congo, demonstrated the lack of **size constancy**, which is an important cue in interpreting pictures. Hudson's studies using pictures depicting hunting scenes found that both children and adults from a variety of African cultures, and regardless of educational or social levels, had difficulty perceiving depth.

- Deregowski's account of an African woman who treated a picture of a human face in profile as a 3-D object, rather than a 2-D representation of a face, shows that she was unable to infer depth in the picture.

- By contrast, some members of the Me'en of Ethiopia found it much easier to recognise pictorial material when it was painted on familiar cloth than line drawings on unfamiliar paper. Also, in Hudson's drawings of hunting scenes, only relative size and overlap or superimposition were used, while other depth cues (such as texture gradient) were omitted, making the task more difficult for non-Western peoples: when they were redrawn so as to include other depth cues, the number of 3-D responses increased.

- People from non-Western cultures might be 'rejecting' Western art forms, i.e. expressing a **stylistic preference**, rather than showing an inability to perceive depth in pictures. This is supported by evidence of a preference for 'split' drawings as opposed to the 'orthogonal' or perspective drawings.

- Just as rural African children are unfamiliar with artistic conventions as used in Western cartoons, so Western observers need guidance to understand the art forms of American Indians.

- Most psychologists adopt a **transactional perspective**, according to which although we may be born with capacities to perceive the world in certain ways, stimulation and environmental influences are crucial in determining how and whether these capacities actually develop.

5

FOCUSED ATTENTION

Introduction and overview

In his book *The Principles of Psychology*, William James (1890) defined attention as:

'the taking possession by the mind, in clear and vivid form, of one of what seems several simultaneously possible objects or trains of thought. Focalisation, concentration of consciousness are of its essence. It implies withdrawal from some things in order to deal effectively with others'.

Although several other uses of the word 'attention' have been discussed by researchers, and whilst attention cannot necessarily be equated with consciousness, attention has, as we will shortly see, been used to refer to the *selective* way in which information is processed.

The importance of the study of attention was emphasised by Titchener (1903), a student of the pioneering experimental psychologist Wilhelm Wundt. According to Titchener:

'the doctrine of attention is the nerve of the whole psychological system, and that as men judge of it so shall they be judged before the general tribunal of psychology'.

Other schools of psychological thought were not so favourably disposed towards the study of attention. Because of their belief that the properties of a stimulus array were sufficient to predict the perceptual response to it, *Gestalt* psychologists (see Chapter 1) believed there was no need to invoke the concept of attention. Supporters of a strict *behaviourist* perspective went even further and argued that since 'attention' was unobservable, it was not worthy of experimental study.

Interest in the study of attention re-emerged following the publication of a book entitled *Perception and Communication* written by Donald Broadbent (1958). Broadbent argued that the world is composed of many more sensations than can be handled by the perceptual and cognitive capabilities of the human observer. In order to cope with the flood of available information, humans must *selectively attend* to only some information and somehow 'tune out' the rest. In order to study our ability to selectively attend to things, researchers have studied focused attention. Our aim in this chapter is to consider some of the theory and research concerned with both focused auditory and visual attention.

Focused auditory attention

CHERRY'S DICHOTIC LISTENING AND SHADOWING RESEARCH

At least in part, Broadbent's (1958) book was an attempt to account for what Cherry (1953) had termed the *cocktail-party phenomenon*, that is, how we are able to focus our attention on one conversation (which we might be having at a party) whilst ignoring other conversations going on around us. In his initial experiments, Cherry had participants wear headphones through which pairs of 'messages' (consisting of spoken prose) were presented to both ears simultaneously, a method known as *binaural listening*. Cherry found that various physical differences affected the ability to select one of the messages to attend to, and he identified voice intensity, the speaker's location and the speaker's sex as being particularly important. He also found that when these differences were controlled for in the two messages (so that each message was, say, spoken in an equally intense female voice), they were extremely difficult to separate according to their meaning.

In other experiments, Cherry changed the participant's task. Instead of hearing two messages through both ears, participants were presented with one message to the right ear and, simultaneously, a different message to the left ear, a method called *dichotic listening*. The participant was required to repeat out loud one of the messages. This procedure is known as *shadowing*, and its purpose is to ensure that one of the messages is being attended to (just as happens at a party when we are engaged in conversation with someone). Cherry found that whilst participants were able to carry out the shadowing requirement, they remembered little, if anything, of the material presented to the non-shadowed (or unattended) ear.

Indeed, later research showed that this was the case even when the same word was presented 35 times to the non-shadowed ear (Moray, 1959). It was also found that if the message was spoken in a foreign language or the message changed from English to a different language, participants did not notice this. Also, whilst speech played backwards was reported as having 'something queer about it', the vast majority of participants believed it to be normal speech. However, a pure tone of 400 cycles per second was nearly always noticed by participants, as was a change of voice from male to female or female to male (Cherry and Taylor, 1954). These data, then, suggested that whilst the physical properties of the message in the non-shadowed ear were 'heard', semantic content (or its meaning) was completely lost. As Hampson and Morris (1996) have noted, people quickly gave up Cherry's original question about how we can attend to one conversation and began asking why so little seemed to be remembered about the other conversations.

BROADBENT'S SPLIT-SPAN STUDIES

At about the same time that Cherry reported his findings using dichotic listening tasks, Broadbent (1954) reported the results of a series of studies using what he called the *split-span procedure*. In a typical split-span experiment, three digits (such as 8, 2 and 1) are presented via headphones to one ear at the rate of one every half a second. Simultaneously, three different digits (such as 7, 3 and 4) are presented to the other ear. The participant's task is to listen to the two sets of numbers and then write down as much as he or she can remember.

Essentially, there are two different ways in which the digits can be recalled. First, they can be recalled according to the ear of presentation, that is, the digits to one ear are recalled first followed by recall of the digits presented to the other ear. This is called *ear-by-ear recall*. Thus, the numbers above would be recalled as either 8,2,1,7,3,4 or 7,3,4,8,2,1. The second way in which

the digits can be recalled is according to their chronological order of presentation. Since the digits have been presented in pairs, this would involve recalling the first pair (8,7 or 7,8), followed by the second pair (2,3 or 3,2) and finally the third pair (1,4 or 4,1). This is called *pair-by-pair recall*.

Research had shown that when people are given a list of six digits at a rate of one every half a second, not using a split-span procedure, serial recall is typically 95 per cent accurate. However, Broadbent found that the typical split-span procedure produced accurate recall only 65 per cent of the time. Moreover, pair-by-pair recall was considerably *poorer* than ear-by-ear recall and that, if given a choice, people preferred to recall simultaneously presented lists according to their *ear* of presentation rather than their temporal order of presentation.

Single-channel theories of focused auditory attention

A number of theories have been proposed to explain the data from the early studies described above. The three theories that we will consider next all propose that somewhere in the processing of information there is a 'bottleneck' or *filter* which allows some information to be passed on for further analysis and either discards or processes only to a limited degree the other information. These so-called *single-channel theories* essentially differ over whether the filtering takes place early or late in the processing of information, and hence they differ in terms of the nature of and extent to which processing of the non-attended material occurs.

BROADBENT'S EARLY SELECTION FILTER THEORY

The first systematic attempt to explain how we select one message to attend to was proposed by Broadbent (1958). A diagrammatic representation of Broadbent's attempt to account for both Cherry's findings and those of his own split-span experiments is shown in Figure 5.1.

According to Broadbent's theory, which rests on the

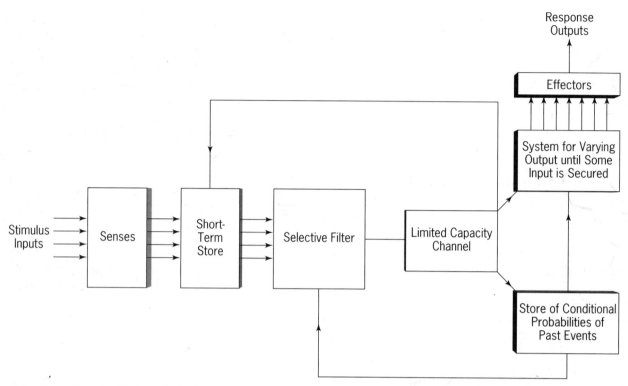

Figure 5.1   Broadbent's theory of the flow of information between stimulus and response.

assumption that our ability to process information is capacity limited, information from the senses passes 'in parallel' (or at the same time) to a *short-term store*. This is a temporary 'buffer system' which holds information until it can be processed further and, effectively, extends the duration of a stimulus (see Chapter 7, page 85). The various types of information presented (such as two or more voices) are then passed, preserved in their original form, to a *selective filter*. The filter operates on the *physical characteristics* of the information presented, selecting one source for further analysis and rejecting all others.

The information that has been allowed through the filter reaches a *limited capacity channel* (and the filter is necessary precisely because the channel is limited in its capacity). The channel corresponds to what William James (1890) called the 'span of consciousness', or what we experience as happening now. A modern analogy would be the central processing unit of a computer. The information that has been allowed to pass through the filter is analysed in that it is recognised, possibly rehearsed, and then transferred to the motor effectors (or muscles) and an appropriate response initiated.

Because Broadbent considered the short-term store to be capable of holding information for a period of time before it decayed away, two simultaneous stimuli *can* be processed provided that the processor can get back to the short-term store soon enough (that is, before the information in it has decayed away). So, attending to one thing does not necessarily mean that everything else is lost. However, Broadbent believed that the switching of attention between channels took a substantial period of time, and so processing information from two channels would always take longer and be less efficient than processing the same information from one channel.

TESTS OF BROADBENT'S THEORY

Broadbent's theory was capable of explaining Cherry's findings concerning the fate of the non-shadowed message because the non-shadowed message is not permitted to pass through the filter. It also explained the data from the split-span experiments by proposing that the location of input (the relevant ear) is the physical property on which the information is selected. However, the theory assumes that because the non-shadowed message is filtered out according to its physical characteristics, the *meaning* of the stimuli presented to the non-attended ear should not be subject to any sort of higher-level analysis.

However, when we are at a cocktail party, or any other party for that matter, our attention sometimes switches from the speaker to whom we are listening to another part of the room if we hear our name mentioned. This phenomenon was demonstrated experimentally by Moray (1959), who found that when the participant's name was presented to the non-attended ear, attention switched to that ear about one-third of the time. Additionally, at least six studies using the shadowing task have presented data inconsistent with the predictions made by Broadbent's theory. These are summarised in Box 5.1.

Box 5.1 Some experimental studies producing data inconsistent with Broadbent's theory

- Gray and Wedderburn (1960) showed that if participants were presented with 'Dear 2 Jane' in one ear and '3 Aunt 8' in the other, they were able to process the information alternately according to the ears, since they typically reported 'Dear Aunt Jane'. Such a finding indicates that the ears do not always function as different channels of information, and that switching between channels is fairly easy to do.

- Treisman (1960) found that if meaningful material presented to the attended ear was switched in mid-sentence to the non-attended ear, participants would occasionally change the focus of their attention to the non-attended ear and shadow the material presented to it before changing back to the attended ear.

- Treisman (1964) discovered that if a French translation of the shadowed material was presented as the non-shadowed material, about half of a group of *bilingual* participants realised that the shadowed and non-shadowed material had the same meaning.

- Corteen and Wood (1972) conditioned participants to produce a galvanic skin response (or GSR, a minute increase in the electrical conductivity of the skin) whenever they heard a particular target word. This was achieved by delivering a small electric shock immediately after the target word was heard. The researchers found that not only did the target

word produce a GSR when presented to the non-attended ear, but *synonyms* of it did as well. These findings were replicated by von Wright et al. (1975) using Finnish participants. However, we should note that in both Corteen and Wood's and von Wright and his colleagues' experiments, GSRs did not occur on anything like all the trials on which the conditioned words were presented.

- Mackay (1973) found that the meaning of ambiguous words could be determined by the information presented to the non-attended ear. Thus, after the word 'bank' had been presented in a sentence and participants subsequently had to recognise the sentence they had heard, recognition was influenced by whether the word 'river' or 'money' had been presented to the non-attended ear.

The studies summarised in Box 5.1 suggest that the meaning of the input to the non-attended ear is processed on at least some occasions. An additional problem for Broadbent's theory is its claim that the non-shadowed message is always rejected at an *early* stage of processing. However, participants in shadowing experiments typically have little familiarity with the task. Underwood (1974) showed that when participants are given *training* at shadowing, they can detect two-thirds of the material presented to the non-attended ear. Additionally, Allport et al. (1972) found that when material used in shadowing tasks is different, such as one being auditory and the other visual, memory for the non-shadowed message is good (presumably because there is less opportunity for interference to occur), indicating that it must have been processed at a higher level than proposed by Broadbent.

TREISMAN'S ATTENUATION OR STIMULUS-ANALYSIS SYSTEM THEORY

According to Treisman (1960, 1964), competing information is analysed for things other than its physical properties. These other things include sounds, syllable patterns, grammatical structure and the meaning of the information (Hampson and Morris, 1996). Treisman suggested that the non-shadowed message was not filtered out early on but that the selective filter *attenuated*

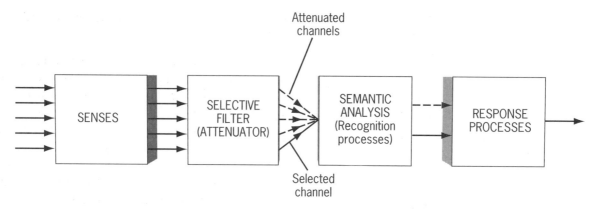

Figure 5.2   Treisman's theory of the processes by which information is selectively attended to.

it. Thus, a message that was not selected on the basis of its physical properties would not be rejected completely, but would be diminished in intensity (or 'turned down') as shown in Figure 5.2.

As Figure 5.2 shows, both the non-attenuated and attenuated information undergo the further analyses we mentioned above. These analyses may result in an attenuated message being attended to, depending on its features. Treisman suggested that stimuli which were biologically relevant and emotionally important may be 'pre-sets' to which our attention is switched irrespective of the content of the attenuated message. This would account for why, when we are attending to one conversation, we are capable of switching our attention to another conversation in which we hear our name mentioned. As Massaro (1989) notes, since Treisman argues that it is the *features* of a stimulus which determine whether or not it is attended to, the concept of *probabilistic filtering* is perhaps a better way of appreciating Treisman's theory than that of attenuation.

THE DEUTSCH–NORMAN LATE SELECTION FILTER THEORY

Another alternative to Broadbent's theory was offered by Deutsch and Deutsch (1963) and Norman (1968, 1976). These researchers did not modify Broadbent's theory, as Treisman's theory effectively does, but completely rejected Broadbent's claim that information is filtered out early on. According to the Deutsch–Norman model, filtering or selection only occurs after *all inputs* have been analysed at a high level (which, in the case of spoken prose, is after each word has been recognised by the memory system and *analysed for*

meaning). The Deutsch–Norman model is shown in Figure 5.3 (see opposite page).

This theory, then, places the filter nearer the *response* end of the processing system, and hence the filter is a 'late' selection one rather than an 'early' selection one. Because the model proposes that processing will have already been undertaken on the information that has been presented before, some information will have been established as *pertinent*, or most relevant, and will have activated particular memory representations (and hence the theory is sometimes known as the 'pertinence theory'). When one memory representation is selected for further processing (and, at any one time, only one can) attention becomes selective. The implication of this theory is that we perceive everything we encounter, but are only consciously aware of some of it (Hampson and Morris, 1996).

TESTS OF TREISMAN'S AND THE DEUTSCH–NORMAN MODELS

Both Treisman's and the Deutsch–Norman model are capable of accounting for the evident processing of non-shadowed material which cannot be explained by Broadbent's theory. If the Deutsch–Norman model was correct, then we would expect to find that participants were able to identify as many target words in the shadowed message as in the non-shadowed message, since the theory claims that both are completely analysed for meaning. Treisman and Geffen (1967), however, found that this was not the case, and that target words were much better detected in the shadowed message (87 per cent) than the non-shadowed message (eight per cent), an outcome which is consistent with

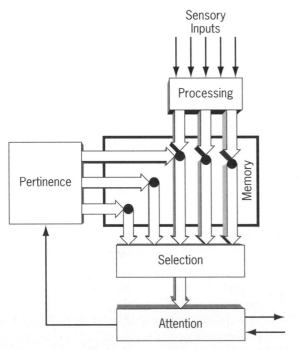

Figure 5.3 The Deutsch–Norman theory of focused attention. All sensory inputs receive perceptual processing and are recognised in the sense that they excite their representations (the black circles) in memory. The information selected is that which has the greatest pertinence (Norman, 1968).

Treisman's view that the non-shadowed message is attenuated.

Treisman and Geffen's findings depend on the assumption that the shadowed and non-shadowed messages are *equally important*. Deutsch and Deutsch (1967) argued that this assumption was not met because the requirement to shadow one message made that message (and hence the target words in it) more important. Treisman and Riley (1969) overcame this problem by requiring participants to *stop* shadowing whenever a target word was heard in either the attended or non-attended ear. They found that under such circumstances, performance was still better for the shadowed message (76 per cent) than for the non-shadowed message (33 per cent).

This finding is consistent with Treisman's theory, but inconsistent with the Deutsch–Norman claim that performance should not differ given that the targets were equally pertinent irrespective of the ear they were presented to. We should however, note that the detection rate for the non-attended ear in Treisman and Riley's study (33 per cent) was much higher than that in the Treisman and Geffen study (eight per cent), a finding

which provides some support for the Deutsch–Norman theory.

Although Treisman's theory has experimental support, some researchers (e.g. Govier, 1980) have questioned its *parsimony*. In Govier's view, the attenuation process appears to be redundant. Because of the existence of 'pre-sets', it is much more economical to have Treisman's filter do its work *after* a high level of analysis of the input. As Govier remarks, since all inputs are analysed to a high level, the bottleneck is apparently a function of consciousness, not analysis.

The Deutsch–Norman theory has also received experimental support. The theory predicts that participants should know the words being presented to the non-attended ear, and so if they are asked immediately should be able to repeat back the words presented to that ear. However, because information to the attended ear absorbs attention, the non-shadowed message cannot be processed any further than recognition. So, the non-shadowed message gets into short-term memory for only a brief period and is then forgotten very quickly.

Consistent with the Deutsch–Norman theory, Norman (1969) found that participants *could* remember the last couple of words presented to the non-attended ear only if tested *immediately* rather than after a short continuation of the shadowing task, a finding replicated by Glucksberg and Cowan (1970). Neisser (1967) has called the system which briefly holds unprocessed auditory information *echoic memory*, and it is discussed further in Chapter 7. The Deutsch–Norman theory is also supported by the studies summarised in Box 5.1 (see page 57) which show that words in the non-shadowed message are processed according to their meaning.

The major problem for the Deutsch–Norman model concerns its claim that the meaning of *every* input is subjected to higher-level analysis, because this makes the processing of information rigid and inflexible. Wilding (1982) has argued that the data indicate that whilst not as much is known about information presented in the non-attended ear as is predicted by the Deutsch–Norman model, more is known about such information than is predicted by either Broadbent's or Treisman's theories!

Alternatives to single-channel theories of focused auditory attention

The lack of *flexibility* of the three single-channel theories discussed above has been the single most important factor that critics of such theories have challenged. Several more 'flexible' theories have been advanced as alternatives to single-channel theories. According to Johnston and Heinz (1978), for example, attentional selectivity can occur at several different stages of processing. The stage at which selectivity does occur is dependent upon the demands made by the task a participant is carrying out. In order to minimise demands on capacity, selection is made as early as possible.

Johnston and Heinz (1979) and Johnston and Wilson (1980) have presented findings which are consistent with their view that processing is more flexible than predicted by single-channel theories. For example, Johnston and Wilson showed that participants processed words presented to *both* ears when they did not know to which ear particular target words would be presented, but did not do this when they knew which ear the target words would be presented to. These data suggest that non-target words are processed only to the extent that they are necessary to perform a task.

Like Johnston and Heinz's theory, other theories (e.g. Kahneman, 1973; Norman and Bobrow, 1975) which have been proposed in light of the perceived inadequacies of single-channel theories can also be applied to the phenomenon of *divided attention*. We shall delay our consideration of them until the next chapter, when we look at research into the ability to perform two tasks simultaneously.

Focused visual attention

According to Driver (1996):

'the cluttered scenes of everyday life present more objects than we can respond towards simultaneously, and often more than we can perceive fully at any one time. Accordingly, mechanisms of attention are required to select objects of interest for further processing. In the case of vision, one such mechanism is provided by eye movements, which allow us to fixate particular regions so that they benefit from the greater acuity of the fovea'.

The fovea is a very small area of the retina which, because it contains very sensitive *cone* cells, provides maximum acuity for visual stimuli. So, when we fixate on an object the eyes are arranged in such a way that maximum visual processing is given to the object that projects its image onto the fovea, whilst the resources given to the other part of the visual field are 'attenuated' (Anderson, 1995a).

Research conducted by Michael Posner and his colleagues (1978, 1980) has shown that when people are told to fixate on one part of the visual field, it is still possible to attend to stimuli seven or so degrees either side of the fixation point, and that attention can be shifted more quickly when a stimulus is presented in an 'expected' rather than an 'unexpected' location. What these experiments show, then, is that visual attention is *not* identical to the part of the visual field which is processed by the fovea. Rather, attention can be shifted without corresponding changes in eye movements. So whilst we ordinarily move our eyes so that the fovea receives information from the stimulus we are attending to, attention to stimuli can occur without eye movements, and such shifts in attention frequently precede the corresponding eye movement (Anderson, 1995a). Posner (1980) has called this phenomenon *covert attention*.

The internal mental spotlight and the zoom lens

Posner likened the phenomenon of covert attention to an internal spotlight that 'illuminates' any stimulus in the attended region so that it is perceived in greater detail. According to this 'spotlight metaphor', covert attention essentially duplicates the functions of eye movements internally, by allowing a particular region of space to be perceptually enhanced (Driver, 1996).

In one experiment conducted by LaBerge (1983), participants were required to judge whether the middle letter of five letters (such as LACIE) came from the beginning or end of the alphabet. On some occasions, however, a stimulus such as +7+++ was presented, and the participant's task was to determine whether the

7 was one of two letters (T or Z). LaBerge found that the speed of judgement was a function of the distance from the centre of attention. Thus, reaction times were fastest for items at the centre of the stimulus and slower at its periphery, even though all items were within the region of the fovea.

On the basis of this finding, LaBerge concluded that visual attention is most concentrated at the centre of the internal spotlight and least concentrated at its periphery. When material beyond the spotlight's centre needs to be processed, the spotlight must be shifted to ensure maximal processing. Because this takes time, it is hardly surprising that participants in Posner et al.'s experiments took longer to judge a stimulus when it appeared in an 'unexpected' location (Eriksen and Yeh, 1987).

In a second experiment, LaBerge found that when participants were required to attend to the whole five-letter word string, the 'width' of the spotlight's 'beam' increased as indicated by the lack of difference in reaction times for items at the centre and periphery. LaBerge's findings led Eriksen (1990) to propose the *zoom-lens model of visual attention*. This model accepts the existence of an internal mental spotlight but suggests that it has a beam which may be very narrow (in the case of LaBerge's letter task) or broad (in the case of LaBerge's word task).

There is evidence to suggest that, consistent with the spotlight model, little or no processing occurs beyond the spotlight (Johnston and Dark, 1986). However, the claims made by both the spotlight model and the zoom-lens extension of it have been contradicted in a number of studies, some of which pre-date the models (e.g. Neisser and Becklen, 1975; Juola et al., 1991). In Neisser and Becklen's study, for example, visual selective attention was studied by superimposing a film of three people playing a ball game on a film which showed two people's hands clapping, as shown in Figure 5.4.

The participant's task was to follow one of the films and press a key to indicate that a 'critical event', such as the ball being thrown, had occurred. Neisser and Becklen reported that whilst adults found it difficult to follow both events simultaneously, they were able to attend selectively to one or other of the films easily. The finding that some things within the visual environment can be attended to and others ignored is difficult for the zoom-lens model to explain, since the model

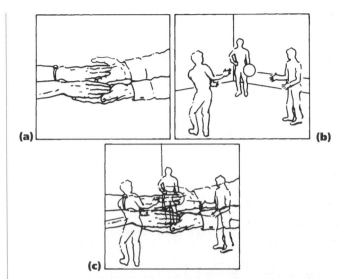

Figure 5.4   A film of two people clapping hands (a) and three people playing a ball game (b) which have been superimposed (c).

proposes that the focus of attention is a given *area* in visual space rather than objects within that area (Eysenck and Keane, 1995). Interestingly, Neisser and Becklen's methodology has been used to study visual selective attention in infants. It seems that infants as young as four months can selectively follow one of the two episodes and, as a result, that selective visual attention is a characteristic which is innate rather than learned (Bahrick et al., 1981).

The fate of unattended visual stimuli

Whether unattended visual stimuli undergo any sort of processing has been the subject of much debate. For some researchers (such as Johnston and Dark, 1986), stimuli beyond the focus of visual attention are subject to no or virtually no semantic processing because of the finding that the nature of the unattended stimuli does not affect stimuli that are attended to. Any such processing as does occur is thought to be limited to mainly simple physical features. Other researchers (such as Driver, 1996) disagree.

Driver and his colleagues (e.g. Tipper and Driver, 1988) have shown that when a picture is shown as the unattended stimulus on one trial, it slows the processing of an attended word with an identical or similar meaning on the next trial. This phenomenon is known as *negative priming*. The fact that processing of the attended stimulus is lessened suggests that the meaning of the unattended stimulus must have been subject to some sort of processing.

TREISMAN'S FEATURE-INTEGRATION THEORY

One who agrees with the view that some processing of unattended material takes place is Treisman (1988). Treisman's theory was developed on the basis of a number of findings using the *visual search procedure*. In this, participants are presented with an array of visual material in which a target item is embedded on some trials but absent on others, and the 'distractor' items can be varied so that they are similar to the target letter or different. The participant's task is to decide if the target is present or absent, as shown in Figure 5.5.

```
X   P   T   L   A   B   N   T

A   R   H   N   J   I   F   R

E   W   R   N   P   A   Z   X

A   H   Y   5   Y   T   E   S

A   N   H   C   E   S   T   I

G   D   T   K   D   Y   U   I
```

Figure 5.5   A visual search array. The task is to find the number five in amongst the letters.

Neisser (1967) argued that when people perform a visual search task, they process many items simultaneously without being fully 'aware' of the exact nature of the distractor items. However, the processing of visual information possibly does occur *pre-attentively* as a result of the nature of the stimuli presented (such as whether they have angular or curved features when the task is to detect a particular letter).

According to Treisman, attention must be focused on a stimulus before its features can be synthesised into a pattern. Evidence in support of this claim was presented by Treisman and Gelade (1980). In one experiment, participants were required to detect the presence of the letter T in amongst an array of I's and Y's. Because the horizontal bar at the top of a T distinguishes it from an I and a Y, Treisman and Gelade predicted that this task could be done fairly easily just by

looking for the horizontal bar. Their results showed that participants took around 800 milliseconds to detect the T's presence and also that the detection time was not affected by the *size* of the array (that is, the number of I's and Y's).

In a second experiment, the T was embedded in an array of I's and Z's. Here, looking for a horizontal bar on its own does not aid detection since the letter Z also has a horizontal bar on top of it. To detect a T, participants need to look for the *conjunction* of a horizontal and vertical line. Treisman and Gelade found that participants took around 1200 milliseconds to detect the T, that is, they took *longer* to recognise the conjunction of features than was the case when the recognition of just one feature was necessary. Moreover, the time needed to detect the T was *longer* when the size of the array was increased.

In further experiments, Treisman and Gelade found that when participants were required to search for a blue letter in amongst different coloured letters, detection time was quicker than when the task was to search for a green letter T in among brown letter T's and green X's with, again, detection time being linked to the size of the array. On the basis of these findings, Treisman proposed her feature-integration theory which is summarised in Box 5.2 (opposite).

According to Treisman's theory, then, focused attention is needed to detect targets which are defined by a combination of features (that is, the second stage of processing identified in Box 5.2 is necessary), whilst objects defined by a single feature can be detected in the absence of focused attention (since only the first stage identified in Box 5.2 is necessary). Additionally, because objects defined by a single feature do not require focused attention, the size of the array will not affect detection time (see above).

CRITICISMS OF TREISMAN'S THEORY AND ALTERNATIVES TO IT

There has been much debate over Treisman's theory. For example, Duncan and Humphreys (1992) have argued that the time taken to detect a target depends on the target's *similarity* to the distractors and the distractors' *similarity to one another*. According to Duncan and Humphreys' *attentional-engagement theory*, all of the visual items in a display are initially segmented and analysed in parallel. After this, selective attention occurs in which items that are well matched to the

According to Treisman, it is possible to distinguish between *objects* (such as a strawberry) and the *features* of those objects (such as being red, possessing curves, and being of a particular size). In the first stage of visual processing, we process the features of stimuli in the visual environment and we do so rapidly and in parallel (or simultaneously) without attention being required.

Next, the features of a stimulus are combined to form objects (such as a small, red strawberry). This second stage of processing is a slow and serial process (that is, features are combined one after another). Processing is slower in this stage when several stimuli must be processed.

Focusing our attention on the location of an object provides the 'glue' which allows unitary features to be formed into their various objects, although features can also be combined on the basis of knowledge stored in memory (such as the knowledge that strawberries are typically red). When relevant stored knowledge is not available or focused attention absent, feature combination occurs in a random way. This can produce *illusory conjunctions* (for example, a blue banana) or odd combinations of features.

(based on Anderson (1995a) and Eysenck and Keane (1995))

description of the target item enter short-term visual memory (see Chapter 7, page 82).

Distractors which are similar to the target will *slow* the search process, as will non-targets that are dissimilar to each other but similar to the target. In the case of distractors that are similar to the target, this is because they are likely to be selected for short-term visual memory. In the case of distractors that are dissimilar to each other but similar to the target, this is because items which are perceptually grouped (because, say, they are similar) will either be selected or rejected together for short-term visual memory. Since dissimilar distractors cannot be rejected together, the search process is slowed (Eysenck and Keane, 1995).

Evidence exists which suggests that *irrespective of the size of the display*, visual search can be fast when the non-targets are the same (Humphreys et al., 1985). Since Humphreys and his colleagues' task was to detect an upright T (a target which has a conjunction of fea-

tures) in amongst inverted T's, Treisman's theory would have predicted that the display size would affect detection time. Equally, though, Treisman (1991) has shown that target similarity can be kept constant but that detection times are still affected by the requirement to perceive conjunctions.

Treisman has also claimed evidence for the occurrence of *illusory conjunctions* (see Box 5.2) in her visual search experiments. Treisman and Schmidt (1982), for example, required participants to identify two black digits flashed in one part of the visual field. In another part of the visual field, letters in various colours were presented (such as a blue T or a red S). After having reported the digits, participants were asked what letters they had seen and the colour of those letters. Most of the participants reported seeing illusory conjunctions (such as a blue S) almost as frequently as correct conjunctions were reported. Such a finding lends support to the view that accurate perception only occurs when attention is focused on an object. When attention is not focused, the features of objects are processed but not always combined accurately.

Treisman and Sato (1990) have acknowledged that the degree of similarity between the target and the distractors is important and, as Eysenck and Keane (1995) have commented, the distance between her theory and that of Duncan and Humphreys appears to be narrowing, although the role of conjoining features and the importance of the similarity between non-targets remain important points of difference. There is also some evidence concerning attention to moving displays which is troublesome for Treisman's theory. In these sorts of experiments, moving items are intermingled with static items. For example, McLeod et al. (1991) asked participants to search for the presence or absence of a single moving X in amongst static X's and moving O's as shown in Figure 5.6 (see page 64).

In this study, the target is defined only by its specific conjunction of form and movement, since its shape is shared with the static X's and its movement with the O's. Treisman's theory would predict that serial attention was necessary for each item when searching the target, and hence that decision times would increase with an increasing number of distractors. In fact, McLeod and his colleagues reported that the target could be easily found regardless of the size of the display. Such an outcome implies a parallel process at work, and in other experiments the researchers showed

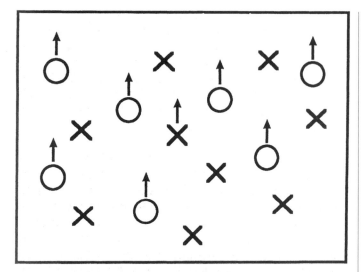

Figure 5.6 A schematic representation of the display used by McLeod et al. (1991). The arrows indicate motion, and the task is to search for a single moving X among moving Os and intermingled static Xs.

that the parallel search arose because attention could be restricted to just the group of items with common motion to the exclusion of the static items. Because the target has a unique shape, it can be detected in parallel.

Visual attention and damage to the brain

Research into visual attention is currently very exciting, and a large number of researchers are looking at the regions of the brain which play a role in attention (e.g. Muller and Maxwell, 1994; Halligan, 1995; Driver, 1996). In a phenomenon called *unilateral neglect*, people who have suffered a right-hemisphere stroke that involves the parietal cortex may completely ignore stimuli which occur on the opposite side to the affected hemisphere. For example, in the case of right-hemisphere damage, they may fail to eat food from the left side of their plate and be unaware of their body on that side. The fascinating thing about unilateral neglect is that these effects occur even though the pathways from the receptors to the central nervous system for the neglected information can be demonstrably intact.

Exactly why these deficits occur is not yet known, but it is possible that the internal attentional 'spotlight' may, as a result of the stroke, become biased towards the side on which the stroke has occurred. Further discussion of this possibility and other recent relevant research can be found in Driver and Mattingley (1995).

Conclusions

Research into focused auditory and visual attention indicates that we are able to attend selectively to certain information, and a number of theories have been advanced to explain how we are able to do this. It is generally accepted that some degree of processing of unattended material takes place in both the auditory and visual modalities, although the exact mechanisms by which this occurs have yet to be determined.

SUMMARY

- The word 'attention' has been used in a variety of ways, including the **selective** processing of information.
- While Titchener saw attention as of central importance to psychology as a whole, **Gestalt psychologists** thought it unnecessary to use the concept of attention, and **behaviourists** rejected it on the grounds that it is unobservable and so not worthy of experimental study.
- According to Broadbent, in order to cope with the flood of available sensory information, humans must **selectively attend** to only some informa-

tion and 'tune out' the rest. He was partly trying to account for Cherry's **cocktail-party situation**.
- Using **binaural listening**, Cherry found that voice intensity, the speaker's location and sex were especially important physical differences affecting the ability to selectively attend to one of the two messages. When these differences were controlled for, it was very difficult to separate the two messages in terms of their meaning.
- In other experiments, Cherry used **dichotic listening**, in which a different message is presented to each ear. In addition, participants had to

shadow one of the messages. While being able to shadow, participants remembered little, if anything, of the non-shadowed message, even when the same word was presented 35 times.

- Later research also found that participants failed to notice if the non-shadowed message was spoken in a foreign language, changed from English to a foreign language or was played backwards. However, a pure tone of 400 cps was almost always noticed, as was a change of voice from male to female or vice-versa. So while the physical properties of the non-attended message were 'heard', its meaning was completely lost.

- In Broadbent's **split-span studies**, each ear was presented with different information. Typical accuracy of recall was 65 per cent (compared with 95 per cent when the split-span procedure was not used) and **pair-by-pair** recall was considerably **poorer** than **ear-by-ear recall**. Also, people preferred ear-by-ear recall if given a choice.

- Three of the **single-channel theories** proposed to explain these findings share the belief in a 'bottleneck' or **filter** which allows some information to be passed on for further processing, and either discards the rest or processes it only to a limited degree. They differ mainly in terms of how early or late the filtering takes place, and hence the nature and extent of the processing of the non-shadowed material.

- According to Broadbent's **early selection filter theory**, sensory information passes 'in parallel' to a **short-term store**, a temporary 'buffer system' which holds information until it is passed in its original form to a **selective filter**. The filter operates on the **physical characteristics** of the selected source, rejecting all the others.

- Information allowed through the filter reaches a **limited capacity channel**, where it is recognised, possibly rehearsed, and then transferred to the muscles, initiating an appropriate response.

- The switching of attention between channels takes a substantial period of time: processing information from two channels will always take longer and be less efficient than processing the same information from a single channel.

- Broadbent's theory could account for Cherry's findings and the split-span data. It also assumes that the **meaning** of the non-shadowed message will not be subjected to any higher-level analysis. However, Moray's demonstration that people will switch attention to the non-attended ear when their name was spoken (about one third of the time) challenges Broadbent's theory.

- Several other studies have also produced data inconsistent with Broadbent's theory, such as Gray and Wedderburn's demonstration that the ears do not always function as two separate channels of information and that switching between them is quite easy. Similarly, Treisman found that participants could sometimes switch attention to the non-attended ear if meaningful material was transferred, mid-sentence, from the attended ear.

- Treisman also found that **bilingual** participants could recognise that the non-shadowed (French) and shadowed (English) messages had the same meaning, while Corteen and Wood found that a conditioned GSR sometimes occurred in response to both a target word and **synonyms** of it appearing in the non-shadowed message.

- These studies suggest that the meaning of the input to the non-attended ear is at least sometimes processed. Additionally, Underwood found that **training** could improve detection of non-shadowed material, and Allport et al. found that when the shadowed and non-shadowed messages are sufficiently different, memory for the latter is good.

- According to Treisman's **stimulus-analysis system theory**, competing information is analysed not just for its physical properties, but for sounds, syllable patterns, grammatical structures and meaning. The selective filter **attenuates** ('turns down') the non-shadowed message: if this includes biologically and emotionally relevant stimuli ('pre-sets'), such as mention of our name, our attention will switch to the non-shadowed message.

- The **Deutsch–Norman late selection filter theory/pertinence theory** completely rejects Broadbent's claim that information is filtered out early on. Instead, selection only occurs after **all inputs** have been analysed at a high level (e.g. after each word has been recognised and **analysed for meaning**). The filter is nearer the **response** end of the processing system, i.e. it is a late-selection filter.

- Since the presented information will have already been processed, some will have been established as **pertinent** and will have activated particular memory representations: when one of these is selected for further processing, attention becomes selective. The implication is that we perceive everything we encounter but are consciously aware of only some of it.

- The Deutsch–Norman model predicts that as many target words would be identified in the non-shadowed as the shadowed message, since both are completely analysed for meaning. However, Treisman and Geffen's study failed to support this prediction. Deutsch and Deutsch in turn criticised the study for wrongly assuming that the shadowed and non-shadowed messages are equally important, but when Treisman and Riley controlled this variable, they replicated the original results (although the detection rate for the non-attended ear was much higher in the second experiment, thus providing some support for Deutsch and Norman).

- According to the Deutsch–Norman theory, participants should be able to repeat back the words presented to the non-attended ear if asked to do so **immediately**; otherwise, they will be lost rapidly from short-term memory. Studies by Norman and Glucksberg and Cowan support this prediction, and the theory is further supported by studies which show that words in the non-shadowed message are processed according to their meaning.

- The major problem for the Deutsch–Norman model concerns its claim that **every** input is analysed at a higher level, making it rigid and inflexible. Although more processing of the non-shadowed message takes place than is claimed by either Broadbent or Treisman, it falls short of what is predicted by Deutsch and Norman.

- The **inflexibility** of single-channel models has led to alternative models, such as Johnston and Heinz's proposal that attentional selectivity can occur at several different stages of processing, depending on the demands made by the experimental task.

- Mechanisms involved in **focused visual attention** include eye movements that allow us to fixate specific regions of the visual field which can be projected on to the **fovea**. This contains very sensitive **cone** cells, providing maximum acuity for visual stimuli.

- When people are told to fixate on one part of the visual field, they can still attend to stimuli seven or so degrees either side of the fixation point. Also, attention can be shifted more quickly when a stimulus is presented in an 'expected' location. This shows that visual attention is **not** identical to the part of the visual field processed by the fovea: attention can be shifted without corresponding eye movement changes (**covert attention**).

- According to Posner, covert attention is like an **internal mental spotlight**, which essentially duplicates the functions of eye movements internally by allowing a particular region of space to be perceptually enhanced. For example,

LaBerge found that reaction times were fastest for items at the centre of a stimulus (the centre of the internal spotlight) and slower at its periphery, even though all items fell within the fovea region.

- When we need to process material beyond the spotlight's centre, the spotlight must be shifted to ensure maximal processing; this will take more time when a stimulus appears in an unexpected location. According to Eriksen's **zoom-lens model of visual attention**, the internal spotlight has a beam which may be very narrow or very broad.

- While there is evidence that little or no processing occurs beyond the spotlight, there is evidence that is inconsistent with both the spotlight and zoom-lens models. For example, Neisser and Becklen showed that participants could easily attend selectively to one or other of two superimposed films. This is difficult for the zoom-lens model to explain, since the focus of attention is supposedly a given **area** in visual space, rather than objects within that area. Evidence also exists which suggests that selective visual attention is innate.

- The finding that the nature of the unattended stimuli has no effect on those that are attended to suggests that the former receive little or no semantic processing. However, demonstration of **negative priming** suggests that processing of meaning of non-attended stimuli does take place.

- According to Neisser, when people are tested using a **visual search procedure**, they process many items simultaneously without being fully aware of the exact nature of the distractor items. However, visual information may be **pre-attentively** processed.

- According to Treisman's **feature-integration theory**, we can distinguish between **objects** and their **features**. In the first stage of visual processing, we process the features of environmental stimuli, rapidly and in parallel, without attention being required. We then combine the features to form objects; this is done slowly and serially. Focusing our attention on an object's location allows unitary features to be formed into their various objects, although these can also be combined on the basis of stored knowledge. **Illusory conjunctions** can arise in the absence of relevant stored knowledge or focused attention.

- Objects defined by a single feature can be detected without focused attention, which explains why the size of the array in visual search experiments does not affect detection time.

- According to Duncan and Humphreys' **atten-**

tional-engagement theory, detection time depends on the **similarity** between the target and distractors and on their **similarity to one another**. All the visual items in a display are initially segmented and analysed in parallel, followed by selective attention, with items that match description of the target entering short-term visual memory.

- While Treisman's theory would predict that time taken to detect an upright T in a display of inverted T's would be affected by array size, Humphreys et al. found that visual search can be fast when the distractors are the same, **irrespective of display size**.

- However, Treisman has shown that target similarity can be kept constant but that detection times are still affected by the requirement to perceive conjunctions. She has also claimed evidence for **illusory conjunctions**, supporting the view that accurate perception requires focused attention on an object, i.e. accurate combination of features.

- Although there appears to be convergence between the theories of Treisman and Duncan and Humphreys, there are still disagreements over the role of combining features and the role of similarity between distractors. There is also evidence from studies of attention to moving displays that is inconsistent with Treisman's theory.

- Current research is investigating areas of the brain involved in visual attention. In **unilateral neglect**, stroke victims ignore stimuli which occur on the opposite side to the affected hemisphere, even though the pathways from the receptors to the central nervous system remain intact.

6

DIVIDED ATTENTION

Introduction and overview

In the previous chapter, we looked at studies which require people to process the information from one of two stimulus inputs. Researchers interested in divided attention also typically present people with two stimulus inputs, but require both of them to be responded to. From our everyday experience, we know that sometimes we are able to do two things at once easily. For example, most of us can drink a pint of beer whilst simultaneously listening to someone talking. Indeed, as we saw in the previous chapter (see page 57), simultaneously attending to two conversations is difficult, but not impossible (Underwood, 1974). In some cases, though, it is extremely difficult to perform two tasks simultaneously.

Our aims in this chapter are threefold. The first is to look at research findings into divided attention. We will begin by briefly reviewing some of the relevant findings and then consider the factors that affect so-called *dual-task performance*. Our second aim is to look at some of the theories which have been advanced to explain how we manage to divide our attention between two tasks. Some theorists have argued that, with sufficient practice, many processes become automatic and make no demands on our attention. Our third aim in this chapter is to review the evidence for and against the claim of automatic processing and to consider how such argument and evidence may help us understand 'action slips', that is, the performance of behaviours that were not intended.

Some demonstrations of dual-task performance

In a study conducted in 1972, Allport and his colleagues showed that skilled pianists were able to successfully read music whilst shadowing speech. Later, Shaffer (1975) reported the case of an expert typist who could accurately type from sight whilst shadowing speech. However, perhaps the most striking example of dual-task performance comes from a study conducted by Spelke et al. (1976).

Spelke and his colleagues had two students spend five hours a week training at performing two tasks simultaneously. Initially, the students were required to read short stories whilst writing down dictated words. At first, this was difficult for them, and both their comprehension of what they had read and their writing down of the words they had heard suffered. After six weeks of training, however, they could read as quickly and comprehend as much of what they read as when reading without dictation. Interestingly, though, they could remember very little of what they had written down, even though thousands of words had been dictated to them over the course of the experiment.

At this point, the task was altered so that the students had to write down the category to which a word belonged, a task which required more processing of the words, whilst at the same time reading the short stories. Again, the task was initially difficult. However, the students were eventually able to perform this task without any loss in their ability to comprehend the stories.

Figure 6.1   Can two or more tasks be performed at the same time to the same level as they would be individually?

Factors affecting dual-task performance

According to Hampson (1989), factors which make one task easier also tend to make the other easier because:

'anything which minimises interference between processes or keeps them "further apart" will allow them to be dealt with more readily either selectively or together'.

Eysenck and Keane (1995) identify three factors which have been shown to affect our ability to perform two tasks at once. These are *difficulty, practice* and *similarity*. Their effects are summarised in Box 6.1.

Box 6.1   The effects of difficulty, practice and similarity on dual-task performance

Difficulty: As a general rule, the more difficult tasks are, the less successful dual-task performance is. However, it is hard to define task difficulty in an objective way, since a task that is difficult for one person might not be difficult for another (and this relates to practice: see below). Also, the demands made by two tasks individually are not necessarily the same when they are performed concurrently. Thus, performing two tasks together may introduce fresh demands and require interference to be avoided.

Practice: As the studies described at the beginning of this section show, practice improves dual-task performance. This could be because people develop new strategies for performing each of the tasks and this minimises the interference between them. Another possibility is that practice reduces the attentional demands a task makes. Finally, practice may produce a more economical way of functioning using fewer resources (a point which we will address in the section on automatic processing).

Similarity: As we saw in both this and the previous chapter, Allport et al. (1972) showed that when people are required to shadow one message and learn pictorial information, both tasks can be performed successfully, presumably because they do not involve the same stimulus modality. Two tasks also disrupt performance when both of them rely on related memory codes (such as visual memory), make use of the same

stages of processing (such as the input stage) or require similar responses to be made.

(based on Eysenck and Keane, 1995)

A brief introduction to theories of divided attention

The theories of selective attention we described in the previous chapter assume the existence of a limited capacity filter which is capable of dealing with one channel of information at a time. As Hampson and Morris (1996) have observed, these theories:

'imply a series of stages of processing, starting with superficial, physical analysis, and working "upwards" towards the "higher" cognitive analyses for meaning'.

In Hampson and Morris's view, these processes are better thought of as an integrated mechanism with the high and low levels interacting and combining in the recognition of stimuli, and that as a result it is better to look at the *overall processing* by the system.

Limited capacity theories of divided attention

KAHNEMAN'S THEORY

According to Kahneman (1973), humans possess only a limited amount of processing capacity, and the extent to which tasks can be performed successfully depends on how much demand they make on the limited capacity processor. Some tasks require little processing capacity and leave plenty of capacity available for performing another task simultaneously. However, other tasks require much more capacity and leave little 'spare' processing capacity available.

Kahneman refers to the process of determining how much capacity is available as 'effort'; and effort is involved in the allocation of that capacity. How much capacity is needed for a task depends on variables such as its difficulty and a person's experience of it. How capacity is allocated depends on *enduring dispositions,*

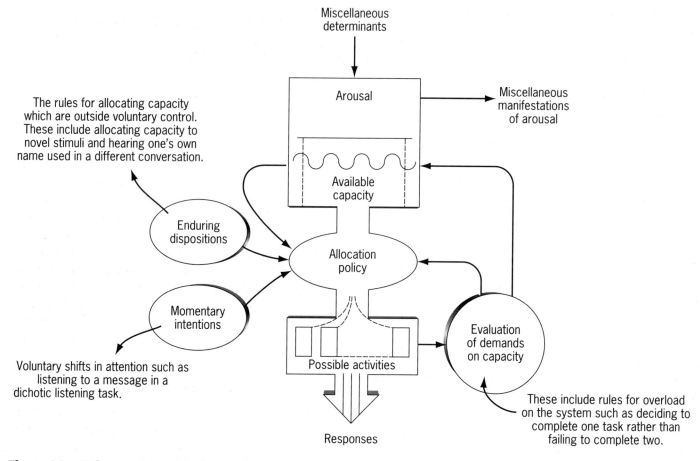

The rules for allocating capacity which are outside voluntary control. These include allocating capacity to novel stimuli and hearing one's own name used in a different conversation.

Voluntary shifts in attention such as listening to a message in a dichotic listening task.

These include rules for overload on the system such as deciding to complete one task rather than failing to complete two.

Figure 6.2   Kahneman's model of attention.

momentary intentions and the *evaluation of the attentional demands* as shown in Figure 6.2. The central processor is responsible for the allocation policy and constantly evaluates the level of demand. When the demand is too high, the central processor must decide how available attention should be allocated.

As Figure 6.2 shows, Kahneman sees *arousal* as playing an important part in determining how much capacity is available. At least up to a point, more attentional resources are available when we are aroused and alert than when we are tired and lethargic. Kahneman argues that attention can be divided between tasks as long as the total available capacity is not exceeded. This can explain the findings from the dichotic listening tasks we discussed in the previous chapter by assuming that shadowing is a task which requires almost all of the capacity available. As a result, the non-shadowed message receives little attention because sufficient

capacity is not available. Kahneman's theory also predicts that as skill on a task increases, so less capacity is needed for it and more becomes available for other tasks. Thus, in Underwood's (1974) study (see page 57), when people are *trained* at shadowing, they become able to shadow *and* attend to the non-shadowed message.

Kahneman's theory suggests that attention is a much more flexible and dynamic system than suggested by the theories of focused attention we described in the previous chapter. Despite this, the theory has important drawbacks (reviewed by Hampson and Morris, 1996). For example, it does not address the issue of how decisions are made to channel attention and, as we will see shortly, the difficulty in defining the general limits of capacity has led some researchers to suggest that the concept of a limited capacity should be abandoned.

NORMAN AND BOBROW'S THEORY

Following on from Kahneman, Norman and Bobrow (1975) have offered a *central capacity interference* account of attentional phenomena. The central feature of their theory is its distinction between *resource-limited* and *data-limited* processes. On a complex task, performance is related to the amount of resources that are devoted to a task. As more resources are allocated to the task, so performance of it improves up to some point. Performance is thus resource-limited. On some tasks, though, applying more resources does not lead to an improvement in performance because of external influences, as when participants are required to identify a quiet tone in amongst loud, masking 'white' noise. This sort of task is data-limited because performance can only be improved by altering the stimuli (such as by making the tone louder and/or the masking noise quieter).

Norman and Bobrow argue that the data-limited and resource-limited difference between tasks can explain findings from both the focused attention and divided attention literature. For example, Treisman and Geffen (1967: see pages 58–59) found that participants shadowing words in one ear had difficulty recognising target words presented simultaneously to the other ear. Lawson (1966), however, found that under similar conditions, participants were able to detect target *tones* presented in the non-attended ear. Such a finding can be explained by proposing that the tone-detection process becomes data-limited much *sooner* than the word-recognition process.

Norman and Bobrow's theory can explain the *data* obtained in various attention studies simply by talking about tasks in terms of their being data-limited or resource-limited. The theory's inability to predict *beforehand* the data an experiment is likely to produce is, however, its biggest weakness. Additionally, because the theory allows for *differential* allocation of resources to tasks, an experimenter can never know the level of resources that has been allocated to a particular task. Any data, therefore, can be interpreted in a way which is consistent with the theory, and no data can ever be taken as negative evidence.

Multi-channel theories of divided attention

Supporters of limited-capacity models argue that their approach is best because of the fact that the attentional system has to break down as more and more is demanded from it, and that if the data from divided-attention studies are considered carefully (see, for example, Hirst et al.'s (1980) extension of Spelke et al.'s (1976) experiment), it is *not* actually the case that two tasks can be performed together with no disruption at all (Broadbent, 1982). However, and as we noted earlier, several researchers have rejected the concept of a general purpose, limited-capacity processor completely. For Allport (1980, 1989, 1993), the concept of attention is often used synonymously with 'consciousness', with no specification of how it is supposed to operate, and this has done little to increase our understanding of the very problems it is meant to explain.

MODULES AND MULTIPLE RESOURCES

According to Allport, it is difficult to see how the neurology of the brain could produce a system of processing capacity that was completely open to any of the tasks that might be presented (Hampson and Morris, 1996). Allport argues that it is much more profitable to view the data in terms of tasks competing for the same specialised processing mechanisms or *modules*, each of which has a limited capacity but none of which is uniquely 'central'.

Allport argues that when two tasks are highly similar, they compete for the same modules, and this leads to performance impairments. However, because dissimilar tasks use different modules, both can be performed simultaneously. A virtually identical theoretical account has been proposed by Navon and Gopher (1979) and Wickens (1992) in their *multiple-resource theory*. Certainly, the findings of the various dual-task studies we have described previously (e.g. Allport et al., 1972) are consistent with the idea of different processing mechanisms handling the requirements of different tasks.

Given the variation in the amount of interference that two tasks can produce for each other, it is plausible to propose that modules or multiple resources exist. However, this approach too cannot be falsified, since any pattern of data can be explained by proposing the existence of a particular pattern of modules (Navon, 1984). Additionally, the *number* of modules has yet to be specified, nor has any attempt been made to explain how people evaluate and integrate multiple sources of information. Lastly, if multiple resources operate in parallel, they must do so in a highly integrated way, given that our behaviour is typically coherent (Eysenck and Keane, 1995).

Attempts at synthesising capacity and module accounts

According to Eysenck (1982, 1984) and Baddeley (1986), a much better way of accommodating the data from divided-attention studies is to see capacity and module accounts as being complementary rather than competitive. So-called *synthesis models* propose the existence of a modality-free central capacity processor, which is involved in the co-ordination and control of behaviour, and specific processing systems. In Baddeley's (1986) model, for example, two independently operating and specific systems (what Baddeley calls an *articulatory loop* and a *visuo-spatial scratchpad*) are proposed. These systems would explain why overt repetition of an overlearned sequence of digits does not interfere with verbal reasoning, since the former is held to use the articulatory loop and the latter the central processor. We shall return to Baddeley's proposals and modifications to them in Chapter 8 when we consider his theory about the structure of human memory.

Automatic processing

As we have noted elsewhere in this chapter, both laboratory evidence (e.g. Spelke et al., 1976: see page 68) and everyday experience testifies to the fact that we can learn to perform two tasks simultaneously and perform highly efficiently on both. For some researchers, this is because many processes become *automatic* (in the sense that they make no attentional demands) if they are used (or practised) frequently enough. Two important theoretical contributions have been made by Schneider and Shiffrin (1977) and Norman and Shallice (1986).

SCHNEIDER AND SHIFFRIN'S MODEL

According to Schneider and Shiffrin (1977; Shiffrin and Schneider, 1977), it is possible to distinguish between attentional processing which is *controlled* and that which is *automatic*. Schneider and Shiffrin argue that, amongst other things, controlled processing makes heavy demands on attentional resources, is slow, capacity limited, and involves attention being consciously directed towards a task. Automatic processing, by contrast, makes no demands on attentional resources, is fast, unaffected by capacity limitations, unavoidable and difficult to modify (in the sense that such processing always occurs in the presence of an appropriate stimulus) and is not subject to conscious awareness.

A number of researchers have contrasted the effects of controlled and automatic processing (e.g. Gleitman and Jonides, 1978; Schneider and Fisk, 1982). Essentially, the results of these studies are consistent with Schneider and Shiffrin's view and show that if people are given practice at a task, they are able to perform it quickly and accurately, but their performance is resistant to change. An example of apparent automaticity in real life occurs when we learn to drive a car. At first, focused attention is required for each component of the skill of learning to drive, and any sort of distraction can disrupt performance. Once we have learned to drive, and as we become more experienced at driving, our ability to simultaneously attend to other things increases (see Figure 6.3).

Figure 6.3   A learner driver exhibits controlled processing to begin with; this will become automatic processing as their competence as a driver increases.

Logan (1988) has suggested that automaticity develops through practice because automatic responses involve an almost effortless retrieval of an appropriate and well-learned response from memory. This does not involve conscious memory because no thought processes intervene between the presentation of a stimulus and the production of an appropriate response. In Logan's view, then, automaticity occurs when stored information about the sequence of responses necessary to perform a task can be accessed and retrieved rapidly.

Despite its intuitive appeal, a number of serious criticisms have been made of Schneider and Shiffrin's model (Eysenck and Keane, 1995). For example, it is not clear whether automaticity results from a speeding up of the processes involved in a task or a *change* in the nature of the processes themselves. Also, the view that automatic processing makes *no* demands on attention has been challenged by findings indicating that allegedly automatic tasks *do* influence the performance of simultaneously performed tasks (e.g. Hampson, 1989). Additional problems occur with what is known as the 'Stroop effect', as shown in Box 6.2.

The application of Schneider and Shiffrin's views beyond the cognitive psychological domain have also met with limited success. One example of this is in the area of research into social facilitation and impairment effects. For over one hundred years, social psychologists have tried to explain why people perform some tasks better (a facilitation effect) and other tasks more poorly (an impairment effect) when other people watch their performance (Guerin, 1993).

According to Manstead and Semin (1980), 'simple' tasks are under what Adams (1976) calls *open-loop control* (a term which is equivalent to Schneider and Shiffrin's automatic processing). With tasks under open-loop control, sequences of responses are run off without them being monitored on a continuous basis. Abrams and Manstead (1981) have argued that when we perform simple tasks, our performance is suboptimal because we do not pay enough attention to relevant feedback (an argument which, as we will see, has also been advanced to explain action slips: see page 75). Abrams and Manstead suggest that when someone watches us engage in a simple task, our attention is focused sharply on the performance which causes feedback to be monitored more closely and performance to be improved (or facilitated). According to this account, social facilitation effects will only occur when the task

---

Box 6.2   The Stroop effect

In an experiment conducted in 1935, J.R. Stroop showed that if a colour word (such as 'blue') is presented in a colour with which the word conflicts (such as the word 'blue' being presented in red), then participants find it difficult to name the *colour* the word has been presented in. Presumably, because reading is such a well learned, unavoidable and automatic activity, the word interferes with the requirement to name the colour it has been presented in.

An analogue of the Stroop effect can be tried here. The task is to say as quickly as you can the *number of characters* in each of the following rows:

```
        5   5   5
      1   1   1   1
              2
      3   3   3   3   3
            4   4
          5   5   5
      4   4   4   4   4
        5   5   5   5
              3
          4   4   4
        2   2   2   2
            3   3
          4   4   4
      1   1   1   1
              3
          2   2   2
```

Flowers et al. (1979) found that people have difficulty in resisting saying the numbers that make up each row rather than counting the numbers because recognition of numbers is much more automated relative to counting numbers. Kahneman and Henrik (1979) found that the Stroop effect is much greater when the conflicting colour word is in the same location as the colour that has to be named than when it is in an adjacent location within the central fixation area (Eysenck, 1993). As Eysenck notes, this finding suggests that automatic responses are *not* always unavoidable.

being performed is so well learned that continuous monitoring of it is not ordinarily required.

Manstead and Semin propose that 'complex' tasks are under what Adams calls *closed-loop control* (a term which is equivalent to Schneider and Shiffrin's controlled processing). Here, the performer is consciously monitoring feedback concerning performance and modifying performance in the light of such feedback. The set-backs which inevitably occur during the learning of complex tasks (such as failures at stages of performance which had temporarily been 'mastered') distract the performer's attention away from the immediate requirement of monitoring a subsequent stage of the task, thereby interrupting the steady progression of learning, leading to increased errors. When performance is observed, the observer acts as an additional source of distraction from the task at hand (especially when set-backs occur), presumably because of the performer's concern about being evaluated by those observing the performance. This distraction places further demands on an already-stretched attentional system and thereby results in an increase in the number of errors.

According to this account of social facilitation and impairment effects, then, the effects of being observed will only be obtained at or near the extremes of what Abrams and Manstead (1981) have termed a *task mastery continuum*. For them:

'the presence of a critical audience should improve the driving of a highly experienced driver, but impair that of a novice driver, since the latter would suffer from attentional overload whereas the former has spare attentional capacity which can be devoted to considering the audience's reaction to the task performance'.

Such a theoretical account helps to explain the occurrence of social facilitation and impairment effects, and can explain the failure to find any effects of observer presence that have been reported by many researchers (see, for example, Guerin, 1993) by proposing that the tasks employed in such studies represented neither the closed- nor the open-loop ends of the task mastery continuum.

Unfortunately, data exist which indicate that 'simple' task performance can be impaired by the presence of others whilst 'complex' task performance can be improved in the presence of others. As we have noted before (see Box 6.1), defining task difficulty in an objective way is not an easy thing to do. However, unless it is assumed that the 'simple' tasks in such experiments were actually 'complex' and 'complex' tasks actually 'simple', the application of automatic and controlled processing to social facilitation and impairment is not strongly supported by the evidence.

NORMAN AND SHALLICE'S MODEL

In order to overcome what Eysenck (1993) calls the 'unavoidability criterion', Norman and Shallice (1986) have proposed that processing involves *two* separate control systems, which they call *contention scheduling* and the *supervisory attentional system*. Norman and Shallice accept that some behaviours involve *fully automatic processing* and that this occurs with little conscious awareness of the processes involved, since it is controlled by *schemas* (or organised plans for behaviour: see also pages 110–112).

However, such processes are capable of disrupting behaviour, and so contention scheduling occurs as a way of resolving conflicts among schemas. This produces *partially automatic processing* which generally involves more conscious awareness than fully automatic processing, but occurs without deliberate direction or conscious control. A third type of processing, called *deliberate control*, involves the supervisory attentional system. This is involved in decision-making and trouble-shooting and allows flexible responding to occur in novel situations.

According to Eysenck and Keane (1995), Norman and Shallice's model is superior to that of Schneider and Shiffrin because it:

'provides a more natural explanation for the fact that some processes are fully automatic whereas others are only partially automatic'.

The feature-integration theory proposed by Treisman that we discussed in the previous chapter can be seen as an attempt to identify processing which is completely free from capacity limitations.

Action slips

Action slips have been defined as the performance of actions that were not intended, and they have been extensively researched by James Reason (1979, 1992). In his original research, Reason asked 35 participants to keep a diary record of the action slips they made over a two-week period. The participants recorded 433 action slips between them. Reason was able to categorise 94 per cent of these as belonging to one of the five categories shown in Box 6.3.

Box 6.3   Reason's five categories of action slips

1 Storage failures

These were the most common form of action slip and accounted for 40 per cent of those that were recorded. These involve performing again an action that has already been completed. An example of a storage failure would be pouring a second kettle of boiling water into a tea pot of freshly made tea without any recognition of having made the tea already.

2 Test failures

These involve forgetting the goal of a particular sequence of actions and switching to a different goal. An example would be intending to turn on the radio but walking past it and picking up the telephone instead. This type of action slip, which accounted for 20 per cent of those recorded, presumably occurs because a planned sequence of actions is not monitored sufficiently at some crucial point in the sequence.

3 Sub-routine failures

Accounting for 18 per cent of the action slips recorded, sub-routine failures involve either omitting or re-ordering the stages in a sequence of behaviour. An example would be making a pot of tea but failing to put any tea bags in it.

4 Discrimination failures

These involve failing to discriminate between two objects involved in different actions. Mistaking toothpaste for shaving cream would be an example of a discrimination failure. These action slips accounted for 11 per cent of the total recorded.

5 Programme assembly failures

This was the smallest category of action slips, accounting for five per cent of the total recorded. Programme assembly failures involve incorrectly combining actions. An example would be unwrapping a sweet, putting the paper in your mouth, and throwing the sweet in the waste-paper bin.

(based on Reason (1992) and Eysenck (1997))

Paradoxically, action slips seem to occur with actions that are highly practised and over-learned (and which should, therefore, be least subject to errors). Reason (1992) has proposed that when we first learn to perform a behaviour, our actions are subject to *closed-loop control* (see page 74). In this, a central processor or attentional system guides and controls behaviour from its start to its finish. Once we have become skilled at a behaviour, it comes under *open-loop control* (see page 73). In this, the behaviour is controlled by motor programs or other automatic processes.

Closed-loop control is slow and effortful whereas open-loop control is fast and allows attentional resources to be given over to other activities. However, closed-loop control is less prone to error and responds more flexibly to environmental demands than open-loop control. As a result, action slips occur because of an over-reliance on open-loop control when closed-loop control (selectively attending to the task) should be occurring.

We know from the data obtained in studies of focused attention which were considered in the previous chapter, that material which is not attended to is typically poorly remembered because it does not get stored in long-term memory. The most common type of action slip, storage failures, can thus be explained in terms of open-loop induced attentional failures leading to a

"Damn! I keep forgetting it's AD not BC now..."

Figure 6.4   What kind of action slip do you think this is?

failure to store (and hence recall) previous actions. As a result, an action may be repeated. Other slips also seem amenable to explanation in terms of open-loop control (Eysenck, 1997).

An alternative theoretical account of action slips has been advanced by Norman (1981) and elaborated by Sellen and Norman (1992). Their theory is based on the concept of the *schema*, a concept first proposed by Bartlett (1932). We shall consider schema theory in detail in Chapter 9. Briefly, though, a schema is an organised mental representation of everything we understand by a given object, concept or event, based on our past experience (see Chapter 7, page 110).

Sellen and Norman's theory distinguishes between *parent* and *child* schemas. Parent schemas are the highest-level schemas and correspond to an overall intention or goal (such as going to a football match). At a lower level are child schemas, which correspond to the actions involved in accomplishing the overall intention or goal (such as driving the car to the football ground, buying a ticket and so on). Each schema has a particular activation level, and a behaviour is produced when the activation level is reached (which depends on the current situation and current intentions) and appropriate 'triggering' conditions exist.

Sellen and Norman argue that if (a) there is an error in the formation of an intention, (b) an incorrect schema is activated, (c) activation of the correct schema is lost, or (d) there is faulty triggering of an active schema, then an action slip occurs. Thus, a regular beer drinker may decide, because he or she is driving, not to drink alcohol on a visit to the pub with friends. However, without realising it, the drinker finds he or she has ordered a pint of beer in the pub as a result of faulty triggering.

Reason and Mycielska (1982) believe that a thorough understanding of the nature of action slips is necessary to avoid potential disaster occurring in the real world (see, for example, Box 16.5 in Chapter 16). Eysenck (1994) makes the valid point that action slips would be eliminated if we were to use closed-loop control for all of our behaviours. However, this would be a waste of

valuable attentional resources! The frequency of action slips reported by Reason's (1979) participants (an average of about one per day) suggests that people alternate between closed-loop and open-loop control as the circumstances dictate. For Eysenck (1994):

'the very occasional action slip is a price which is generally worth paying in order to free the attentional system from the task of constant monitoring of our habitual actions'.

Whether the theoretical accounts of action slips proposed by Reason and Sellen and Norman are accurate remains to be seen. It is possible that each type of action slip might require its own explanation, because whilst the mechanisms underlying them may *appear* to be similar, they might *actually* be very different (Eysenck and Keane, 1995).

We should also note that any theoretical account depends on the validity of the data it attempts to explain. The diary method employed by Reason may supply weak data because participants might not have detected some of their action slips or remembered to record them when they did (Eysenck, 1997). As a result, the percentages reported by Reason may be inaccurate. Finally, in Eysenck and Keane's (1995) words:

'the frequency of a particular action slip is meaningful only when we know the number of occasions on which the slip might have occurred but did not. Thus, the small number of discrimination failures (reported by Reason) may reflect either good discrimination or a relative lack of situations requiring anything approaching a fine discrimination'.

Conclusions

Whilst it is sometimes possible to divide our attention between two different tasks, the way in which this is achieved has not yet been satisfactorily explained. The idea that many processes become automatic and make no demands on our attention has some support and may help to explain why we sometimes perform behaviours that we did not intend to.

SUMMARY

- Researchers interested in divided attention typically present people with two stimulus inputs, but, unlike studies of focused attention, they are required to respond to both (**dual-task performance**). Doing two things at once often proves extremely difficult.
- Demonstrations of dual-task performance include Allport et al.'s study of skilled pianists, Shaffer's study of an expert typist, and Spelke et al.'s study in which students were first trained to read short stories while writing down dictated words, and later to categorise dictated words.
- Eysenck and Keane identify three factors which have been shown to affect dual-task performance: **task difficulty**, **practice** and **similarity**.
- Generally, the more difficult tasks are, the less successful dual-task performance is, but difficulty is hard to define objectively, and performing two tasks simultaneously may introduce interference not present when they are performed separately.
- Minimising interference between tasks through the development of new strategies might account for how practice improves dual-task performance. Alternatively, practice might reduce a task's attentional demands or produce a more economical way of functioning.
- Two tasks disrupt performance when they both involve the same stimulus modality, rely on related memory codes (such as visual memory), make use of the same processing stages (such as the input stage) or require similar responses to be made.
- Theories of selective attention assume the existence of a limited capacity filter, capable of dealing with one information channel at a time. They imply a series of stages of processing which Hampson and Morris prefer to see as an integrated mechanism, i.e. we should consider the **overall processing** by the system.
- According to Kahneman, humans possess only a limited amount of processing capacity. Different tasks require different amounts of processing capacity, leaving different amounts of 'spare' capacity available for performing other tasks. The amount of 'effort' needed for a task depends on factors such as its difficulty and a person's experience of it, and how capacity is allocated depends on **enduring dispositions**, **momentary intentions** and the **evaluation of the attentional demands.**
- The central processor controls the allocation policy and constantly evaluates the level of demand. **Arousal** is important for determining how much capacity is available, with more attentional resources available when we are alert.
- Kahneman argues that attention can be divided between tasks as long as the total available capacity is not exceeded. Also, the more skilled we are at a particular task, the less capacity is needed.
- Despite the greater flexibility of the attentional system as proposed by Kahneman's theory compared with theories of focused attention, it fails to address the issue of how decisions are made to channel attention. It also faces the problem of trying to define the general limits of capacity.
- According to Norman and Bobrow's **central capacity interference** theory, performance on a complex task is related to the level of resources devoted to a task: as more resources are allocated, so performance on the task improves up to some point (performance is **resource-limited**). But some tasks are **data-limited**, where performance can only be improved by changing the stimuli.
- This distinction can explain findings from both focused and divided-attention studies. The finding that **tones** (but not **words**) can be detected in the non-attended ear can be explained by proposing that the tone-detection process becomes data-limited much **sooner** than the word-recognition process. However, a major shortcoming of Norman and Bobrow's theory is its inability to predict **beforehand** whether an experiment is likely to produce data-limited or resource-limited data.
- Several researchers, such as Allport, have rejected the concept of a general purpose, limited-capacity processor altogether. Allport argues that the most useful way of interpreting the data is in terms of tasks competing for the same **modules** (specialised processing mechanisms), each of which has a limited capacity but none of which is uniquely 'central'.
- Two highly similar tasks compete for the same modules, leading to performance deficits, while dissimilar tasks use different modules and thus do not compete. This is also the view taken by **multiple-resource theory**. However, it is impossible to falsify these claims, and the **number** of modules remains unspecified, as does the way in which they are integrated.
- Eysenck and Baddeley believe that capacity and

module accounts are complementary. **Synthesis models** propose the existence of a modality-free central capacity processor, which co-ordinates and controls behaviour, plus specific processing systems, as in Baddeley's **articulatory loop** and **visuo-spatial scratchpad**. These are independent and help explain why certain dual tasks do not interfere with each other.

- Another explanation of our ability to perform two tasks together is that many processes become **automatic**, i.e. they make no attentional demands, if used or practised often enough.

- According to Schneider and Shiffrin, **controlled processing** makes heavy demands on attentional resources, is slow, capacity limited and involves attention being consciously directed towards a task. By contrast, **automatic processing** makes no demands on attentional resources, is fast, unaffected by capacity limitations, unavoidable and inflexible and not subject to conscious awareness.

- Several studies have shown that practice makes performance fast and accurate, but resistant to change. Learning to drive a car illustrates apparent automaticity.

- According to Logan, practice leads to automaticity through effortless retrieval from memory of an appropriate and well-learned response, with no conscious thought processes intervening between the presentation of the stimulus and production of the appropriate response.

- Schneider and Shiffrin's model does not make it clear whether automaticity results from a **speeding up** of the processes involved in a task or a **change** in the nature of the processes themselves. Also, the 'Stroop effect' shows that well-learned, unavoidable and automatic skills (such as reading) can interfere with other tasks (such as naming the colour of a written word).

- Schneider and Shiffrin's model has been applied to social psychological processes such as social facilitation and impairment. According to Manstead and Semin, 'simple' tasks are under **open-loop control** (equivalent to automatic processing), while 'complex' tasks are under **closed-loop control** (controlled processing).

- Abrams and Manstead suggest that when someone watches us perform a simple task, we closely monitor the feedback, which facilitates our performance. Social facilitation will only occur when the task is so well learned that continuous monitoring of it is not normally required. When learning a complex task, being observed by others adds to the distraction, placing further demands on an already-stretched attentional system and leading to an increase in the number of errors.

- According to Norman and Shallice, processing involves two separate control systems: **contention scheduling** and the **supervisory attentional system**. Contention scheduling occurs as a way of resolving conflicts among **schemas** which control **fully automatic processing** and produces **partially automatic processing**. The supervisory attentional system is involved in **deliberate control**, which allows flexible responses in novel situations.

- **Action slips** were originally studied by Reason, whose participants kept a diary record over a two-week period. A majority of the recorded action slips could be categorised as **storage failures** (the most common), **test failures**, **sub-routine failures**, **discrimination failures** or **programme assembly failures**.

- Paradoxically, action slips seem to involve actions that are highly practised or over-learned. Performance of new behaviours is subject to **closed-loop control**, while skilled performance is under **open-loop control**. The latter is fast and frees attentional resources for other activities, but it is more prone to error and is less flexible in response to environmental demands. Action slips reflect an over-reliance on open-loop control when focused attention is needed.

- Sellen and Norman distinguish between **parent schemas** (overall intention or goal) and **child schemas** (the actions involved in achieving the goal). Each schema has a particular activation level, and a behaviour is produced when the activation level is reached and appropriate 'triggers' exist.

- An error in the formation of the intention activates an incorrect schema, prevents activation of the correct schema or mistakenly triggers an active schema. The resulting action slips could be avoided if we used closed-loop control for all our behaviours, but they are the price we pay for freeing our attentional system from constantly having to monitor our actions.

- Different types of action slip may require their own explanation. Also, Reason's diary method may provide weak data because participants might not have detected some of their action slips or remembered to record them. We also need to know when a particular slip did *not* happen and not just how many times it did.

PART 2
Memory

THE NATURE OF MEMORY AND AN INTRODUCTION TO THE MULTI-STORE MODEL OF MEMORY

Introduction and overview

Reber (1985) identifies three meanings of the word 'memory'. First, it is the mental function of retaining information about events, images, ideas and so on after the original stimuli are no longer present. Second, memory is a hypothesised 'storage system' that holds such information. Third, the word 'memory' can also be used to describe the actual information that has been retained. Whatever meaning we consider, few of us would disagree that memory plays a central role in all cognitive processes, and that without memory, life would be impossible.

Psychologists define *learning* as a relatively permanent change in behaviour as a result of experience, and clearly without memory we could not benefit from past experience. The uses we have for memory and the amount of information we can store almost defies belief, and it is astonishing to think that an average brain weighing around three pounds can store more information than the world's most advanced supercomputers (Baron, 1989). Yet at the same time, memory can be frustratingly and painfully fallible, as anyone who has ever forgotten their loved one's birthday will agree. As Blakemore (1988) has remarked:

'Without the capacity to remember and learn, it is difficult to imagine what life would be like, whether we could call it living at all. Without memory we would be servants of the moment, with nothing but our innate reflexes to help us deal with the world. There could be no language, no art, no science, no culture. Civilization itself is the distillation of human memory'.

Our aim in this chapter is to examine the nature of memory and to consider the *multi-store model of memory*, which has been one of the most influential models attempting to describe the memory's structure. However, we will begin this chapter by looking at some 'traditions' and 'approaches' to the study of memory, the ways in which memory can be measured, and the concept of memory as 'information processing'.

'Traditions' and 'approaches' to the study of memory

THE EBBINGHAUS 'TRADITION'

Not surprisingly, the study of memory has been a cen-

79

tral topic in psychology. The systematic scientific investigation of memory can be traced back to 1885, and the publication of a book entitled *On Memory* by a German philosopher, Herman Ebbinghaus. Ebbinghaus considered using poetry as material to try and commit to memory. However, he dismissed its use on the grounds that it contained material which is:

'now narrative in style, now descriptive, now reflective; it contains a phrase that is pathetic, now one that is humorous; its metaphors are sometimes beautiful, sometimes harsh; its rhythm is sometimes smooth and sometimes rough'.

In order to overcome these difficulties, and study memory in its 'purest' form, Ebbinghaus invented material which he considered to be meaningless, varied and simple. This consisted of three-letter *nonsense syllables*, comprising a consonant followed by a vowel followed by another consonant (such as XUT and JEQ). Ebbinghaus spent several years using only himself as the subject of his research. Between 1879 and 1880, for example, he memorised over 1,200 lists each containing 13 nonsense syllables. Accompanied by the loud ticking of a watch, Ebbinghaus read each list out loud, his pace being dictated by the moving second hand. When he felt that he had recited a list sufficiently to retain it, he tested himself.

If Ebbinghaus achieved two consecutively correct repetitions of a list, he considered it to be learnt. After recording the time taken to learn a list, he then began another one. After specific periods of time, Ebbinghaus would return to a particular list and attempt to memorise it again. The amount he had forgotten could be expressed in terms of the number of attempts (or *trials*) it took him to relearn the list, as a percentage of the number of trials it had originally taken to learn it. If this figure is subtracted from 100 per cent, an indication of the amount 'saved' (*savings score*) is obtained. As Figure 7.1 illustrates, memory declines sharply at first, but then levels off, a finding which has been subsequently replicated numerous times.

Ebbinghaus carried out many experiments of this sort, and his experimental rigour showed that memory could be scientifically investigated under carefully controlled conditions. He suspected, for example, that memory may not be the same at different times of the day, a suspicion which contemporary researchers have confirmed. In studies conducted between 1883 and 1884, Ebbinghaus *always* tested himself between 1 p.m. and 3 p.m.

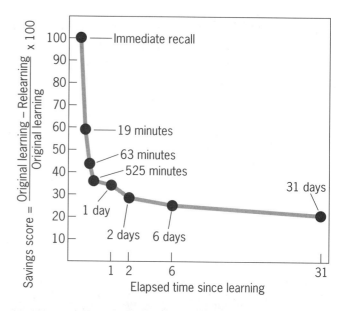

Figure 7.1   The forgetting curve obtained by Ebbinghaus. The savings score declined very rapidly in the first day, but then levelled off.

THE BARTLETT 'APPROACH'

The Ebbinghaus 'tradition' (Baddeley, 1976) remains popular with today's memory researchers. Some psychologists, though, were critical of Ebbinghaus's methodology. In his book *Remembering*, Bartlett (1932) argued that the Ebbinghaus tradition excluded 'all that is most central to human memory'. According to Bartlett, the study of 'repetition habits' had very little to do with memory in everyday life. If anything, argued Bartlett, research should examine people's active search for meaning rather than their passive responses to meaningless stimuli presented by an experimenter.

Although Bartlett accepted that meaningful material would be more complex than meaningless material, Bartlett's 'approach' (Baddeley, 1976) was to argue that it too could be studied experimentally. In one series of experiments, participants were asked to recall an American Indian folktale (*War of the Ghosts*) they had been told after various periods of time. Bartlett found that participants tended to modify the tale in such a way as to make it more consistent with their own frames of reference (Clifford, 1980).

Borrowing the terms *schema* and its plural *schemata* from the neurologist Sir Henry Head, Bartlett suggested that the learning of new things is based on already-existing knowledge (or schemata) of the world.

As Baddeley (1976) has noted, Bartlett saw both learning and remembering as an *active process* involving 'effort after meaning'. When existing schemata conflict with new information, distortions occur, as happened with the participants' recall of the folk tale. Whether schemata distort the reconstruction of material during retrieval of it, as Bartlett seemed to believe, is debatable. For Eysenck (1993), it is far more likely that schemata exert their effect on the understanding of material at the time of learning. We shall examine the role of schemata in more detail in Chapter 9, when we look at the organisation of information in memory.

There are advantages and disadvantages to both the Ebbinghaus 'tradition' and the Bartlett 'approach'. As Baddeley (1976) has noted, memory research has been torn between Ebbinghaus's insistence on simplification (with its attendant danger of trivialisation) and Bartlett's emphasis on memory's complexities (with its danger of being difficult to work with). However, in common with other researchers active in this area, Baddeley sees the conflict as being a healthy one. Neither methodological approach is uniquely correct and, as will become evident over the course of this and the following four chapters, both are useful depending on what aspect of memory is being studied.

The measurement of memory

A number of techniques for assessing memory have been devised. As we mentioned, Ebbinghaus's major method of measuring memory involved *relearning*, that is, recording the number of repetitions needed to learn some material and comparing this with the number of repetitions needed to relearn the material. Another technique is *recognition*, and involves having to decide whether or not a particular piece of information has been encountered before (that is, whether or not it is recognised).

In *recall* tasks, participants are required to recall items either in the order in which they were presented (*serial recall*) or in any order they like (*free recall*). One version of serial recall is the *memory-span procedure*. In this, a person is given a number of unrelated digits or letters and then required to immediately repeat them back in the order they were heard. The number of items on the list is successively increased until an error

in recall is made. The maximum number of items that can be consistently recalled correctly is a measure of *immediate memory span*.

In *paired-associates* recall tasks, participants are required to learn a list of paired items (such as the word 'chair' being paired with the word 'elephant'). When one of the words (e.g. 'chair') is re-presented, the participant must recall the word it was paired with.

Which of these techniques is used depends on what a researcher is interested in investigating. A more detailed description of these and other methods can be found in Gross (1996).

Memory as information processing

The concept of information processing derives partly from computer science and its related fields (Baron, 1989). For some researchers, memory can best be understood in terms of the three basic operations involved in the processing of information by modern computers. These operations are termed *registration* (or *encoding*), *storage* and *retrieval*. It is important to note that advocates of an information-processing approach do not believe that memory operates in *exactly* the same way as a computer does. Rather, the view is taken that the approach is a helpful way of conceptualising what we would all agree is an extremely complex phenomenon.

Registration
This involves the transformation of sensory input (such as a sound or image) into a form which will allow the input to be entered into (or registered in) memory. With a computer, for example, information can only be encoded if it is presented in a format recognisable to the computer.

Storage
This is the operation of holding or retaining the information in memory. Computer data are stored by means of changes in the system's electrical circuitry. With people, the changes occurring in the brain allow information to be stored, though exactly what these changes involve is not precisely known.

Retrieval
This is the name given to the process by which the

information that has been stored is extracted from memory. Another process, which we will consider in Chapter 10, is *forgetting*. This is the inability to recall accurately what has been presented. As we will see, forgetting can occur at the encoding, storage or retrieval stage.

Registration can be thought of as a *necessary* condition for storage to take place. However, it is not *sufficient*, that is, not everything which registers on the sensors is stored. Similarly, storage can be seen as a necessary but not sufficient condition for retrieval. Thus, we can only recover information that has been stored (we cannot remember something we do not know), but the fact that something has been stored is no guarantee that it will be remembered on any particular occasion. This suggests that it is possible to make a distinction between *availability* (whether or not the information is actually available) and *accessibility* (whether or not it can be retrieved). As we will see in Chapter 10 (see page 117), this distinction is especially relevant to theories of forgetting.

The nature of memory

As long ago as 1890, the philosopher William James commented on the fact that whilst some information seems to be stored in memory for a lifetime, other information is lost very quickly:

> 'The stream of thought flows on, but most of its elements fall into the bottomless pit of oblivion. Of some, no element survives the instant of their passage. Of others, it is often confined to a few moments, hours or days. Others, again, leave vestiges which are indestructible, and by means of which they may be recalled for as long as possible'.

James distinguished between two structures or types of memory which he called *primary* and *secondary memory*. These relate to the psychological *present* and *past* respectively (Eysenck, 1993). Today, what James called primary memory is referred to as *short-term memory*, and what he called secondary memory is referred to as *long-term memory*. To these two types of memory, a third can be added. This is *sensory memory*.

THE NATURE OF SENSORY MEMORY

The world is full of sensory information. Sights, sounds and so on are constantly stimulating our senses. Not all

of this information is important, though, and an efficient memory system would be one which retained only that information which was 'significant' in some way. It seems that the function of sensory memory (sometimes called the *sensory register*) is to retain information for a period of time long enough to enable us to decide whether the information is worthy, or otherwise, of further processing. The encoding of information in sensory memory is related to the process of *transduction*. This is the transformation of sensory information from the environment into neural impulses that can be processed by our sensory systems and the brain. In the case of the eye, the excitation on the retina lasts for a few tenths of a second after the image has gone.

Mostly, we are unaware of sensory memory. However, if you watch someone wave a lighted cigarette in a darkened room, a streak rather than a series of points will be seen (Woodworth, 1938), indicating the persistence of an image when the stimulus has disappeared (the same effect can be achieved with a sparkler on bonfire night). If there was no sensory register, we would only be able to react to a given stimulus at a given time, and tracing our own name with a sparkler would be impossible. Since humans have several sensory systems, it is likely that a sensory memory exists for *all* sense modalities. Most research, though, has concentrated on visual and auditory sensory memory.

Visual sensory memory

Much of what we know about visual sensory memory (or *iconic memory*) comes from experiments conducted by George Sperling (1960). Sperling used a *tachistoscope* to flash visual displays to participants for very brief periods of time (around 50 to 100 milliseconds). In the *whole-report procedure*, Sperling asked his participants to identify as many of nine letters (which were arranged in three rows of three) as they could. He found that participants could typically identify a maximum of four or five correctly. The participants, though, claimed that they could actually remember more than that, but that after naming four or five, the image of them had faded completely.

To test his participants' claims, Sperling devised a slightly different experiment which used the *partial-report procedure*. In this, the three rows of three letters were again presented tachistoscopically, but were immediately followed by a high-, medium- or low-pitched tone. The tone was the signal for the participant to recall the top, middle or bottom row of letters respectively. Sperling had found that when the tone *preceded* the presentation of the visual display, recall was (not unexpectedly) just about faultless. When the tone *followed* the display's presentation, recall was almost as good, even though participants had to retrieve the information from the sensory register. On the basis of this finding, Sperling concluded that the capacity of sensory memory is large, and may even be large enough to hold brief representations of virtually everything that impinges on the visual sensory system (Reeves and Sperling, 1986).

In other experiments, Sperling delayed the sounding of the tone after the visual display had been presented. With a delay of half a second, recall was only 63 per cent accurate, and after one second very little was recalled, suggesting that visual sensory memory is like a 'rapidly decaying mental photograph' (Hassett and White, 1989). Because information decays so rapidly, then, it is hardly surprising that participants in the whole-report procedure were unable to recall more items than they did (and this also explains why 'Bob' might be able to trace his name completely with a sparkler but 'Constantine' cannot!). Figure 7.2 shows the partial-report method (a) and the same method with a half-second delay (b).

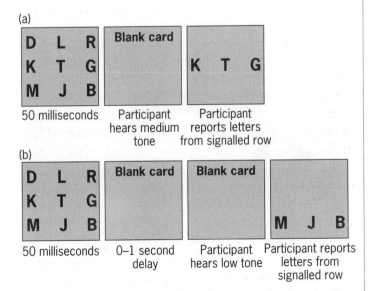

Figure 7.2 (a) shows Sperling's partial-report method, and (b) shows the partial-report method with a delay.

Auditory sensory memory

Auditory sensory memory (*echoic memory*, or what Morton (1970) calls the *pre-categorical acoustic store*) is very similar, if not identical to Broadbent's *sensory buffer store* that we discussed in Chapter 5 (see page 56). Echoic memory enables us to hear a sound after it has stopped. Since we cannot identify a word until we have heard all the sounds that make it up, echoic memory is necessary to hold a representation of an initial sound until the whole word has been heard. Only then can the sound be put into context (Baddeley, 1995). Probably for this reason, echoic memory persists for longer than iconic memory. Cowan (1984) suggests that the duration can be as long as ten seconds, depending on the method of measurement used. Darwin et al. (1972) suggest that an upper limit of around four seconds is more realistic.

Two additional points should also be noted. First, and as we mentioned earlier on, sensory registration is a *necessary* but not sufficient condition for the storage of information. The mere fact that something has been registered does not necessarily mean that it will be stored. Something must be done with the information and, as Box 7.1 shows, done very quickly, if the material is to be passed on for further processing. We shall discuss what needs to be done shortly. Second, whilst it is likely that there is a sensory memory for all sense modalities, it is unlikely that these reside in some central system, because if visual information follows visual information, visual sensory memory is impaired (and the same is true for auditory information). However, if auditory information follows visual information, visual sensory memory is not impaired. This implies that information is held by the sensory system that received it, that is, sensory memory is *modality specific*.

Box 7.1   The 'attentional gate'

Reeves and Sperling (1986) asked participants to watch a stream of letters appearing in their left visual field. Participants were instructed to shift their attention to their right visual field whenever a target (the letters C, U or a square) appeared in their left visual field. A stream of numbers was already being presented in the right visual field, and the participants had to report the first four numbers they saw. The time between the occurrence of a target and the reporting of a number was taken as a measure of how quickly attention could be shifted, and the researchers assumed that this interval would indicate how long an 'attentional gate' between sensory memory and short-term memory (STM) remained open. The data showed that the gate remained open for around 0.4 of a second, and that participants could not report the numbers they saw in the correct order, even though they thought they could, suggesting a loss of information during the transfer from sensory memory to STM.

SHORT-TERM MEMORY

According to Lloyd et al. (1984), probably less than one-hundredth of all the sensory information that impinges every second on the human senses reaches consciousness, and of this, only about five per cent achieves anything like stable storage. Clearly, if we possessed only sensory memory, our capacity for retaining information would be extremely limited and very precarious. Information that has not been lost from the sensory register is claimed to be passed on to a second storage system called short-term memory (STM). The encoding of information in STM was actually studied as long ago at 1887 by Joseph Jacobs who remarked that:

> 'It is obvious there is a limit to the power of reproducing sound accurately. Anyone can say Bo after once hearing it; few could catch the name of the Greek statesman M. Papamichalopolous without the need of a repetition'.

The capacity of STM

Jacobs argued that STM could only hold a limited amount of information, that is, its capacity was finite. In a classic paper entitled *The magical number seven, plus or minus two; Some limits on our capacity for processing information*, Miller (1956) showed that most people could store only about seven *independent* items (numbers, letters, words or tones with particular pitches). Miller used the word *chunk* to refer to a discrete piece of information. So, when people attempt to remember an *unrelated* string of letters, each constitutes one chunk of information. However, Miller also showed that the capacity of STM could seemingly be enlarged if it was possible to *combine* separate pieces of information into a larger piece of information.

For example, the sequence 246813579 can be 'chunked' by applying a rule concerning odd and even numbers. The amount that can be held in STM, then, depends on the *rules* which are used to organise the information. As far as Miller is concerned, the capacity of STM is seven plus or minus two chunks rather than individual pieces of information (remember, once pieces of information have been 'chunked', they can no longer be considered independent). Miller's views are discussed further in Box 7.2.

Box 7.2   Miller and the concept of 'chunking'

Miller argues that chunking is a *linguistic recoding* which is 'the very lifeblood of the thought process'. In his view, chunking is not a surprising phenomenon given how lexical information is normally processed. Thus, our capacity to read and understand is largely based on the chunking of letters into words, words into phrases, and phrases into sentences. So the capability of STM to deal with a vast amount of information is facilitated by our ability to chunk information. However, we cannot do this until certain information in long-term memory (LTM) has been activated and a match made between incoming information and its representation in LTM.

Miller and Selfridge (1950) showed this by giving participants 'sentences' of varying lengths which approximated (to different degrees) to true English, and asking them to recall the words in their correct order. The closer a 'sentence' approximated true English, the better immediate recall of it was. This suggests that knowledge of semantic and grammatical structure (which is presumably stored in LTM) is used to facilitate recall from STM.

In a conceptually similar study, Bower and Springston (1970) presented some participants with a letter sequence in which the letters were presented in a way that formed a well-known group (e.g. fbi, phd, twa, ibm). Other participants were presented with the same letters but in a way that did not form a well-known group (e.g. fb, iph, dtw, aib, m). The former recalled many more letters than the latter, the material to the former being clustered in acronyms familiar to most American college students. In effect, the pause after 'fbi' and so on allowed participants to 'look up' the material in their mental lexicon and so encode the letters in one chunk.

Coding in STM

The way in which information is coded or stored in STM has been the subject of much research. Conrad (1964) visually presented participants with a list of six consonants (such as BKSJLR), each of which was seen for about three-quarters of a second. Following presentation, participants were instructed to write down what they had seen. Conrad found that the errors made by participants tended to be linked to a letter's *sound*. For example, there were 62 instances of B being mistaken for P, 83 instances of V being mistaken for P, but only two instances of S being mistaken for P. These *acoustic confusion errors* suggested to Conrad that STM must code information according to its sound. When information is presented visually, it must somehow be *transformed* into its acoustic code.

Although most verbal input appears to be stored primarily in an acoustic form, STM also codes information in other ways. For example, Shulman (1970) visually presented participants with lists of ten words. They were then tested for their recognition of the words using a visually presented 'probe word'. The probe word was a *homonym* of one of the words on the list (such as 'bawl' instead of 'ball'), a *synonym* of one of the words (such as 'talk' instead of 'speak') or was identical to the test word. Shulman found that homonym and synonym probes produced similar error rates, implying that some *semantic coding* (or coding for meaning) had taken place in STM, since if an error was made on a synonym probe, some matching for meaning must have taken place. Other research has shown that visual images (in the form of abstract pictures, which would be hard to store in the form of an acoustic code) can be maintained in STM, if only for a brief period of time.

The duration of STM

The length of time that information can be held within STM was studied by Brown (1958) and Peterson and Peterson (1959) using what is known as the *Brown-Peterson technique*. By repeating something that has to be remembered (a method called *maintenance rehearsal*), information can be held in STM almost indefinitely. The Brown-Peterson technique involves participants hearing various *trigrams* (such as XPJ). Immediately afterwards, they are instructed to recall what they heard or to count backwards in threes from some specified number for a pre-determined period of time (the *retention interval*). The function of this so-called *distractor* task is to prevent rehearsal. At the end of the time period, the trigram must be recalled. Figure 7.3 shows the results obtained by Peterson and Peterson.

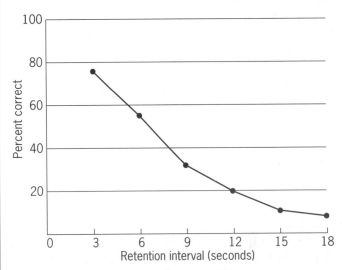

Figure 7.3   The data reported by Peterson and Peterson in their experiment on the duration of STM.

As we can see, the average percentage of correctly recalled trigrams was high with short delays, but decreased as the delay interval lengthened. After only 18 seconds, the average percentage of correctly recalled trigrams was a mere six per cent. In the absence of rehearsal, then, it would seem that the duration of STM is very short, and other research has shown that it can be made even shorter if a more difficult distractor task is used (Reitman, 1974).

LONG-TERM MEMORY

Long-term memory (LTM) has been conceptualised as a vast storehouse of information in which memories are stored in a relatively permanent way, and it is to this storage system that information not lost from STM passes. Exactly how much information can be stored in LTM is not known, and most psychologists would agree that there is no evidence for any limit to LTM's capacity. In contrast with STM, then, the *capacity* of LTM is much, much larger. Since memories are held to be stored in LTM in a relatively permanent way, the *duration* of LTM is also considerably longer than that of STM.

As far as verbal material is concerned, the *coding* of material in LTM appears to be primarily according to its *meaning* (that is, semantic coding). For example, Baddeley (1966) presented participants with words which were acoustically similar (such as 'mad', 'man' and 'mat'), semantically similar ('big', 'broad' and 'long'), acoustically dissimilar ('foul', 'old' and 'deep') or semantically dissimilar ('pen', 'day' and 'ring'). When recall from STM was tested, acoustically similar words were recalled less well than acoustically dissimilar words (supporting the claim that acoustic coding occurs in STM). Semantically similar words were significantly less well recalled than semantically dissimilar words, although this difference was very small (64 per cent compared with 71 per cent), a finding which suggests that whilst some semantic coding occurs in STM, it is not the dominant method.

When an equivalent study was conducted on LTM, semantically similar material impaired long-term recall, but acoustically similar material had no effect. As Baddeley (1976) has noted, such findings do not imply that LTM codes material in no form other than semantically. The fact that we can conjure up the image of a place we visited on holiday or an old school friend indicates that at least some information is stored or coded in *visual* form. Although we may not want to, most of us who have heard it would be able to sing the chorus to Kylie Minogue's song 'I should be so lucky', indicating that some types of information are coded *acoustically* in LTM. Yet other memories, such as smells and tastes, for example, are also stored in LTM, suggesting that as well as being large and long-lasting, it is also a very flexible system. We shall have more to say about the structure of LTM in the following chapter.

The multi-store model of memory

The multi-store model of memory (which is sometimes known as the *dual-memory model* because of its emphasis on STM and LTM) was an attempt by Atkinson and Shiffrin (1968, 1971) to explain the flow of information from one system to another. The model, which is shown in Figure 7.4, sees sensory memory, STM and LTM as *permanent structural components* of the memory system, and intrinsic features of the information-processing system of humans. In addition to these structural components, our memory system is seen as comprising relatively transient processes (called *control processes*).

One important transient process is *rehearsal*, which is seen as having two functions. First, it acts as a buffer between sensory memory and LTM by maintaining incoming information within STM. Second, it enables information to be transferred to LTM. Although Atkinson and Shiffrin saw rehearsal as the most common method of transfer, they accepted that there were a number of other ways in which material could be transferred. Indeed, they suggested that it was even pos-

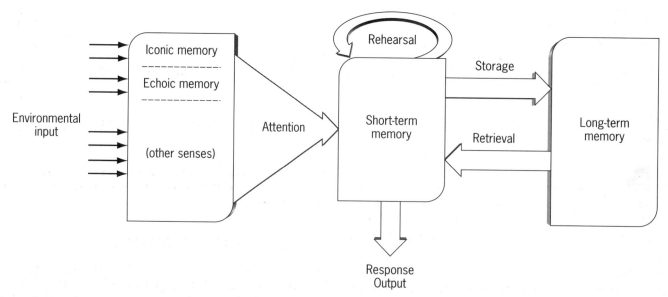

Figure 7.4   The multi-store/dual-memory model of memory proposed by Atkinson and Shiffrin.

sible for information to bypass STM and enter LTM directly from the sensory register, a point which some of their fiercest critics have tended to ignore (see below).

Two lines of evidence which support Atkinson and Shiffrin's view that STM and LTM may be considered to be separate and distinct storage systems come from *experimental studies of STM and LTM* and *clinical studies of amnesics*.

EXPERIMENTAL STUDIES OF STM AND LTM

In a study conducted by Murdock (1962), participants were presented with a list of words at a rate of about one per second. After presentation, the participants were required to free recall as many of the words as they could. Murdock found that the words did not have an equal chance of being recalled and that some words, namely those which appeared at the beginning and the end of the list, were much more likely to be recalled than those that appeared in the middle of the list. Murdock called this the *serial position effect*, and examples of *serial position curves* for word lists of different lengths are shown in Figure 7.5.

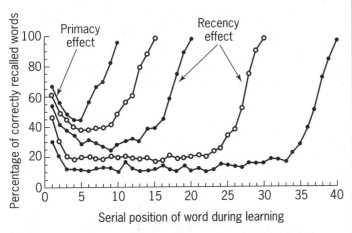

Figure 7.5   Serial position curves for word lists of different lengths.

The superior recall of the items that appeared at the beginning of the list is termed the *primacy effect*, whilst the superior recall of the items that appeared at the end is called the *recency effect*. This seems to be good evidence for the separation of STM and LTM. The primacy effect is held to occur because the items that appeared at the beginning of the list have presumably been subject to some rehearsal and have been trans-

ferred to LTM from where they have been recalled. To test the idea that the passage of items occurs through rehearsal, Rundus and Atkinson (1970) asked participants performing a Murdock-type task to rehearse out loud the list they were presented with. Tape recordings indicated that words from the beginning of the list were more likely to be rehearsed than later ones. The recency effect can be explained in terms of items currently held in STM being recalled from that system. Because STM's capacity is limited and can only hold items for a brief period of time, words in the middle of the list are thought to be either lost from the system completely or otherwise unavailable for recall.

In a variation of Murdock's study, Glanzer and Cunitz (1966) showed that delaying recall for 30 seconds and preventing rehearsal (by means of the counting task used by Peterson and Peterson: see page 85) of a list of presented words resulted in the recency effect disappearing, but the primacy effect remaining, as shown in Figure 7.6. Presumably, the earlier words had been transferred to LTM (from where they were recalled) whilst the most recent words were what Eysenck (1993) terms 'vulnerable' to the counting task. Other research (e.g. Murdock and Walker, 1969) has shown that under certain conditions, the recency effect can be left intact, but the primacy effect massively depressed.

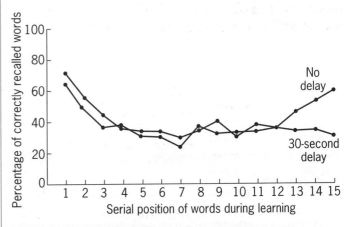

Figure 7.6   Data from Glanzer and Cunitz's study showing serial position curves after no delay and a delay of 30 seconds.

CLINICAL STUDIES OF AMNESICS

Amnesics are people who suffer memory loss, most usually as a result of damage to the brain. If STM and LTM are distinct and separate storage systems, then certain types of damage which affect only one of the systems should leave the other intact, and this would be reflected in the affected person's ability to remember. One example of amnesia occurs in *Korsakoff's syndrome*, which is often found in chronic alcoholics. In people with this syndrome, STM appears to be intact and it is, for example, possible to carry on a normal conversation with them, and they are capable of reading a newspaper. However, the transfer of information to LTM is seriously impaired, and Korsakoff's amnesics may have no memory of a conversation taking place or of a paper having been read.

In a study of amnesia not caused by chronic alcohol use, Shallice and Warrington (1970) reported the case of K.F., a man who had suffered brain damage as a result of having been involved in a motorbike accident. K.F.'s STM was severely impaired, and he could often recall no more than one or two digits on a digit span test. However, his LTM for events occurring after the accident was normal. As well as supporting the view that STM and LTM are separate and distinct, this finding suggests that information can find its way into LTM even if STM is severely impaired.

Other research, using PET and MRI scanning devices, has also produced evidence of multiple memory systems. Periani et al. (1993), for example, reported differential changes in brain structure metabolism according to the type of amnesia a person was experiencing. Periani and his colleagues identified the hippocampus, thalamus and cingulate gyrus as being important, although the cerebral circuitry connecting these structures has yet to be clearly established. A dramatic case of amnesia caused by damage to the hippocampus is described in Box 7.3.

Box 7.3   A case of amnesia caused by damage to the hippocampus

In March 1985, Clive Wearing, former chorus master of the London Sinfonietta, suffered a brain infection caused by the herpes simplex (cold sore) virus. As well as damaging parts of his cortex, the virus destroyed Wearing's hippocampus. The consequence of this is that Wearing appears to be unable to transfer new information from STM to LTM, and as a result lives in a 'snapshot' of time constantly believing that he has just awoken from years of unconsciousness. Thus, he reacts to people as if they had been parted for years, even though those people might have paid him a visit minutes earlier.

Wearing can still speak and walk, as well as play the organ and conduct, and his musical ability is remarkably well preserved. He is capable of learning some new skills, and these appear to be stored in LTM. However, whenever he is asked to perform the skill, he reacts as though he has never attempted to learn the skill before. His memory of his early life is patchy, and his ability to recall details of his life extremely poor. When shown pictures of Cambridge, where he had studied, he recognised King's College chapel (the most well known and distinctive building in Cambridge) but did not recognise his own college. He could not remember who wrote *Romeo and Juliet*, and identified the Queen and the Duke of Edinburgh as singers he had known from a Catholic church.

Wearing's lack of *conscious* recollection is, in his own words, 'Hell on earth – it's like being dead – all the bloody time'.

(adapted from Blakemore (1988) and Baddeley (1990))

Several other cases of hippocampal damage leading to effects similar to those seen in Clive Wearing have been documented. For example, Farenhah Varga-Khadem at the Institute of Child Health, has described three cases, all of whom had suffered hippocampal damage early in life. All three were unable to remember everyday events, such as where their belongings were located or what day it was. Incredibly, though, all three had attended mainstream schools and learned to read and write with average competency (Highfield, 1997).

Some challenges to the multi-store model of memory

Along with the evidence from experimental studies of verbal learning, clinical studies of amnesics offer support for the multi-store model of memory and the model continues to be influential in the area of memory research. However, some psychologists have argued that there is no real need to make a distinction between the various storage systems and that it is far more profitable to view them as being different phases of a continuous process. Moreover, Atkinson and Shiffrin's 'compartmentalisation' of memory into units from which information flows has also been challenged.

Certainly, studies suggest that it seems highly unlikely that STM contains only *new* information. What seems more likely is that information is retrieved from LTM for use in STM. For example, the string of numbers 18561939 may appear to be independent. However, they can be 'chunked' into one unit according to the rule 'the years in which Sigmund Freud was born and died'. If we can impose meaning on a string of digits, we must have learned this meaning *previously*, the previously learned rule presumably being stored in LTM. In this case, information has flowed not only from STM to LTM but also in the opposite direction. A vivid example of this comes from studies of people who are experts in some particular domain. de Groot (1966), for example, showed that expert chess players had a phenomenal STM for the position of chess pieces on a board *provided* they were organised according to the rules of chess. When the pieces were randomly arranged, the recall of experts was no better than that of non-chess players. In the case of chess experts, information from LTM about the rules of chess were used to aid recall from STM.

Other researchers have challenged the role that rehearsal is held to play by the multi-store model. In one experiment, Craik and Watkins (1973) asked participants to remember only certain 'critical' words (those beginning with a particular letter) from lists presented either rapidly or slowly. The position of the critical words relative to the others determined the amount of time a particular word spent in STM and the number of potential rehearsals it could receive. The researchers found that retention over long periods was unrelated to either the amount of time a word had spent in STM or the number of explicit or implicit rehearsals.

On the basis of this and other findings (e.g. Glanzer and Meinzer, 1967), Craik and Watkins argued that in addition to *maintenance rehearsal* (see page 85), in which material is rehearsed in 'rote' fashion, that is, the form in which it was presented, another type of rehearsal exists. They called this *elaborative rehearsal* (or *elaboration of encoding*), describing it as a form of rehearsal in which the material is elaborated in some way (such as by giving it a meaning or linking it with pre-existing knowledge). According to Craik and Lockhart (1972), it is the *kind* of rehearsal or processing that is important rather than the *amount* of rehearsal. We shall consider the evidence in support of this distinction in the following chapter.

Conclusions

In this chapter, we have discussed some of the findings relating to the nature of memory and considered the multi-store model as a way of conceptualising how various storage systems are linked. Although influential, and supported by evidence, the multi-store model has, as we saw in the last section of this chapter, been the subject of criticism. As a result, alternatives to it have been advanced. In the following chapter we will consider these alternatives.

SUMMARY

- The word 'memory' has a variety of meanings. It plays a vital role in all cognitive processes and without it, **learning** and, indeed life itself, would be impossible.
- The systematic study of memory began with Ebbinghaus in the 1880s. He invented **nonsense syllables** in order to study memory in its 'purest' form, using himself as the sole subject of his research. Measuring memory in terms of a **savings score**, he found that it declines rapidly at first before levelling off, a finding which has been replicated many times since.
- Bartlett criticised Ebbinghaus's approach for being largely irrelevant to memory in everyday life: research should examine people's active search for meaning rather than passive 'repetition habits'.

Meaningful material, while more complex, could also be studied experimentally, as in the recall of *The War of the Ghosts* after various time intervals.

- Bartlett believed that learning new material is based on already-existing **schemata**, which can result in distortions of the former. Both learning and remembering are **active processes** involving 'effort after meaning'.
- Many memory researchers, including Baddeley, regard the conflict between the Ebbinghaus and Bartlett traditions as healthy: both are useful depending on what aspect of memory is being studied.
- Ebbinghaus's technique for assessing memory involved **relearning**. Others include **recognition**, **serial** or **free recall** (an example of the former being the **memory-span procedure**, a measure of **immediate memory span**) and **paired associates** recall tasks.
- For some researchers, the best way of understanding memory is in terms of the three basic operations involved in the **processing of information** by modern computers (**registration/encoding**, **storage** and **retrieval**).
- **Registration**, which involves the transformation of sensory input into a form which allows entry into memory, is necessary for **storage**, which refers to the retention of the information in memory (i.e. **availability**) and involves some kind of physical change in the brain. Just as not everything that is registered on the senses is stored, so not everything that is stored can be **retrieved** (i.e. is **accessible**).
- William James distinguished between **primary** (referred to today as **short-term**) and **secondary (long-term) memory** relating to the psychological **present** and **past** respectively.
- The function of **sensory memory** (or the **sensory register**) is to retain information just long enough to enable us to decide whether it is worthy of further processing or not. Through **transduction**, sensory information is transformed into neural impulses for processing by the sensory systems and the brain.
- Although we are mostly unaware of sensory memory, the image of a stimulus must persist for a brief time after the stimulus has been removed, otherwise we would be unable to respond to it. It is likely that there is a sensory memory for **each** sense modality, but research has concentrated on visual (**iconic**) and auditory (**echoic**) sensory memory.
- Sperling used a **tachistoscope** to study **iconic memory**. The **whole-report procedure** typically showed that participants could remember four or five of the nine letters presented, while the **partial-report procedure** produced almost perfect retrieval. This suggests that sensory memory has a large capacity. Other studies showed that information decays very rapidly (most is lost after one second).
- **Echoic memory** (or the **pre-categorical acoustic store**), which is very similar to Broadbent's **sensory buffer store**, enables us to hear a sound after it has stopped. This is necessary for identifying spoken words. It persists for longer than iconic memory, with estimates ranging from four to ten seconds.
- Something must be done very quickly with the information in sensory memory if it is to be passed on for further processing. The **'attentional gate'** between iconic memory and short-term memory (STM) remains open for about two-fifths of a second, with information being lost during the transfer between them.
- Information appears to be held by the sensory modality that received it, i.e. sensory memory is **modality specific**.
- Only a tiny fraction of all the sensory information that reaches the senses at any one time is actually stored: if memory were limited to sensory memory, our capacity for retaining information would be extremely restricted.
- Information that has not been lost from the sensory register is passed on to short-term memory. According to Miller, the **capacity** of STM is seven plus or minus two **chunks** of information: if unrelated or independent items of information are **combined** ('chunked'), the capacity of STM can be increased.
- Miller sees chunking as a **linguistic recoding**. Our capacity to read and understand is largely based on the chunking of letters into words, words into phrases and phrases into sentences, but this depends on the activation of knowledge of semantic and grammatical knowledge stored in LTM and its being matched with incoming information. This was demonstrated by Miller and Selfridge's experiment, using different approximations to English, and Bower and Springston's study, in which letters could be chunked into familiar acronyms.
- According to Conrad and Baddeley, **acoustic confusion errors** indicate that STM **codes** information **acoustically**. But Shulman and Baddeley also found some evidence of **semantic coding**, and other research suggests that visual images can be briefly maintained in STM.

- Using **maintenance rehearsal**, information can be held in STM almost indefinitely. The **Brown-Peterson technique** has shown that, by using a **distractor** task to prevent rehearsal, almost no information is recalled after an 18-second **retention interval**.
- LTM's **capacity** is far greater than that of STM: most psychologists believe that it is limitless. Its **duration** is also considerably longer, with information probably being stored permanently.
- According to Baddeley, the **coding** of verbal material in LTM is primarily **semantic**, but clearly some information is coded in **visual** form (as when we recall someone's face), while other information is stored **acoustically** (as when we remember a melody). LTM is a very flexible system.
- According to Atkinson and Shiffrin's **multi-store/dual-memory model**, sensory memory, STM and LTM are **permanent structural components** of the memory system, with STM and LTM being distinct storage systems. **Rehearsal** is an example of a transient **control process**.
- Rehearsal acts as a buffer between sensory memory and LTM (by maintaining incoming information within STM) and also aids the transfer of information to LTM. But it is possible for information to enter LTM directly from the sensory register.
- According to Murdock's **serial position effect**, free recall of a list of words produces better recall of words at the **beginning** and the **end** of the list (the **primacy** and **recency effect** respectively) compared with those in the middle. The primacy effect is taken to reflect recall from LTM (based on rehearsal of those items), while the recency effect reflects recall from STM.
- Glanzer and Cunitz found that delaying recall for 30 seconds caused the disappearance of the recency effect, while the primacy effect was unaffected. This outcome can be reversed under certain conditions.
- **Clinical studies of amnesics** provide an additional source of evidence regarding the distinction between STM and LTM. In people with **Korsakoff's syndrome**, STM appears to be intact, but the transfer of information to LTM is seriously impaired.
- K.F., who suffered brain damage as a result of a motorbike accident, had a severely impaired STM, but his LTM for events that occurred after the accident was normal.
- Studies using PET and MRI scanning devices also support the idea of multiple memory systems, with the hippocampus, thalamus and cingulate gyrus all appearing to play an important role. A dramatic case of amnesia caused by hippocampal damage is that of Clive Wearing.
- Although the multi-store model continues to be influential in memory research, some psychologists believe that it is unnecessary to distinguish between the various storage systems. Rather than seeing STM as containing only **new** information, it is likely that information is retrieved from LTM for use in STM, as in chunking and the chess experts studied by de Groot.
- The kind of rehearsal proposed by the multi-store model is what Craik and Watkins call **maintenance rehearsal**, which they distinguish from **elaborative rehearsal or elaboration of encoding**. While the multi-store model stresses the **amount** of (maintenance) rehearsal or processing, Craik and Lockhart argue that what matters is the **kind** of rehearsal or processing.

8

SOME ALTERNATIVES TO THE MULTI-STORE MODEL OF MEMORY

Introduction and overview

As we noted in the previous chapter, the multi-store model of memory has attracted considerable support but has also been the subject of some criticism. Our aim in this chapter is to consider three major efforts to revise Atkinson and Shiffrin's model. The first is an attempt by American psychologists Fergus Craik and Robert Lockhart to argue against the multi-store model's claim that memory can be 'compartmentalised'. The second is an attempt by British psychologist Alan Baddeley and his associates to reconceptualise the nature of short-term memory. The third is the challenge to the multi-store model's claim that long-term memory is unitary in nature, and is associated with a number of North American and European psychologists, most notable among whom is Endel Tulving. Whilst the alternatives we will discuss are critical of the claims made by the multi-store model, it is important to note that none represents an outright rejection of it. Rather, they all share the view that the multi-store model is an oversimplified account of our highly complex memory.

The levels-of-processing model

The first major challenge to the multi-store model came from Craik and Lockhart (1972). Although they accepted that the multi-store model accommodated the research findings reasonably well, they argued that there was also evidence to directly contradict it. As we noted in the previous chapter (see page 89), the concept of rehearsal was criticised for being too general and unnecessary. The distinction between maintenance and elaborative rehearsal allowed Craik and his colleagues to argue that the number of rehearsals *per se* was less important in determining the transfer of information than the type of rehearsal engaged in by participants, and the study conducted by Craik and Watkins (1973) (see page 89) is consistent with such a claim.

As we saw in Chapter 7, the multi-store model distinguishes between the *structural components* of memory (sensory memory, STM and LTM) and *control processes* (such as rehearsal and coding), with the latter being tied to the former. So, the multi-store model places its emphasis on the sequence of stages that information goes through as it passes from one structural component to another when being processed. Craik and Lockhart, however, began with the hypothesised processes and then formulated a memory system (the structural components) in terms of these operations.

According to Craik and Lockhart, memory is a by-product of perceptual analysis. Crucial to their model is the concept of a *central processor*, capable of analysing data on a variety of levels. The processor is seen as being of finite capacity and therefore incapable of dealing with all aspects of a stimulus. The extent to which analysis can be controlled is determined by which features of the stimulus are paid attention to. The surface features of a stimulus (such as whether a word is in lower case or upper case letters) are analysed superficially or, to use Craik and Lockhart's phrase, processed at a *shallow level*. The semantic features of a stimulus (such as a word's meaning) are analysed more extensively, that is, they are processed at a *deep level*. Lying between these two ends of a processing continuum, a verbal stimulus can also be analysed according to its sound. Such processing occurs at a *phonemic (or phonetic) level*.

Which level is used depends on both the nature of the stimulus and the time available for processing. The model proposes that the more deeply information is processed, the more likely it is to be retained. In one test of this proposal, Craik and Tulving (1975) used a tachistoscope to present participants with a list of words. After each word had been presented, participants were asked one of four questions to which they had to respond 'yes' or 'no'. The four questions were:

1 Is the word (e.g. TABLE/table) in capital letters?
2 Does the word (e.g. hate/chicken) rhyme with 'wait'?
3 Is the word (e.g. cheese/steel) a type of food?
4 Would the word (e.g. ball/rain) fit in the sentence 'He kicked the . . . . . . into the tree'?

Question (1) corresponds to structural processing, (2) to phonetic processing, and (3) and (4) to semantic processing. Later on, participants were unexpectedly given a test in which the words they had seen appeared amongst words they had not seen. The participants' task was to identify which words had been presented earlier. The researchers found that there was significantly better recall of words that had been processed at the deepest (semantic) level. Additionally, recognition was superior when the answer to the question was 'yes' rather than 'no'.

Several researchers have also found that *elaboration,* that is, the *amount* of processing of a particular kind at a particular level is also important in determining whether material is stored or not. For example, Craik and Tulving (1975) asked participants to decide if a particular word would be appropriate in simple sentences such as 'She cooked the . . . . . .' or complex sentences such as 'The great bird swooped down and carried off the struggling . . . . . .'. When participants were later given a test of *cued recall,* in which the original sentences were again presented but without the particular words, recall was much better for the words compatible with the complex sentences. Since the same depth of processing (semantic) occurred with both types of sentence, some additional factor (namely elaboration) must also be involved.

Bransford and his colleagues (1979) have shown that the *nature* of the elaboration is more important than the amount of elaboration. In their study, minimally elaborated sentences such as 'A mosquito is like a doctor because they both draw blood' were better remembered than multiply elaborated similies like 'A mosquito is like a racoon because they both have hands, legs and jaws'. One possible reason for this is that material which is distinctive or unique in some way is more likely to be remembered. This is another

way of conceptualising 'depth' – it may be that it is the non-distinctiveness of shallow encodings (as opposed to their shallowness *per se*) which leads to their poor retention (Eysenck and Keane, 1995).

Eysenck (1993) has argued that it is often difficult to choose between level of processing, elaboration and distinctiveness because they can occur together. We know that retention cannot be predicted solely on the basis of level of processing because more elaborate or distinctive semantic encodings are usually better remembered than non-elaborate or non-distinctive ones. Thus, Eysenck and Eysenck (1980) found that a shallow level of processing could result in remembering that was almost as good as a deep level of processing, as long as it was also distinctive. Quite possibly all three make separate contributions to remembering, but distinctiveness, which relates to the nature of processing and takes account of relationships between encodings, is likely to be more important than elaboration, which is only a measure of the amount of processing (Eysenck, 1986).

Evaluating the levels-of-processing model

Craik and Lockhart advanced their model as a new way of interpreting existing data and to provide a conceptual framework for memory research. It is generally accepted that the model contains a grain of truth, and that perception, attention and memory are interdependent. Prior to 1972, very few studies had compared the effects on memory of different kinds of processing, because it was implicitly assumed that any particular stimulus would typically be processed in a very similar way by all participants on all occasions. For Parkin (1987), the model is to be applauded because it has led to general acceptance of the idea that *processing strategies* may provide at least the basis for an understanding of memory.

The model has not, however, escaped criticism. For many researchers, it is a rather simplistic model which is predominantly descriptive rather than explanatory (Eysenck and Keane, 1995). For example, the model fails to address the question of *why* deeper processing leads to better recall. Another problem concerns the difficulty of defining or measuring depth independently of a person's actual retention score. So, if 'depth' is defined as 'the number of words remembered', and 'the number of words remembered' is taken as a measure of 'depth', the model's logic has a *circular quality* to it. Although attempts have been made to provide an independent measure to depth (e.g. Hyde and Jenkins, 1973), Baddeley (1990) notes that there is no *generally accepted* way of independently assessing depth and that this 'places major limits on the power of the levels-of-processing approach'.

Finally, the model has been directly contradicted by some studies. For example, Morris (1977) has shown that rhyming recognition tests produce better recall when they are processed at the 'shallow' than the 'deep' level. It seems that the *relevance* of the processing is influential. If material is ordinarily processed at a shallow level, recall is better at that level. According to Parkin (1993), the different instructions participants are given vary in terms of the extent to which they require them to treat the stimulus as a word (compare, for example, 'Is a "tiger" a mammal?' with 'Does "tiger" have two syllables?'), yet retention tests always require participants to remember words. Since semantic tasks, by definition, require attention to be paid to stimuli as words, the superior retention they produce could reflect the bias of the retention test towards the type of information being encoded.

Reconceptualising short-term memory: the working-memory model

The multi-process model's concept of a *unitary* short-term memory (STM) was criticised by Baddeley and Hitch (1974). Although they did not reject the multi-store model's view of STM as rehearsing incoming information for transfer to LTM, they argued that it was much more complex and versatile than the multi-store model's conception of it as a passive 'stopping-off station' for information. For example, and as we noted earlier, information can flow from LTM to STM as well as in the other direction. Whenever we begin a sentence, we think about what we are going to say (which must be based on information stored in LTM) as well as what we have just said.

According to Cohen (1990), Baddeley and Hitch's concept of STM as a *working-memory store* emphasises that it is an active store used to hold information which

is being manipulated. For Cohen, working memory is 'the focus of consciousness – it holds the information you are consciously thinking about now'. The original model has been modified and elaborated by Baddeley and his colleagues (e.g. Baddeley, 1981, 1986; Salame and Baddeley, 1982). In its present form, it consists of a system in 'overall charge', which is called the *central executive*, and a number of sub-systems or *slave systems* whose activities are directed by the central executive. These slave systems are the *articulatory loop*, the *visuo-spatial scratch pad* (or *sketch pad*) and the *primary acoustic store*. These are shown in Figure 8.1.

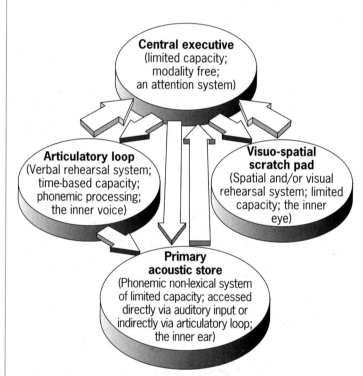

Figure 8.1   The working-memory model.

The central executive

The central executive is used whenever we deal with any task which makes cognitive demands. Although it is of limited capacity, it is a very flexible system that can process information in any sense modality (that is, it is *modality free*) and in a variety of ways. For Baddeley (1981), the central executive approximates to a *pure attentional system*.

The articulatory loop

The articulatory (or *phonological*) loop can be regarded as a verbal rehearsal loop that we use when, for example, we try to remember a telephone number for a few seconds by saying it to ourselves. It is also used to hold the words we are preparing to speak aloud. Because it uses an *articulatory/phonological code*, in which information is represented as it would be spoken, it is sometimes referred to as the *inner voice*.

The visuospatial scratch pad

The visuospatial scratch pad can also rehearse information, but it deals with visual and/or spatial information as, for example, is used when we drive along a familiar road, approach a bend, and think about the spatial layout of the road beyond the bend (Eysenck, 1986: see Figure 8.2). Because it uses a *visual code*, representing information in the form of its visual features such as size, shape and colour, it is sometimes referred to as the *inner eye*. Baddeley (1986) has described the visuospatial scratch pad as:

'a system especially well adapted to the storage of spatial information, much as a pad of paper might be used by someone trying, for example, to work out a geometric puzzle'.

Figure 8.2   The visuospatial scratchpad is where we store information about familiar roads, so we know what is round the bend.

The primary acoustic store

The primary acoustic store receives auditory input directly, but visual input can only enter it indirectly, after it has been processed by the articulatory loop and *converted* to a phonological form. Because it uses an *acoustic/phonemic code*, representing information in the form of auditory features such as pitch and loudness, it is sometimes referred to as the *inner ear*.

Baddeley (1995) suggests that one way of understanding how working memory operates can be gained from trying to determine the number of windows you have in your house. Most of us attempt to determine this by forming a visual image of our house and then either 'looking' at the house from the outside or taking a 'mental journey' through the various rooms of the house. To set up and manipulate the image, we need the visuospatial scratch pad, and to sub-vocally count the number of windows we need the articulatory loop. The whole operation is organised and run by the central executive.

Much of the research into working memory has used the *concurrent* or *interference-* (or *dual-*) *task method* (similar to the studies on divided attention we described in Chapter 6). On the assumption that each of the slave systems has a limited capacity, then with two tasks making use of the same component or components, performance on one or both should be worse when they are performed together than when they are performed separately (Baddeley et al., 1975). If two tasks require different slave systems, it should be possible to perform them as well together as separately. Some researchers have used *articulatory suppression*, in which the participant rapidly repeats out loud something meaningless (such as 'hi-ya' or 'the'). This uses up the resources of the articulatory loop, and so it cannot be used for anything else. If articulatory suppression produces poorer performance on another task that is being performed at the same time, then we can infer that this task also uses the articulatory loop (Eysenck and Keane, 1995).

An evaluation of the working-memory model

It is generally accepted that it is much more profitable to see STM as being composed of a number of relatively independent processing mechanisms than as the single unitary store proposed by the multi-store model. It is also generally accepted that attentional processes and STM are part of the *same* system, mainly because they are probably used together much of the time in everyday life. The idea that any one component of working memory (such as the articulatory loop) may be involved in the performance of apparently very different tasks (such as memory span, mental arithmetic, verbal reasoning and reading) is also a valuable insight.

For Gilhooly (1996), the working-memory model also has practical applications which extend beyond its theoretical importance. For example, Baddeley (1990) has proposed that the articulatory loop is 'not just a way of linking together a number of laboratory phenomena'. Rather it (or some similar system) plays an important part in learning to read. According to Gathercole and Baddeley (1990), one of the most striking features of children with specific problems in learning to read (despite being of normal intelligence and having a supportive family background) is that they have an impaired memory span. They also tend to do rather poorly on tasks which do not directly test memory, such as judging whether words rhyme. It is possible that such children experience some form of phonological deficit (detectable before the child has even begun to read) that seems to prevent them from learning to read. This deficit might be related to the development of the phonological loop system, although as Baddeley (1990) has noted, we do not yet know enough to draw any firm conclusions.

As Hampson and Morris (1996) have observed, one weakness of the model is that we know *least* about the component that is *most* important, namely the central executive. The central executive can apparently carry out an enormous variety of processing activities in different conditions. This poses problems in terms of describing its *precise* function, and it might even be that the idea of a single central executive is as inappropriate as that of a unitary STM (Eysenck, 1986). According to Baddeley (cited in Groeger, 1994):

> 'I talk about it (the central executive) as if it is a single unitary system; it probably is a system, but I do not know how unitary it is. It is almost certainly the case that what one will end up with is a number of interrelated executive processes, and indeed it may be possible ... to do away with the central executive as an entity. I don't really have a strong view about whether you have a system with a dictator at the top, or an oligarchy or a syndicalist system, but it is important to recognise that there does appear to be some form of overall executive control'.

Reconceptualising long-term memory

In the previous chapter (see Box 7.3, page 88), we noted that whilst Clive Wearing was severely impaired as a result of his brain damage, he was still able to use many skills and was capable of learning some new ones (even though he did not know he had learnt them). These findings would suggest that certain parts of his LTM were still intact whilst other parts were not. This is difficult for the multi-store model to explain, since the view of that model is that LTM is a *unitary* entity.

Squire (1987) suggests that it is possible to distinguish between two basic types of LTM. These are *declarative memory* and *procedural memory*. Declarative memory has been called 'fact' memory, since it is held to store our knowledge of specific information. Put another way, declarative memory is concerned with *knowing that*, for example, we first learned to ride a bike when we were three and that bicycles have two wheels. Procedural memory, by contrast, has been called 'skill' memory, since it is held to store our knowledge of *how to*, for example, ride a bicycle.

DECLARATIVE MEMORY

According to Endel Tulving (1972, 1985), declarative memory can be divided into *episodic memory* (EM) and *semantic memory* (SM).

Episodic memory

Episodic memory is an autobiographical memory system responsible for storing a record of the events, people, objects and so on which we have personally encountered. This typically includes details about times and places in which things were experienced (so the example we gave above of knowing that we learned to ride a bike at the age of three is an example of EM). Although EMs have a subjective or 'self focused' reality, most of them (such as knowing what we had for breakfast) can, at least in theory, be verified by others.

Semantic memory

Semantic memory (SM) is our store of general factual knowledge about the world, including concepts, rules and language. Tulving (1972) describes it as 'a mental thesaurus, organised knowledge a person possesses about words and other verbal symbols, their meanings and referents'. SM can be used without reference to where and when the knowledge was originally acquired. Most of us, for example, do not remember 'learning to speak'. Rather we 'just know' our native language. SM can, however, also store information about ourselves. This would include things like the number of sisters and brothers we have, and with memories like this we do not have to remember specific past experiences in order to retrieve this information. In the same way, much of our SM is built up through past experiences. For example, a 'general knowledge' about word processors is built up from past experiences with particular word processors through abstraction and generalisation (and such experiences are, of course, examples of EMs).

Originally, Tulving conceived of EM and SM as being distinct systems within LTM. However, the example we used about a 'general knowledge' of word processors being built up from past experiences with particular word processors, suggests that a better way to view SM is as a collection of EMs (Baddeley, 1995). We should also note that Tulving believed EM to be synonymous with *autobiographical memory* (AM), that is, our *involvement* in an event that is stored in memory, and suggested that when we try to recall a list of words we have been presented with, EM is being assessed (since our exposure to the words was an episode in our life). Cohen (1993), however, argues that this is not what most people understand by the term 'autobiographical' memory. In her view, AM is a special kind of EM which is concerned with specific life events that have personal significance. Cohen calls this *autobiographical EM* and distinguishes it from *experimental EM* which is assessed when we take part in experiments that require us to learn lists of words.

Flashbulb memories

These have been considered as a special kind of EM. Just before the turn of the century, Colegrove (1899) asked a number of Americans if they remembered where they were when they heard that Abraham Lincoln (16th president of the United States) had been assassinated. One person replied: 'I was standing by the stove getting dinner; my husband came in and told me', whilst another said: 'I was fixing the fence, can go within a rod of the place where I stood. Mr W. came along and told me. It was nine or ten o'clock in the morning'. Colegrove found that of the 179 people he asked, 127 claimed to recall precisely where they were, what they were doing and what time it was when they heard of the assassination. Considering they were asked the question 33 years after the event, such recall is remarkable.

Brown and Kulik (1977) coined the termed *flashbulb memory* to refer to a special kind of EM in which we are able to supply a vivid and detailed recollection of where we were and what we were doing when we heard about or saw some major public event. Brown and Kulik conducted a study in which a number of participants were asked about their memories of various actual or attempted assassinations which had occurred in the previous 15 years. These included the assassination of John F. Kennedy, Martin Luther King and Robert Kennedy. Additionally, participants were asked if they had flashbulb memories for shocking events of a personal nature.

Of the 80 participants, 73 reported a flashbulb memory associated with a personal shock, the most common being the sudden death of a relative. The assassination of John F. Kennedy was recalled most vividly, with all but one of the participants reporting a memory of that event, although other successful or unsuccessful assassinations also produced detailed memories. Additionally, Brown and Kulik found that flashbulb memories were more likely to be formed if an event was unexpected and personally consequential. The importance of consequentiality was shown in participants' memories of the death of the black politician Martin Luther King. Whilst 75 per cent of black participants reported a flashbulb memory for King's assassination, only 33 per cent of white participants reported such a memory. Similar findings have been obtained by Palmer et al. (1991) concerning memories for earthquakes amongst those living in the affected area and those living well beyond it.

The flashbulb memory phenomenon is so called because it is as though the brain has recorded an event like the scene caught in the glare of a camera's flashlight. Indeed, Brown and Kulik (1982) have argued for the existence of a special neural mechanism which is triggered by events that are emotionally arousing, unexpected or extremely important, with the result that the whole scene becomes 'printed' on the memory. One way of explaining such memories is in evolutionary terms. In prehistoric times, when memory was the only record-keeping device, an event of an unexpected and consequential nature that threatened survival would need to be retained for future reference in order to decrease the chance of harm from recurrence of that event. Thus, a special memory for storing events of physical significance would benefit an organism that possessed it and, according to Brown and Kulik, this system was expanded to incorporate survival-threatening events that the organism was only a witness to.

The claims made about flashbulb memories have attracted considerable interest. Box 8.1 describes some other important findings that have been obtained.

PROCEDURAL MEMORY

As we noted above, procedural memory (PM) has been referred to as a 'skill' memory, since it is held to store our knowledge of *how to*, for example, ride a bicycle. Unlike EM and AM, PM cannot be inspected consciously and its contents described to another person because it is concerned with complex skills that are difficult to describe. According to Anderson (1983), when we initially learn something, it is learned and encoded declaratively. With practice, however, it becomes compiled into a procedural form of knowledge, and corre-

According to Wright, people reconstruct events *post hoc* with recall altering over time, and such memories may not require a 'special' flashbulb mechanism.

Conway et al. (1994) have argued that in studies failing to find evidence of flashbulb memories, it is not entirely clear whether the events had personal consequences for those asked about them (and remember that personal consequences were identified by Brown and Kulik as being a key characteristic of flashbulb memories). Since, for most British people, the resignation in 1990 of the then prime minister Margaret Thatcher was of some personal consequence, a flashbulb memory for this event might be expected to be found. The researchers found that this was indeed the case with 86 per cent of British participants having a flashbulb memory after 11 months. Also important was the finding that only 29 per cent of participants from other countries (for whom the event was presumably of less personal consequence) had a flashbulb memory after the same period of time.

Box 8.1   Some important findings relating to flashbulb memories

According to Neisser (1982), the durability of flashbulb memories stems from their frequent rehearsal and reconsideration after the event, and the detail of people's memories and their vividness are not necessarily signs of their accuracy. For example, Neisser and Harsch (1992) asked college students to report how they learned about the explosion of the space shuttle *Challenger* the day after the disaster occurred. When the students were asked about the disaster three years later, none produced an entirely accurate report of their original learning of it, and over one-third produced a report which was *completely* inaccurate, even though they believed it to be completely accurate.

Similar findings have been obtained by Wright (1993) in a study of recall of the Hillsborough football disaster in 1989 when 95 spectators were crushed to death at an FA Cup semi-final between Liverpool and Nottingham Forest. Wright found that five months after the disaster, participants could remember little of it and, with the passage of time, they were more likely to say they were watching television when the event occurred.

sponds to the distinction between controlled/automatic processing and focused/divided attention which we discussed in Chapter 6.

In Clive Wearing's case (see page 88), it seems that most aspects of his PM were intact, but his EM and SM were impaired. Another amnesic patient similarly affected was H.M., whose limitations are similar to those of Clive Wearing. The case of H.M. is described in Box 8.2.

When Gabrieli et al. (1988) gave H.M. extensive training every day for ten days in acquiring the meaning of unfamiliar words which had come into popular use since his operation, he made very little progress. Eysenck and Keane (1995) suggest that this failure to update SM to take account of changes in the world is characteristic of most amnesics who do not, for example, know the name of the current prime minister or recognise the faces of people who have become famous subsequent to the onset of the amnesia.

When new learning does occur in amnesics, such as problem-solving and acquiring psychomotor skills, they typically *deny* having encountered the task before, despite (as we saw in the case of Clive Wearing) simul-

Box 8.2   The case of H.M.

H.M. had suffered epileptic fits since the age of 16. Because they became so devastating, he underwent surgery at the age of 27 to try to effect a cure. The surgery, which involved removal of the hippocampus on both sides of the brain, was successful in treating the epilepsy, but left H.M. with severe amnesia. Although he had a near-normal memory for things he had learned prior to the operation, his ability to store memories of events that occurred after the surgery was very poor. Although H.M.'s STM was generally normal, he either could not transfer information into LTM or, if he could, he could not retrieve it from there. Thus, he had almost no knowledge of current affairs because he forgot the news shortly after having read it in a newspaper. Unless he looked at his clock, he had no idea what time of day it was.

Whilst H.M. could recognise his friends, state their names and relate stories about them, he could do so only if he knew them before his operation. Those he met after the operation remained, in effect, total strangers, and H.M. had to 'get to know them' afresh each time they came to his house. Although H.M. could learn and remember perceptual and motor skills, he had to be reminded each day just what skills he possessed. But as Blakemore (1988) has remarked:

'new events, faces, phone numbers, places, now settle in his mind for just a few seconds or minutes before they slip, like water through a sieve, and are lost from his consciousness'.

taneously displaying evidence of learning it. These examples of learning share one crucial characteristic, namely that they allow the amnesic to demonstrate learning without the need for conscious awareness of the learning process. As Baddeley (1995) has noted, declarative memory involves conscious recollection of the past, and its adequate functioning seems to be disrupted by damage to a number of cortical and sub-cortical areas (including the temporal lobes, hippocampus, thalamus and mamillary bodies).

For example, Kaushall et al. (1981) describe the case of N.A., a young man who suffered damage to the left side of his thalami as a result of a fencing foil being accidentally thrust through one of his nostrils. Since his injury, N.A. has been unable to store any new declarative knowledge, as evidenced by his inability to read a book or follow a television programme. However, he is still able to store new procedural knowledge and has learned to ride a horse, swing a golf club and swim. This finding suggests that 'fact' knowledge and 'skill' knowledge must be stored in different parts of the brain, and as we saw in the previous chapter, PET studies have lent considerable support to the view that different clusters of cerebral areas are associated with primary components of memory function (Periani et al., 1993).

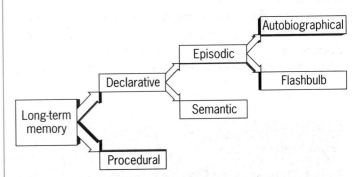

Figure 8.3   A summary of the different kinds of LTM.

Conclusions

As influential as the multi-process model of memory has been, our consideration of research in this chapter has shown that it is seriously deficient in a number of respects. Whilst it is an elegant model of memory, the evidence indicates that it is far too simplistic to accommodate a large number of research findings, although much work remains to be done before we can confidently claim that the structure of memory has been determined.

SUMMARY

- All the major alternatives to the multi-store model regard it as an oversimplified account of our highly complex memory, but they do not represent rejections of it.
- Based on the distinction between **maintenance** and **elaborative rehearsal**, Craik argued that the **amount** of rehearsal as such was less important than the **type** of rehearsal.
- While the multi-store model stresses the sequence of stages that information goes through as it passes from one **structural component** to another, driven by rehearsal and other **control processes**, Craik and Lockhart's **levels-of-processing model** sees memory as a by-product of these processes, specifically of perceptual analysis.
- A finite-capacity **central processor** is capable of analysing data at various levels. The surface features of a stimulus are analysed at a **structural/shallow level**, its semantic features are analysed at a **semantic/deep level** and, intermediate between these two, the sound of a verbal stimulus can also be analysed at a **phonemic/phonetic level**. The level used depends both on the nature of the stimulus and the time available for processing.
- The more deeply information is processed, the more likely it is to be retained. This was demonstrated in Craik and Tulving's experiment in which participants were given an unexpected test of word recognition after having earlier been asked questions about the words; the questions corresponded to the structural, phonetic and semantic levels of processing.
- **Elaboration** (i.e. the **amount** of processing) was also shown to be an important determinant of retention in Craik and Tulving's experiment. In a test of **cued recall**, recall for words compatible with complex sentences was much better than for words compatible with simple sentences, despite semantic processing being involved in both types of sentence.
- According to Bransford et al., the **nature** of the elaboration is more important than the amount. Material that is distinctive in some way may be more easily remembered; this represents another way of thinking about the concept of 'depth'.
- Level of processing, elaboration and distinctiveness often occur together, making it difficult to choose between them. Although all three con-

tribute to remembering, Eysenck believes that distinctiveness, which relates to the nature of processing, is probably more important than elaboration, which is only a measure of 'how much'.
- The levels-of-processing approach, which sees perception, attention and memory as interdependent, challenged the implicit and long-held assumption that any stimulus would typically be processed similarly by all participants on all occasions. It is now generally accepted that **processing strategies** may help in understanding memory.
- However, the model is seen as largely descriptive, as opposed to explanatory. For example, **why** is deeper processing more effective and **how** can depth be defined or measured independently of actual retention scores?
- Morris's demonstration that when rhyming recognition tests are used, shallow processing can produce better recall than deep processing, contradicts the levels-of-processing model and suggests that the **relevance** of the processing is influential. Also, the superior retention produced by semantic tasks could reflect the bias of the retention test towards the type of information being processed (i.e. words in both cases).
- Baddeley and Hitch criticised the multi-store model's view of STM as **unitary.** They saw it as much more complex and versatile than simply rehearsing incoming information for transfer to LTM, with information flowing in both directions between them.
- The **working-memory model** sees STM as an active store, holding information which is being manipulated. It is the 'focus of consciousness'.
- It comprises a **central executive**, which has overall control of the activities of several sub-systems or **slave systems: articulatory/phonological loop, visuospatial scratch pad/sketch pad** and **primary acoustic store**.
- The limited-capacity central executive, used whenever a task makes cognitive demands, is a very flexible system and is **modality free**. It resembles a **pure attentional system**.
- The articulatory/phonological loop uses an **articulatory/phonological code**, in which information is represented as it would be spoken (the **inner voice**).
- The visuospatial scratch pad uses a **visual code**,

- representing information in the form of its visual features (the **inner eye**).
- The primary acoustic store receives auditory input directly, but visual input can only enter it indirectly after **conversion** by the articulatory loop. It uses an **acoustic/phonemic code** (the **inner ear**).
- Much of the research into working memory has used the **concurrent** or **interference-/dual-task method**: if two tasks performed together require the same slave systems, then performance on one or both should be worse than when performed separately or compared with two concurrent tasks requiring different slave systems. If **articulatory suppression** decreases performance on a concurrent task, we can infer that this task uses the articulatory loop.
- The working-memory model's view of STM as comprising a number of relatively independent processing mechanisms is preferable to the multi-store model's view of a unitary store. It is also widely accepted that attentional processes and STM are part of the **same** system, and seeing any one component as involved in apparently different tasks is a valuable insight.
- An important practical application of the working-memory model is in helping us to understand children with specific problems in learning to read. They share an impaired memory span and tend to do poorly on tests of word rhyme, suggesting some phonological deficit related to development of the phonological loop.
- Unfortunately, **least** is known about the **most** important component, i.e. the central executive. Its versatility makes it difficult to describe its **precise** function and the idea of a single central executive might simply be wrong.
- The multi-store model, with its **unitary** LTM, has difficulty explaining cases like that of Clive Wearing, whose LTM appeared to be intact in certain respects but not others.
- Squire distinguishes between **declarative** ('fact') **memory**, which is concerned with **knowing that**, and **procedural** ('skill') **memory**, which is concerned with **knowing how.**
- Tulving distinguishes two kinds of declarative memory: **episodic memory (EM)** and **semantic memory (SM)**. Episodic memory is autobiographical and stores personal experiences which, despite their 'self-focused' nature, can usually be verified by others. Semantic memory is our store of general factual knowledge about the world, a 'mental thesaurus', but it can also store information about ourselves.

- Rather than EM and SM being distinct systems within LTM, it might be better to view SM as a collection of EMs, as when we build up general knowledge through particular past experiences.
- Tulving believed that EM is synonymous with **autobiographical memory (AM)**, denoting our **involvement** in the event that is stored. But Cohen argues that AM is a special kind of EM concerned with personally significant life events and she distinguishes between **autobiographical** and **experimental EM.**
- **Flashbulb memory** refers to another kind of EM, in which we have vivid and detailed recollection of the circumstances in which we learned of some major public event, such as the assassination of President Kennedy. Brown and Kulik found that such memories were more likely if the event was unexpected and personally consequential, as was the assassination of Martin Luther King for black participants.
- Brown and Kulik believe that there is a special neural mechanism which is triggered by events that are emotionally arousing, unexpected or especially important. This makes sense from an evolutionary perspective: a special memory for survival-threatening events would benefit organisms that possessed it, and this has expanded to include such events that are only witnessed.
- Neisser believes that flashbulb memories are so durable because they are often rehearsed and reconsidered after the event. Also, the detail and vividness of such memories do not necessarily indicate their accuracy: people may reconstruct events **post hoc** with recall altering over time, without a special flashbulb mechanism being needed.
- Unlike EM and SM, **procedural memory (PM)** cannot be inspected consciously and its contents described to another person. According to Anderson, learning is initially declarative (controlled processing/focused attention), but with practice becomes compiled into a procedural form of knowledge (automatic processing/divided attention).
- In the case of Clive Wearing, most aspects of his PM were intact, while his EM and SM were impaired. Similarly, H.M. was unable to learn the meaning of unfamiliar, newly popularised, words despite extensive training; this failure to update SM is typical of most amnesics.
- When amnesics do acquire psychomotor skills, they typically **deny** having encountered the task before. These examples of learning all allow the amnesic to display learning without the need for conscious awareness of the learning process. By

contrast, declarative memory involves conscious recollection of the past and is disrupted by damage to several cortical and sub-cortical areas, including the hippocampus.

- N.A.'s failure to store any new declarative knowledge but successful acquisition of procedural knowledge, suggests that 'fact' and 'skill' knowledge are stored in different parts of the brain. This is supported by the finding of PET studies, which show that different clusters of cerebral areas are associated with primary components of memory function.

9

THE ORGANISATION OF INFORMATION IN MEMORY

Introduction and overview

In Chapter 7, we discussed the limited capacity of STM and noted that 'chunking' is a way of apparently increasing its capacity by imposing meaning on the information presented. 'Chunking' is achieved by integrating and relating the incoming information to knowledge that we already possess in LTM. In chunking, then, we *organise* information, giving it a structure it does not otherwise have. For Baddeley (1995), the secret of a good memory is, like a library, organisation. He also notes that:

'good learning typically goes with the systematic encoding of incoming material, integrating and relating it to what is already known'.

One line of evidence which indicates that memory is stored in a highly organised way comes from a case study reported by Hart et al. (1985). Two years after suffering a stroke, M.D. appeared to have made a complete recovery, his only problem being that he could not remember the names of fruits or vegetables or sort pictures of fruits or vegetables into proper categories. The fact that he could identify other things and sort, for example, types of food or vehicles into categories, does suggest that related information in memory is stored together, and may even be stored in specific areas of the brain. Our aim in this chapter is to look at the role of organisation in memory and to consider some specific models of the way in which information is represented in semantic memory.

Some experimental studies of organisation in memory

In a classic experiment, Bousfield (1953) asked participants to try to learn 60 words. The word list consisted of four categories (animals, people's names, professions and vegetables) with 15 examples of each, all mixed up. Bousfield found that when participants free-recalled the list, they tended to cluster items from particular categories. For example, if a participant recalled 'onion', it was very likely that other vegetables followed. Although the participants had not been told of the categories, the fact that they recalled words in clusters suggested that they had tried to organise the material to which they were exposed. Bousfield called this phenomenon *categorical clustering*. Other researchers have reported categorical clustering in more naturalistic settings. For example, Rubin and Olson (1980) asked students to recall the names of as many members of staff as they could remember. The researchers found a strong tendency for names to be recalled by department.

It has also been found that instructions to organise material will facilitate learning, even when participants are not trying to remember material. Mandler (1967) used a pack of 100 cards, each of which had a word printed on it. Participants were told to arrange the cards into categories that 'went together'. Half were told to try to remember the words, but the other half were not. Participants continued the sorting task until the cards they put into each category were 95 per cent the same from one trial to the next. The cards were then taken away, and the participants asked to remember as many of the words as they could.

Mandler found that people tended to recall the words according to the categories they used for sorting the cards, that is, categorical clustering occurred. Also, those who were instructed just to sort the cards into categories recalled *as many* as those instructed to try and remember them, suggesting that once we become involved in working with material, we tend to organise it.

Tulving (1968) has argued that people will tend to create their own categories when the items they are pre-

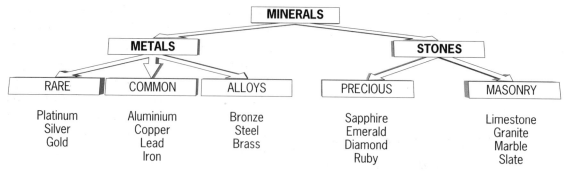

Figure 9.1   A conceptual hierarchy as used by Bower et al. (1969).

sented with do not obviously fall into categories. Tulving calls this *subjective organisation* (SO) and distinguishes it from *experimenter organisation* (EO) in which organisation is imposed by the experimenter. One of the best-known studies of experimenter-imposed organisation was conducted by Bower et al. (1969). Their participants were required to learn a list of words which were arranged into conceptual hierarchies as shown in Figure 9.1. For one group, the words were organised in a *hierarchical* form. The other group were presented with the same words, but these were arranged randomly. The results showed that the first group recalled an average of 65 per cent of words correctly, whilst the other recalled an average of only 19 per cent correctly.

Imagery as a form of organisation

Imagery is the basis of many kinds of *mnemonic devices* or memory aids (which we will discuss further in Chapter 11), and there is a large amount of evidence indicating that verbal material can be better remembered if it can be associated in some way with a visual image. This is true for both initial learning (how the material is encoded) and retrieval. The use of imagery as a way of organising information can be traced back at least as far as the first century BC, and the writing of Cicero. Cicero tells the story of the Greek poet Simonides who lived around 500 BC. Cicero's story is retold in Box 9.1.

Simonides' *method of loci* ('loci' is the Greek for 'places') became popular with classical orators and is still used by people today in various forms. One variation of this way of organising information is called the *narrative story method* in which the items to be remembered are incorporated into a meaningful story which is then retold in order to remember the items (Bower and Clark, 1969). Perhaps the most famous person who used the narrative story method was a Russian newspaper reporter called Shoresheveski (or 'S'), studied by

Luria (1968). S's memory appeared to have no limits and included the ability to recall lists of more than a hundred digits and elaborate scientific formulae, even though he was not a scientist. S's use of the narrative story method is described in Box 9.2.

Box 9.2   S's use of the narrative story method

'When S read through a long series of words, each word would elicit a graphic image, and since the series was fairly long, he had to find some way of distributing these images in a mental row or sequence. Most often (and this habit persisted throughout his life) he would "distribute" them along some roadway or street he visualised in his mind ... Frequently he would take a mental walk along that street ... and slowly make his way down, "distributing" his images at houses, gates and in store windows ... This technique of converting a series of words into a series of graphic images explains why S could so readily reproduce a series from start to finish or in the reverse order; how he could rapidly name the word that preceded or followed one I'd selected from the series. To do this he would simply begin his walk, either from the beginning or end of the street, find the image of the object I had named and "take a look at" whatever happened to be situated on either side of it'.

(taken from Luria, 1968)

One experimental study of mental imagery was reported by Bower (1972) who presented participants with 100 different cards one at a time. Each card had two unrelated words printed on it (such at 'cat' and 'brick'). Participants in one group were instructed to form mental images to *link* the unconnected words, the more vivid the image the better. Participants in the other group were simply instructed to memorise the words. After the words had been presented, each participant was shown a card with the first word of each pair, the task being to recall the second word. Bower found that those who used imagery recalled 80 per cent of the words whilst the non-imagers recalled only 45 per cent.

Research has shown that *bizarre, interacting* and *vivid* images are most effective (Anderson, 1995b), possibly because such images tend to be more distinctive or novel than plausible images and take more time to

form. The extra time and effort taken in constructing such images may help them to be remembered better. According to Paivio (1986), the effects of imagery can be explained in terms of what he calls a *dual-code model of memory*, which sees memories as being stored in either *sensory codes* (as visual images or sounds) or *verbal codes* (as words). Within the latter, each known word is assumed to be represented by a *logogen*. Within the former, images are represented in the form of *imagens*.

The two systems are held to be connected by means of *referential links* which allow a word to be associated with its relevant image (and vice versa). This can explain the finding that it is easier to form images of *concrete* words (such as 'apple') than *abstract* words (such as 'nourishment'). Abstract words may be processed by, and represented in, the verbal system only, whereas concrete words may be processed by, and represented in, both systems (Parkin, 1993).

A special type of mental imagery is called *eidetic imagery*, and involves a persistent and clear image of some visual scene which enables the scene to be recalled in astonishing detail. According to Haber (1969), eidetic imagery is more common in children than adults, but even so only about five per cent of children display it. The ability declines with age, and has all but disappeared by early adulthood. Interestingly, children with eidetic imagery (who are called *eidetikers*) perform no better than their non-eidetic classmates on other tests of memory, and eidetic imagery appears to be an essentially perceptual phenomenon in which the coding of information is not a factor (Haber, 1980).

An overview of semantic-network models

The various studies we have described in the preceding sections clearly indicate the importance of organisation, but they say little about the kind of organisation that occurs in memory. Semantic-network models are an attempt to address this issue. Although the various models that have been proposed differ in important ways, they share two main features. First, all are concerned with the way in which meaningful material (rather than meaningless material, such as nonsense syllables) is organised. Second, they all assume that the best way to think about semantic organisation is in terms of multiple, interconnected associations, relationships or pathways. The models assume that information is embedded in an organised, structured network composed of semantic units and their functional relationships to one another (Houston et al., 1991).

Hierarchical-network models

One of the best-known hierarchial-network models of the way in which semantic memory is organised is the so-called *Teachable Language Comprehender* devised by Collins and Quillian (1969, 1972) and based on work carried out by Quillian for his doctoral dissertation. Like other models, Collins and Quillian's is primarily concerned with *lexical memory*, that is memory for particular words rather than grammar or sentences. It would be impossible to portray the interrelationships among *all* the words in a complete lexicon. As a result, we will consider only the *nature* of the overall lexical structure proposed.

Collins and Quillian see semantic memory as being organised in the form of a hierarchical network. Major concepts are represented as *nodes*, and each node has a number of properties or features associated with it. Each node is also associated with other concepts elsewhere in the hierarchy, as shown in Figure 9.2.

In the example shown in Figure 9.2, the concept 'animal' and the properties or features associated with animals appear at the top of the hierarchy. The concept 'animal' is also associated with the concepts of 'bird' and 'fish' which appear at the next level in the hierarchy. In turn, these concepts are associated with yet other concepts lower down in the hierarchy. Thus, the 'bird' concept is associated with 'canary' and 'ostrich' (and presumably many others) whilst the 'fish' concept is associated with 'shark' and 'salmon' (and presumably many others as well). Since almost all birds, for example, have wings, feathers and can fly, it is not necessary for these features to appear lower down the hierarchy as properties of canaries and ostriches. This hierarchical arrangement means that a great deal of information can

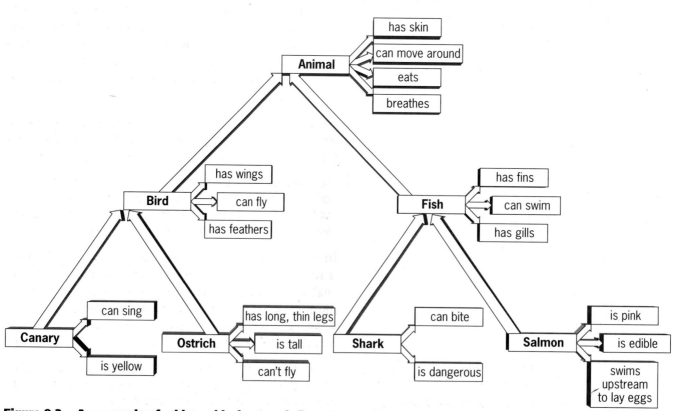

Figure 9.2   An example of a hierarchical network (based on Collins and Quillian, 1969, 1972).

be stored in a very economical way with little redundancy.

Experimental tests of the model's usefulness have typically involved *sentence verification tasks*. In these, participants are given a sentence such as 'A canary can sing' or 'A canary can fly' and asked to verify whether the sentence is true or not, and the time the participant takes to verify each sentence is recorded. The model predicts that with a sentence like 'A canary can sing', reaction time should be shorter as compared with the sentence 'A canary can fly'. The reason for this is that verifying the first sentence does not involve moving beyond the concept, since the property 'can sing' is associated with the concept 'canary'. However, the property 'can fly' is associated with the concept 'bird', and so one level of the hierarchy must be traversed. A sentence like 'A canary breathes' should take even longer to verify, since this involves traversing two levels of the hierarchy.

Consistent with their model, and as shown in Figure 9.3, Collins and Quillian found that the time taken to decide whether a statement was true increased as a function of the number of levels of the hierarchy that had to be traversed to verify it. However, the findings are open to alternative explanations. For example, it might take longer to verify 'A canary is an animal' because there are more animals than birds. In other words, Collins and Quillian's findings could be explained in terms of the relationship between *category size* and reaction time.

Also, some members of a category are judged to be much more typical than others. For example, whilst 'canary' and 'ostrich' both belong to the category 'bird', canaries are judged to be a more typical bird than ostriches. The evidence suggests that the sentence 'A canary is a bird' (in which the canary is a *typical* instance) is verified *more* quickly than 'An ostrich is a bird' (in which the ostrich is an *atypical* instance) (Baddeley, 1990). Since both sentences involve traversing the same number of levels, Collins and Quillian's model would predict that there should be no difference in verification time for the two sentences.

Yet other findings cast doubt on the usefulness of the model. For example, Conrad (1972) found that response time may reflect the *relative frequency* with which certain attributes are commonly associated with a particular concept. In her experiment, frequency was controlled for, and there was no evidence for longer response times to categories supposedly stored at a higher level. What this suggests is that 'semantic relatedness' (or the attributes that are commonly associated with particular concepts) could account for the original findings. According to Collins and Quillian, all attributes of a concept are *equally important* or salient in determining the members of a concept, but Conrad's data suggest that they are not. Other research (e.g. Rips et al., 1973) has shown that it takes longer to verify the sentence 'A bear is a mammal' than 'A bear is an animal'. Since 'animal' is higher up in the hierarchy than 'mammal', this is the opposite of what Collins and Quillian's model predicts.

Another, more complicated, hierarchical-network model has been proposed by Lindsay and Norman (1977). As Bower and Hilgard (1981) have noted:

'a realistic memory, of course, contains thousands of . . . concepts, each with very many connections, so that the actual topographical representation would look like a huge "wiring diagram" '.

In Lindsay and Norman's model, an example of which is shown in Figure 9.4, just a fragment of information enables many questions to be answered. For example, if the system was asked to compare the similarities and differences between beer and wine, it could do this. As Bower and Hilgard have observed:

'the number of factual relationships derivable and possible questions that can be answered increases exponentially as the number of encoded predicates or "bits of knowledge" increases'.

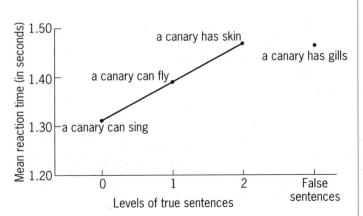

Figure 9.3   Data from Collins and Quillian's sentence verification tasks.

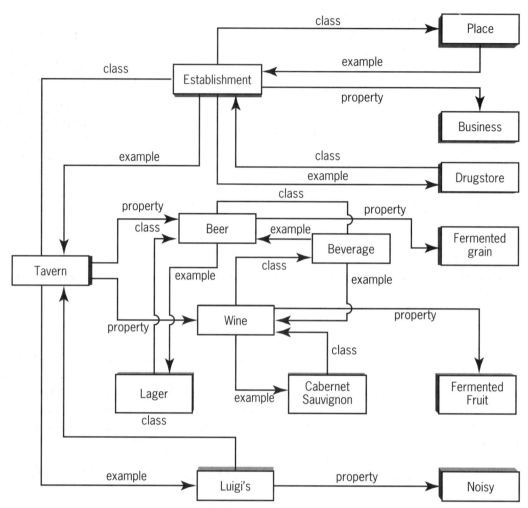

Figure 9.4   An example of a hierarchical-semantic network surrounding the concept of a 'tavern' (based on Lindsay and Norman, 1977).

Matrix models

In an experiment conducted by Broadbent et al. (1978), participants were given a list of 16 words to remember. For one group of participants (the control group), the words were presented in a random order. For a second group, they were organised hierarchically. A third group were presented with the words in the form of a matrix. The two forms of presentation given to the experimental groups are shown in Figure 9.5.

The results showed that those participants presented with the words in a hierarchical form or in the form of a matrix remembered significantly more words than those presented with the words in random order. However, the hierarchical and matrix group did not differ from one another, suggesting that both are

equally helpful as forms of organisation. So whilst hierarchical models represent one way in which semantic information may be represented in memory, *matrices* offer another possibility.

Feature models

As we saw earlier, Rips et al. (1973) found that it took participants longer to verify the sentence 'A bear is a mammal' than 'A bear is an animal', and we noted that this is inconsistent with the predictions from Collins and Quillian's model. Smith et al.'s (1974) *feature approach* is an attempt to address this weakness in the Collins and Quillian model, and is concerned with our ability to decide whether certain nouns belong to certain categories.

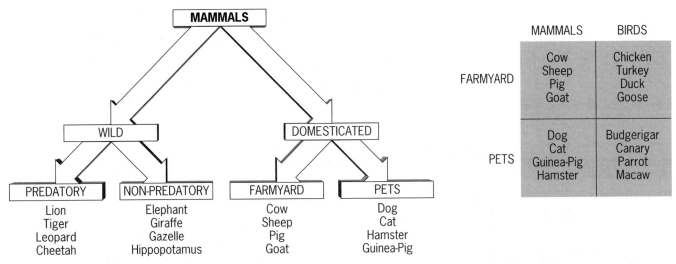

Figure 9.5   The hierarchical organisation of words in Broadbent et al.'s experiment (left), and the same words presented in matrix form (right).

Suppose, for example, we are asked to verify the sentence 'A cat is an animal'. For Smith and his colleagues, the crucial factor is not the spatial relationship between the two concepts, but the number of *features* they have in common. A cat and an animal have a large number of features in common (such as both can breathe, have skin and so on) and as a result, it should not take long to verify the sentence. The same would be true of the sentence 'A cat is sand', since these two concepts have very little in common. So, when there are either a large number of features in common between concepts or none at all, decisions are made very quickly.

In some cases, though, the number of common attributes is what Smith and his colleagues call *intermediate*. In the sentence 'A mould is a plant', the two concepts share some features, but it is difficult to generate enough to enable a decision to be reached quickly. According to Hampton (1979), in such circumstances we look at *defining features* and *characteristic features*. A defining feature is a necessary *and* sufficient condition for reaching a decision, whilst a characteristic feature is a typical attribute of an item belonging to a category, but is not itself sufficient to determine whether something belongs to a category. For example, any animal that has feathers is a bird since there are no featherless birds and no non-birds that have feathers. However, whilst birds characteristically fly, not all do, and some things that do fly are not birds. In Hampton's view, when the number of common attributes belonging to a category is intermediate, and a decision is difficult to

reach, we consider *only* defining features. Since this involves time, the decision process is inevitably slowed down. This feature approach to semantic memory could explain some of the data that are difficult for the Collins and Quillian model to explain.

Spreading-activation models

In light of the criticisms made of the hierarchical-network model, Collins and Loftus (1975) proposed a revised network model. There are several differences between this and the hierarchical network, as can be seen in Figure 9.6. First, the network is not limited to hierarchical relationships between concepts. Second, the *semantic distance* between concepts varies. The longer the distance, the weaker the relationship between the concepts. Thus, highly related concepts are located close together. Third, when a particular item is processed, activation spreads out along the pathways from a concept in all directions. Although the concept of 'activation' has not been defined precisely, the basic idea is that an activated item can be more easily processed (in the sense of being retrieved, judged, recognised or evaluated) than an unactivated one.

Several studies have provided data consistent with the model (e.g. Jones and Anderson, 1987). In *lexical-decision experiments*, participants are first shown a

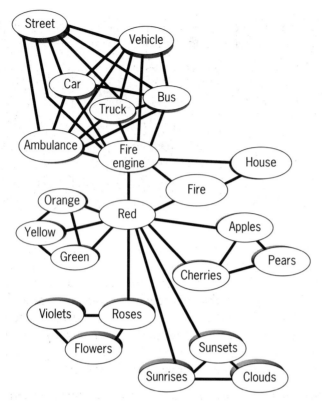

Figure 9.6   An example of a spreading-activation model. The length of each line (or link) represents the degree of association between particular concepts (based on Collins and Loftus, 1975).

prime, such as the word 'dog'. Then, a *target* word is shown for a very brief period of time. The target word may be related to the prime word (e.g. 'dalmatian'), unrelated (e.g. 'banana') or even a nonsense word (e.g. 'grilf'). The participant has to make a judgement about the target word such as whether it actually is a word or whether it belongs to a certain category. The data indicate that the speed with which a decision is reached is increased the closer the relationship between the target and prime. In terms of the spreading-activation model, this is because the prime activates material in the semantic network, and the closer the prime is to the target, the more activated and more easily processed it is.

Despite apparent support for the model, Johnson-Laird and his colleagues (1984) have pointed out that there are many examples where the interpretation offered by the network will tend, in actual discourse, to be overridden by the constraints of real-world knowledge. Consider, for example, the sentence 'The ham sandwich was eaten by the soup'. Whilst this sentence may

be nonsensical to some of us, for waiters and waitresses (who often label customers in terms of their orders), the sentence is quite understandable. Johnson-Laird et al. call this 'failure to escape from the maze of symbols into the world' the *symbolic fallacy*: a person has to know the relationship between symbols and what they refer to (see also Chapter 17).

Schemas

Although the various models of organisation in semantic memory we have reviewed are helpful, it is clearly the case that semantic memory must contain structures considerably larger than the simple concepts those models consider. This 'larger unit' of semantic memory is the *schema*, a term introduced to memory research by Sir Frederick Bartlett (see Chapter 7, page 80). Bartlett was the first to recognise that memory can be seen as a *reconstructive* process in which information we have already stored affects the remembering of other events. In his research, Bartlett found that people frequently add or delete details to make new information more consistent with their conception of the world. So rather than being like a computer, with output matching input, Bartlett's view of memory is as an 'imaginative reconstruction' of our experience.

Our schemas provide us with preconceived expectations, and they operate in a 'top-down' way to help us interpret the 'bottom-up' flow of information reaching our senses. Schemas are useful because they help to make the world more predictable. They can, however, also lead to significant distortions in our memory processes, because they have a powerful effect on the way in which memories for events are encoded (Crooks and Stein, 1991). For example, in a study conducted by Allport and Postman (1947), white participants were shown a picture of two men evidently engaged in an argument, as shown in Figure 9.7.

After briefly looking at the picture, participants were asked to describe the scene to someone else who had not seen the picture. This person was then required to pass the information on to another person and so on. As the information was passed, so features of it changed. The most important of these was that the knife was reported as being in the black man's hand.

Other research has demonstrated the apparently powerful effects of schemas on recall outside the laboratory. Ulric Neisser (1981) studied the testimony given by

Figure 9.7 **The stimulus material used by Allport and Postman (1947). The two men are engaged in an argument. The better-dressed man is black, and the white man has a cutthroat razor in his left hand.**

John Dean, a key figure in the Watergate conspiracy. Dean testified to a committee that was trying to determine whether President Nixon had been involved in a plan to 'bug' the Democratic National Committee headquarters about an event that had occurred nine months earlier. Dean's testimony and Neisser's analysis are shown in Box 9.3.

Box 9.3   Neisser's (1981) analysis of John Dean's testimony

According to Dean:

'When I arrived at the Oval Office, I found Haldeman and the President. The President asked me to sit down. Both men appeared to be in very good spirits, and my reception was warm and cordial. The President then told me that Bob (Haldeman) had kept him posted on my handling of the Watergate case. The President told me that I had done a good job and he appreciated how difficult a task it had been and the President was pleased that the case had stopped with Liddy.'

A comparison of this statement with transcripts of

the tape-recording Nixon *secretly* made of the meeting revealed the following discrepancies:

- Nixon had not asked Dean to sit down.
- Nixon had not said that Haldeman had 'kept him posted'.
- No compliment was paid by Nixon on the job Dean had done.
- Nixon did not say that he 'appreciated how difficult a task it had been'.
- There was no reference made to Liddy and the case by Nixon.

Neisser points out that, in terms of a central schema, concerning Nixon's involvement in the Watergate cover-up, Dean's recollections *were* accurate, and Neisser suggests that his specific recollection described in Box 9.3 might have come from *another* schema, namely the one that describes what generally happens when people enter a room (viz., the host greets the guest, and the guest is invited to sit down).

Schemas can also act at a powerful enhancement to memory, as was shown by Bransford and Johnson (1972). In their study, participants were asked to read the passage shown in Box 9.4.

Box 9.4   The passage read by participants in Bransford and Johnson's (1972) experiment

The procedure is actually quite simple. First you arrange items into several different groups. Of course, one pile might be sufficient, depending on how much there is to do. If you have to go somewhere else due to lack of facilities, that is the next step; otherwise you are pretty well set. It is important not to overdo things. That is, it is better to do a few things at once than too many. In the short run, this may not seem important but complications can easily arise. A mistake can be expensive as well. At first, the whole procedure will seem complicated. Soon, however, it will become just another fact of life. It is difficult to see any end to the necessity of this task in the immediate future, but then one can never tell. After the procedure is completed, one arranges the material into different groups again. They then can be put into their appropriate places. Eventually, they will be used once more and the whole cycle will have to be repeated. However, that is part of life.

Bransford and Johnson's participants found the passage difficult to understand and could later recall only a few of the 18 distinct ideas it contains. This was because they lacked an appropriate schema, that is, they could not relate the material to what they already knew. However, when another group of participants were told in advance that the passage was about *washing clothes*, they found it more understandable and recalled twice as many ideas as the first group of participants.

Schema theories

According to Cohen (1993), schema theory is one of the most influential approaches to the problem of understanding the complex pattern of remembering and forgetting. Several schema theories have been advanced (e.g. Rumelhart, 1975; Schank, 1975; Schank and Abelson, 1977), and there is considerable overlap between them. The broad characteristics shared by the various theories are summarised in Box 9.5.

Box 9.5   Similarities between schema theories

- Schemas are viewed as 'packets of information' which consist of a fixed compulsory value and a variable (or optional) value. Our schema for buying things has fixed slots for the exchange of money and goods, and variable slots for the amount of money and the nature of the goods. In some cases, a slot may be left unspecified and can often be filled with a 'default' value, or 'best guess' given the available information.

- Schemas are not mutually exclusive packets of information but can be related together to form systems. A schema for a picnic, for example, might be part of a larger system of schemas including 'meals' and 'outings'.

- Schemas can relate to abstract ideologies, abstract concepts (such as 'justice') as well as concrete objects (such as the appearance of a face).

- Rather than representing definitions and rules about the world, schemas represent knowledge and experience of the world.

- Schemas are active recognition devices which enable us to try to make sense of ambiguous and unfamiliar information in terms of our existing knowledge and understanding (as we have already seen).

Schank and Abelson argue that we develop schemas or *scripts* which represent the sequence of actions we go through when carrying out commonly experienced social events such as going to a restaurant, and the objects and people we are likely to encounter. These scripts enable us to fill in much of the detail which might not be specified in a piece of information. Consider, for example, the sentences 'We had a tandoori chicken at the Taj Mahal last night. The service was slow, and we almost missed the start of the play.' These sentences can only be interpreted by bringing in additional information (Baddeley, 1990). We need to have schemas that predict what would happen next and to fill in those aspects of the event which are left implicit. Such scripts are essential ways of summarising common cultural assumptions which not only help us to understand text and discourse, but also enable us to predict future events and behave appropriately in given social situations.

Schank and Abelson (1977) built their scripts into a computer program called *SAM*. The program, whose 'restaurant script' is shown in Table 9.1, can evidently 'answer' questions and 'understand' stories about restaurants. Bower et al. (1979) have shown that there are certain actions and events that form part of people's knowledge about what is involved in going into a restaurant and that these broadly agree with Schank and Abelson's restaurant script. Bower and his colleagues also found that when people are asked to recall a passage of text concerning 'restaurant behaviour', they falsely recall aspects which were not explicitly included but which are consistent with a 'restaurant script' *and* change the order of events so as to make them consistent with such a script (exactly as Bartlett would have predicted).

An evaluation of schema theories

Schema theories have been criticised on a number of grounds (Cohen, 1993). First, the whole idea of a schema appears to be so vague as to be of little practical use. Second, schema theories have tended to emphasise the inaccuracies of memory and overlook the fact that complex events are sometimes remembered very accurately (especially the unexpected and unusual aspects of

Table 9.1   A simplified version of Schank and Abelson's schematic representation of activities involved in going to a restaurant

Name	Restaurant	Roles	Customer
Props	Tables		Waiter
	Menu		Cook
	Food		Cashier
	Bill		Owner
	Money		
	Tip		
Entry conditions	Customer is hungry	Results	Customer has less money
	Customer has money		Owner has more money
			Customer is not hungry
Scene 1	Entering	Scene 3	Eating
	Customer enters restaurant		Waiter gives food to customer
	Customer looks for table		Customer eats food
	Customer decides where to sit		
	Customer goes to table		
	Customer sits down		
Scene 2	Ordering	Scene 4	Exiting
	Customer picks up menu		Waiter prepares bill
	Customer looks at menu		Waiter goes over to customer
	Customer decides on food		Waiter gives bill to customer
	Customer signals waiter		Customer gives tip to waiter
	Waiter comes to table		Customer goes to cashier
	Customer orders food		Customer gives money to cashier
	Waiter goes to cook		Customer leaves restaurant
	Waiter gives food order to cook		
	Cook prepares food		

(based on Bower, et al., 1979).

them). Third, the theories have very little to say about the acquisition of schemas. Without schemas, we are unable to interpret new experiences, and we need new experiences in order to build up schemas.

Schank (1982) has attempted to address these (and other) criticisms with his *dynamic-memory theory*. As its name suggests, this is an attempt to take account of the more dynamic aspects of memory and is a more elaborate and flexible version of his original theory. The theory attempts to clarify the relationship between general knowledge schemas and memories for specific episodes, based on a hierarchical arrangement of memory representations. At the bottom of the hierarchy are *Memory Organisation Packets* (MOPs) which store specific details about specific events. At higher levels in the hierarchy, the representations become more and more general and schema-like. MOPs are not usually stored for very long, and become 'absorbed' into the 'event schemas' that store those features which are common to repeated experiences. Details of unusual or atypical events, however, are retained (Cohen, 1993).

According to Alba and Hasher (1983) and Bahrick (1984), whilst there is some evidence for schema theories, schemas themselves are unlikely to be involved in things like the retrieval of general knowledge, that is, things like remembering one's name, facts and rules. Bahrick's own research concerns what he calls *replicative memory*, that is, memory which closely resembles the original content. Bahrick has found that even people who studied a particular language (Spanish) 50 years earlier, and have never used it since, remembered 'large portions of the originally acquired information'. This suggests that at least some types of information can be stored for very long periods of time and recalled in their *original* form.

Conclusions

In this chapter, we have shown that evidence exists to support the view that memory is highly organised. The organisation of information can be achieved by a variety of methods, and several models have been proposed to explain the kind of organisation that occurs in memory, although there is insufficient evidence as yet to support any particular model.

SUMMARY

- Chunking represents a way of **organising** information by giving it a structure it does not otherwise have. Baddeley believes that organisation is the secret of a good memory, such that new material is integrated with what we already know.
- M.D.'s inability to remember the names of fruits or vegetables and to sort them into categories suggests that related information is stored together in memory. This storage may even take place in specific areas of the brain.
- Bousfield's classic experiment found that participants free-recalled a list of randomly presented words in clusters (**categorical clustering**), despite not being told of the categories into which they fell. This suggested that they had tried to organise the words.
- Mandler's study using words printed on cards showed that instructions to organise material will facilitate learning, even when participants are not trying to remember it. Not only did categorical clustering occur, but participants instructed just to sort the cards into categories remembered as many as those instructed to remember them.
- According to Tulving, people will tend to create their own categories when the items they are presented with do not fall into obvious categories (**subjective organisation (SO)**), which he distinguishes from **experimenter organisation (EO)**. Bower et al.'s experiment showed that when words were presented in the form of conceptual **hierarchies**, they are recalled significantly better than when they are presented randomly.
- **Imagery** represents a form of organisation and is the basis of many kinds of **mnemonic devices**. Verbal material can be both better learned and retrieved if it can be linked in some way with a visual image.
- The use of imagery can be traced to the ancient Greek poet Simonides, who used the **method of loci**. This became popular with classical orators and is still used in various forms today, such as the **narrative-story method**, which was used by 'S', the Russian newspaper reporter studied by Luria. He commonly took a mental walk down a street, 'distributing' graphic images (each linked to a word in the list to be remembered) at various places along the way.
- Bower's experimental study showed that participants instructed to **link** pairs of unrelated words through visual images performed much better on a test of recall than those simply instructed to memorise the words. Other research suggests that **bizarre**, **interacting** and **vivid** images are most effective, possibly because they are more distinctive and require extra time and effort.
- According to Paivio, the effects of imagery can be explained in terms of a **dual-code model of memory**, with memories being stored in either **sensory codes** (as visual images or sounds – **imagens**) or **verbal codes** (as words – **logogens**). The two systems are connected by **referential links** which can explain why it is easier to form images of **concrete** words (which can be processed by or represented in both systems) than **abstract** words (processed by or represented in the verbal system only).
- **Eidetic imagery** is more common in children than adults, although only about five per cent of all children display it. **Eidetikers** perform no better than non-eidetikers on other tests of memory and, according to Haber, it is basically a perceptual phenomenon in which the coding of information plays no part.
- **Semantic-network models** attempt to identify the kind of organisation that occurs in memory. They are concerned with the organisation of meaningful material, and assume that information is embedded in an organised structural network composed of semantic units and their functional relationships to one another.
- Collins and Quillian's **Teachable Language Comprehender** is, like other models, mainly concerned with the **nature of lexical memory.**

They see semantic memory as organised in the form of a **hierarchical** network, with major concepts (e.g. 'animal') represented as **nodes**, each of which has several properties or features associated with it and which is linked with other concepts at a lower level in the hierarchy (e.g. 'bird'/'fish'). The latter are also linked with other concepts lower down in the hierarchy (e.g. 'canary'/'shark').

- Using **sentence verification tasks**, Collins and Quillian confirmed the model's prediction that the more levels that have to be traversed, the longer it will take to verify the truth or falsity of a sentence. However, their findings could be explained in terms of the relationship between **category size** and reaction time, and some members of a category are much more **typical** than others (with more typical instances being easier to verify).
- Response time may also reflect the **relative frequency** with which certain attributes are commonly associated with a particular concept ('semantic relatedness'). While Collins and Quillian's model sees all attributes of a particular concept as of **equal importance**, studies by Conrad and Rips et al. suggest that this is not so.
- In Lindsay and Norman's more complex hierarchical model, a small fragment of information allows many questions to be answered, such as the similarities and differences between beer and wine.
- In Broadbent et al.'s experiment, participants presented with words in either a hierarchical form or in the form of a matrix remembered significantly more of them than participants presented with the words in a random order. However, the first two groups did equally well, suggesting that semantic memory (SM) may be organised in the form of **matrices.**
- According to Smith et al.'s **feature model**, the crucial factor in deciding whether a sentence is true is the number of features the concepts have in common (e.g. a cat and an animal). When the number of common features is **intermediate**, the task becomes more difficult and time consuming, and we look for what Hampton calls **defining features** (as opposed to **characteristic features**).
- Collins and Loftus's **spreading-activation model** represents a revision of the original hierarchical-network model. The network is no longer limited to hierarchical relationships between concepts, the **semantic distance** between concepts now varies, and when a particular item is processed, activation spreads out along the pathways from a concept in all directions.

- Despite any precise definition of 'activation', the basic idea is that an activated item can be more easily processed (retrieved/judged/recognised/ evaluated) than an inactivated one. **Lexical-decision experiments** tend to confirm the prediction that the **prime** activates material in the semantic network, and that the closer it is to the **target**, the more activated it is.
- According to Johnson-Laird et al., the interpretation offered by the network will often be overridden by the constraints of real-world knowledge: we need to know the relationship between symbols and what they refer to, otherwise we may be guilty of the **symbolic fallacy.**
- SM must contain structures considerably larger than the simple concepts proposed by the various models of SM. **Schemas** represent this larger unit, a term first introduced into psychology by Bartlett, who was the first to recognise the **reconstructive** nature of memory.
- Schemas provide us with preconceived expectations and operate in a 'top-down' fashion to help us interpret the 'bottom-up' flow of information reaching our senses. As well as making the world more predictable, they may also distort our memories, as demonstrated by Allport and Postman using a picture of two men engaged in an argument.
- Schemas have also been shown to have powerful effects on recall outside the laboratory, as illustrated by Neisser's analysis of the testimony given by John Dean in the Watergate investigation.
- Bransford and Johnson showed that schemas can also enhance memory quite powerfully: without an appropriate schema, it is sometimes difficult to relate certain material to what we already know, but being provided with such a schema can aid both understanding and recall.
- According to Cohen, **schema theory** is one of the most influential approaches to the study of remembering and forgetting. Different theories share a common view of schemas as interrelated 'packets of information' comprising both a fixed compulsory value and a variable or optional value. They can refer to both abstract concepts and concrete objects and are active recognition devices which help make sense of ambiguous or unfamiliar information.
- Schank and Abelson believe that we develop **scripts** regarding the sequence of actions involved in commonly experienced social events, such as going to a restaurant. Scripts help us to fill in missing details from a piece of information by allowing us to predict what would happen next,

as well as enabling us to behave appropriately in given social situations.

- Schank and Abelson built their scripts into a computer program called **SAM**, which apparently can answer questions and understand stories about restaurants. Support for their program comes from a study by Bower et al., who found that people's recollections of a passage of 'restaurant text' reflected their 'restaurant script'.

- The schema concept has been criticised for being too vague. Also, schema theories tend to emphasise the limitations of memory and overlook the sometimes accurate recall of complex events, as well as failing to explain how we initially acquire schemas.

- Schank's **dynamic-memory theory** tries to address these criticisms by identifying the relationship between general knowledge schemas and memories for specific episodes. At the bottom of a hierarchy are **Memory Organisation Packets (MOPs)**, and representations become increasingly general and schema-like at higher levels in the hierarchy. MOPs gradually become absorbed into the 'event schemas'.

- While there is some support for schema theories, they cannot account for the retrieval of general knowledge. Also, according to Bahrick's concept of **replicative memory**, certain types of information can be stored over long periods of time and recalled in their **original** form.

THEORIES OF FORGETTING

10

Introduction and overview

As we mentioned in Chapter 7 (see page 82), forgetting can occur at the encoding, storage or retrieval stage. In order to understand why we forget, we need to examine the distinction between *availability* and *accessibility*. Availability refers to whether or not the material has been stored in the first place, whereas accessibility refers to being able to retrieve what has been stored. In terms of the multi-store model of memory, since information must be transferred from STM to LTM for permanent storage, availability mainly concerns STM and the transfer of information from it into LTM. Accessibility, by contrast, mainly concerns LTM. Memory loss may be caused by a number of factors, including physical trauma and drug abuse, in which actual brain cells or systems are destroyed (Clifford, 1991). Research into findings relating to these causes can be found in Eysenck and Keane (1995) and Hayes (1996). Our aim in this chapter, though, is to review the various psychological explanations of forgetting that have been advanced and the evidence relating to them.

Motivated-forgetting theory

According to this theory, forgetting is a motivated process rather than a failure in terms of learning or other processes. Sigmund Freud used the word *repression* to refer to an unconscious process in which certain memories are made inaccessible. According to Freud, those memories which are likely to elicit guilt, embarrassment, shame or anxiety are repressed from consciousness as a form of *defence mechanism*. For example, Freud (1901) reported the case of a man who continually forgot what came after the line 'with a white sheet' even though he was extremely familiar with the poem from which the line came. Freud found that the man associated 'white sheet' with the linen sheet that is placed over a corpse. An overweight friend of the man's

had recently died from a heart attack, and the man was worried that because he was a little overweight, and his grandfather had died of heart disease, the same fate would befall him. For Freud, the apparently innocent forgetting of a line from a poem involved the repression of unconscious conflicts over a fear of death.

Evidence for repression and the 'return of the repressed' has been claimed in a number of studies. Anderson (1995b) has argued that there is little doubt that traumatic experiences can produce memory disturbances, but much more doubt as to whether a Freudian explanation best accounts for them. Certainly, clinical evidence exists which is at least consistent with Freud's theory, an example being *psychogenic amnesia*, that is, amnesia which does *not* have a physiological cause. One common form of this is *event-specific* amnesia, or loss of memory for events occurring over some particular time frame.

Event-specific amnesia was apparently shown by Sirhan Sirhan, the assassin of United States presidential candidate Robert F. Kennedy. Sirhan claimed that he could not recall committing the crime, and it was only under hypnosis that these events were recalled (Bower, 1981). Although it is possible that Sirhan was faking, supporters of a motivated-forgetting theory would argue that he was repressing his memory because to recall his actions would elicit guilt and anxiety about them. Psychogenic amnesia is linked to stressful events, and may last for hours or years. Interestingly, it may disappear as suddenly as it appeared, although the motivated-forgetting theory does not offer a ready explanation as to why this occurs.

Parkin (1993) has pointed out that repressive mechanisms may play a beneficial role in enabling people experiencing *post-traumatic stress disorder* to adjust. For example, Kaminer and Lavie (1991) found that survivors of the Holocaust who were judged to be better adjusted to their experiences were less able to recall their dreams when woken from REM sleep than those judged to be less well adjusted. As Parkin notes, though, when the term 'repression' is used, it does not necessarily imply a strict Freudian interpretation. Instead, Parkin sees the use of the word as:

'simply acknowledging that memory has the ability to render part of its contents inaccessible as a means of coping with distressing experiences' and that 'the mechanism by which memory achieves this . . . is an elusive one'.

A survey conducted by the British Psychological Society (1995) points to a similar view as regards *recovered memories* concerning child sexual abuse. One difficulty with accepting recovered memories as literal interpretations of past events is that they might have (supposedly) happened at a very early age, when experience is not verbalised as it is later on in life. Child sexual abuse which occurs before the age of four and doesn't continue beyond that age might not be retrievable in a narrative (describable in words) form. Very early memories are implicit rather than explicit and are reflected in behaviour outside conscious awareness. This means that we don't need repression to explain the 'forgetting' of childhood experiences, but it also implies that some recovered memories could be either false or inaccurate.

A survey of 810 chartered psychologists indicated that 90 per cent believed recovered memories to be sometimes or 'essentially' correct, a very small percentage believed that they are always correct, about 66 per cent believed that they are possible, and 14 per cent believed that one of their own clients has experienced false memories (BPS, 1995). Readers interested in a detailed consideration of what has been termed *false memory syndrome* are directed to Toon et al. (1996).

Distortion and decay theories of forgetting

THE GESTALT THEORY OF FORGETTING

The Gestalt theory of forgetting (which is also known as *systematic distortion of the memory trace*) is closely related to the Gestalt theory of perception (see Chapter 1). According to this theory, memories undergo *qualitative changes* over time rather than being lost completely, and become distorted towards a 'better', more regular, symmetrical form (that is, they are distorted in the direction of 'good form'). A number of studies have

claimed to support this theory, mainly using participants' reproduction by drawing of material seen earlier (e.g. Wulf, 1922; Irwin and Seidenfeld, 1937; James, 1958). Such studies have supposedly shown that genuine changes in memory occur with the passage of time.

However, several researchers (e.g. Baddeley, 1968) have found that research supporting the Gestalt position can be explained in terms of experimental artefacts and biases (such as the supposed changes in the memory trace actually being due to a limitation in participants' ability to accurately draw the figures they had seen). Despite the work that has gone into it, Baddeley (1976) has concluded that the Gestalt theory of forgetting has proved to be 'both experimentally and theoretically sterile'.

DECAY THEORY OF FORGETTING

Decay (or *trace decay*) theory is essentially an attempt to explain why forgetting increases with time. The ancient Greek philosopher Plato advanced an early version of this theory when he likened the formation of a memory to the fresh imprint on a seal of wax. In the same way that wax loses it shape over time, so, argued Plato, do memory traces. Initially, memory traces are held to lose their sharp detail. Eventually, they are thought to fade beyond recognition.

Clearly, memories must be stored somewhere, the most obvious location being the brain. Presumably, some sort of structural change occurs when learning takes place, this change being called the *engram*. According to decay theory, metabolic processes occur over time which degrade the engram (unless the engram is maintained by repetition and rehearsal), and the consequence of this is that the memory contained within it is no longer available.

Hebb (1949) argued that whilst learning is taking place, the engram which will eventually be formed is very delicate and liable to disruption. Hebb called the developing engram an *active trace*. With learning, the engram grows stronger until a permanent engram is formed through neurochemical and neuroanatomical changes. Hebb called this the *structural trace*. The active trace corresponds roughly to STM, and forgetting from STM is held to be due to the disruption of the active trace. Although Hebb himself did not apply the idea of decay to LTM, other researchers have argued that it can explain forgetting from LTM if it is assumed that decay occurs through *disuse*. So, if certain knowledge or skills are not used or practised for long periods of time, the engram corresponding to them will eventually decay away (Loftus and Loftus, 1980).

There is, however, evidence to indicate that even if they are not practised, certain motor skills (such as driving a car or playing the piano) are not lost. Bahrick's (1984) study (which we described in Chapter 9) is evidence of this, as is a study reported by Bahrick and Hall (1991) who showed that even if people haven't used something like algebra for years, it can be remembered *if* they follow a 'refresher' course in it at college. Additionally, the ability of a delirious person to remember a foreign language not spoken since childhood also testifies against a simple 'decay through disuse' explanation of forgetting.

One study which has been used as support for the role of decay in forgetting from STM is that conducted by Peterson and Peterson (1959) which was described in Chapter 7 (see page 85) when we considered the duration of STM. If decay did occur in STM, then we would expect to find poorer recall of information with the passage of time, which is exactly what the Petersons reported. However, the difficulty with the Petersons' study in particular, and decay theory in general, is that other possible effects need to be excluded before an account based on decay can be accepted. As we will see in the following sections, the data obtained by the Petersons are open to at least two alternative explanations.

An ideal way to study the role of decay in forgetting would be to have people receive information and then do *nothing* physical or mental for a period of time. If recall was poorer with the passage of time, it would be reasonable to suggest that decay had occurred. Such an experiment is, of course, an impossibility. However, Jenkins and Dallenbach (1924) were the first to attempt to *approximate* it. These researchers had participants learn a list of ten nonsense syllables. In one condition, participants then went to sleep immediately, a condition approximating to the ideal 'do nothing' state. Other participants continued with their normal activities. After varying intervals of one, two, four or eight hours, participants were tested for their recall of the syllables.

As Figure 10.1 shows, Jenkins and Dallenbach found that the period spent asleep did not result in greater forgetting, which led them to conclude that:

'forgetting is not so much a matter of decay of old impressions and associations as it is a matter of interference, inhibition or obliteration of the old by the new'.

Although some data exist which indicate that neurological breakdown occurs with age and disease (an example being Alzheimer's disease), it is generally accepted that the major cause of forgetting from LTM is *not* neurological decay (Solso, 1995).

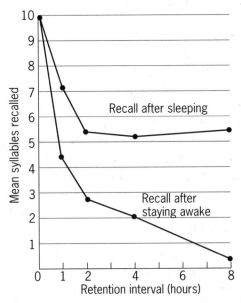

Figure 10.1   Mean number of syllables recalled by participants in Jenkins and Dallenbach's experiment.

Interference theory of forgetting

According to interference theory, forgetting is influenced more by what we do before or after learning than by the passage of time. Two types of interference can be identified. In *retroactive interference* (or *retroactive inhibition*), later learning interferes with the recall of earlier learning. Suppose, for example, a person originally learned to drive in a car in which the gears are changed manually. That person then learned to drive a car with an automatic gearing system. When returning to a car with manual gears, the new learning might interfere with the old, resulting in the person

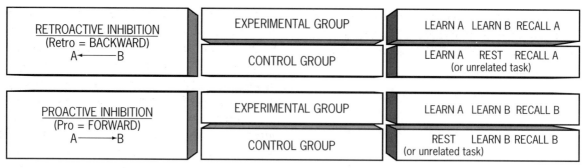

Figure 10.2   Experimental procedures for investigating retroactive and proactive interference.

attempting to drive the car as though it had an automatic gear system.

In *proactive interference* (or *proactive inhibition*), earlier learning interferes with the recall of later learning. Suppose, for example, a person learned to drive in a car in which the indicator lights are turned on using the stalk on the left of the steering wheel, and the windscreen wipers by the stalk on the right. After passing his or her driving test, the person then buys a car in which this arrangement is reversed. Proactive interference would be shown by the windscreen wipers being activated just before the person signalled his or her intention to turn left or right!

Interference theory has been extensively studied in the laboratory using *paired-associates lists*, and the usual procedure for studying interference effects is shown in Figure 10.2.

Usually, the first member of each pair in list A is the same as in list B, but the second member of each pair is different in the two lists. In retroactive interference (RI), the learning of the second list interferes with the recall of the original list (so, as its name indicates, retroactive interference works *backwards* in time). In proactive interference (PI), the learning of the original list interferes with the recall of the later learned second list (so, as its name indicates, proactive interference works *forwards* in time).

Interference has been suggested as an alternative way of explaining the data obtained by Peterson and Peterson (1959) (see page 85). Having noted that the Petersons administered two *practice trials* before their test, Keppel and Underwood (1962) looked at what happened after these trials in the actual experiment. As Figure 10.3 shows, they found that the first two trials did have an

effect on those that followed, in that there was no evidence of forgetting on the first trial, some on the second and yet more on the third. Other researchers (e.g. Baddeley and Scott, 1971) have shown that forgetting *can* occur on the first trial, an observation which supports decay theory. However, Keppel and Underwood's finding that performance did not decline until the second trial does suggest that proactive interference did occur in the Petersons' experiment.

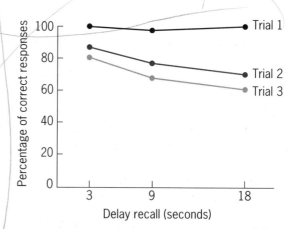

Figure 10.3   Mean percentage of items correctly recalled on trials 1, 2 and 3 for various delay times (based on Keppel and Underwood, 1962).

It has been suggested that the most important cause of proactive interference is interference with the process of *retrieval*. Like Keppel and Underwood, Wickens (1972) found that participants became increasingly poor at retaining information in STM on successive trials. However, when the *category* of information was changed, participants performed as well as they had done on the first list. So, performance with lists of numbers was increasingly poor over trials, but if the task was changed to lists of letters, it improved. This phenomenon is called *release from proactive inhibition*, and is shown in Figure 10.4.

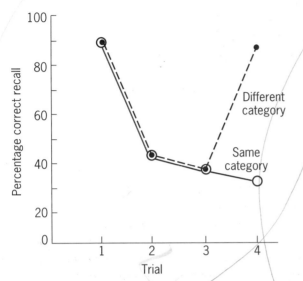

Figure 10.4   The effect on recall of being presented with a list of stimuli from a different category.

Gardiner et al.'s (1972) experiment showed that when people are told about a change of category *either before or after it occurs*, release from proactive inhibition occurs. This is important because it indicates that the major cause of proactive interference must be interference with the retrieval of information from STM rather than with its storage, since telling participants about a change in category *after* they have heard the words cannot possibly affect the way these words are stored in STM. It can, however, affect the way in which participants attempt to retrieve these words.

The strongest support for interference theory comes from studies conducted in the laboratory. However, Baddeley (1990) has pointed out that in such studies, learning does not occur in the same way as it does in the real world. Our learning of potentially interfering material in the real world is spaced out over time. In the laboratory, though, learning is artificially compressed in time, and this maximises the likelihood of interference occurring. What this suggests is that laboratory studies of interference lack *ecological validity*.

Additionally, Solso (1995) has pointed out that most laboratory-based investigations supportive of interference theory have used nonsense syllables as the stimu-

lus material, and that when meaningful material is used, interference is more difficult to demonstrate. When people have to learn the response 'bell' to the stimulus 'woj', the word 'bell' is not actually learned in the laboratory since it is already part of people's *semantic memory*. Rather, what has to be learned is that 'bell' is the response word to 'woj', and this is stored in *episodic memory*, since the learning is taking place in a specific laboratory situation. Solso suggests that experimental studies of interference are largely based on episodic memory and hence that interference effects apply only to that type of LTM. Since semantic memory is much more stable and structured, it is also much more resistant to the effects of interference.

As we mentioned above, the strongest support for interference theory has been obtained in laboratory studies of it. However, there is some evidence of interference outside of the laboratory. For example, Barry Gunter and his colleagues (1980) found that if participants viewed successive television news broadcasts, they experienced retroactive interference, whilst Chandler (1989) has shown that if students have to study more than one subject in the same time frame, subjects that are as dissimilar as possible should be chosen to minimise the possibility of interference occurring (see Chapter 11, page 135). A tragic example of the effects of apparent interference is described in Box 10.1.

Box 10.1   Some devastating effects of apparent interference

In August 1995, a light aircraft crashed at Fyfield, near Andover, Hampshire, shortly after take-off from Thruxton airfield. An official enquiry into the accident suggested that the pilot may have pulled the wrong control. The pilot, who had little training on the Beechcraft Baron aircraft, sounded a warning five minutes after take-off, reporting that a door was open. He told air-traffic controllers he would make one circuit and land. However, as he tried to pull the aircraft around, it banked sharply and dived, crashing onto the edge of a cornfield, 30 yards from a children's playing field. Witnesses saw the pilot struggling to steer the dual-controlled plane away from houses shortly before it crashed.

No evidence of engine failure was found, and investigators believe that the pilot, unfamiliar with the controls, inadvertently pulled the wrong lever. The investigators noted that the pilot had

319 hours' flying experience, but had flown only 34 hours in the Beechcraft Baron aircraft. According to the report from the Air Accidents Investigation Branch:

'the Beechcraft Baron is unusual in that the engine controls are grouped in the order propellers, throttles and mixtures in pairs from left to right. The conventional layout is throttles, propellers and mixtures from left to right'.

Quite probably, the pilot attempted to throttle back the engines to reduce acceleration. However, the lever he believed to control the throttle actually controlled the propellers, resulting in a far greater reduction in power than expected.

Displacement theory of forgetting

One way in which forgetting might occur in a memory system with *limited capacity* is through displacement of material. Presumably, when the system is 'full', the oldest material in it is displaced (or 'pushed out') by incoming and new material. The possibility that displacement occurs in forgetting from STM was explored by Waugh and Norman (1965) using what is known as the *serial probe task*. In this, participants were presented with 16 digits at the rate of either one per second or four per second. One of the digits (the 'probe') was then repeated and participants had to say which digit *followed* the probe.

Presumably, if the probe digit was one of the digits presented at the beginning of the list, the probability of recalling the digit that followed would be small, because later digits would have displaced earlier ones from the limited capacity STM system. However, if the probe digit was one of the digits presented towards the end of the list, the probability of recalling the digit that followed it would be high, since the last digits to be presented would still be available in STM.

As Figure 10.5 shows, Waugh and Norman found that when the number of digits following the probe was small, recall was good. However, when the number of digits following the probe was large, recall was poor, a

finding which is consistent with the idea that the earlier digits have been displaced by the later ones. Interestingly, Waugh and Norman also found that recall was generally better with the faster (four-per-second) presentation rate, a finding which could be taken as support for decay theory. Since less time had elapsed between presentation of the digits and the probe in the four-per-second condition, there would be less opportunity for those digits to have decayed away.

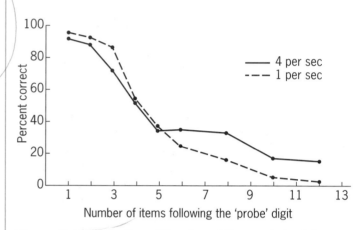

Figure 10.5   Data from Waugh and Norman's serial probe experiment.

Waugh and Norman's findings were later confirmed by Shallice (1967), although Shallice found that elapsed time was *less* important than the number of subsequent items in determining the probability of recall. Despite the evidence favouring displacement theory, it is far from clear that displacement refers to a process distinct from either decay or interference or, indeed, some combination of the two.

Retrieval-failure theory of forgetting

According to retrieval-failure theory, memories cannot be recalled because the correct *retrieval cues* are not being used. If the correct retrieval cues can be used, the individual should be capable of remembering the information. The role of retrieval cues in the recall of information was demonstrated by Brown and McNeill (1966) in their investigation of the *tip-of-the-tongue phenomenon*, in which we know that we know something but cannot retrieve it at that particular point in time. William James (1890) described the phenomenon most eloquently:

> 'Suppose we try to recall a forgotten name. The state of our consciousness is peculiar. There is a gap therein: but no mere gap. It is a gap that is intensely active. A sort of wraith of the name is in it, beckoning us in a given direction, making us at moments tingle with a sense of closeness, and then letting us sink back without the longed for term'.

In Brown and McNeill's study, participants were given dictionary definitions of unfamiliar words and asked to provide the words themselves. Most of the participants either knew the word or knew that they did not know it. Some, however, were sure they knew the word but could not recall it (it was on the tip of their tongue). About half of these participants could give the first letter of the word and the number of syllables in it, and they often offered words which sounded like the word or had a similar meaning to the word. Brown and McNeill's findings suggest that the required words were in memory, but the absence of a correct retrieval cue prevented them from being recalled. An example of a tip-of-the-tongue test is shown in Box 10.2.

Box 10.2   An example of a tip-of-the-tongue test

For each of the six examples below, try and identify the word that fits each definition. You may find that you cannot think of the word yet you know that it is on the verge of coming to you. When a word is on the tip-of-your-tongue, see if you can prompt its retrieval by writing down (1) the number of syllables in the word, (2) the initial letter of the word, (3) words which sound similar, and (4) words of similar meaning.

1 A small boat used in the harbours and rivers of Japan and China, rowed with a scull from the stern, and often having a sail.

2 A navigational instrument used to measure angular distances at sea, especially the altitude of the sun, moon and stars.

3 Favouritism, especially governmental patronage extended to relatives.

4 The common cavity into which the various ducts of the body open in certain fishes, reptiles, birds and mammals.

5 An opaque, greyish, waxy secretion from the intestines of the sperm whale, sometimes found floating on the ocean or lying on the shore, and used in making perfumes.

6 An extending portion of a building, usually semicircular with half a dome; especially the part of a church where the altar is located.

(based on Brown and McNeill (1966) and adapted from Carlson (1987); the answers are given on page 125)

Other evidence supporting retrieval failure theory comes from a study conducted by Tulving and Pearlstone (1966). These researchers read participants lists of varying numbers of words (12, 24 or 48 words) containing categories of one, two or four exemplars per list along with the category name. Participants were instructed only to try to remember the exemplars (such as category name = animal, exemplar = dog). Half of the participants free-recalled the words and wrote these down on a blank piece of paper. The other half were provided with the category names. As can be seen in Figure 10.6, the results showed that those participants given the category names recalled significantly more words, and that the difference was most pronounced on the 48-item list. However, when the category names were provided for those who had written their responses on the blank sheet of paper, their recall

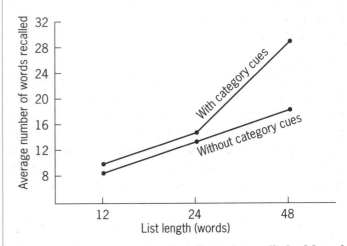

Figure 10.6   Average number of words recalled with and without category cues in Tulving and Pearlstone's (1966) experiment.

improved, indicating that the category names helped to make information that was available for recall accessible.

Tulving (1968) has also shown that retrieval failure offers a better account of forgetting from LTM than either decay or interference theory. In Tulving's experiment, participants were shown a list of words and then asked to write down as many as they could remember in any order they liked. Later, and without being presented with the list again or seeing the words they had written down previously, participants were again asked to recall as many of the words as they could. Even later, Tulving asked the participants to once again recall the words on the original list. A (hypothetical) set of results produced by a participant is shown in Table 10.1.

Table 10.1   Hypothetical results of Tulving's experiment (1968)

Trial 1	Trial 2	Trial 3
Table	Table	Table
Driver	Escalator	Driver
Escalator	Apple	Escalator
Apple	Railway	Apple
Railway	Pen	Pen
Pen		Fountain

As Table 10.1 shows, the same words were *not* recalled across the three trials. This finding is difficult for decay theory to explain, because that theory would not predict the recall of a word on trial 3 if it was not recalled on either trial 1 or 2. The fact that some words were recalled on the second and third trials, but not on the first, is difficult for interference theory to explain because, as Clifford (1991) has noted, it would have to be assumed that what had been unlearned on trial 1 was learned on trial 2 and/or trial 3. Retrieval-failure theory, however, can explain these findings by arguing that different retrieval cues were in operation across the three trials (perhaps, in the example shown in Table 10.1, 'pen' somehow acted as a retrieval cue for 'fountain' on trial 3 but not on trial 1 or 2). Unfortunately, the precise way in which retrieval cues act is not known (Hampson and Morris, 1996) although researchers have attempted to identify when successful recall will occur.

According to Tulving and Thomson's (1973) *encoding specificity principle*, recall improves if the same cues are present during recall as during the original learning. Tulving (1974) used the term *cue-dependent forgetting*

to refer jointly to *context-dependent* and *state-dependent* forgetting. Forgetting or, more accurately, being unable to retrieve something from memory, is held to be a failure of retrieval cues to match the encoded nature of items in memory (Solso, 1995). Environmental or contextual variables represent *external cues* whilst psychological or physiological *states* represent *internal cues.*

One study supporting the idea of context-dependent forgetting was conducted by Abernathy (1940). In his experiment, one group of participants learned and then recalled material in the same room, whilst a second group learned material in one room but recalled it in another. Abernathy found that recall was better in the first than second group of participants, a finding which has also been obtained by some other researchers (e.g. Smith, 1979). Similarly, Godden and Baddeley (1975) had divers learn word lists either on land or 15 feet under water and then tested their recall in either the same or a different context. The results showed a 30 per cent decrement when recall was tested in a different context. The researchers also found that cue-dependent forgetting applies only to recall, since when recognition is used, no effects of context are observed.

According to Baddeley (1995), large effects of context on memory are only found when the contexts in which encoding and retrieval occur are very different. Although less marked changes can produce some effects, studies looking at the effects of context on examination performance, other than Abernathy's and Smith's, have *tended* to show few effects of context. Quite possibly, this is because when we are learning, our surroundings are not a particularly *salient* feature of the situation. However, our internal state is more salient, and several studies claim to have found that people's internal state can have a powerful effect on recall. For example, Clark et al. (1987) have argued that victims' inability to recall details of a violent crime may be due at least in part to the fact that recall occurs in a less emotionally aroused state, whilst McCormick and Mayer (1991) have suggested that the important link is between mood and the sort of material being remembered. Thus, we are more likely to remember happy events when we are feeling happy rather than sad.

THE PERMANENCE OF MEMORY

In a number of studies conducted in the 1930s, a Canadian neurosurgeon, Walter Penfield, electrically stimulated the cerebral cortex of conscious and alert patients who were about to undergo brain surgery. Penfield found that stimulation of certain cortical areas seemed to produce a 'memory' in his patients. Although these 'released memories' were not perfectly detailed, Penfield (1969) concluded that 'each succeeding state of consciousness leaves its permanent imprint on the brain'. In 1980, Loftus and Loftus found that 84 per cent of psychologists surveyed by them believed that memories were permanently stored, as did 69 per cent of non-psychologists.

The claim that permanent storage of information occurs and that all forgetting results from the failure to use appropriate retrieval cues is a provocative one. But as Eysenck (1993) has noted, the evidence from Penfield's studies are not particularly supportive of such a claim. For example, of the 520 patients studied by Penfield, only 40 reported the recovery of an apparently long-forgotten memory, and those memories that were recovered were typically far from vivid and detailed. For Eysenck (1993):

'in view of the evidence, it is surprising that the permanent-memory hypothesis remains popular. Part of the reason for its popularity is that none

of the evidence produced in this field disproves the hypothesis. We must also admit that much (or even most) forgetting is cue-dependent rather than trace dependent. However, the fact that there is no compelling evidence at all in favour of the permanent memory hypothesis indicates that we should be careful about aligning ourselves with the 84 per cent of psychologists who agree with it'.

Conclusions

This chapter has considered several psychological explanations of forgetting. Of the various theoretical accounts we have looked at, some are better supported by the evidence than others. Of those theories that have survived experimental investigation, some are better applied to forgetting from STM whilst others are better applied to forgetting from LTM.

Answers to the tip-of-the-tongue test presented in Box 10.2

1 sampan, 2 sextant, 3 nepotism, 4 cloaca, 5 ambergris, 6 apse

SUMMARY

- While **availability** refers to whether or not the material has been stored in the first place, **accessibility** refers to being able to retrieve what has been stored. In terms of the multi-store model, availability mainly concerns STM and the transfer of information from STM into LTM, while accessibility mainly concerns LTM.
- According to Freud's **motivated-forgetting theory**, memories that are likely to elicit guilt, embarrassment, shame or anxiety are made inaccessible through **repression** as a **defence mechanism.**
- According to Anderson, there is little doubt that traumatic experiences can produce memory disturbances (as in **psychogenic amnesia**, one form of which is **event-specific amnesia**). But Freud's theory would have trouble explaining why psychogenic amnesia sometimes disappears as suddenly as it appeared.
- According to Parkin, repression may help people experiencing **post-traumatic stress disorder** to cope, as in better-adjusted survivors of the

- Holocaust being less able to recall their dreams. However, 'repression' does not necessarily imply a strict Freudian interpretation.
- One difficulty with taking **recovered memories** of child sexual abuse literally is that they may relate to a time before memories become retrievable in a narrative form (i.e. describable in words). Because very early memories are implicit (outside conscious awareness), we don't need repression to explain 'forgotten' childhood experiences. By the same token, some recovered memories may be either false or inaccurate (**false memory syndrome**).
- According to the **Gestalt theory of forgetting/systematic distortion of the memory trace**, memories undergo **qualitative changes** over time, becoming distorted in the direction of 'good form'. Despite some apparent empirical support, the findings can often be explained in terms of experimental artefacts and biases, and the theory is of little value.
- **Decay/trace decay theory** tries to explain why

forgetting increases over time. Like wax, memory traces initially lose their sharp detail, then fade beyond recognition. Some sort of structural change occurs in the brain when learning first occurs (the **engram**) and, unless this is maintained by rehearsal, the memory contained within it will cease to be available.

- Hebb argued that the engram at first is very delicate and liable to disruption (an **active trace**) but grows stronger and becomes permanent (the **structural trace**) through neurochemical and neuroanatomical changes. The active trace corresponds roughly to STM, so that forgetting is seen as caused by disruption of the engram.

- Decay can also explain LTM forgetting, on the assumption that decay occurs through **disuse**. However, there is also evidence that certain motor – and other – skills are not lost, even if they are not practised for long periods of time, and the generally accepted view is that the major cause of LTM forgetting is **not** neurological decay.

- Peterson and Peterson's findings that poorer recall of information occurs with the passage of time appears to support the view that decay occurs in STM, but they are open to alternative explanations.

- Jenkins and Dallenbach were the first to try to **approximate** an experiment in which people receive information and then do **nothing** for a period of time by having people go to sleep after learning a list of nonsense syllables. The period spent sleeping did not result in greater forgetting, which led them to conclude that rather than decay, it is interference that is the major cause of forgetting.

- According to **interference theory**, forgetting is influenced more by what we do before or after learning than by the passage of time. In **retroactive interference/inhibition (RI)**, later learning prevents the recall of earlier learning (and so works **backwards**), while in **proactive interference /inhibition (PI)**, earlier learning prevents recall of later learning (and so works **forwards**).

- Interference theory has been extensively studied in the laboratory using **paired-associates lists**. The first member of each pair in list A is usually the same as in list B, but the second member of each pair is different.

- According to Keppel and Underwood, the two **practice trials** used in the Peterson and Peterson study had an effect on subsequent trials, which suggested proactive interference.

- The most important cause of PI may be interference with **retrieval**, as shown by Wickens' partici-pants who became increasingly poor at retaining information in STM on successive trials. But when the **category** of information was changed (from numbers to letters), participants did as well as on the first list (i.e. numbers); this is called **release from PI**.

- Release from PI also occurs when people are told about a change of category **either before or after it occurs**, indicating that interference with retrieval is the crucial factor involved, as opposed to storage.

- While the strongest support for interference theory comes from laboratory studies, where learning is artificially compressed, our learning of potentially interfering material in the real world is spaced out over time. Hence, laboratory studies make interference much more likely to occur and lack **ecological validity**. Nevertheless, there is some evidence of interference in the real world, a particularly tragic example being the fatal crash involving the Beechcraft Baron light aircraft in Hampshire.

- Most laboratory studies also tend to use nonsense syllables rather than meaningful material, which is more resistant to interference. Learning to pair words (already part of **semantic memory (SM)**) with nonsense syllables is stored in **episodic memory (EM)**, and so interference effects apply mainly to EM. SM is more resistant to interference.

- According to **displacement theory**, in a **limited-capacity** system such as STM, the oldest material is pushed out by incoming new material. Using the **serial-probe task**, Waugh and Norman found that when the number of digits following the probe was small, recall was good, while when the number was large, recall was poor. This is consistent with displacement theory. They also produced evidence supportive of decay theory.

- Despite Shallice's confirmation of these findings, it is unclear whether displacement is distinct from either decay or interference; it may be a combination of the two.

- According to **retrieval-failure theory**, memories cannot be recalled because the correct **retrieval cues** are not being used. The role of retrieval cues was demonstrated by Brown and McNeill's study of the **tip-of-the-tongue phenomenon**.

- Tulving and Pearlstone found that when category names were provided as a recall cue, participants recalled significantly more words (exemplars) than participants simply asked to free-recall the exemplars. The difference was most marked on the longest list. When the free-recall participants were provided with the category names, their recall improved, indicating that available information was now being made accessible.

- Tulving asked participants to free-recall a list of words on three separate occasions and found that the same words were **not** recalled across the three trials. According to retrieval-failure theory, different retrieval cues were operating on each trial, and this seems to provide a better account of LTM forgetting than either decay or interference theories.
- According to the **encoding specificity principle**, recall improves if the same cues are present during recall as during the original learning. **Cue-dependent forgetting** refers jointly to **context-dependent** and **state-dependent** forgetting, in which **external cues** (environmental/contextual variables) or **internal cues** (psychological/physiological **states**) respectively fail to match the encoded nature of items in memory.

- Context-dependent forgetting was demonstrated by Abernathy and in Godden and Baddeley's study of divers. However, large context effects are only found when the encoding and retrieval contexts are very different. During learning, our internal state, such as how emotionally aroused we are, may be much more **salient**, which might also explain why victims often fail to recall details of a violent crime.
- Penfield's discovery of 'released memories' when electrically stimulating the cortex led him to conclude that memories are permanently stored, a view shared by a majority of psychologists. However, Penfield's evidence is far from convincing, and Eysenck argues that there is no compelling evidence to support the permanent-memory hypothesis.

11

SOME PRACTICAL APPLICATIONS OF RESEARCH INTO MEMORY

Introduction and overview

As interesting as the various laboratory studies of memory we have discussed in the previous four chapters are, such studies tend, as Hampson and Morris (1996) have noted, to 'minimise many of the features that may be central to our memory in everyday life'. 'Everyday' things that have been researched include the 'mental maps' of the world in which we live that develop through our experiences (e.g. Smith et al., 1994), our memory for medical information (e.g. Ley, 1988), 'prospective memory' or our memory for things we *have* to do rather than things we have done (e.g. Morris, 1992), memories across our lifetimes (e.g. Schuman and Rieger, 1992) and our memory for familiar objects such as coins and postage stamps (e.g. Richardson, 1993).

Other areas that have attracted interest include eyewitness testimony (e.g. Loftus, 1974), strategies for improving memory (e.g. Higbee, 1996) and memory expertise (e.g. Valentine and Wilding, 1994). Limitations of space prevent us from considering all of the various practical applications we have identified. In this chapter, we will confine ourselves to an examination of research findings concerning eyewitness testimony, memory improvement and memory expertise.

Eyewitness testimony

In 1973, the British government established a committee, headed by Lord Devlin, to look at the legal cases in England and Wales that had involved an identification parade. The committee found that of those people who were prosecuted after being picked out from an identification parade, 82 per cent were convicted. Of the 347 cases in which prosecution occurred when eyewitness testimony was the *only* evidence against the defendant, 74 per cent were convicted (Devlin, 1976). Although eyewitness testimony is regarded as being important evidence in legal cases, the evidence that memory is reconstructive has led some researchers to question its usefulness (e.g. Fruzzetti et al., 1992; Wells, 1993; see Figure 11.1).

One example of a miscarriage of justice as a result of eyewitness testimony was the case of Lonnie and Sandy Sawyer. In 1975, the Sawyers were convicted of kidnapping the assistant manager of a department store in North Carolina. Although the brothers maintained their innocence, they were sentenced to between 28 and 40 years in prison, mainly on the testimony of the man who had been kidnapped, Robert Hinson. Hinson only glimpsed his kidnappers before they put on stocking masks, but his testimony was sufficient to convince a jury of the Sawyers' involvement. Two years later, the Sawyers were released from jail after private detectives

Figure 11.1   Eyewitness testimony may not be as useful as we would like.

tracked down one of the men who did commit the kidnapping (Loftus, 1979). Even law-abiding psychologists have been the victims of misidentification, as Box 11.1 shows.

Box 11.1   The dangers of being a psychologist interested in eyewitness testimony

A psychologist in Australia who had appeared in a TV discussion on eyewitness testimony was arrested some time later, picked out in an identity parade by a clearly very distraught woman and told he was being charged with rape. It became clear that the rape had been committed at the same time as he was taking part in the TV discussion. When the psychologist told the police that he had a large number of witnesses including an Assistant Commissioner of Police, the policeman taking the statement replied: 'Yes, and I suppose you've also got Jesus Christ and the Queen of England too!'. It turned out that the woman had been watching the TV programme when the rape had occurred and she had correctly recognised that she had seen the face at the time, but not the circumstances.

The leading researchers in the area of eyewitness testimony are Elizabeth Loftus and her colleagues. As we saw in the previous chapter, memory may involve fiction as well as fact, as a result of our tendency to 'fill in the gaps' of our knowledge or to modify memories so as to match existing schemas. Loftus and her colleagues have posed questions like 'Is eyewitness testimony influenced by people's tendency to reconstruct their memory of events to fit their schemas?', 'Can subtle differences in the wording of a question cause witnesses to remember an event differently?' and 'Can witnesses be misled into remembering things that did not actually occur?' On the basis of numerous studies into eyewitness testimony, Loftus and her colleagues have argued that the evidence given by witnesses in court cases is highly unreliable. The data relating to this claim are considered below.

THE IMPORTANCE OF EYEWITNESS TESTIMONY, EVEN WITH A DISCREDITED WITNESS

In one experiment, Loftus (1974) asked a group of students to judge the guilt or innocence of a man who was accused of robbing a grocer's and murdering the owner and his five-year-old granddaughter (note that

the case was fictitious). On the evidence presented, only nine of the 50 students considered the man to be guilty. Another group of students was presented with precisely the same case, but were also told that an assistant in the store had testified that the accused was the man who had committed the crimes. This resulted in 36 of the 50 students judging the accused to be guilty, suggesting that eyewitness testimony does influence juror decisions.

A third group of students was presented with the original evidence and the eyewitness testimony of the assistant. However, this group was told that the eyewitness had been *discredited* by the defence lawyer, who had shown that the shortsighted eyewitness was not wearing his glasses when the crime occurred, and could not possibly have seen the face of the accused from his position in the store. Loftus and her colleagues reasoned that if the students were totally fair in their decisions, about the same number should consider the accused to be guilty as was observed in the first group of students. In fact, 34 of the 50 students judged the man to be guilty, suggesting that a mistaken eyewitness is better than no eyewitness at all.

Wells (1993) has reviewed research which indicates that there are a number of factors concerning suspects that are particularly important in influencing the accuracy of eyewitness testimony. Two of the most important are described in Box 11.2.

Box 11.2   Two important factors influencing the accuracy of eyewitnesses

Race: Errors are more likely to occur when the suspect's race differs from that of the witness's (Brigham and Malpass, 1985). Luce (1974), for example, found that African American, white American and Chinese American participants recognised members of their own race extremely well. However, participants of *all* races were significantly poorer at recognising faces of people of other races. Perhaps this is why we sometimes hear people say 'They all look the same to me' when referring to members of different races. Social psychologists call this phenomenon *the illusion of outgroup homogeneity*.

Clothing: According to Sanders (1984), witnesses pay more attention to a suspect's clothing than to more stable characteristics such as height and facial features. Sanders conducted an experiment in which participants saw a video of a crime in which the criminal wore glasses and a T-shirt. Afterwards, they were asked to select the criminal in an identification parade; the participants were more likely to select a person wearing glasses and a T-shirt. Evidently, criminals are aware of this, since they change their appearance prior to an identity parade (Brigham and Malpass (1985)).

THE EFFECTS OF 'LEADING QUESTIONS' ON EYEWITNESS TESTIMONY

According to Loftus and her colleagues, it is the form of questions that witnesses are asked which mainly influences how they 'remember' what they 'witnessed'. 'Leading questions' are of particular interest because they can introduce new information which can alter a witness's memory of an event. By either their *form* or their *content*, such questions can suggest to a witness the answer that *should* be given. Lawyers, of course, are skilled at deliberately asking such questions, and it is likely that the police also use such questioning when interrogating suspects and witnesses to a crime.

Loftus and Palmer (1974) tested experimentally the effect of changing a single word in certain critical questions on the judgement of speed. Participants were shown a 30-second videotape of two cars colliding, and were then asked several questions about the collision. One group of participants was asked 'About how fast were the cars going when they *hit*?'. For other participants, the word 'hit' was replaced by *smashed, collided, bumped* or *contacted*. These words have very different connotations regarding the speed and force of impact, and this was reflected in the judgements given by the participants. Those who heard the word 'hit' produced an average speed estimate of 34.0 mph. For 'smashed', 'collided', 'bumped' and 'contacted', the average estimates were 40.8 mph, 39.3 mph, 38.1 mph, and 31.8 mph respectively (see Figure 11.2).

Loftus and Palmer wanted to know if memory itself undergoes change as a result of misleading questions or whether the existing memorial representation of the accident is merely being supplemented by the misleading questions. From a theoretical perspective, this is an important issue, since the idea of *memory as reconstruction* is that memory itself is transformed at the time of retrieval, that is, what was originally encoded changes when it is recalled.

(a)

(b)

Figure 11.2   Assessments of speed of crashing vehicles can be influenced by the verb used to describe the impact. While (a) represents 'two cars hitting', (b) represents 'two cars smashing'. Which word is used in a question about speed can influence people's estimates of how fast the cars were travelling at the time of impact.

This issue was tested in a follow-up experiment in which those participants who had heard the words 'smashed' and 'hit' returned to the laboratory one week after seeing the film. Without the film being seen again, the participants were again asked a series of questions, one of which was whether they remembered seeing *any* broken glass (even though there was none in the film). If 'smashed' really had influenced participants such that they remembered the accident as more serious than it was, then they might also 'remember' details that they did not actually see but which are consistent with an accident occurring at high speed (broken glass being an example, of course).

The results showed that of the 50 participants who were asked about the 'smashing' cars, 16 (32 per cent) reported that they had seen broken glass. Only seven (14 per cent) of the 50 participants who were asked about the 'hitting' cars reported that they had 'seen' broken glass. This finding suggests that the answer to the question about the glass was determined by the earlier question about speed, which had changed what was originally encoded when seeing the film.

In other research, Loftus and her colleagues looked at ways in which 'after-the-fact' information can change memory for an event. For example, Loftus (1975) had participants witness a short videotape of a car travelling through the countryside. Half of the participants were asked 'How fast was the white sports car going while travelling along the country road?' whilst the other half were asked 'How fast was the car going when it passed the barn while travelling along the country road?' The second question, of course, *presupposes* that the car actually passed a barn. In fact, it didn't. A week later, participants were again questioned about what they had seen. Loftus found that of those who had previously answered the question that presupposed there was a barn on the videotape, 17.3 per cent answered 'yes' to the question 'Did you see a barn?'. Only 2.7 per cent of the other participants (who had heard nothing about a barn when previously questioned) claimed to have seen a barn.

Loftus argues that leading questions may not only produce biased answers, but they actually distort memory. In another study, Loftus and Zanni (1975) showed participants a short film depicting a car accident. After seeing the film, each participant answered questions about what they had witnessed. Some of the participants were asked whether they had seen *a* broken headlight whilst others were asked whether they had seen *the* broken headlight. The results showed that those asked about *the* headlight were far more likely to report having seen one than those asked about *a* headlight.

The same effect has been obtained in settings beyond the laboratory. For example, Loftus (1979) staged a fake crime at a busy train station. Two of Loftus's female students left a large bag unattended on a bench, and while they were gone, a male student reached inside the bag, pretended to pull out an object and place it under his coat. He then walked away. When the two females returned, one cried out: 'Oh my God, my tape recorder is missing!'. The two females then began to talk to potential eyewitnesses, most of whom agreed to give them their phone number in case their testimony was needed.

A week later, a student posing as an 'insurance agent' phoned the witnesses and asked them to remember details about what they had seen. The questioning ended with the witness being asked 'Did you see the tape recorder?'. Although there was no tape recorder, more than half of the eyewitnesses 'remembered' seeing it, and most were able to give 'details' about it such as its colour, shape and even the height of the aerial on it. Additionally, most eyewitnesses claimed that they would be able to recognise the thief again.

Loftus and her colleagues believe that the findings of their studies are disturbing, particularly when viewed in the light of what often does happen to eyewitnesses who are questioned by the police, who may introduce incorrect information by asking leading questions. For Loftus and her colleagues, the answer to the question 'are eyewitnesses reliable?' is 'sometimes' at best, and 'no' at worst.

An evaluation of Loftus's research on eyewitnesses

According to Tversky and Tuchin (1989):

'there is now substantial support for the view that misleading information affects memory for the original information'.

However, Loftus's view that memories about what has been witnessed can be changed has been challenged. For example, Bekerian and Bowers (1983) have argued that if witnesses are asked questions that follow the order of events in strict sequence, rather than being asked in the relatively unstructured way employed by Loftus and her colleagues, they are *not* influenced by the bias introduced by subsequent questions. For Baddeley (1995), the 'Loftus effect' is not due to the destruction of the memory trace. Rather, it is due to interfering with its retrieval.

Other researchers (e.g. McCloskey and Zaragoza, 1985) have challenged the claim that eyewitnesses are as unreliable as Loftus claims. Even Loftus has acknowledged that in some cases, such as when misleading information is 'blatantly incorrect', it has no effects on a witness's memory. For example, Loftus

(1979) showed participants colour slides of a man stealing a red purse from a woman's bag. Ninety-eight per cent of those who saw the slides correctly identified the purse as being red, and when they read a narrative description of the event which made reference to a 'brown purse', all but two continued to remember it as red.

This finding suggests that our memory for obviously important information, which is accurately perceived at the time, is not easily distorted, a finding confirmed in studies in which people have witnessed a real (and violent) crime (Yuille and Cutshall, 1986). Cohen (1993) believes that people are more likely to be misled if the false information they are given concerns *insignificant* details which are peripheral to the main event, if the false information is given after a delay (when the memory of the event has had time to fade), and if participants are not aware that they may be deliberately misinformed and so have no reason to distrust the information.

COGNITIVE INTERVIEWS

In order to try to elicit accurate and detailed information from eyewitnesses, an increasing number of police forces are using what Geiselman (1988) has termed the *Cognitive Interview Technique*, which draws on Tulving's research concerning the relationship between encoding and retrieval (see Chapter 10, page 128). The procedures used in the technique are shown in Box 11.3.

Box 11.3   The four procedures of the Cognitive Interview Technique

1 Reinstating the context
This involves the interviewer and interviewee attempting to recreate the context (the surrounding environment, such as the temperature, and the witness's own state) in which the incident occurred before any attempt is made to recall what happened.

2 Reporting the event
Once the context has been recreated, the witness is then required to report any information he or she can remember, even if it is not considered to be important.

3 Recalling the event in a different order
The third step is for the witness to try to recall the events in, say, the reverse order or by starting from whatever was most memorable about the event.

4 Changing perspectives
Finally, the witness is asked to try to recall the event from, say, the perspective of a prominent figure in the event (such as the cashier in the case of a bank robbery), and to think about what the cashier must have seen.

(adapted from Hampson and Morris, 1996)

In a number of studies, Geiselman and his colleagues have shown that the Cognitive Interview Technique does produce significantly better recall than the usual interview techniques employed by the police, a finding which has also been obtained by other researchers (e.g. Roy, 1991).

Despite continued debate about eyewitness testimony, there is little doubt that Loftus and other researchers have shown that our knowledge of the processes involved in memory can be usefully applied in the 'real world'. The report of the Devlin Committee (see page 128), for example, recommended that the trial judge be required to instruct the jury that it is not safe to convict on a single eyewitness testimony alone, unless (a) the circumstances are exceptional (such as the witness being a close friend or relative), or (b) when there is substantial corroborative evidence. The Devlin Committee's safeguards are much stronger than those of the US supreme court, but similar to those of American legal experts (see Gross (1994) for a further discussion of this and other issues in eyewitness testimony).

Improving memory

MNEMONICS

Techniques for aiding recall from memory, which most people consider to be unusual and artificial, are termed mnemonics (the word 'mnemonic' derives from Mnemosyne, the Greek goddess of memory). According to Belezza (1981), mnemonics have two fundamental characteristics. First, they are not inherently connected to the material that has to be learned. Instead, they impose meaning and structure on material that is otherwise not very meaningful and structured. Second, they typically involve adding something to the material to create meaningful associations between what is to be learned and what is already stored in long-term memory.

Mnemonic devices do not therefore simplify information, but make it more elaborate, with the result that more, rather than less, information is stored in memory. However, the additional information makes the material easier to recall, and the mnemonic device organises new information into a cohesive whole so that the retrieval of part of the information ensures the retrieval of the rest of it. As we saw in Chapter 9 (see pages 104–105), the use of mnemonic devices is not new (even though commercial packages promising memory improvement may be), and there is plenty of evidence to suggest that mnemonic devices are not simply limited to the learning of lists of words.

For example, Snowman et al. (1980) taught college students on a 'study skills' course to use the method of loci (see page 104) to remember the central concepts from a 2,200-word passage of prose. As compared with students taught more traditional study skills, the group that used the loci method recalled significantly more ideas from the passage. The method of loci has also been used successfully by special populations such as the blind, brain damaged and elderly (Yesavage and Rose, 1984).

In addition to those we considered in Chapter 9, there are many other mnemonic devices that can be used as aids to recall. One of these was devised by Henry Herdson in the 17th century (Hunter, 1957) and involves imagining numbers as objects. For example, 1 might be imagined as a pencil, 2 as a swan and so on. The items to be remembered are then imagined interacting with their relevant number. For example, if the first item to be remembered was 'clock', an image of a clock with a pencil for the minute hand might be formed.

Higbee (1996) has distinguished between visual mnemonic *systems* (those which use imagery) and verbal mnemonic *techniques*, which make associations with words. Verbal mnemonics include *rhymes* ('In fourteen hundred and ninety-two, Columbus sailed the ocean blue'), *acrostics* (a verse in which the first letters correspond with the material that needs to be remembered, as in 'Richard Of York Gave Battle In Vain' for the colours of the rainbow), *acronyms* (such as HOMES for the five great lakes (Huron, Ontario, Michigan, Erie

and Superior)) and *association* ('my PAL the princiPAL, to distinguish its spelling from principLE as a ruLE).

Other mnemonic methods consist of both a verbal and a visual process (and note that since these are neither 'systems' nor 'techniques', we have used the word 'method' instead). One such method, similar to that devised by Herdson (see above), is the *key-* or *peg-word system* which was introduced to England in the late 19th century by John Sambrook (Paivio, 1979). In this, a rhyme such as 'one is a bun, two is a shoe, three is a tree' and so on is used to associate an object (the key or peg word) with each number in the rhyme. The items to be remembered are then individually paired with a key word by means of a mental image. For example, if the first word to be remembered is 'clock', an image of a bun with a clock face might be formed. For each of the items, the rhyme is recited and the mental image previously formed is 'triggered' with the result that the item is recalled.

A variation on the key- or peg-word method is called the *link-word method*. First systematically studied by Atkinson (1975), the method has been used extensively in the teaching of foreign languages (e.g. Gruneberg, 1992). The method involves initially constructing a concrete link word or words to represent the foreign word to be learned. For example, the Greek word for 'worm' is 'skooleekee'. This could be represented by two words which sound similar, namely 'school' and 'leaky'. Next, a verbal image is formed connecting the link word or words with its English meaning. For example, the learner could picture his or her school leaky and worms falling through the roof. Once the image has been formed, which involves the learner thinking very hard about it for at least ten seconds, the meaning of the Greek word can be obtained by retrieving the link words 'school' and 'leaky' and then the stored image that links these words to 'worm' (see Figure 11.3).

The link-word method appears to be highly effective as a mnemonic method for learning a foreign language (Young, 1971), and it has also been successfully used by medical students to store the names of the numerous things they must remember. Bower (1973) gives an example of a method by which the twelve cranial nerves can be stored:

'At the oil factory (*olfactory nerve*), the optician (*optic*) looked for the occupant (*oculomotor*) of the truck (*trochlear*). He was searching because

Figure 11.3   An example of the link-word method being used to remember the word *skooleekee*, the Greek for 'worm'.

three gems (*trigeminal*) had been abducted (*abducens*) by a man who was hiding his face (*facial*) and ears (*auditory*). A glossy photograph (*glossopharyngeal*) had been taken of him, but it was too vague (*vagus*) to use. He also appeared to be spineless (*spinal accessory*) and hypocritical (*hypoglossal*)'.

OTHER APPROACHES TO MEMORY

IMPROVEMENT

As we saw in Chapter 9, an important factor that influences memory is *context*, and context can taken on many forms. A large number of studies have shown that it is easier to recall an event or experience if we are in the same location or context in which the information was first encoded (Estes, 1972). This would suggest that if we learn material in a particular place, the best way to try and recall that material would be to go to the same place (revising in the examination hall in roughly the position you would expect to be sitting in the examination, perhaps?). At least some evidence suggests that students do perform better if they are tested in the room in which they were taught (Wingfield, 1979), and evidence even exists to suggest that it is helpful to *imagine* that we are in that place when we try to recall information (Smith, 1979).

We also saw in Chapter 9 that researchers have claimed that our *internal state* (our emotions or physiological condition) can act as a context which influences recall. For example, some studies have reportedly shown that when people encode material under the influence of drugs like alcohol and marijuana, recall is better when the intoxicated state is re-created as compared with recall in a non-intoxicated state. The evidence concerning moods is also inconclusive. Some studies appear to have shown that people remember things better when they are in the same mood or emotional state as when the information was encoded (e.g. Eich and Metcalf, 1989), whilst other research has found little evidence of this (e.g. Bower and Mayer, 1985: see also Chapter 9, page 124).

STUDY SKILLS

A number of textbooks (including this one) offer both an introduction and overview to each chapter and a summary of the material that has been covered. Reder and Anderson (1980) found that of two groups of students who spent the same amount of time studying, those who read only the summary of the material remembered more than those who read the whole text, and that this was true when questions were taken directly from the text or required the combination of material and the drawing of inferences! Moreover, the difference was maintained even when the main points to be remembered were underlined for the students reading the whole text. Clearly, we would not wish to advocate reading only the summaries of each chapter in this book, but Reder and Anderson's findings do suggest that summaries can be useful as revision aids.

The findings reported by a number of researchers in this regard have led to the development of study guides designed to help the reader retain as much information as possible from a book. One of the most popular of these is Thomas and Robinson's (1972) *PQ4R method*. In this, the reader begins by **p**reviewing the material to familiarise him/herself with the range of topics covered in a chapter. Next, the reader prepares **q**uestions that focus on key concepts and issues. With these questions in mind, the chapter is then **r**ead, with time being taken to **r**eflect on the meaning of the information and its relation to what is already known. Once the chapter has been read, the reader **r**ecites what has been read, using the questions as reminders (with those parts that are difficult being re-read). Finally, the reader **r**eviews the entire material in his/her mind, again using questions to structure this task.

Some other applications of memory research to studying are summarised in Box 11.4.

Box 11.4   Practical strategies for maximising learning

- **Reduce the material to a manageable amount**
  It is unlikely that every single point in a chapter is important. Therefore, try to reduce the material to its salient points.

- **Impose meaning on the material**
  As we saw in Chapter 8, *elaborative rehearsal* is much more effective than maintenance rehearsal in producing retention. An example would be making something you have read about relevant to your own experiences.

- **Learn the whole**
  Recall tends to be better if material is reviewed as a whole rather than being broken into smaller parts. Only when material is particularly long and complicated is breaking it into segments effective.

- **Use periodic retrieval**
  Instead of passively reading and re-reading material, engage in periodic retrieval to determine if the material has been effectively encoded. If it has not, review the material again.

- **Engage in overlearning**
  Ebbinghaus (see Chapter 7, page 80) found that he could improve his retention of material by repeatedly reviewing it after he had reached 100 per cent accuracy. Once something has been mastered, it should be reviewed at least once or twice.

- **Use study breaks and rewards**
  We can only function so long at maximum efficiency before our concentration begins to wane. Taking a break every so often, and doing something rewarding in between, allows us to return to work refreshed.

- **Space study sessions**
  Two three-hour or three two-hour study sessions usually result in better retention than a single six-hour session.

- **Avoid interference**
  Competing material produces interference effects. If you have to work on two or more subjects in the same time frame, try to make them as dissimilar as possible to reduce pro-active and retroactive interference. Planning study sessions to avoid this possibility is obviously helpful.

- **Use time effectively**
  Try to develop a time management schedule (incorporating spaced study sessions) in which certain times are devoted to study and certain others to leisure. Once the schedule has been constructed, stick to it!

(based on Crooks and Stein, 1991)

Understanding memory expertise

We mentioned some studies of memory expertise in Chapter 9 (see page 105). People with 'supernormal' memories have long been of interest to both the general public and professional psychologists. Two researchers who have been particularly concerned with understanding memory expertise are Elizabeth Valentine and John Wilding (e.g. Wilding and Valentine, 1994; Valentine and Wilding, 1994). One rich source of study for Valentine and Wilding has been the World Memory Championships (the 'Memoriad') which were first staged in 1991. The feats of some of the competitors are truly astonishing. For example, Hideaki Tomoyori was able to recite 40,000 digits of pi in 17 hours and 21 minutes (including 255 minutes for breaks!), whilst one of the feats of the 1993 winner was to recall in correct order 416 playing cards (or eight complete packs).

Valentine and Wilding's research has shown that outstanding performers can be divided into *strategists*, that is, those people who use particular methods to store information (such as the mnemonic techniques we described in the previous section) and *naturals*, who do not (and who appear to have a yet-to-be-understood 'natural ability'). The former tend to perform better on 'strategic' tasks, such as face recognition and the recall of words, whilst the latter tend to perform better on 'non-strategic' tasks, such as the recognition of snow crystals and the temporal order of pictures.

Whilst Valentine and Wilding have also found evidence that some people appear to have a superior memory across a wide range of tasks, other research also indicates that in some 'strategists', performance is confined to tasks for which their methods are best suited (e.g. Biederman et al., 1992). Valentine and Wilding believe that the principles employed by strategic memorisers are those on which normal memory processes are founded, namely *semanticization* (or making the meaningless meaningful), *imagery* and *association*. Strategists, however, use these methods in a conscious and intentional way.

Whilst we know a lot about strategic memory, the study of naturally good memory is in its infancy. Valentine and Wilding believe that progress can be made by looking at the development of natural memory and the possibility of a critical period for its development, the relationship between memory and cognitive abilities such as intelligence, and the neurophysiological and biochemical bases of natural memory. In connection with the neurophysiological and biochemical bases, Valentine and Wilding suggest that

developments in imaging techniques rather than biochemical techniques (such as drugs) may be a more useful way of furthering our understanding of memory expertise.

Conclusions

In this chapter, we have looked briefly at just some of the ways in which our knowledge of human memory has been applied practically. As we have seen, a number of important insights into 'everyday' memory have been obtained. Although such research has been criticised for using methodologies which fall short of those employed in laboratory studies of memory (e.g. Banaji and Crowder, 1989), what Eysenck and Keane (1995) term a 'balance sheet' on the advantages and disadvantages of research into the practical applications of memory research seems to show it to be very much in the black.

SUMMARY

- Laboratory studies of memory tend to minimise many aspects of 'everyday memory'. Those aspects of everyday memory which have been researched include 'mental maps' of the world, memory for medical information, 'prospective memory', memories across our lifetimes, memory for familiar objects, eyewitness testimony, strategies for improving memory and memory expertise.
- The Devlin Committee investigated the role of identification parades as evidence in criminal cases. Even when this was the **only** evidence against the defendant, conviction rates were very high, which is worrying given the reconstructive nature of memory and known miscarriages of justice resulting from eyewitness testimony.
- According to Loftus and her colleagues, the evidence given by witnesses in court cases is highly unreliable. In one experiment, a **discredited** eyewitness influenced the student-jurors to almost the same extent as a non-discredited witness, and both groups were much more likely to find the defendant guilty than jurors given no eyewitness testimony at all. This suggests that a mistaken eyewitness is better than no eyewitness.

- According to Wells, several factors concerning suspects have been shown to influence the accuracy of eyewitness testimony. Errors are more likely to occur when the suspect's **race** differs from the witness's, reflecting **the illusion of outgroup homogeneity. Clothing** also seems to be more influential than height or facial features.
- Loftus believes that **leading questions** are especially important in influencing how eyewitnesses 'remember' what they 'witnessed' because they can introduce new information which can alter memory of the event. Such questions, used by both lawyers and the police, can suggest the answer the witness **should** give, either by their **form** or their **content**.
- Loftus and Palmer showed the effects of changing a single word in certain critical questions concerning the speed of a car that 'hit'/'smashed'/'collided'/'bumped'/'contacted' another. These words have very different connotations regarding speed and force of contact which were reflected in the speed estimates given by different groups of participants.
- The view of **memory as reconstruction** implies

that memory itself, at the time of retrieval, under-goes change as a result of misleading questions. Loftus and Palmer found support for this in a fol-low-up experiment in which participants in the 'smashed' group were more likely to 'remember' having seen broken glass than those in the 'hit' group, despite there being none in the original videotape.

- Loftus also investigated how 'after-the-fact' infor-mation can change memory for an event. Participants who were asked a question which (falsely) **presupposed** that a car passed a barn were more likely, a week later, to claim they had seen a barn as compared with participants whose original question did not make this presupposi-tion.

- A similar effect was found by Loftus and Zanni when they asked questions about **a** or **the** broken headlight. The naturalistic study at a train station produced similar findings when witnesses were asked about 'the tape recorder'.

- Contrary to the claim that there is now substantial support for the view that misleading information can change memory for the witnessed event, Baddeley argues that the 'Loftus effect' is due to interfering with retrieval of the memory trace, not to its destruction.

- According to Bekerian and Bowers, if witnesses are asked questions that follow the sequence of events, rather than in the unstructured way used by Loftus, they are **not** influenced by the bias introduced by subsequent questions.

- The unreliability of witnesses has also been chal-lenged, and Loftus herself has demonstrated that our memory for obviously **significant** details which are accurately perceived at the time is not easily distorted. People are more likely to be mis-led if the false information concerns insignificant details, is delayed, and if they have no reason to believe that they might be misinformed.

- An increasing number of police forces are using Geiselman's **Cognitive Interview technique**. This involves four procedures: **reinstating the context, reporting the event, recalling the event in a different order** and **changing per-spectives**. This technique produces significantly better recall than traditional interviews used by the police.

- Loftus's research has shown that knowledge of memory processes can be usefully applied in the real world. For example, the Devlin Committee report recommended that the trial judge should instruct the jury about the dangers of convicting on the basis of eyewitness testimony unless there is a very good reason for doing so.

- According to Belezza, **mnemonics** are not inher-ently connected to the material that has to be learned but impose meaning and structure on rel-atively meaningless or unstructured material. They also typically involve adding something to the material by way of meaningful associations with what is already stored in LTM.

- This elaboration of material makes it easier to recall by organising it into a cohesive whole, so that retrieving part of it ensures retrieval of the rest. It is not confined to learning lists of words, and the method of loci has been applied in the form of a 'study skills' course to help students remember the central concepts from a lengthy prose passage, as well as with blind, brain dam-aged and elderly people.

- Higbee distinguishes between visual mnemonic **systems** (using imagery) and verbal mnemonic **techniques** (using word associations), such as **rhymes, acrostics, acronyms** and **association**. Other methods combine verbal and visual compo-nents, such as the **key-** or **peg-word system** and the related **link-word method**, which has been widely used in the teaching of foreign languages and by medical students.

- Many studies have shown that it is easier to recall something in the same **context** in which it was originally encoded, such as students being tested in the classroom in which they were taught. Even **imagining** that we are in that place when we try to recall information can help.

- Our **internal state**, such as being under the influ-ence of drugs like alcohol and marijuana, can act as a context influencing recall, but the evidence is inconclusive, as it is in relation to mood or emo-tional state.

- Many textbooks include an introduction and overview to each chapter, plus a summary of the chapter content, as aids to learning. Reder and Anderson found that reading just the chapter summaries can be more useful than reading the whole text.

- A popular form of study guide is Thomas and Robins's **PQ4R method**, in which the reader begins by **p**reviewing the material, followed by preparing **q**uestions that focus on key concepts and issues. The chapter is then **r**ead, with **r**eflec-tion on the meaning of the information, followed by **r**eciting what has been read. Finally, the reader **r**eviews the entire material in his/her mind.

- Other practical strategies for maximising learning include: **reducing the material to a manage-able amount, imposing meaning on the**

material (elaborative rehearsal), learning the whole, periodic retrieval, overlearning, using study breaks and rewards, spacing study sessions, avoiding interference and **using time effectively**.

- People with supernormal memories have long been of interest both to the general public and psychologists. Valentine and Wilding have studied the feats of contestants in the World Memory Championships and have divided outstanding performers into **strategists** and **naturals**. The former use **semanticization**, **imagery** and **association**, the basic principles of normal memory processes.

- Less is known about naturally good memory than about strategic memory. There may be a critical period for its development, and it would be useful to know how it is related to cognitive abilities, such as intelligence. Studying the neurophysiological and biochemical bases of natural memory through imaging techniques is another useful way of increasing our understanding of **memory expertise**.

PART 3
Language and thought

DESCRIBING LANGUAGE DEVELOPMENT

Introduction and overview

Until recently, the study of language was largely the domain of *linguistics*. Linguistics is an area of study concerned primarily with the *structure* of language – the sounds that compose it, their relation to words and sentences, and the rules which govern such relations. In the last 20 or so years, however, psychologists have become interested in language from the perspective of how it develops, whether it is unique to humans, and how it is related to learning, memory and thought.

The 'marriage' between psychology and linguistics is called *psycholinguistics*, a discipline which studies the perception, understanding and production of language, together with the development of these activities. In this and the chapters that follow, we will look at some of the major issues concerning language. Our aim in this chapter is to look at the course of language development in humans. We will begin, however, by looking at what language is and what its major components are.

What is language?

According to the psycholinguist Roger Brown (1965), language is an arbitrary set of symbols:

'which, taken together, make it possible for a creature with limited powers of discrimination and a limited memory to transmit and understand

an infinite variety of messages and to do this in spite of noise and distraction'.

Whilst other species are able to *communicate* with each other (see Chapter 14), they can do so only in a limited way, and it is, perhaps, the 'infinite variety of messages' part of Brown's definition that sets humans apart from non-humans. For example, wild chimpanzees use over 30 different vocalisations to convey a large number of meanings, and repeat sounds in order to intensify their meaning. However, they do not string these sounds together to make new 'words' (Calvin, 1994). As we will see in Chapter 14, the claims that chimpanzees are capable of using language are based largely, and until recently, on *deliberate training*. In humans, language is mastered spontaneously and quite easily within the first five years of life.

In a later definition of language, Brown (1973) pointed out that humans do not simply learn a repertoire of sentences but:

'acquire a rule system that makes it possible to generate a literally infinite variety of sentences, most of them never heard from anyone else'.

Psycholinguists call the rule system *grammar* (or *mental grammar*). However, for psycholinguists, grammar is much more than the parts of speech we learn about in school. For them, grammar is concerned with the description of language, the rules which determine how a language 'works', and what governs our patterns of speech (Jackendoff, 1993).

The major components of grammar

Grammar consists of *phonology, semantics* and *syntax* as shown in Figure 12.1.

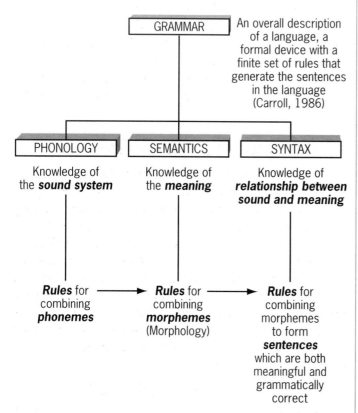

Figure 12.1   The major components of grammar (adapted from Gross, 1996).

PHONOLOGY

Phonologists are concerned with the sound system of a language, that is, what counts as a sound and what constitutes an acceptable sequence of sounds. Basic speech sounds are called *phones* or *phonetic segments* and are represented by enclosing symbols inside square brackets. For example, [p] is the initial phone in the word 'pin'. Different languages have different numbers and combinations of these basic sounds. Some languages have as few as 15 distinguishable sounds and others as many as 85. The English language has some 46 phones (Solso, 1995).

Although all phones are different, only those which affect the meaning of what is being said matter. For example, the [p] phone can be pronounced slightly differently each time without changing the perception of the 'p' in 'pin'. However, the difference between [p] and [d] does matter because that difference alone can lead to two words with different meanings (such as 'pin' and 'din'). Because [p] and [d] cannot be interchanged without changing a word's meaning, they belong to different functional classes of phones called *phonemes*.

Phonemes or *phonological segments* are a language's functionally important classes of phones. The phones [p] and [d] belong to the different phonemes /p/ and /d/. As well as differing in terms of the number of phones, languages also differ in terms of the number of phonemes they have. For example, [l] and [r] belong to different phonemes in English, but not in Japanese (hence our mirth when asked if we want 'flied lice' with our meal). *Phonological rules* constrain the permitted sequence of phonemes. For example, 'port' is an *actual* sequence of phonemes, 'plort' is a *possible* sequence, but 'pbort' is a *prohibited* sequence in English.

In themselves, phonemes have no meaning and are just sounds, and they correspond roughly to the vowels and consonants of a language's alphabet. However, and as is the case with English, languages can have more phonemes than letters in the alphabet (see above). The reason for this is that some letters, such as the vowel 'o', can be pronounced differently (as is the case with 'hop' and 'hope'). The development of speech sounds continues for several years after birth (see page 142) and most children *recognise* sounds in adult speech before they can *produce* them. So, in response to the instruction: 'I am going to say a word two times and you tell me which time I say it right and which time I say it wrong: *rabbit, wabbit*', a child might reply: '*Wabbit* is wight and *wabbit* is wong', indicating that the 'r' sound can be recognised but not yet produced (Dale, 1976).

SEMANTICS

Although meaningless in themselves, phonemes are important for meaning. Semantics (from the Greek 'sema' meaning 'sign') is the study of the meaning of language, and can be analysed at the level of *morphemes* and *sentences*. Morphemes are the basic units of meaning in a language and consist mainly of *words*. Other morphemes are *prefixes* (letters attached to the beginning of a word, such as 'pre' and 're') and *suffixes* (letters attached to the end of a word, such as 's' to make a plural). The plural 's' is a morpheme which is 'bound', that is, it only takes on meaning when it is attached to other morphemes. However, most morphemes are 'free', that is, they have meaning when they stand alone, as most words have. Single words, however, have only a limited meaning and are usually combined into longer strings of phrases and sentences, the other level of semantic analysis.

SYNTAX

Syntax (from the Greek 'syntassein' meaning 'to put together') refers to the rules for combining words into phrases and sentences. Although often taken to be the same as grammar, syntax is, as we have seen, only one part of it. One example of a *syntactic rule* is word order. This has great significance for understanding language development and, as we will see in Chapter 14, for evaluating the claim that non-humans can acquire language. Clearly, the sentences 'The dog bit the postman' and 'The postman bit the dog' have very different meanings, and a competent language user will recognise this.

Another example of a syntactic rule occurs in the sentence 'The dog chased the . . . . . .' In English, only a noun can complete this sentence. Some sentences may be syntactically correct but have no semanticity. For example, 'The player scored a goal' and 'The goal post scored a banana' are both syntactically correct, but one has much more meaning than the other. A sentence like 'Breakfast English full enjoy I a' breaks syntactic rules and is also meaningless. From these examples, then, we can see that syntax and semantics are closely related, but distinct. Also, whilst sentences have sounds *and* meanings, syntax refers to the *structures* which relate the two. We shall return to psycholinguistics in the following chapter when we look at theories which attempt to explain language development.

Stages in the development of language

For many psychologists, language development follows a universal timetable, that is, regardless of their language or culture, all children are believed to pass through the same sequence of stages at approximately the same ages (although there may be differences between children with respect to the rate of their development). Whilst this belief stresses the role of *maturation*, environmental factors are also necessary in that children can only come to speak a language if they are exposed to it. The claim that children are *programmed* to develop language if exposed to it is one of the competing theoretical views that we will examine in the following chapter.

It is generally agreed that there are three major stages in language development. These are the *pre-linguistic stage* (0–12 months), the *one-word stage* (12–18 months) and the *stage of two-word sentences*. This third stage is divided into two sub-stages, these being *stage 1 grammar* (18–30 months) and *stage 2 grammar* (30 months and beyond).

THE PRE-LINGUISTIC STAGE (0–12 MONTHS)

In the first year of life, babies are essentially pre-linguistic. They make various sounds with their vocal organs (including crying) long before they can talk. Crying tends to dominate in the first month of life, with parents gradually learning to discriminate between the various cries (Gustafson and Harris, 1990). By one month of age, babies are able to distinguish between phonemes (such as 'ba' and 'pa') and other sounds, even though these may be physically and acoustically almost identical (Aslin et al., 1983). Quite possibly, this perceptual ability (which is called *categorical speech perception*) is innate (see Chapter 13).

At about six weeks of age, *cooing* begins. These sounds are associated with pleasurable states and do not occur when babies are hungry, tired or in pain. Although vowel sounds may be produced at this age, these are different from those that will later be made and from which the first words will be formed. This is because the baby's oral cavity and nervous system are not sufficiently mature to enable it to produce the sounds necessary for speech.

The major development in the first year of life is *babbling*, which usually begins between six and nine months. In this, phonemes are produced and take the form of combinations of consonants and vowels (such as *ma* and *da*). These may be repeated to produce *reduplicated monosyllables* (such as *mama* and *dada*). Although these are very different from the earlier cooing sounds, they have no meaning (despite the claim of parents that their child is trying to communicate some message).

Babbling and pre-babbling vocalisations differ in two main ways. First, babies spend more time making noises, especially when *alone* in their cots (a phenomenon called *spontaneous babbling*), and they seem to enjoy exercising their voices for the sake of it. To borrow from Tartter (1986), they:

'appear to be playing with the sounds, enjoying the tactile and auditory feel of vocalisation'.

Second, babbling has intonational patterns, just as speech has, with rising inflections and speech-like rhythms. By 11 to 12 months, syllables are often produced over and over again (as in *dadadada*), a phenomenon called *echolalia* (this term is also used to refer to the repeating back of other people's speech, as occurs, for example, in autism).

Because babbling occurs at around the same age in all babies, regardless of their culture or whether the baby is deaf and its parents deaf-mute, its onset is probably based on maturation. However, since smiling, soft sounds and pats on the abdomen can all increase the frequency of babbling, experience can play a role in modifying it (Rheingold et al., 1959).

Babies initially produce only a few phonemes, but within a short period almost every available phoneme is produced, whether or not it is a phoneme in what will become the baby's native language. Like babbling, the onset of this *phonemic expansion* is probably maturational. At around nine or ten months, *phonemic contraction* begins, and phoneme production is restricted to those used in the baby's native language, a restriction which is probably based on the baby's sampling of phonemes used in its 'linguistic environment'. Thus, babies whose native languages will be different can be distinguished on the basis of the sounds they produce. Additionally, deaf babies usually *stop* babbling at around nine or ten months, presumably because of the lack of feedback from their own voice.

Whilst phoneme production is now restricted to those necessary for production of the baby's native language, this does not mean that *all* phonemes have been mastered. By two and a half years of age, only about 60 per cent of the phonemes used in English are mastered, and complete mastery will not be achieved until around the age of seven.

ONE-WORD STAGE

Typically, children produce their first word at around the age of one, although there is considerable variability in this (Rice, 1989). Babies do not, of course, suddenly switch from babbling to the production of words. Rather, the two merge, and non-words (or *jargon*) continue to be produced for up to another six months. The baby's first words involve only a few phonemes, a hardly surprising finding given that they have come shortly after phonemic contraction.

These first words (or articulate sounds) are often invented, and not like 'adult words' at all. Scollon (1976) has defined a word as 'a systematic matching of form and meaning'. On this definition, 'da' is a word if it is consistently used to refer to a doll, since the same sound is being used to label the same thing or kind of thing, and there is a clear intention to communicate.

As Barrett (1989) has noted, though, an infant's earliest words are usually *context bound* in nature, and are produced only in very limited and specific situations or contexts in which particular actions or events occur. For example, Barrett (1986) reports the case of an infant who, at least at first, only produced the word 'duck' whilst hitting a toy duck off the edge of a bath. The word was never used in any other context.

Barrett has argued that an infant's first words often do not serve a communicative purpose as such. Rather, because they typically occur as accompaniments to the occurrence of particular actions or events (as in the case above) they function as 'performatives'. The utterance of some words may, as Barrett's term 'performatives' suggests, be more like the performance of a ritualised action than the expression of a lexical meaning to another person. However, words seem to have either an *expressive function*, in that they communicate internal states (such as pleasure and surprise) to others, or a *directive function*, in which the behaviour of others is directed (by, for example, requesting or obtaining and directing attention).

The one-word stage is also characterised by the use of *holophrases*. In holophrastic speech, a single word (such as 'milk') is used to convey a much more complex message (such as 'I want some more milk' or 'I have spilt my milk'). Because holophrases are accompanied by gestures and tone of voice to add full meaning to an individual word, they may be seen as precursors of later, more complex sentences (Greenfield and Smith, 1976). They are, however, dependent upon the recipient of the holophrase making the 'correct' interpretation.

The kinds of words that babies acquire were studied by Nelson (1973). Nelson identified six categories and calculated the percentage of the babies' first 50 words (typically acquired by 19 to 20 months) that fell into each category. These are shown in Table 12.1.

Table 12.1 Nelson's six categories and the percentage of children's first 50 words falling into each of them

1	*Specific nominals.* Names for unique objects, people or animals (14 per cent).
2	*General nominals.* Names for classes of objects, people or animals, e.g. 'ball', 'car', 'milk', 'doggie', 'girl', 'he', 'that' (51 per cent).
3	*Action words.* Describe or accompany actions or express or demand attention, e.g. 'bye-bye', 'up', 'look', 'hi' (13 per cent).
4	*Modifiers.* Refer to properties or qualities of things, e.g. 'big', 'red', 'pretty', 'hot', 'all gone', 'there', 'mine' (9 per cent).
5	*Personal-social words.* Say something about a child's feelings or social relationships, e.g. 'ouch', 'please', 'no', 'yes', 'want' (8 per cent).
6	*Function words.* Have only grammatical function, e.g. 'what', 'is', 'to', 'for' (4 per cent).

(taken from Gross (1996))

On the basis of her findings, Nelson argued that it is not just the amount of exposure to objects and words that is important in the acquisition of words. Rather, given that specific and general nominals and action words make up the vast majority of those produced, it is the child's active involvement within its environment that determines many of its first words.

We should note that children *understand* more words than they can produce. For example, a child who uses 'bow-wow' to refer to all small animals will nonetheless pick a picture of a dog rather than any other animal when asked to select a 'bow-wow' (Gruendel, 1977). The child's *receptive vocabulary* (the words that can be understood) is therefore much bigger than its *expressive vocabulary* (the words that are used in speech).

Even before the age of two, children begin acquiring words at the rate of about 20 per day (Miller, 1978). Whilst some of these are context bound, they gradually become decontextualised as the one-word stage progresses. Other words are used from the start in a decontextualised way (Barrett, 1989). As the one-word stage progresses, so the child becomes able to ask and answer questions and provide comments on people and objects in the immediate environment. These abilities enable the child to participate in very simple conversations with other people.

STAGE OF TWO-WORD SENTENCES

Like the one-word stage, this stage is universal (although individual differences become more marked) and, like the transition from babbling to the one-word stage, the transition to the two-word stage is also gradual (Slobin, 1979). As well as continued development of vocabulary, the understanding of grammar grows, and it is possible to divide this stage into what Bee and Mitchell (1980) term *Stage 1 grammar* (lasting from 18 to 30 months) and *Stage 2 grammar* (occurring after 30 months).

Stage 1 grammar (18–30 months)

Here, the child's speech is essentially *telegraphic* (Brown, 1965). When telegrams were used to send messages, the sentence was charged by the word. To avoid a hefty bill, the sender tried to convey as much meaning as possible in as few words as possible. The language of children in this stage has this telegraphic quality, and only those words which convey the most information (so-called *contentives*) are used. Purely grammatical terms (or *functors*), such as the verb 'to be', plurals and possessives are left out. For example, children will say 'There cow' to convey the underlying message 'There is a cow'. Table 12.2 shows some two-word combinations produced by children from six different cultures. As Brown (1973) has noted, it seems that irrespective of their culture, children express basic facts about their environment.

Interestingly, the order of the words produced is *rigid*, and this seems to preserve the meaning of the sentence. For example, if a child is asked 'Does John want some milk?', he might reply 'John milk' (or, later on, 'John want milk'). Adult speech, by contrast, does not rely exclusively on word order to preserve meaning. An example is the passive form of a sentence. So, 'John drank the milk' and 'The milk was drunk by John' both convey the same meaning, even though the word order of the two sentences is different.

Children's imitations of adult sentences are also simple and retain the word order of the original sentence. For example, 'John is playing with the dog' is imitated as 'Play dog', a phenomenon Brown (1965) terms *imitation by reduction*. Complementary to this is *imitation with expansion*, which is the adult's imitation of the

Table 12.2   Two-word combinations produced by children in six cultures

English	German	Russian	Finnish	Luo	Samoan
more milk	mehr Milch (more milk)	yesche moloka (more milk)	lisää kakkua (more cake)		
big boat	Milch heiss (milk hot)	papa bol-shoy (papa big)	rikki auto (broken car)	piypiy kech (pepper hot)	fa'ali'i pepe (headstrong baby)
mama dress	Mamas Hut (mama's hat)	mami chashka (mama's cup)	täti auto (aunt car)	kom baba (chair father)	paluni mama (balloon mama)
Bambi go	Puppe kommt (doll comes)	mama prua (mama walk)	Seppo putoo (Seppo fall)	chungu biro (European comes)	pa'u pepe (fall doll)
hit ball		nashla yaechko (found egg)		omoyo oduma (she dries maize)	
where ball	wo Ball (where ball)	gde papa (where papa)	missa pallo (where ball)		fea pupafu (where Punafu)

Source: Crider et al. (1989)

child's utterances. Here, the 'missing' functors are inserted by the adults so that the child's production of 'John milk' becomes 'John would like some milk'. The rigid order of the child's utterances makes it easier to interpret their meaning, but gestures and the context still provide important clues (as was the case in the one-word stage).

Compared with adults talking to one another, adults talking to children tend to use much shorter sentences, simplify the syntax, raise the pitch of their voice for emphasis, and repeat or paraphrase much of what the child says. This *motherese* or *baby-talk register* helps to achieve a mutual understanding with children who have not yet mastered the full complexity of language. Sensitivity to the child's vocabulary and its intellectual and social knowledge is an example of a *pragmatic rule* for ensuring a degree of shared understanding (Greene, 1990) and also supports a social interaction approach to language acquisition (see Chapter 13).

Children's two-word utterances are not just random combinations of words, but systematic expressions of specific semantic relations. Table 12.3 shows the eight most common semantic relationships found during the two-word stage.

Brown (1970) has distinguished between two main types of semantic relations. The first type are those expressed by combining a single constant term or pivot word (such as 'more') with another word which refers

to an object, action or attribute (such as 'milk'). The second type are those that do not involve the use of constant or pivot words. The appearance of two-word utterances can therefore be attributed to the child's acquisition of two different types of combinatorial rule, namely *pivotal* and *categorical rules*. According to Barrett (1989), there is considerable individual variation in the type of two-word utterances which different children produce. Some rely largely on pivotal rules whereas others rely primarily on categorical rules.

Word order in two-word utterances seems to reflect the child's pre-linguistic knowledge. According to Cromer's (1974) *cognition hypothesis*, language structures can only be used correctly when our cognitive

Table 12.3   The eight most common semantic relationships produced by children in the two-word stage

Semantic relationships	Examples
agent + action	mommy give, daddy sit
action + object	give money, open door
agent + object	mommy car, Angel bone
action + location	sit there, fall floor
entity + location	plane rug, phone table
possessor + possession	my mommy, baby bed
entity + attribute	truck red, house pretty
demonstrative + entity	dat tree, dis mop

Source: Brown (1973)

structures enable this. Children form schemata to understand the world and then talk about them. A good example of this is object permanence, which is a prerequisite for understanding that words can represent things. If a child did not already understand the relationships between objects, people and events in the real world, its first words would be like random unconnected lists. These are important concepts in Piaget's developmental theory (see McIlveen and Gross, 1997) and are consistent with his views of language development reflecting the child's stage of cognitive development (see Chapter 13).

Stage 2 grammar (from about 30 months)

This stage lasts until around the age of four or five, and whilst it may be different for different languages, the rule-governed behaviour in language development is universal. Over-extension begins to disappear as the child's vocabulary grows rapidly and sentences become longer and more complex. Researchers use a measure called *mean length of utterance* (MLU) which is defined as the number of words in a sentence divided by the total number of sentences produced. So, a child who produced 100 sentences with 300 words would have a MLU of 3.00. Figure 12.2 shows the increase in MLU for three children.

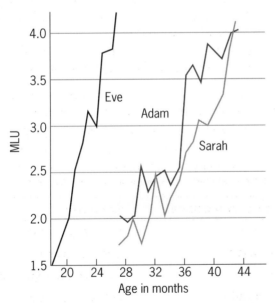

Figure 12.2   Mean length of utterance (MLU) plotted against age in months for three children (after Brown, 1973).

The increase in MLU is due largely to the inclusion of the functors that are left out of the telegraphic speech evident in Stage 1 grammar. For example, 'Daddy hat' may become 'Daddy wear hat' and finally 'Daddy is wearing a hat'. Sentences also become longer because conjunctions (such as 'and' and 'so') are used to form compound sentences like 'You play with the doll and I play with the ball'. Stage 2 grammar, then, really begins with the first use of purely grammatical words. There does not appear to be a 'three-word' stage.

Brown (1973) has found that there is a distinct regularity among English-speaking children in terms of the order in which grammatical complexities are added. Similarly, de Villiers and de Villiers (1979) have found that, irrespective of their culture, children seem to acquire functional words in the same general order but at different rates. Each function word corresponds to a syntactic rule. We know from a number of studies, including that described in Box 12.1, that when children begin to apply these rules (such as the rule for forming plurals), they are not just imitating others.

Box 12.1   Berko's (1958) study of rule formation in children

Berko showed children a picture of a fictitious creature called a wug and told the children 'This is a wug'.

The children were then shown a second picture in which there were two of the creatures and told 'Now there is another one. There are two of them.'

The children were asked to complete the sentence 'There are two ......' Berko found that three- and four-year-olds answered 'wugs' despite never having seen a 'wug' before. Although the children could not have been imitating anybody else's speech, and had not been told about the rule for forming plurals, they were able to apply this rule. Significantly, the children were not consciously aware of having acquired the rule for forming a plural and could not say what the rule they were using was.

The rule-governed nature of language is also shown in the grammatical mistakes that children make. For example, whilst the rule 'add an "s" to a word to form a plural' usually works, there are exceptions to this rule. Such exceptions include 'sheep' rather than 'sheeps' and 'geese' rather than 'gooses'. In the same way, the rule 'add "ed" to form the past tense' usually works. So, 'pass' becomes 'passed' and 'kick' becomes 'kicked'. In the case of 'cost' and 'go', however, it does not. The observation that children use words like 'costed' and 'goed', without ever having heard others use them, suggests that they are applying a rule rather than using imitation. In these cases, however, the rule is being overgeneralised or the language over-regularised. Even subtle attempts at correcting the misapplication of rules fail to work, as shown in Box 12.2.

> **Box 12.2   An example of how the misapplication of a rule is greater than any desire to imitate**
>
> Jean Berko Gleason (1967) has shown how the misapplication of a rule is greater than any desire to imitate. The following is a transcript of an interaction between a mother and her child:
>
> CHILD: My teacher holded the baby rabbits and we patted them.
>
> MOTHER: Did you say your teacher held the baby rabbits?
>
> CHILD: Yes.
>
> MOTHER: What did you say she did?
>
> CHILD: She holded the baby rabbits and we patted them.
>
> MOTHER: Did you say she held them tightly?
>
> CHILD: No, she holded them loosely.

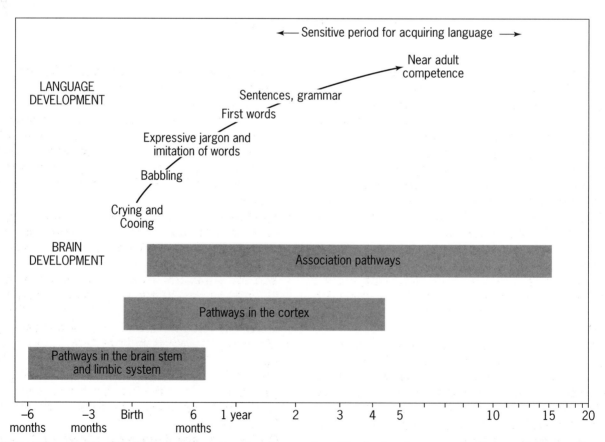

Figure 12.3   The relationship between language development and brain development. Early speech is associated with development of pathways in the cortex, but more complex speech depends on the development of association pathways in the cortex (Fischer and Lazerson, 1984).

By the age of four or five, basic grammatical rules have been acquired, and by the age of five or six, children have acquired most of what they need to know about phoneme construction. For example, if four-year-olds are asked to say which of two made-up speech sounds would be a better name for a toy, and one of the names is consistent with the rules for combining phonemes in the English language (such as 'Klek') and the other is not (such as 'Lkel'), most will choose the former. However, a typical five-year-old will have difficulty understanding passive sentences. For example, if asked to act out the sentence 'The horse is kissed by the cow', most five-year-olds will reverse the meaning and make the horse do the kissing. There are also a great number of irregular words still to be learned, and this aspect of grammatical development will take several more years.

By the age of 13, most English-speaking children have a vocabulary of 20,000 words, and by the age of 20, this will have risen to 50,000 or more (Aitchison, 1996), a vocabulary which Templin (1957) has calculated is acquired at an *average rate* of nine words per day. Not surprisingly, the development of language and the development of the brain are closely related. Figure 12.3 shows the relationship between language development and brain development.

Conclusions

The present chapter has described the course of language development. From what we have seen, there does, as many psychologists contend, appear to be a 'timetable' for language development amongst speakers of English and other languages. Thus, at particular ages, children have particular linguistic capabilities. The importance of this finding is explored in the following chapter.

SUMMARY

- Until recently, the study of language was dominated by **linguistics**, which, combined with psychology, is called **psycholinguistics**, the study of the perception, understanding and production of language and their development.
- While non-human species can **communicate** with each other only in a limited way, human beings are capable of transmitting and understanding an infinite variety of messages, and language is mastered spontaneously early in life, without the need for **deliberate training**.
- Language involves the acquistion of a rule system (**grammar/mental grammar**) which is concerned with the description of language, how it 'works' and what governs our patterns of speech. Grammar consists of phonology, semantics and syntax.
- **Phonology** refers to the sound system of a language. Different languages have different numbers and combinations of **phones/phonetic segments** and **phonemes/phonological segments**, the functionally important classes of phones. **Phonological rules** constrain the permitted sequence of phonemes.
- Phonemes themselves are meaningless sounds but they are important for meaning. Most children **recognise** sounds in adult speech before they can **produce** them themselves.
- **Semantics** refers to the meaning of language. **Morphemes** are the basic unit of meaning, consisting mainly of **words** (which are 'free') but also including **prefixes** and **suffixes** (which are 'bound'). Single words have only limited meaning and are usually combined into phrases and **sentences**.
- **Syntax** refers to the rules for combining words into phrases and sentences. Word order is an example of a **syntactic rule** which is very important for understanding language development and for evaluating claims regarding the language abilities of non-humans. Syntax and meaning are closely related but are distinct: syntax refers to the **structures** which relate sound and meaning.
- Many psychologists believe that language development follows a universal timetable, reflecting the role of **maturation**. But being '**programmed**' to develop language still requires exposure to language, which is an environmental influence.
- During the **pre-linguistic stage** (0–12 months), babies make various sounds with their vocal organs but cannot yet talk. Crying dominates the

first month, after which they begin to display **categorical speech perception**.

- **Cooing** begins at about six weeks, but the baby's oral cavity and nervous system are not sufficiently mature to produce speech sounds. **Babbling** (starting at six to nine months), however, involves the production of phonemes, although these still lack meaning. Consonants and vowels may take the form of **reduplicated monosyllables**.
- Babbling differs from pre-babbling in that babies seem to enjoy exercising their voices for the sake of it (**spontaneous babbling**), and their speech sounds have intonational patterns as in real speech. Babbling also involves **echolalia** and is probably based on maturation, although it can also be modified through experience.
- **Phonemic expansion**, the onset of which is also probably maturational, is replaced at around nine or ten months by **phonemic contraction**, which reflects the baby's sampling of phonemes used in its 'linguistic environment'. Babies from different language backgrounds can now be distinguished, and deaf babies **stop** babbling. It will still take another six years or so for **all** phonemes in the child's native language to be mastered.
- The transition from babbling to the **one-word stage** is gradual, and there is continued production of non-words/**jargon** for several months after the first word (articulate sound) is produced (typically at around age one).
- The child's first words are often invented and **context bound**, denoting specific actions, events or objects. According to Barrett, they perform less of a communicative function and more of a performative function, although they can be categorised as having either an **expressive** or a **directive function**.
- The one-word stage is also characterised by **holophrases**, whose full meaning is provided by accompanying gestures and tones of voice. They can be thought of as precursors of later, more complex sentences.
- According to Nelson, a baby's first 50 words tend to fall into six categories: **specific nominals**, **general nominals**, **action words**, **modifiers**, **personal-social words** and **function words**. The first three categories account for 78 per cent of the total, suggesting that it is the child's active involvement in its environment that determines many of its first words.
- The child's **receptive vocabulary** outstrips its **expressive vocabulary**, but the latter increases rapidly before the age of two. Words become increasingly decontextualised and the child

becomes increasingly capable of participating in simple conversations.

- Like the one-word stage, the **two-word stage** is universal, and transition to it is also gradual. Bee and Mitchell divide it into **Stage 1 grammar** (18–30 months) and **Stage 2 grammar** (30 months and beyond).
- The child's language in Stage 1 grammar is **telegraphic**, consisting of **contentives** but no **functors**. The child is expressing certain basic facts about its environment, and this occurs regardless of the child's cultural background.
- Telegraphic speech involves a **rigid word order**, which helps adults to interpret the meaning of a sentence (unlike adult speech). This is also true of the child's imitation of adult speech (**imitation by reduction**), which is complemented by the adult's **imitation with expansion**.
- **Motherese/baby-talk register** involves sensitivity to the child's immature vocabulary and knowledge and represents a **pragmatic rule** for ensuring mutual understanding. It also supports a social-interaction approach to language acquisition.
- Two-word utterances represent systematic expressions of specific semantic relations, the most common examples being **agent + action**, **action + object**, **agent + object**, **action + location**, **entity + location**, **possessor + possession**, **entity + attribute** and **demonstrative + entity**.
- Brown distinguishes two main types of semantic relations, **pivotal rules** and **categorical rules**. These are combinatorial rules, and children show considerable individual variation in which type they use for forming their two-word utterances.
- Word order seems to reflect the child's pre-linguistic knowledge, as claimed by Cromer's **cognition hypothesis**, according to which children form schemata (such as object permanence) and then talk about them. Similarly, Piaget believes that language development reflects the child's stage of cognitive development.
- The rule-governed nature of **Stage 2 grammar** is universal. There is rapid growth of vocabulary, with sentences becoming longer and more complex, as measured by the **mean length of utterance (MLU)**. The increase in MLU is due largely to the inclusion of functors missing from Stage 1 telegraphic speech.
- There appears to be a universal sequence of development of grammatical complexities/functional words, although the rates may differ. Each functor corresponds to a syntactic rule, which are

not simply imitations of others' speech, as shown by Berko's 'Wug' study of the rule for forming plurals.

- The rule-governed nature of language is also illustrated in children's grammatical mistakes, which often involve the overgeneralised/over-regularised application of a rule. Even subtle attempts to correct this misapplication of rules are likely to fail.

- By age four or five, basic grammatical rules have been acquired. Later development involves understanding the difference between active and passive sentences, learning a great number of irregular words, and continuing expansion of vocabulary.

13

THEORIES OF LANGUAGE DEVELOPMENT

Introduction and overview

In the previous chapter, we looked at the major 'milestones' in the development of language. Our aim in this chapter is to consider some of the theories that have been advanced to explain the mechanisms by which children develop their native language. Two main theoretical accounts have been advanced. According to one, language development can be attributed primarily to environmental input and learning. The leading theorists in this respect are B.F. Skinner and Albert Bandura.

Another position argues that whilst the environment may supply the *content* of language (such as the specific words that children use), the *structure* of language (its *grammar*) is an inherent, biologically determined capacity of human beings. According to this position, which has been most strongly put by Chomsky, Lenneberg and McNeill, the process of language development is essentially one of *acquisition* (as distinct from *learning*).

Our main aim in this chapter is to consider the evidence for and against the learning theory and biological approaches. However, as well as reviewing these approaches, we will also consider some alternatives to them. Prominent amongst such alternatives have been those which see the relationship between language and children's cognitive development, and children's interactions with other language users, as being important.

Learning theory and language development

CLASSICAL CONDITIONING

The earliest theory implicating learning principles suggested that much of our language is developed through *classical conditioning* (Houston et al., 1991). Consider, for example, the development of the sound 'mama'. If this initially neutral sound (which will eventually become a *conditioned stimulus*) is repeatedly paired with the *unconditional stimulus* of the mother and her actions, then the baby's responses to the mother's actions become classically conditioned to the 'mama' sound. In the same way, words like 'hot' may acquire their meaning through repeated pairings with a certain class of unconditional stimuli such as fires, radiators and so on (Houston et al, 1991).

OPERANT CONDITIONING

According to Skinner (1985):

'verbal behaviour evidently came into existence when, through a critical step in the evolution of the human species, the vocal musculature became susceptible to operant conditioning'.

Skinner first applied the principles of operant conditioning to explain language development in his book *Verbal Behaviour* (1957) in which he argued that:

'a child acquires verbal behaviour when relatively unplanned vocalisations, selectively reinforced, assume forms which produce appropriate consequences in a given verbal community'.

Whilst Skinner accepted that pre-linguistic vocalisations such as cooing and babbling were probably inborn, he argued that adults *shape* the baby's sounds into words by *reinforcing* those sounds which approximate the form of real words. Through selective reinforcement, words are shaped into sentences with correct grammar being reinforced and incorrect grammar being ignored. According to Whitehurst (1982), this language learning is put together into:

'a patchwork of thousands of separately acquired frames, patterns, responses, rules and small tricks. The elegance of the final product belies the chaos of its construction'.

One way in which positive reinforcement is given is in the form of the child getting what it asks for. For example, 'May I have some water?' produces a drink that reinforces that form of words. Skinner termed these requests *mands*. Reinforcement may also be given by parents becoming excited and poking, touching, patting and feeding children when they vocalise. Indeed, as we saw in the previous chapter (see page 142), the evidence suggests that babbling does increase when it results in adult smiles, strokes and so on. The mother's delight on hearing her child's first real word is exciting for the child, and so acquiring language becomes reinforcing in itself.

Skinner also saw *imitation* as playing an important role. When children imitate, or produce *echoic responses* of verbal labels (which Skinner calls *tacts*), they receive immediate reinforcement in the form of approval from parents and significant others to the extent that the imitations resemble correct words. As children continue to learn new words and phrases through imitation, so their language becomes progressively more like that of adults (Moerk and Moerk, 1979).

An evaluation of Skinner's theory

There is some evidence to support Skinner's views. For example, Brodbeck and Irwin (1946) found that, compared with institutionalised children who received less attention, children whose parents reinforced their early attempts at meaningful sounds did tend to vocalise more. As any parent will testify, parents often do reinforce children when they imitate adult language (and the laughter of adults when children produce a profanity increases the probability of that profanity being produced in the future!). We should also note that using *behaviour modification*, Lovaas (1987) has shown that selective reinforcement can be used successfully to teach language to emotionally disturbed or developmentally delayed children.

Skinner's views on the importance of reinforcement in the development of language have, however, been challenged by a number of researchers. Box 13.1 illustrates some of the criticisms that have been made.

The role of imitation in language development has also attracted much criticism. Whilst imitation must be involved in the learning of accent and vocabulary, its role in complex aspects of language (syntax and seman-

---

Box 13.1   Does selective reinforcement have any influence on children's grammar?

- According to Brown et al. (1969), mothers respond to the 'truth value' or presumed meaning of their children's language rather than to its grammatical correctness or complexity. Brown and his colleagues argue that mothers extract meaning from, and interpret, their children's incomplete and sometimes primitive sentences.

- Tizard et al. (1972) have argued that attempts to try to correct grammatical mistakes or teach grammar have little effect (see also Chapter 12, page 146). Indeed, Nelson (1973) has claimed that vocabulary develops more slowly in children of mothers who systematically correct poor word pronunciation and reward good pronunciation.

- Slobin (1975) found that children learn grammatical rules *despite* their parents, who usually pay little attention to the grammatical structure of their children's speech and, moreover, often reinforce incorrect grammar. According to Slobin, 'a mother is too engaged in interacting with her child to pay attention to the linguistic form of (its) utterances'.

What the studies cited above suggest is that whilst parents usually respond to (or reinforce) true statements and criticise or correct false ones, they pay little regard to grammatical correctness. Even if they do, this has little effect on language development.

---

tics) is less obvious. As we saw in the previous chapter (see page 143), when children do imitate adult sentences, they tend to reduce or convert them to their own currently operating grammar. So, between 18 and 30 months, the child's imitations are as telegraphic as its own spontaneous speech. Furthermore, since at least some adult language is ungrammatical, imitation alone cannot explain how children ever learn 'correct language'. Even if we do not always speak grammatically ourselves, we still know what is good grammar and what is not.

By way of defence against these criticisms, Bandura (1977), amongst others, has broadened the concept of imitation. Accepting that the *exact* imitation of particular sentences plays a relatively minor role in language development, Bandura argues that children may imitate the *general* form of sentences, and fill in these general forms with various words. Snow (1983) uses the term *deferred imitations* to refer to those sequences of words and language structures that are stored in a child's memory for long periods before being used (and are often used in the same situation in which they were first heard). What Snow calls *expanded imitations* are repetitions of sentences or phrases that were not present in the original form. In Snow's view, children's language production sometimes exceeds their competence in that they imitate forms of language they do not understand. By storing examples of adult language in memory, children have a sort of 'delayed replay' facility that enables them to produce language forms after they have been acquired, and this aids the development of language.

In spite of attempts to defend the view that language development can best be explained in terms of learning theory, there are (based on what we said in the previous chapter) at least four reasons for disputing its usefulness. These are summarised in Box 13.2.

Box 13.2   Some reasons for disputing learning theory's explanation of language development

- If language is established through reinforcement, then we would expect that all children living under widely varying social conditions would acquire language in different ways. The fact that there seems, as we saw in Chapter 12, to be a culturally universal and invariant sequence in the stages of language development, which occurs under highly variable conditions, goes against this. Indeed, even children born to, and raised by, deaf parents seem to acquire language in the same sequence as other children (Slobin, 1986).

- Learning theory also fails to explain the *creativity of language*, that is, the fact that native speakers of a language can produce and understand an infinitely large number of sentences never heard or produced before by anyone. As Chomsky (1968) has put it:

  'the normal use of language is innovative, in the sense that much of what we say in the course of normal language use is entirely new (and) not a repetition of anything that we have heard before'.

- It is difficult for learning theory to explain the child's spontaneous use of grammatical rules which they have never heard or been taught. As we saw in the previous chapter (see page 146), these rules are often overgeneralised and incorrectly used, and children are largely impervious to parental attempts to correct grammatical errors.

- Finally, learning theory cannot account for children's ability to understand the meaning of sentences as opposed to word meaning. The meaning of a sentence is not simply the sum of the meanings of the individual words. As Neisser (1967) has observed, the structure of language is comparable to the structure of perception as described by the Gestalt psychologists (see Chapter 1). Learning theory may be able to account for how children learn the meaning of individual nouns and verbs since these have an obvious reference. It cannot, however, explain how the meaning of grammatical terms is acquired.

Chomsky's LAD and the biological approach to language development

Of course, language cannot develop without some form of environmental input. For some psychologists, however, the role played by the environment in the development of language is only a minor one and could never explain language development adequately. The major advocates of this view are Chomsky (1957, 1965, 1968), Lenneberg (1967) and McNeill (1970). According to Chomsky, children are born already programmed to formulate and understand all types of sentences even though they have never heard them before.

Chomsky proposed the existence of an innate *language acquisition device* (LAD). Whitehurst (1982) has likened the LAD to a street map. Whilst a stranger in a city eventually learns, through trial and error, to find their way around, someone with a map has an overview of what roads lead where. Whitehurst argues that this is the case with children and the LAD, which gives them an 'internal street map' of language and enables, for example, the distinction to be made between verbs (what things do) and nouns (the things themselves).

According to Chomsky, language is much more complex and much less predictable than Skinner believed. In his book *Syntactic Structures,* Chomsky (1957) outlined his theory of *transformational grammar* (TG). Critical to the theory of TG are a set of rules called *phrase-structure rules* which specify what are and are not acceptable utterances in a speaker's native language. When applied systematically, these rules generate sentences in English or any other language. Some of Chomsky's phrase-structure rules are shown in Figure 13.1 which also shows how a sentence is produced using these rules.

Rule (1) An S (sentence) consists of (or can be broken down into) NP (noun phrase) and VP (verb phrase)

Rule (2) NP ──────▶ Article + (Adjective) + Noun

(The brackets denote 'optional')

Rule (3) VP ──────▶ Verb + NP

Rule (4) Article ──────▶ a(n), the

Rule (5) Adjective ──▶ big, small, red, etc.

Rule (6) Noun ──────▶ boy, girl, stone, etc.

Rule (7) Verb ──────▶ hit, threw, helped, etc.

} These are *Lexical Rewrite Rules.*

The commas imply that only *one* word should be selected from the list

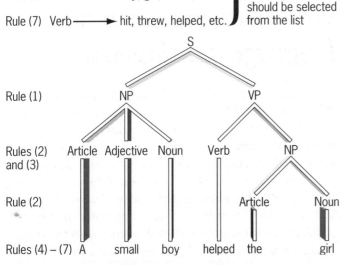

Figure 13.1   Some of Chomsky's phrase-structure rules and an example of a sentence produced by using them.

Whilst phrase-structure rules specify *some* important aspects of language, Chomsky recognised that they do not specify them all. Some sentences (such as 'A small boy helped the girl') share the same meaning as other sentences (such as 'The girl was helped by a small boy')

but have different phrase structures. Also, two sentences (such as 'Performing fleas can be amusing' and 'Playing tiddlywinks can be amusing') may have the same superficial structure but different meanings. In the case of the first example, 'performing' describes the fleas, whereas in the second example, 'playing' is a verb. As a result, the word 'are' can replace 'can be' in the first example but not in the second. The reverse is true for the word 'is'. Finally, certain sentences (such as 'The missionary was ready to eat') can have ambiguous meanings.

Examples such as these led Chomsky to distinguish between a sentence's *deep structure* and its *surface structure.* A sentence's surface structure is its grammatical structure, that is, the actual words or phrases used. The deep structure of a sentence more or less corresponds to the sentence's meaning. Chomsky argued that when we hear a spoken sentence, we do not 'process' or retain its surface structure. Instead, we transform it into its deep structure. Chomsky called the understanding or knowledge of how to transform the meaning of a sentence into the words that make it up (and vice versa) *transformational grammar.* In Chomsky's view, this understanding or knowledge is an innate *language acquisition device* and is what enables us to produce an infinite number of meaningful sentences.

A single surface structure may have more than one deep structure, as in the sentence 'The missionary was ready to eat'. In one representation it is the missionary who is ready to consume a meal, whilst in another the missionary has been made ready for consumption by others. Figure 13.2 shows how a political cartoonist has exploited two deep structures of a single surface structure. Conversely, different surface structures can have the same deep structure (as in the sentences 'A small boy helped the girl' and 'The girl was helped by a small boy').

Our ability to understand the various meanings of a single sentence and the single meaning of two superficially different sentences is also a result of the LAD. For Chomsky, then, children are equipped with the ability to learn the rules to transform deep structure into various surface structures, and they do this by looking for certain kinds of linguistic features which are common to all languages. For example, all languages make use of consonants and vowels, syllables, modifiers and so on. Collectively, these linguistic features provide the deep structure.

Figure 13.2   As 'New Labour' takes over from 'Old Labour', two veteran socialists (Arthur Scargill and Tony Benn) contemplate the party's future. Scargill's question has two deep structures and, given all the 'Old Labour' policies that have, along with Scargill and Benn, been put in the dustbin, we might expect Benn's reply simply to be 'No'. Benn's reply to the alternative deep structure is out of context and hence the cartoon is funny.

Chomsky calls these features *linguistic universals*. In his view, they must be universal because all children can learn any language to which they are exposed with equal ease. So, a child born in England of English parents who went to live in China soon after birth would learn Chinese if brought up by a Chinese-speaking family just as easily as a native-born Chinese child. Chomsky argues that only some kind of LAD can account for the child's learning and knowledge of grammatical rules in view of the limited and often ungrammatical and incomplete samples of speech that a child hears.

Chomsky did not claim that his theory explained how we construct and utter sentences, that is, he did not suggest that we go through the procedures of phrase structure and transformational grammar when we prepare to speak a sentence (Hampson and Morris, 1996). For Chomsky, a language's grammar is an idealised description of the *linguistic competence* of native speakers of the language. Any model of how this competence is applied in actual *performance* must take into account certain psychologically relevant factors such as memory, attention, the workings of the nervous system and so on (Lyons, 1970).

The evidence we identified in Box 13.2 disputing

learning theory's account of language development is supportive of Chomsky's theory, as is the fact that the human vocal organs, breathing apparatus, auditory system and brain are all specialised for spoken communication. Other evidence favouring Chomsky is briefly summarised in Box 13.3.

Box 13.3   Some evidence supporting Chomsky's theory

- Research conducted by Eimas (1975) suggests that babies do not need to learn to discriminate between different speech sounds. Eimas showed that babies as young as two days old can discriminate between 'ba' and 'pa' sounds. According to Chomsky, these phonetic discriminations can be thought of as the first linguistic universals which the baby discovers.

- All adult languages appear to have certain linguistic universals (see text on pages 153–4) and transformational grammar is acquired in some form by all people (unless brain damaged or reared in isolation) irrespective of their culture and despite enormous variations in the ability to learn other skills (Lenneberg, 1967). The fact that a person with an IQ of 50 may have difficulty in learning simple tasks but still learns to talk indicates that language develops independently from factors that affect the learning of other tasks. For Lenneberg, this indicates that language acquisition must be controlled by genetic factors that are independent (at least to a degree) of those that control general intelligence.

- In some studies of twins, the existence of a 'private language', intelligible only to the twins, has been observed (Malmstrom and Silva, 1986). Likewise, recent studies of some deaf children in Nicaragua have revealed a parallel phenomenon with sign language (Gerrard, 1997). These languages do not appear to be a variation of ordinary language, but do have the characteristics of ordinary languages (such as verbs, nouns and syntax). The existence of 'private languages', with a set of structures comparable to all known languages, supports the view that humans are born with an already-formed knowledge of syntax.

- Studies of congenitally deaf children have shown the emergence of 'gestural language' even though the children received no encouragement or training from their parents

---

(Goldin-Meadow and Feldman, 1977). This suggests that language is very difficult to suppress even in adverse environmental circumstances, provided the individual has someone with whom they can communicate.

Lenneberg has argued that the years leading to puberty constitute a *critical period* for language development. Lenneberg's argument centres around the brain's relative lack of specialisation while it is still developing. Children who are born brain damaged and who lose their language abilities can relearn at least some of them because other, non-damaged parts of the brain seem to take over the language function. However, adolescents or adults who experience an equivalent amount of damage are unable to regain abilities corresponding to the site of the injury because the brain is now specialised (or 'committed') and no longer 'plastic'.

Evidence exists, however, which suggests that the first ten years or so may not necessarily be the critical period Lenneberg has argued for. For example, Curtiss (1977) reports the case of Genie, an American child raised in conditions of extreme (de)privation until her discovery at the age of 13 years and seven months. Amongst other appalling treatment, Genie was beaten if she made any noise, and she had learned to suppress almost all vocalisations except for a whimper. According to Curtiss, 'Genie was unsocialised, primitive, hardly human'.

Genie could understand a handful of words (including 'rattle', 'bunny' and 'red') but she always responded to them in the same way. Essentially, then, Genie had to learn language at the age of nearly 14. She never developed normal language skills and by the age of 18 could produce only short sentences which lacked important aspects of grammar (the use of pronouns being an example). Her vocabulary expanded, and she could hold a conversation, but her use of intonation was poor and only those who knew her well could understand much of what she said. Genie herself had great difficulty in understanding complex syntax. Nonetheless, the fact that she was capable of learning any language at all weakens Lenneberg's claim for a critical period. However, the obvious retardation of her language abilities is consistent with the idea of there being a *sensitive period* for language development.

An evaluation of Chomsky's theory

As we noted earlier (see page 154), Chomsky did not suggest that we actually go through the processes of phrase structure and transformational grammar when we prepare to speak a sentence. However, and as Hampson and Morris (1996) have observed, if phrase structure and transformational grammar do describe language, it is not unreasonable to investigate whether the actual processes in preparing to speak actually do follow the same steps. In general, experimental investigations have failed to find strong evidence for the application of Chomsky's rules when people speak and listen (Hampson and Morris, 1996).

Aitchison (1983) has argued that Chomsky's assumption that children are 'wired' with the knowledge that language is rule governed, and that they make a succession of hypotheses about the rules underlying the speech they hear, is substantially correct. Aitchison, though, disputes the claim that the LAD consists of *both* a hypothesis-making device *and* transformational grammar. In her view, the claim about transformational grammar (or what she calls 'Content Cuthbert') is mistaken. Aitchison prefers what she calls 'Process Peggy', a process approach in which children are seen as having inbuilt puzzle-solving equipment which enables them to process linguistic data along with other sorts of data.

By contrast, Chomsky (1979) argues that an innate language ability exists *independently* of other innate abilities, because the mind is constructed of 'mental organs' which are:

'just as specialised and differentiated as those of the body ... and ... language is a system easy to isolate among the various mental faculties'.

Some alternatives to learning theory and biological approaches

In recent years, there has been a growing acceptance that neither learning theory nor nativist approaches offers a complete account of language development. The general view of integrative theoretical positions is that children cannot acquire language until an appropriate maturational level has been reached, but that language development is more closely related to environmental input and cognitive development than a strict Chomskyan view proposes. Maratsos (1983) has identified several assumptions made by integrative theorists. These are summarised in Box 13.4.

> **Box 13.4   Some assumptions made by integrative theorists**
>
> - Children are highly motivated to communicate and therefore are *active* rather than *passive* learners of language.
>
> - Children can learn the major aspects of grammar because they have already acquired important concepts on which grammar is based (namely that events involve agents, actions, objects of actions and so on). For this reason, learning a grammar does not require much information processing.
>
> - Other aspects of language can be explained by the language parents use to talk to children.
>
> - Those rules of grammar that do not fit in with children's natural cognitive processes, and are not conveyed adequately through parental input, are unnatural and difficult for the child. They are also acquired very late (the passive voice in English being a good example).

THE LANGUAGE AND SOCIAL-INTERACTION APPROACH

One alternative explanation of the rule-bound nature of children's speech, which represents a departure from the grammatical competence approach inspired by Chomsky, is that it arises from the child's *pre-linguistic knowledge*. During the 1970s, psychologists began to look at language development in the first 12 to 18 months of life because the basic skills acquired in the first 18 months contribute substantially to the syntactic skills characteristic of adult language.

A purely syntactic analysis of language cannot answer the question of how children 'discover' their language, that is, how they learn that there is such a thing as language which can be used for communicating, categorising, problem-solving and so on. However, Smith and Cowie's (1991) *language and social-interaction approach* sees language as being used to communicate needs and intentions and as an enjoyable means of entering into a community.

Several studies have indicated how babies initially master a social world onto which they later 'map' language. Snow (1977), for example, notes that adults tend to attach meaning to a baby's sounds and utterances. As a result, burps, grunts, giggles and so on are interpreted as expressions of intent and feeling, as are non-verbal communications (such as smiling and engaging in eye contact). Snow sees this as a kind of primitive conversation (or *proto-conversation*) which has a rather one-sided quality in that it requires a 'generous' adult attributing some kind of intended meaning to the baby's sounds and non-verbal behaviours. From this perspective, the infant is an inadequate conversational partner.

Much more two-way exchanges are what Collis and Schaffer (1975) call *visual co-orientation* (or joint attention) and *formats*. Visual co-orientation refers to the process whereby two individuals come to focus on some common object. This puts an infant's environmental explorations into a social context, so that an infant-object situation is converted into an infant-object-mother situation (Schaffer, 1989). The joint attention that this entails provides opportunities for learning how to do things. So, as parents and children develop their mutual patterns of interaction and share attention to objects, some of their activities recur, as happens in joint picture-book reading.

Bruner (1975, 1978) uses Collis and Schaffer's term 'formats' to refer to rule-bound activity routines in which the infant has many opportunities to relate language to familiar play (as when the mother inserts name labels into a game or activity), initially in indicating formats and later in requesting formats. These ritualised exchanges stress the need for turn-taking and so help the baby to discover the social function of communication. As a result, the infant can learn about the structures and demands of social interaction and prepare and rehearse the skills that will eventually become essential to successful interchanges such as conversation.

LASS: THE ACTIVE ADULT

According to Bruner (1983), formats comprise what he calls the *language acquisition support system* (LASS). Bruner is more concerned with the pragmatics and functions of language, that is, what language is used for. In Bruner's view:

'entry into language is entry into discourse that requires both members of a dialogue pair to interpret a communication and its intent. Learning a language ... consists of learning not only the grammar of a particular language, but also learning how to realise one's intentions by the appropriate use of that grammar'.

The emphasis on intent requires a far more active role on the part of the adult in helping a child's language acquisition than that of just being a 'model' or merely providing the input for the child's LAD. Moerk (1989) has argued that 'the LAD was a lady', i.e. the lady who does most of the talking to the child (namely its mother). Mothers not only simplify linguistic input, but also break it down into helpful, illustrative segments for the child to practise and build on. As Durkin (1995) notes, this view sees language development as being a very sophisticated extension of the processes of meaningful interaction that the caregiver and child have constructed over several months.

THE ACTIVE CHILD

Another way of looking at the 'partnership' between adults and infants is to see the infant (rather than the adult) as being the more 'active' partner in the relationship between them. The view of language as a *cause-effect analytic device* has been summarised by Gauker (1990) according to whom:

'the fundamental function of words is to bring about changes in the speaker's environment ... Linguistic understanding consists of a grasp of these causal relations'.

According to this perspective, language is a form of tool use, a tool being a set of symbols whose use results in a change of behaviour in the listener. The use of words as communicative tools is shown in what has been called the *emergence of communicative intentionality*. During the pre-linguistic stage, children have no awareness that they can gain a desired effect indirectly by changing somebody else's behaviour. So, they may cry and reach for something but not direct the cry towards the caregiver or look back at the caregiver. The cry merely expresses frustration and is not a communicative signal designed to affect the other's behaviour. This 'analysis' of means-ends relationships, that is, what causes what, solely as a product of one's own actions, is called *first-order causality*.

The emergence of communicative intentionality involves *second-order causality*, or the awareness that it *is*

possible to bring about a desired goal by using another person as a tool. Pointing gestures and glances now rapidly proliferate as a means of asking others to look at or act upon an object. According to Savage-Rumbaugh (1990), the child is beginning to understand in a general sense:

'that it is possible to "cause" others to engage in desired actions through the mechanism of communication about those actions'.

This use of animate tools (other people) parallels the use of inanimate tools (physical objects), and this is an important feature of what Piaget (1952) calls *sensorimotor intelligence*. Some kind of *instrumental understanding* (what leads to what) seems to underlie both activities.

It is, however, more difficult to analyse language *comprehension* in terms of a cause-effect analysis than it is to analyse *language production*, since what do we cause to happen when we understand things that have been said to us? Based on her work with chimpanzees, Savage-Rumbaugh (1990) concludes that language comprehension is clearly becoming the driving force underlying the language acquisition process and that under normal circumstances, language production is just one outcome of the development of language comprehension.

PIAGET AND LANGUAGE DEVELOPMENT

According to Piaget (1952), the growth of language can be predicted from an understanding of children's cognitive skills. Piaget believed that children must first understand concepts before they can use words that describe those concepts. Piaget's views are an important contribution to the debate concerning the relationship between language and thought, and we shall consider them in more detail in Chapter 17.

Conclusions

Explanations of language development range from Skinner's account based on operant conditioning to the view that language is biologically determined. The evidence suggests that Skinner's account is unlikely to be true. Whilst biologically based accounts of language development are probably closer to the truth, it is unlikely that they offer a complete account of language development.

SUMMARY

- According to **learning theory**, language development can be attributed primarily to environmental input and learning. The first such theory, **classical conditioning**, claims that certain sounds (words) become **conditioned stimuli** through repeatedly being paired with particular **unconditioned stimuli**, such as the mother's actions or physical objects.

- According to Skinner, verbal behaviour is acquired through a process of **operant conditioning**. While cooing and babbling are probably inborn, adults **shape** these into words by **reinforcing** those sounds which approximate real words. Selective reinforcement is used to shape words into grammatically correct sentences.

- Positive reinforcement may take the form of the child getting what it asks for (**mands**), parental excitement at the child's vocalisations, physical contact or food rewards.

- Immediate reinforcement may also come following children's successful **imitation (echoic responses)** of verbal labels (**tacts**), helping to make their language progressively more like that of adults.

- There is some evidence that children whose parents reinforce their early attempts at meaningful sounds tend to vocalise more, compared with institutionalised children. Also, Lovaas has used **behaviour modification** to teach language to emotionally disturbed or developmentally delayed children.

- There is also evidence that contradicts Skinner, such as the finding that mothers respond to the 'truth value' of their children's language rather than to its grammatical correctness or complexity. Indeed, evidence suggests that children learn grammatical rules **despite** their parents, who often reinforce incorrect grammar.

- Attempts to correct grammatical mistakes have little effect and may even slow down the development of vocabulary.

- While **imitation** is necessary for the learning of accent and vocabulary, some adult speech is ungrammatical, making imitation an insufficient explanation for the development of syntax and semantics. Also, imitation of adult speech reflects the child's currently operating grammar, as in the telegraphic imitations of stage 1 grammar.

- Taking a broader view of imitation, Bandura argues that, while the **exact** imitation of particular sentences plays a minor role, children may imitate the **general** forms of sentences and fill these in with various words. According to Snow, **deferred imitations** are stored in long-term memory and provide a 'delayed replay' facility; these are complemented by **expanded imitations**.

- Learning theory fails to explain the culturally universal and invariant sequence in the stages of language development, and even children raised by deaf parents seem to pass through this same sequence. It also fails to explain the **creativity of language** and the child's spontaneous use of grammatical rules never heard or taught.

- Learning theory also cannot explain children's ability to understand the meaning of sentences, which is greater than the sum of the meaning of the individual words. While individual nouns and verbs have an obvious reference, grammatical terms do not.

- While not denying the role of some form of environmental input, Chomsky, Lenneberg and McNeill argue that this is an inadequate explanation of language development.

- According to Chomsky, children are innately programmed to formulate and understand all types of sentences they have never heard before in the form of a **language acquisition device (LAD)**. Whitehurst likens this to a street map, and it consists essentially of **transformational grammar (TG)**.

- Critical to TG are **phrase-structure rules** which specify what are/are not acceptable utterances in a speaker's native language. However, these rules are unable to specify **all** aspects of language, as when two sentences have the same meaning but different phrase structures, or the same superficial structure but different meanings. Also, the same sentence can have ambiguous meanings.

- Chomsky distinguishes between a sentence's **surface structure** (the actual words or phrases used) and its **deep structure** (its meaning). TG is what enables us to transform a spoken sentence into its deep structure, as well as to transform the meaning of a sentence into the words that compose it.

- LAD is used to look for certain kinds of linguistic features common to all languages (**linguistic universals**), such as consonants and vowels, syllables, and modifiers. Collectively, these provide the deep structure.

- Linguistic universals must exist for children to be able to learn any language to which they are exposed with equal ease. Only some kind of LAD can account for the children's learning of grammatical rules in light of the limited and often ungrammatical speech to which they are exposed.

- For Chomsky, grammar represents an idealised description of native speakers' **linguistic competence** as opposed to actual **performance**, the latter being influenced by memory, attention, operation of the nervous system and other psychologically relevant factors.
- The human vocal organs, breathing apparatus, auditory system and brain are all specialised for spoken communication and two-day-old babies are capable of making phonetic discriminations (the first linguistic universals the baby discovers).
- All adult languages have certain linguistic universals, and TG is acquired by everyone, including those with very low IQs. Lenneberg takes this to indicate that language acquisition is controlled by genetic factors that are distinct from those that control general intelligence.
- The existence of 'private languages' among twins with the characteristics of ordinary languages supports the claim the humans are born with some knowledge of syntax. Studies of 'gestural language' in congenitally deaf children suggest that language is very difficult to suppress even in adverse environmental conditions.
- Lenneberg's proposed **critical period** for language development is based on the finding that only in adolescents and adults does brain damage result in permanent loss of the corresponding abilities, since the brain is now specialised, unlike the child's 'plastic' brain.
- Curtiss's study of Genie suggests that the period up to adolescence may not be critical after all. However, her obviously retarded language abilities is consistent with the idea of a **sensitive period**.
- In general, experimental studies have failed to find convincing evidence for the application of Chomsky's phrase-structure rules and TG when people speak and listen.
- Aitchison disputes Chomsky's claim that LAD comprises **both** a hypothesis-making device **and** TG ('Content Cuthbert'). Instead, she prefers 'Process Peggy', according to which linguistic data are just one kind of data to which inbuilt puzzle-solving equipment is applied. Chomsky believes that innate language ability represents an **independent** 'mental organ', distinct from other innate abilities.
- According to **integrative theorists**, children are

active learners of language. Their learning of grammar is based on important concepts already acquired, and so little information processing is required. However, some grammatical rules (such as the passive voice) do not fit in with their natural cognitive processes and are not conveyed adequately through parental input, making them difficult.

- The **language and social-interaction approach** represents an alternative to Chomsky's grammatical competence approach and emphasises the child's **pre-linguistic knowledge**. It sees language as being used to communicate needs and intentions and as an enjoyable means of entering into a community.
- Babies initially master a social world onto which they later 'map' language, as demonstrated by **proto-conversations**, in which adults tend to attach meaning to a baby's non-speech sounds and non-verbal behaviour. Other, more two-way, exchanges include **visual co-orientation** (such as joint picture-book reading) and **formats**.
- According to Bruner, formats comprise the **language acquisition support system (LASS)**, which reflects his concern with the functions of language, i.e. how we use appropriate grammar in order to realise our intentions. Adults are not merely 'models' or providers of input for the child's LAD, but they simplify linguistic input, breaking it down into segments that the child can practise and build on.
- One way of seeing the child as the more 'active' partner is to see language as a **cause-effect analytic device**, according to which words are used as a tool for bringing about a change in the listener's behaviour. This **emergence of communicative intentionality** involves **second-order causality**, the awareness that it is possible to achieve a desired goal by using another person as a tool, as in pointing gestures and glances.
- The use of other people as tools parallels the use of physical objects, an important feature of Piaget's **sensorimotor intelligence**, with some kind of **instrumental understanding** underlying both activities. More generally, Piaget believes that children must first understand concepts before they can use words that describe them.
- According to Savage-Rumbaugh, language **comprehension** is becoming the driving force underlying the language acquisition process, with language **production** being just one outcome of the development of comprehension.

14

LANGUAGE IN NON-HUMANS

Introduction and overview

As we saw in the previous chapter, some psychologists see language as being a species-specific behaviour common to all humans and found only in humans. Chomsky (cited in Wyman, 1983) has put this view most strongly:

'Language is a property of humans. If any other animal had a language capacity, they'd be using it. It's like thinking humans have an undiscovered capacity to fly'.

For other researchers, Chomsky and his followers are seriously mistaken, and what Rumbaugh and Savage-Rumbaugh (1978) have termed our 'egocentric view' that humans are unique from other forms of life is 'being jarred to the core'.

Rumbaugh and Savage-Rumbaugh's view comes from their own and other researchers' attempts to teach language to our closest evolutionary relatives, chimpanzees and gorillas. Clearly, if non-humans can be taught to use language, then they must have the *capacity* for language, and whilst such an ability obviously does not appear spontaneously (as Chomsky has correctly observed), it must be *latent* in them. Such a finding would have serious implications for Chomsky and his followers and would necessitate a dramatic revision of views about what makes humans different from other species.

Our aim in this chapter is to describe and evaluate attempts to teach language to non-humans. Before we review the various attempts, however, we need to look at the distinction between communication and language, and the criteria for a 'true' language.

The communication/ language distinction and early attempts to teach non-humans language

As we noted in Chapter 12, many non-human species are, like humans, able to *communicate*. Honey-bees, for example, communicate the location, distance and quantity of a pollen source to one another by means of elaborate 'waggle dances' (von Frisch, 1974), whilst other species use vocalisations, odours or body posture to communicate with one another. A communication system, though, is not necessarily a language. For example, human language can be modified by experience and is adaptable to novel situations. Non-human communication systems, by contrast, are quite inflexible and, whilst usually well adapted to a particular habitat, can be inaccurate when there are changes to the environment. Thus, the information supplied by a honey-bee is inaccurate when the honey-bee has to fly upwind to its hive (Moffett, 1990).

Many people treat *speech* as being synonymous with language. As is the case with the ability to communicate, though, the ability to speak does not necessarily mean that language is being used. Parrots can 'talk', but most of us would agree that they are not capable of language because there is no meaning or understanding in the sounds they make. To borrow from Chomsky, parrots do not display *linguistic competence* (but see page 167 for an alternative view about this). Early research into the possibility of non-human language did, however, involve attempts to teach chimpanzees to speak (e.g. Yerkes and Learned, 1925; Kellogg and Kellogg, 1933; Hayes and Hayes, 1951).

Kellogg and Kellogg, for example, raised a chimpanzee called Gua alongside their own son, Donald. Although Gua displayed some of the same abilities as Donald, such as moving around and grasping objects, she did not display any evidence of vocalising in the way Donald did, and whilst she could understand a few words, she failed to utter a single one. Keith and Cathy Hayes' research involved a chimpanzee called Viki who was raised from infancy in the Hayes' home. Viki wore nappies, followed Cathy Hayes (her 'mother') around the house, and was generally treated as though she was a human infant. Like human infants, she behaved mischievously, scribbling on walls and opening windows. However, she never mastered toilet training and, unlike most human infants, bit her 'parents' visitors. Despite the intensive training she was given over three years, Viki managed to utter only a few simple words, namely 'mam', 'pap', 'cup' and 'up', and even these were difficult for her human trainers to understand. She did, however, learn to light a cigarette (see Figure 14.1).

Figure 14.1   Although she did not learn to speak, Viki acquired some human behaviours, not all of them desirable.

The failure of the Kelloggs and the Hayes followed that of Yerkes and Learned. As an explanation for their failure, Yerkes and Learned suggested that:

'if the imitative tendency of the parrot were combined with the calibre of intellect of the chimpanzee, the latter undoubtedly would possess speech, since he has a voice mechanism comparable to man's as well as an intellect of the type and level to enable him to use sounds for the purpose of real speech'.

As Vygotsky (1962) has noted, Yerkes and Learned confused human language with human speech. Kellogg (1968) pointed out that chimpanzees' vocal apparatus is unsuitable for making English speech sounds, and subsequent research has shown that the brain mechanisms by which we are able to control our vocal apparatus are not present in chimpanzees.

The criteria for 'true' language

One way of evaluating attempts to teach language to non-humans who do not speak is by using criteria that are generally agreed by researchers to be attributes of language. One set of criteria was devised by Hockett (1960) who proposed 13 *design features* of language. Working within Hockett's framework, Aitchison (1983) has proposed that four of these features distinguish between true language (that is, language as used by humans) and the communication systems of animals. These four criteria, which have been used as the basis for evaluating attempts to teach language to non-humans, are shown in Box 14.1.

> **Box 14.1   Aitchison's four criteria for a true language**
>
> 1 **Semanticity:** This is the use of symbols to mean or refer to objects, actions, relational concepts (such as 'over', 'in' and 'more') and so on.
>
> 2 **Displacement:** This refers to the ability to make reference to events and objects in another time or place. For example, displacement allows us to talk about a person we met last week and a person we will be meeting next week.
>
> 3 **Creativity:** This is the capacity to combine symbols so as to produce (and understand when the symbols are combined by someone else) 'original' language. Brown (1973) calls this *productivity*, and 'original' means the production and understanding of novel combinations of symbols, that is, a combination that has *never* been produced before.
>
> 4 **Structure dependence:** To be creative, an individual must have some understanding of the patterned nature of language and the use of 'structured chunks' such as word order. This appreciation of *syntax* (see Chapter 12, page 141) is what is meant by structure dependence.

Studies of 'linguistic primates'

Speech is not the only way in which language can be expressed. The profoundly deaf use *sign language*, which is a gestural form of language that makes use of hand signals. The mere fact that chimpanzees cannot talk does not exclude the possibility that they are capable of learning some form of language. This was very much Vygotsky's view, and he argued that using sign language to teach language to chimpanzees would be a more sensible approach to adopt because the actions involved in sign language are very much within a chimpanzee's competence. Also, because our own hand and finger dexterity and that of a chimpanzee are more or less the same, any limitations in acquiring language would be purely cognitive (Carlson, 1987).

WASHOE

Vygotsky's proposal was taken up by Allan and Beatrice Gardner (Gardner and Gardner, 1969, 1977). The Gardners' 'Project Washoe' began in the 1960s using an eight-month-old female chimpanzee called Washoe (named after the county in Nevada where the Gardners worked). Using a variety of methods, including modelling and physically guiding Washoe's hands, as well as operant conditioning, the Gardners attempted to teach her *Ameslan* (an acronym of 'American sign language') which is the sign language used by the hearing impaired in North America. In Ameslan (or ASL), many gestures visually represent aspects of a word's meaning, and Ameslan is a 'true' language in that it contains function words and content words along with regular grammatical rules. Indeed, Ameslan is fully adequate for expressing everything that can be spoken. The most efficient method of teaching turned out to be placing Washoe's hands and fingers in the desired position and repeatedly guiding her through a sign (a procedure known as *moulding*).

Washoe was a year old when her formal training began. She was tutored in an environment in which she was only ever communicated to in sign language, and her trainers communicated to one another exclusively in sign language. Whenever Washoe made a correct sign, she was positively reinforced for it. At age two, Washoe had learned 38 signs, and the Gardners observed that her progress was similar to that of human one- and two-year-olds. Thus, she used signs to communicate the location of objects, the individual to whom objects belonged and the properties of those objects.

By the age of four, Washoe could use over 130 signs, and by the age of five could use 160 signs. Just as young children do, Washoe also generalised particular signs. For example, 'more' was signed to request 'more tickling', 'more food' and so on. Although she initially used single signs (much like young children use spoken language), she began to use two and more signs in order to make a single 'sentence' such as 'Washoe sorry', 'Gimme flower', 'More fruit' and 'You tickle me'. According to the Gardners, these combinations were made on her own, without specific teaching. Washoe also appeared to produce combinations of signs that suggested a creative use of language. For example, after seeing a swan, she signed 'water-bird' and after being menaced by an aggressive monkey, she made the sign 'dirty-monkey'.

Washoe could apparently understand simple sentences. For example, when asked 'Who good?', she signed 'good me', and she occasionally produced syntactically correct sentence phrases like 'gimme tickle'. In addition to being able to initiate commands and answer questions, Washoe also appeared to be able to apologise, make assertions and do the sorts of things that children do when they are learning language. The immediate interest in the Gardners' research was reflected by the comments of a reporter from the *New York Times* whose first language was sign language, which he had learned from his deaf parents. After meeting Washoe, he was moved to comment that 'suddenly I realised I was conversing with a member of another species in my native tongue'.

Washoe displayed some evidence of displacement, since she could ask for or refer to absent objects or people. Although she was as likely to sign 'sweet go' as 'go sweet' in the early stages of her training, Gardner and Gardner (1978) reported that her use of word order eventually became consistent. By the age of five, Washoe's command of language was roughly equivalent to that of a three-year-old child. As Carlson (1987) has observed, though, we cannot really compare Washoe's progress with that of ordinary human children. The fairest comparison would be with deaf children learning to use sign language. Whilst Washoe's accomplishments were impressive, she did not learn language as readily as deaf human children do (although such readiness has been claimed in other chimpanzees: see below).

SARAH

Similar findings to those obtained by the Gardners were reported by a research team led by David Premack (e.g. Premack, 1971; Premack and Premack, 1972). Rather than using sign language, Sarah was taught to communicate using a technique that required her to substitute variously shaped plastic pieces for objects and actions. These pieces differed in size, shape and colour and had a magnetic backing so that they could be put onto a 'language board' to form a vertical picture, as shown in Figure 14.2.

Figure 14.2   Using plastic shapes to teach language to a non-human.

As a result of being positively reinforced by means of bananas and jam, Sarah very quickly learned symbols for her favourite things and for the humans who looked after and trained her. She also learned symbols for relationships such as 'give'. To do this, her trainers placed a piece of fruit out of her reach, and only when she placed the symbol for 'give' on the magnetic board did she receive her reward. Sarah learned over 100 symbols and also appeared to understand complex sentences such as 'Sarah insert banana in pail, apple in dish'. She also showed evidence of learning concepts. Thus, when asked to compare a banana and a yellow ball, she arranged the symbols to indicate 'the same', which requires an understanding of the concept of colour (Crooks and Stein, 1991).

Interestingly, Sarah learned how to use word order to denote subject-verb-object, and this rule could be applied to new sentences such as 'Debbie cut banana'. Sarah even learned how to construct sentences involv-

ing conditional relationships, as in 'If Sarah take apple, then Mary give Sarah chocolate' and 'If Sarah take banana, then Mary no give Sarah chocolate'. However, Sarah showed no evidence of displacement, and whilst some of her use of the plastic symbols was impressive, the Premacks were unable to hold 'conversations' with Sarah in the way that the Gardners were with Washoe.

LANA

A slightly more sophisticated approach to the use of symbols was taken by Duane Rumbaugh and his associates (e.g. Rumbaugh et al., 1974; Rumbaugh, 1977; Rumbaugh and Savage-Rumbaugh, 1978). The researchers worked with a female chimpanzee called Lana who was taught to type messages onto a keyboard consisting of 50 keys, each of which displayed a geometric configuration or pattern. The keyboard (or *lexigram*, as the researchers termed it) was connected to a computer. Each geometric symbol had an equivalent in human language, the language itself being called *Yerkish* after the Yerkes Primate Research Centre in Atlanta, Georgia where the research was undertaken.

As noted, each key was labelled with a particular symbol that stood for an object or action. When Lana pressed a sequence of keys, the configurations appeared on a screen in front of her. Because she learned to correct herself after checking the sequence of configurations on the screen, it could be said that she had learned to 'read'. Lana learned to form sentences and was capable of initiating and comprehending quite complex sentences. For example, to one of her trainers called Beverley she once operated the keys to produce 'Beverley move behind room' possibly suggesting that the trainer should leave the cage and go into the room behind it. When Beverley left the cage, Lana typed 'Please machine, make window open', and when Beverley opened the window, Lana was there looking at her.

Lana's comprehension skills were demonstrated in her ability to respond to the question 'What is the name of the object that is green?'. Lana could also create original messages, as in the case of asking her trainer Jim to 'Give apple which is orange' for an orange. Although the word 'orange' was not in her vocabulary as a noun, it was as an adjective, and not having the noun form, she substituted another fruit in order to convey meaning. Similarly, when she saw a ring on the finger of one of her trainers for the first time, she combined two signs she already knew ('finger' and 'bracelet'). Like

Sarah, Lana was trained to use a fixed word order, and like Sarah, she showed some evidence of structure dependence, since she could distinguish between 'Tim groom Lana' and 'Lana groom Tim'.

KOKO

In the studies we have described so far, the non-humans used were chimpanzees. However, Patterson and Linden (1981) attempted to teach a female gorilla, Koko, to use Ameslan. By the age of seven, Koko had mastered some 375 distinctive signs, and was capable of combining these into longer 'utterances'. Like Washoe, she was also able to arrange signs in novel combinations such as 'white tiger' (for 'zebra') and 'elephant baby' (for a Pinocchio doll). According to Patterson (1980), Koko's large vocabulary was accompanied by the ability to express emotions (such as happiness), to refer to past and future events, to do the opposite of what she was told to do and 'bend the truth' to her own advantage. For example, when she once jumped on a sink and pulled it away from the wall, she responded to the accusation that she had caused the damage by blaming one of her trainers.

Koko could also evidently use Ameslan to produce insults such as 'Penny dirty toilet devil' when angry with one of her trainers. Perhaps more remarkably, Koko invented signs of her own such as tucking her index finger under her arm to represent a thermometer (Patterson et al., 1987). Finally, it also appears that Koko could express a sense of self-awareness. When asked the question 'Are you an animal or a person?', she referred to herself as a 'fine animal gorilla'.

Table 14.1 summarises the findings relating to Washoe, Sarah, Lana and Koko in terms of the four criteria for 'true' language we identified earlier.

Table 14.1   Summary of the findings relating to Washoe, Sarah, Lana and Koko

	Washoe	Sarah	Lana	Koko
Semanticity	yes	yes	yes	yes
Displacement	yes	no	yes	yes
Creativity	some evidence	little evidence	yes	yes
Structure dependence	some evidence	some evidence	some evidence	little evidence

As Table 14.1 shows, the evidence is, at least on first inspection, impressive for semanticity and creativity, but less impressive for displacement and structure dependence. Whilst the particular training methods used by researchers may account for the lack of structure dependence, some researchers believe that none of the studies we have described offers compelling evidence that non-humans can acquire language.

Criticisms of the 'linguistic primates' studies

One of the fiercest critics of the view that non-human animals are capable of acquiring language has been Herbert Terrace (1979). Terrace studied a male chimp called 'Nim Chimpsky', a play on words of 'Noam Chomsky'. Like Washoe, Nim was raised much like a human child would be, although because Nim was raised in the Bronx in New York City, he slept in a loft bed and had to commute to Terrace's university! Nim was taught Ameslan, eventually learning 125 basic signs, and Terrace and his co-workers attempted to record every statement that Nim made. Within two years, they had recorded over 20,000 statements consisting of two or more signs, and the research team were initially amazed by Nim's apparent linguistic abilities.

After studying videotapes of Nim, however, Terrace concluded that whilst Nim could produce a large number of combinations of his 125 signs, he was essentially just imitating the signs of his trainers rather than creatively communicating new information. Moreover, what Nim did produce bore no resemblance to sequences produced by human children (Terrace et al., 1979). When Nim did form long sentences, they were produced by an almost random stringing together of signs that roughly applied in a given context, such as 'You me sweet drink give me' (Pettito and Seidenberg, 1979).

According to Terrace, no research, his own included, has shown spontaneous utterances from non-humans which are 'not whole or partial imitations of the teacher's most recently signed utterances' (Terrace, 1985). Joining Terrace, several other researchers have questioned the data obtained from the various studies of non-humans. Some of the criticisms that have been made are summarised in Box 14.2.

Box 14.2   Some criticisms of attempts to teach language to non-humans

- In all studies, chimpanzees and gorillas have acquired their limited vocabularies with great difficulty and only following intensive reinforcement. This contrasts sharply with children who 'effortlessly soak up dozens of new words each week' (Limber, 1977). For Terrace (1979):

  'unlike children who are able readily to add new items to their vocabularies in response to casual instruction (or without any instruction at all), apes are able to do so only in narrowly structured situations and with extensive drill. What appears to be lacking in the case of apes is an understanding of the fact that one can refer to an object by its name'.

- None of the apes has progressed beyond the level of a three-year-old child, particularly in forming *complex syntactic constructions*. So, to a child 'you tickle' and 'tickle you' have different meanings. In general, chimpanzees are likely to use such phrases interchangeably. Thus, word order is unreliable in chimps, yet reliable word orders tend to be used by children as young as one (Terrace et al., 1979).

- Deaf children who learn Ameslan (ASL) outpace chimpanzees taught Ameslan in terms of their ability to ask questions, form negative sentences and so on, even though they are given nowhere near the explicit training in language received by apes (Crider et al., 1989).

- According to Tartter (1986), researchers have been guilty of the *generous interpretation pitfall*. When presented with ambiguous information, we tend to see what we expect or want to see (as we noted in Chapter 2, see page 22). So, when Washoe, for example, signed 'waterbird', the researchers might have generously assumed that she was being creative in naming an object (a swan) for which she did not have a word. A less generous interpretation, though, is that Washoe was first naming 'water' (in which the swan was swimming) and then naming the animal ('bird') using a sign with which she was familiar. Likewise, it may be generous to claim that because Koko's thumb was too short to make the sign for 'eleven', she creatively made the sign for 'lemon o'clock' in a discussion about time.

- When apes are tested by people who are either not familiar with the symbols or signs being used or who do not know the correct answers, they perform far more poorly than when tested by familiar trainers (although it should be acknowledged that the same is true of children performing in front of adults with whom they are not familiar).

- Epstein et al. (1980) have argued that the 'language-driven behaviour' of apes can be explained in terms of imitation and reinforcement, and that an ape putting together symbols for some sort of reward (such as a tickle) is no different to a pigeon pecking a series of buttons in a particular sequence in order to gain some sort of reward (such as a food pellet). In Epstein and his colleagues' experiment, two pigeons called Jack and Jill were operantly conditioned to perform language-like behaviours in which one pecked coloured keys in order to 'answer' the 'questions' selected by the other. In Epstein et al.'s view:

  'we have thus demonstrated that pigeons can learn to engage in sustained and natural conversation without human intervention, and that one pigeon can transmit information to another entirely through the use of symbols'.

In addition to the criticisms described in Box 14.2, some researchers have asked whether the correct use of signs to refer to things is a *sufficient* criterion for semanticity. Even Savage-Rumbaugh et al. (1980) were doubtful whether any apes (including Lana) used individual elements of their vocabularies as *words*. In children, much of their initial vocabulary of names functions as a way of informing another person that they have noticed something. According to MacNamara (1982), no amount of training could ever produce an ape with such an ability, since the act of referring is not learnt, but is what MacNamara terms 'a primitive of cognitive psychology'.

After the publication of Terrace's damaging critique and other criticisms that followed, researchers involved in teaching language to non-humans attempted to defend themselves. For example, Gardner (1981) has suggested that Nim was not brought up in a way comparable to Washoe, being restricted to a 'windowless cell' and having a large number (over 60) of trainers, some of whom lacked competence in sign language.

Additionally, according to Bernstein (1987), Washoe and her companions have been observed spontaneously signing to one another, suggesting they are not merely repeating or reproducing signs in order to obtain a reward. For example, Loulis, a ten-month-old chimpanzee 'adopted' by Washoe, began to imitate Washoe's signs within eight days (Fouts et al., 1989). To ensure that it was Washoe rather than themselves who was being imitated, the trainers limited the signs they used in Loulis' presence. One sign they did not use was that for 'food'. In the words of Fouts (1983):

> 'Washoe was observed to sign "food" repeatedly in an excited fashion when a human was getting her some food. Loulis was sitting next to her watching. Washoe stopped signing and took Loulis' hand in hers, molded it into the "food" sign configuration, and touched it to his mouth several times'.

One beneficial effect of the various criticisms that have been made is that studies have become much more rigorously controlled. For example, Gardner and Gardner (1984) allowed chimpanzees to see a series of slides that were projected in such a way that only the chimpanzees could see them. This ruled out the possibility that intentional or unintentional non-verbal reinforcement by trainers could be responsible for the chimpanzees' performance. Under such circumstances, it has been claimed that chimpanzees can recognise concepts and name them in sign language.

Kanzi

Rather than putting chimpanzees through the rote learning of symbols and building up a vocabulary one symbol at a time, Savage-Rumbaugh (1990) and her colleagues have used a large vocabulary of symbols from the outset. Their aim has been to work with chimpanzees in a way which is much more like the way in which language is used by adults around children. The 'star pupil' of the research has been Kanzi, a rare bonobo chimpanzee. Originally, a chimpanzee called Matata was to be the subject of research, her teaching apparatus consisting of a lexigram of 256 geometrical symbols representing verbs and nouns (see Figure 14.3). When a symbol is touched, the word is spoken

Figure 14.3   Kanzi, Sue Savage-Rumbaugh and the 256-symbol lexigram.

by means of a voice synthesiser, which allows the comprehension of spoken English to be tested.

Matata was a poor learner and only used a handful of the symbols. However, although no attempt was made to teach Kanzi, he 'picked up' the symbols used by Matata as naturally as a human child picks up the words used by adults. By the age of ten, Kanzi had a vocabulary of around 200 words. However, whilst the size of his vocabulary is impressive, the apparent meaning the words have to him is even more impressive. Even under very rigorously controlled conditions in which only Kanzi can hear verbal instructions issued by an experimenter, he correctly responds to many different instructions, even when he has not heard an instruction before (such as 'put the keys in the fridge' or 'put the syringe in the dog'). Interestingly, Kanzi actually performs better when syntactically complex sentences ('Get the orange that is in the colony room') as opposed to syntactically simple sentences ('Go to the colony room and get the orange') are used.

According to Savage-Rumbaugh (1990), language training that is *production based* is sufficiently detrimental that it may be said to disrupt the 'normal course' of language acquisition in the ape, and that:

> 'when the environment is structured in a way that makes it possible for the chimpanzee to acquire language much as does the normal child, by coming to understand what is said before it elects to produce utterances, the perspective of language acquisition and function that emerges is very different from that seen in (other chimpanzees)'.

In the view of some researchers (e.g. Aitchison, 1983), whilst the various apes seem to be able to cope with some of the basic features of language, they do not appear to be predisposed to cope with them, and the ease with which humans acquire language supports the Chomskyan idea that we are innately predisposed to do so. Moreover, although some chimpanzees have grasped some of the rudiments of language, what they have learned and the speed at which they learn it is qualitatively different from that of human beings (Carroll, 1986).

Whilst Aitchison and Carroll might be expressing the view held by a number of researchers, there are a growing number of supporters of the view that language is not confined to human beings. For example, Maratsos (1983) has argued that the criteria we identified earlier on in this chapter for 'true' language are actually relatively new, and that:

> 'apes can probably learn to use signs to communicate meaning ... As this used to be the old boundary for language, it seems unfair to raise the ante and say that (using signs) to communicate meaning is not really language'.

Likewise, Savage-Rumbaugh and her colleagues believe that there is only a difference of degree between human and ape language. Responding to Terrace's criticism that Kanzi still only uses his lexigram symbols to get things done and to ask for things, rather than to share his perception of the world, Savage-Rumbaugh acknowledges that what Terrace says is true, but argues that Kanzi is no different from a young human child in

this respect. Whilst Kanzi does predominantly use symbols for 'requesting', he can also tell his trainers when he is going to be 'good' or 'bad', where he is going on his travels, or what he has just eaten, something Terrace has consistently refused to acknowledge.

The evidence indicates that Kanzi's capacity for comprehension is much better than his capacity for producing language using the lexigram, and that as far as we can tell, he is extremely frustrated by this. But if Kanzi were to talk, what would he say? As Lewin (1991) has observed, 'Maybe the first thing he'd say is that he is fed up with Terrace claiming that apes don't have language'.

Related research with non-humans

There also seems to be evidence that some non-primates might be capable of acquiring certain features of 'true' language. Research conducted by Herman et al. (1990) with dolphins and Pepperberg (1990) with African grey parrots indicates that these non-primates can understand the meaning of individual symbols. Other researchers have used chimpanzees' apparent linguistic abilities to study their cognitive capabilities. Sarah (the chimpanzee originally studied by Premack's research team), for example, has been shown to be able to conserve liquid quantity (Woodruff et al., 1978).

After being trained to use symbols for the words 'same' and 'different', Sarah was presented with two tall vessels containing equal amounts of coloured water. The contents of one of the vessels were then poured into a wider but shallower vessel. Sarah was given the symbols for 'same' and 'different' and, with her trainers out of the room, she placed the 'same' symbol between the two vessels (see Figure 14.4).

Subsequent studies revealed that Sarah did not show any evidence of being able to understand the concept of number (and so could not be tested on her ability to conserve this). According to Marc Hauser and his colleagues (cited in Highfield, 1996), however, the cotton-top tamarin monkey can add and subtract better than human infants. In Hauser's experiments, the monkeys were shown one or two aubergines which were then hidden behind a screen. When the number of aubergines was changed, the monkeys appeared to be aware of the difference. Also, unlike human infants

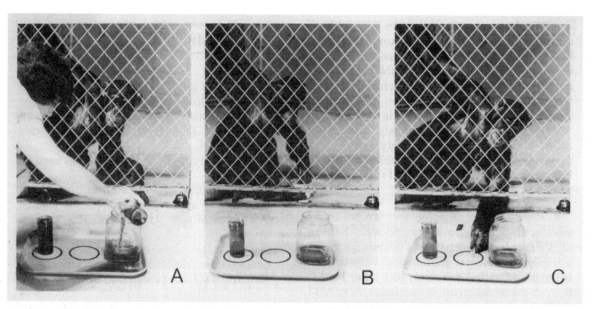

Figure 14.4   The conservation of liquid quantity by a chimpanzee (reprinted with permission from *Science*, 202 (1978) G. Woodruff, D. Premack and K. Kennel, 'Conservation of liquid quantity by the chimpanzee'. Copyright (1997) American Association for the Advancement of Science).

under the age of one, the monkeys were still aware of a change in number when different types of vegetable were used as substitutes.

Conclusions

It seems clear that, despite the various criticisms, chimpanzees and gorillas are capable of satisfying at least some of the criteria used to define 'true' language and that there are clear parallels between the accomplishments of apes' and children's linguistic development. Such findings have important implications for the theories of language development in humans that we described in the previous chapter.

SUMMARY

- Chomsky is one of the most ardent advocates of the view that language is a human species-specific behaviour. Rumbaugh and Savage-Rumbaugh challenge this 'egocentric view' based on attempts to teach language to chimpanzees and gorillas, which may have a **latent capacity** for language.
- While many non-human species are able to **communicate**, as in the honey-bees' 'waggle dance', this does not necessarily constitute a language. Human language is adaptable to novel situations, while non-human communication systems are inflexible and so can be inaccurate in a changing environment.
- **Speech** is **not** synonymous with language, as in the case of parrots whose 'talk' is meaningless, but early attempts to teach language to non-humans did involve attempts to teach chimpanzees to speak, such as the Kelloggs' study of Gua and the Hayes' study of Viki.
- The failure of these and other early studies is now generally taken to reflect the unsuitability of chimpanzees' vocal apparatus for making English speech sounds: they lack the brain mechanisms which enable us to control our vocal apparatus.
- Hockett proposed a set of 13 criteria or **design features** of language. According to Aitchison, four of these distinguish true language as used by humans, namely **semanticity**, **displacement**, **creativity/productivity** and **structure dependence** (i.e. the appreciation of **syntax**). These

four criteria can be used to evaluate attempts to teach language to non-humans.

- Vygotsky argued that chimpanzees' inability to talk does not mean they are incapable of learning some form of language, such as **sign language**, which involves actions very much within their competence. Also, the similarity of human and chimp hand and finger dexterity means that any limitations in acquiring language would be purely cognitive.
- The Gardners used modelling, physical guidance (**moulding**) and operant conditioning to teach Washoe **Ameslan**, in which many gestures visually represent aspects of a word's meaning. This is a 'true' language, containing function and content words and grammatical rules, and allowing expression of everything that can be spoken.
- Washoe was communicated to exclusively in sign language, and by age two, she had learned 38 signs used to communicate the location and properties of objects and who owned them; her progress was similar to a one- and two-year-old child. By age four, she could use 130 signs; by age five, 160.
- Washoe generalised particular signs, initially used single signs but then began spontaneously to combine two or more to make a single sentence, suggesting a creative use of language. She could also understand simple sentences, initiate commands, answer questions and showed some evidence of displacement. Her use of word order eventually became consistent.
- Although the Gardners assessed her progress at age five as equivalent to that of a three-year-old child, the fairest comparison would be with deaf children learning sign language. On this basis, she (and other apes) did not do as well as her human counterparts, especially in view of the amount of training received.
- Similar results were reported for Sarah by Premack, who used pieces of plastic of various shapes, sizes and colours which could be placed on a magnetic 'language board'. She learned over 100 symbols and seemed to understand complex sentences, as well as showing evidence of learning concepts such as colour.
- Sarah also learned how to use word order to denote certain grammatical rules and 'if then' relationships, although she showed no sign of displacement. It was not possible to hold 'conversations' with her as it had been with Washoe.
- Rumbaugh and colleagues taught Lana to type messages onto a 50-key keyboard or **lexigram**, each key displaying a geometric pattern, and each

pattern represented an object or action. The language was called **Yerkish**. Pressing a sequence of keys caused the patterns to appear on a screen and, by correcting the pattern, she learned to 'read'.
- Lana learned to form sentences, could initiate and comprehend quite complex sentences, and she could create original messages by combining two familiar signs to name an unfamiliar object. Like Sarah, Lana was trained to use a fixed word order and showed some evidence of structure dependence.
- Patterson and Linden attempted to teach Ameslan to Koko, a female gorilla. By age seven, she had learnt 375 signs which she could combine to form longer 'utterances'. Like Washoe, she could arrange familiar signs in novel ways. She could also use signs to express emotions, to refer to past and future events, to 'bend the truth' and to insult others. She could even express a sense of self-awareness.
- The overall evidence is impressive for semanticity and creativity, less so for displacement and structure dependence. Some researchers believe that none of the evidence is convincing.
- Chimpanzees and gorillas acquire their vocabularies only in narrowly structured situations and after extensive training that requires intensive reinforcement. This contrasts sharply with children's ability to soak up new words quickly and easily.
- While even one-year-old children use reliable word order, this is very inconsistent among the non-human subjects. Generally, the ability to form **complex syntactic constructions** fails to progress beyond the level of a three-year-old child.
- According to Tartter, researchers have been guilty of the **generous interpretation pitfall**, whereby ambiguous information is interpreted in line with expectations. Also, when tested by people unfamiliar with the symbols or signs being used, apes perform more poorly than when tested by familiar trainers.
- According to Epstein et al., the 'language-driven behaviour' of apes is no different from pigeons pecking a series of buttons: in both cases, the behaviour is rewarded.
- Another area of controversy concerns whether apes use individual signs as **words**, thus raising doubt over whether the semanticity criterion has been satisfied. MacNamara sees the act of referring as 'a primitive of cognitive psychology' which humans possess but which cannot be learnt by apes.

- Based on his study of Nim Chimpsky, Terrace launched a fierce attack on the claims that non-human animals are capable of acquiring language. After initial amazement at Nim's apparent abilities, Terrace concluded that he was essentially imitating his trainers' signs and not showing creativity. When Nim produced long sentences from his 125 basic signs, they were combined almost randomly.
- Gardner defended his findings by noting that Nim was raised very differently from Washoe, being confined to a 'windowless cell' and having over 60 trainers, some of whom lacked competence in sign language. Fouts has also reported evidence that Loulis, 'adopted' by Washoe, began spontaneously imitating her and that she helped Loulis to make new signs.
- The various criticisms have led to more rigorously controlled studies, such as the Gardners' use of slides seen only by the chimps. Under these circumstances, they seem to be able to recognise concepts and name them in sign language.
- Savage-Rumbaugh's method of working with chimps is intended to be much more like the way that adults use language around children than the earlier **production-based** studies. Initially, Matata was taught using a lexigram, such that when a symbol is touched, the word is spoken via a voice synthesiser.
- While Matata proved to be a poor learner, Kanzi, a rare bonobo chimp, learned the symbols as naturally as a child picks up adult speech, without any training, and had a vocabulary of 200 words by age ten. More impressive still is his ability to follow verbal instructions, even when these have not been heard before, and he seems to perform better when syntactically complex sentences are used.
- Savage-Rambaugh believes that production-based studies may actually disrupt the normal course of apes' language acquisition. The approach used with Matata and Kanzi allows the ape to understand what is said before it begins to use any signs itself, much as happens with children.
- A widely held view is that while apes seem to grasp some of the rudiments of language, they do not seem predisposed to do so, as are humans: what and how fast they learn is qualitatively different from human learning. However, the communication of meaning may be the fairest way of defining 'true' language, rather than the four criteria used to evaluate the ape studies.
- Savage-Rumbaugh argues that when Kanzi uses his symbols primarily to get things done and to ask for things, rather than to share his perception of the world, he is doing what young children do. She concludes that the difference between human and ape language is only one of degree.
- Research with dolphins and African grey parrots indicates that some non-primates can understand the meaning of individual symbols, and other researchers have studied the cognitive abilities of chimps, such as Woodruff et al.'s study of Sarah's ability to conserve liquid quantity. Although Sarah was later shown to be unable to conserve number, the cotton-top tamarin monkey can add and subtract better than human infants.

15

SOME ASPECTS OF READING AND WRITING

Introduction and overview

According to Massaro (1989), a literate person faced with a written word is captured by it and seems to have no choice but to read it. One experimental demonstration of this was provided by Stroop (1935) who, as we saw in Chapter 6 (see page 73), showed that when the name of a colour is written in a different colour, and a person is asked to name the colour but ignore the word, the task is difficult to do. Such a finding indicates that reading is such an overlearned skill that it is not easily 'put on hold' (Massaro, 1989).

As early as 1908, Edmund Huey wrote that:

'to completely analyse what we do when we read would almost be the acme of a psychologist's achievements for it would be to describe very many of the most intricate workings of the human mind, as well as to unravel the tangled story of the most remarkable specific performance that civilisation has learned in all its history'.

Much research has gone into attempting to understand the processes involved in reading, and it would be impossible in a book of this size to review all of this research. Our modest aim in this chapter is to consider some of the research concerned with understanding the processes involved in reading.

Complementary to the cognitive skill of reading is writing. Writing is the production and organisation of connected discourse and, like reading, is almost always meaningful (Gagné, 1985). Both reading and writing have been common skills for only a short time (Hampson and Morris, 1996). One of the most active research areas concerned with writing has been an examination of the cognitive processes that are involved in it. Again, it would be impossible to review all of the research that has been conducted. As a result, we will confine our concern to considering one of the most influential theories of the processes involved in writing.

Some basic findings in reading research

Harris and Sipey (1983) have defined reading as 'a meaningful interpretation of written or printed verbal symbols'. Research into how this meaningful interpretation is made began in the 1870s with the invention of the *tachistoscope*, a device which presents visual material under conditions of very brief exposures, and the discovery of *saccadic eye movements*. Prior to Emil Javal's discovery of such movements, it had been assumed that the eye moved smoothly and continuously across the page, identifying each letter as it appeared. What Javal showed was that the eye makes a series of start-stop jumps across a line of print, the jumps being known as *saccades* and the periods of time in which the eyes are at rest being termed *fixations*.

Although researchers have devised several methods for investigating reading (descriptions of which can be found in Rayner and Sereno, 1994), the study of eye movements during the silent reading of words is generally accepted as being the best currently available. Research indicates that each saccade takes only a few milliseconds and covers about seven to nine characters on a line (Just and Carpenter, 1984). The eye is essentially 'blind' during a saccade, and the most important information is processed during fixations.

Fixations last about 250 milliseconds (which is equivalent to about eight letters or spaces) and take up more than 90 per cent of total reading time. For a typical line of print, about five or six fixations are made (Rayner and Sereno, 1994). Although our *perceptual span* (or 'effective field of view': Eysenck and Keane, 1995) can be limited by factors such as print size, the maximal span is around three or four letters to the left of the fixation and in the region of 15 letters to the right (a finding which is reversed in people whose language reads from right to left: Pollatsek et al., 1981).

Whilst most of our eye movements are forward towards new words, some are back to earlier words. These *regressions* occur more frequently in poor readers than in good readers, as shown in Figure 15.1.

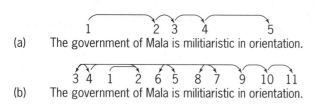

Figure 15.1   Regressions occur in about ten to 20 per cent of eye movements in skilled readers. In poor readers, regressions occur much more frequently. The figure shows the sequence of fixations for a skilled reader (a) and an unskilled reader (b).

Phonological mediation

Whilst we are reading, we sometimes experience hearing an 'inner voice', which speaks the words that are written on a page. One of the oldest questions in research into reading is whether printed language must be translated into some form of speech *before* meaning can be accessed (a process known as *phonological mediation*). The view that reading could be dependent on our cognitive processes, which interpret the words we hear, is supported by the 'inner voice' experience and by the finding that we can use phonological mediation for reading unfamiliar words (such as 'the kurnel sailed his yott': Hampson and Morris, 1996). However, Hampson and Morris have argued that the fact that we are able to use phonological mediation does not necessarily mean that it is the basis of all reading. It may, however, be a useful way of tackling unfamiliar words.

Models of word recognition

Whether or not the recognition of a word first involves identifying the letters that make it up has been addressed in a number of studies. Whilst research (e.g. Cosky, 1976; Reicher, 1969) suggests that not all the letters of a word need to be identified before the whole word is recognised, it is assumed by theories of word recognition that letter recognition does play a role in the process of identifying words.

According to Rayner and Sereno (1994), word identification is a generally automatic process, taking around a mere 50 milliseconds. Research reviewed by Ellis (1993) and Hampson and Morris (1996) suggests that as well as involving recognition of letters, word identification may also involve *spelling* (or *orthographic*) *regularities*, a word's *shape*, its *familiarity* and, in the case of unskilled readers or poorly presented text, the *context*. As we saw in the previous section, there is also evidence to suggest that some information about the sound of words is available during reading, and that such phonological information can play a role in the identification of rare as opposed to common words.

The question of how word identification takes place has been addressed by a number of models, all of which assume the existence of some form of representation of words known by us, and that this representation must be activated for identification to occur (Hampson and Morris, 1996).

THE LOGOGEN MODEL

According to the *logogen model of word recognition* (Morton, 1964, 1969), each word a person knows has a representation (or logogen) in long-term memory. A logogen for a given word has a *resting level of activity* which can be increased by stimulus events (such as hearing or seeing the word). When the level of activity exceeds a logogen's threshold, the logogen fires and the word is recognised. Because high-frequency words are recognised more quickly than low-frequency words (Frederikson and Kroll, 1976), the model assumes that high-frequency words either have a lower threshold of activation or that the meaning of a high-frequency word can be checked more quickly once the logogen has fired (Morton, 1979).

THE COHORT MODEL

An influential approach to the recognition of spoken words which has also been applied to reading is the *cohort model* proposed by Marslen-Wilson (1984). According to this, words are recognised letter by letter in a left-right manner. The model suggests that word recognition occurs by means of the elimination of alternative word candidates (or cohorts). Thus, the recognition of the first letter in the word eliminates all words that do not have that letter in their initial position. Recognition of the second letter eliminates the remaining cohorts that do not have the second letter in the second position and so on, until only one word remains. This is the point at which word recognition occurs.

THE INTERACTIVE-ACTIVATION MODEL

Rumelhart and McClelland's (1982) *interactive-activation model* proposes the existence of three types of recognition unit. The first detects the various features of letters such as vertical and horizontal lines. The second detects the letter that is represented by the combination of letter features. When a letter is recognised as appearing in a particular position in a word, the recognition units for all words which have that letter in a particular position are activated whilst all other word units are inhibited. Following the activation of the word units which have all of the letters making up a particular word and which appear in a particular position, integration occurs in which 'only one word wins and stays active' (Hampson and Morris, 1996).

COMPARING THE MODELS

The three models outlined above differ from one another. Available evidence does not yet generally favour one model over another, and all can claim some experimental support. But as Hampson and Morris (1996) have observed, much of the evidence concerning the information that is used in word recognition comes from studies in which one word is read at a time, and such information may not be necessary to normal reading. Thus the processes involved in reading continuous text, clearly printed, at the reader's own pace may differ from those used when one word is flashed briefly to a participant via a tachistoscope or on a computer screen.

Comprehension

Whilst models of word recognition are important, they tell us little about the comprehension of written language. As Massaro (1989) has noted:

> 'the leap from recognition [*a bottom-up process: see Chapter 1*] to comprehension [*a top-down process: see Chapter 1*] requires certain cognitive prerequisites on the part of the reader. The text must be capable of activating the appropriate knowledge to effect understanding of the message'.

Research indicates that when we read, we draw *infer-*ences in order to help our understanding and use our knowledge and expectations to 'fill in the gaps' (Schank and Abelson, 1977, see Chapter 9).

As we saw in Chapter 9, Bransford and Johnson (1972) found that a particular passage of prose (shown in Box 9.4) was rated as incomprehensible by participants given the passage in isolation, and that their subsequent recall of it was poor. However, if the theme 'washing clothes' was provided, the passage was rated as being more comprehensible and was better recalled. The comprehension of text, then, depends on activating appropriate knowledge sources. Consider, for example, the passage shown in Box 15.1 which was presented to participants by Bransford (1979).

Box 15.1   The passage used in Bransford's (1979) experiment

The man was worried. His car came to a halt and he was all alone. It was extremely dark and cold. The man took off his overcoat, rolled down the window and got out of the car as quickly as possible. Then he used all his strength to move as fast as he could. He was relieved when he finally saw the lights of the city, even though they were far away.

You will probably agree that the passage makes sense, but can you explain *why* the man took off his overcoat or rolled down the window? The actions only make sense if the car is submerged in water. So, whilst we may feel we know something's meaning, we may actually know only a little or nothing!

Towards a theory of reading

Any theory of the cognitive processes involved in reading must accommodate the large amount of data which has accumulated in over 100 years of research. An important model that goes some way towards this is that developed by Marcel Just and Patricia Carpenter (1980, 1992). In their model, shown in Figure 15.2, the reader encounters new information through reading and, after extracting a word's physical features, assigns preliminary meaning to it instead of storing it

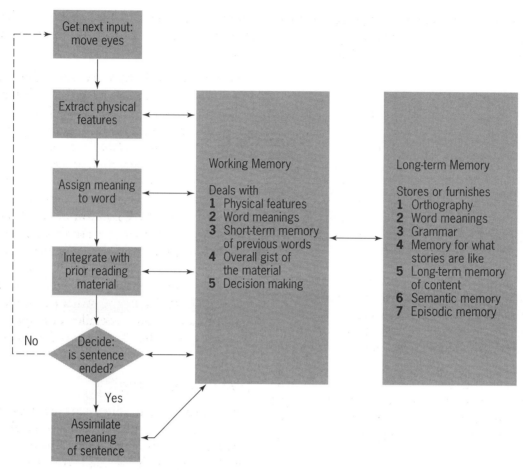

Figure 15.2   Just and Carpenter's model of the cognitive processes in reading.

for later processing. The word is then integrated with the material that has previously been read and if the sentence is ended, its meaning is assimilated.

As Figure 15.2 shows, both long-term memory and working memory (see Chapter 7) contribute to the reading process, although the model sees the main activities of reading (like other cognitive processes) occurring in working memory. Thus, our schemata affect both the information we take in and the way we take it in (that is, the way in which we read). Also, our existing knowledge is modified and transformed by the new content. Like other cognitive processes, then, reading is a dynamic process, and the meaning that is obtained is influenced by the content, prior knowledge, goals and context.

The claim that the processes required to understand each word and its relationship to other words are car-

ried out as soon as a word is encountered is called the *immediacy assumption*, and is held to occur because of working memory's limited capacity. According to Just and Carpenter, individual differences in the capacity of working memory influence how well language is comprehended. Whilst the finding that readers sometimes move their eyes *back* to an earlier part of the text and sometimes *fixate* the same word more than once casts doubt on the immediacy assumption, the assumption about working memory is better supported.

One measure of working-memory capacity is *reading span*, which is defined as the largest number of sentences for which a person can recall all of the final words more than 50 per cent of the time. Just and Carpenter have found that reading span correlates highly with the ability to comprehend written material, and that people with large reading spans read difficult text faster than those with small reading spans. This suggests that people with more processing resources available can carry out forms of processing that those with fewer resources are unable to do (Eysenck and Keane, 1995).

Eysenck and Keane see Just and Carpenter's theory as a 'refreshing change' from much of the theorising on language comprehension that has taken place. However, they note that other differences in comprehension ability which do not depend solely on working-memory capacity (such as the ability to reject inappropriate information), and the model's emphasis on working-memory capacity at the expense of more specific processes involved in comprehension, limit its explanatory power.

Just and Carpenter's model also has little to say about the eye movements that occur during reading (see page 171). Alternative models of reading (such as the *interactive model* proposed by Rayner and Pollatsek, 1989) do incorporate such findings (and a detailed review of these can be found in Eysenck and Keane, 1995). However, Rayner and Pollatsek's model says little about other processes in reading, such as the drawing of inferences. It seems, then, that we are some way from a complete explanation of the cognitive processes involved in reading.

Learning to read

READING READINESS

Harris and Sipey (1983) have argued that learning to read occurs in a number of stages, beginning with 'reading readiness' and culminating in the refinement of reading skills in school and adulthood. 'Reading readiness' is not easy to define. For some researchers (e.g. Spache, 1981), it consists of a large group of characteristics which include visual skills, auditory factors and 'general co-ordination'. For others (e.g. Butler et al., 1985), it can be defined much more narrowly in terms of the possession of *critical pre-reading skills* which include attending to letter order and matching and blending sounds.

Views about the optimum age at which reading instruction should begin have also been the subject of much debate (e.g. Chall, 1983). For a long time, Morphett and Washburne's (1931) view that it is best to postpone reading instruction until children reach a mental age of six years and six months was widely held.

However, Coltheart (1979) has shown that this 'critical stage of reading readiness' viewpoint is unlikely to be true.

Marsh et al. (1981) have identified four stages in learning to read which are found in children taught in British and American schools. These are *glance and guess*, *sophisticated guessing*, *simple grapheme-phoneme correspondence* and *skilled reading*. The four stages themselves have been re-described by Frith (1985) as three skills in learning to read. The first two stages correspond to what Frith calls *logographic skills*, which involve the direct recognition of words as wholes. The third stage corresponds to Frith's *alphabetic skills* which involve using the visual correspondence between particular letters and their sounds. The fourth stage corresponds to Frith's *orthographic skills*, which involve the use of regularities in the structure of words to obtain their pronunciation. A detailed description of the stages and skills can be found in Hampson and Morris (1996).

TEACHING READING

One approach to teaching reading is called the *phonics method*. This method emphasises symbol-sound relationships (such as how to pronounce 'sp', 'st' and 'br'). Another approach, termed the *whole-word method*, encourages the recognition of words by sight. In her book *Learning to Read: The great debate*, Chall (1967) analysed 67 research studies which compared different approaches to reading. Chall cites the conclusions of a special committee held in 1959 into reading, which reported that:

> 'No serious researcher could state with any degree of certainty, on the basis of . . . evidence, that either one or another approach to beginning to read was indeed the best or the worst'.

Thirty years after Chall's book was published, the debate about which strategy produces a better basis for teaching reading continues (Goswami, 1993), although the balance appears to have tipped in favour of phonic methods. For Hampson and Morris (1996), whilst it is difficult to obtain unambiguous evidence concerning the effectiveness of teaching methods, 'it does appear that teaching phonic methods can benefit rather than harm the new reader'.

Writing

The evolution of written language is a relatively recent phenomenon in human history, and the historical development of writing systems is believed to have evolved from *pictorial writing*, a set of pictographic symbols representing a limited number of objects and actions (Gelb, 1952). After that came *logography* (the use of logograms, as in Egyptian hieroglyphics (3000 BC), and Chinese characters (1500 BC)). *Logosyllabic writing* and *syllabic writing* culminated in *alphabetic writing* using letters, as in the Phoenician (1000 BC), Greek (800 BC), Arabic and Gothic (AD 400) and Cyrillic (AD 900) writing systems (Harris and Hodges, 1981).

Some psychologists have approached the processes involved in writing by focusing on individual words, the similarities and differences between written languages and (by studying brain-damaged individuals) the processes involved in spelling (Ellis and Young, 1988). Others have studied writing from a broader per-

spective. The most influential model of the processes involved in writing is that developed by John Hayes and Linda Flower.

Hayes and Flower's model of writing

Hayes and Flower's (e.g. Hayes and Flower, 1980; Flower and Hayes, 1983) information-processing model of writing emphasises the role of working memory, in which three major processes are held to occur. These are *planning, translating* and *reviewing*, as shown in Figure 15.3.

Planning

Planning for writing involves setting goals and organising ideas based on information from the *task environment* and *long-term memory*. Examples of task environments include an essay set by a teacher (such as 'Describe and evaluate any two theories of forgetting'),

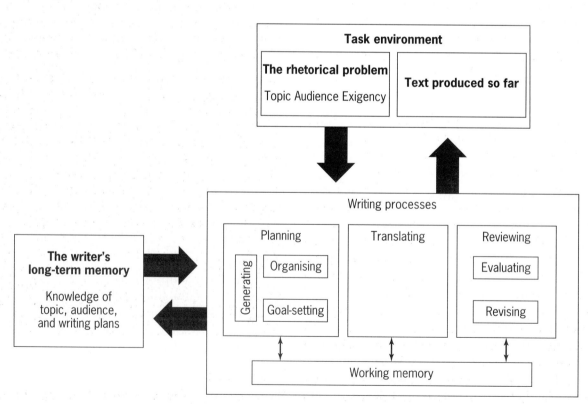

Figure 15.3   Hayes and Flower's model of writing.

receiving feedback from a teacher (such as 'Your essay lacks evaluation of the theories you describe') and knowledge about the intended audience (such as an examiner or a group of fellow students). The particular task environment will, of course, influence the planning of the writing.

Long-term memory is used in several ways in the planning process. For example, we may use our knowledge of different writing forms to, perhaps, begin an essay with a question or a bold statement. Our knowledge of the audience can also influence planning. We may know that a particular teacher likes to see lots of references to experimental research whilst another likes the use of analogies in the explanation of things. Finally, information from long-term memory may incorporate factual information such as the inclusion of certain procedures which, in the case of an essay on theories of forgetting, have been used to study the phenomenon. As Glover and Bruning (1987) have commented, knowledge about writing in general, the particular form that needs to be presented for a given task, the intended audience and specific knowledge about the task can all influence the quality of planning that occurs.

Whilst *knowledge* about a particular task influences the plan that is produced (Voss et al., 1980), other factors are also important. As Figure 15.3 shows, Hayes and Flower's model identifies three sub-processes that are involved in planning, namely *generating, organising* and *goal-setting*.

Generating refers to obtaining information from long-term memory that is relevant to the task in question (such as the names of two theories of forgetting) and the task environment (this essay has to be no longer than 1500 words). *Organising* involves the selection and organisation of information into a writing plan, which can be achieved through the use of *outlines* (Beach and Bridwell, 1984). Thus, an essay on theories of forgetting might begin with an introductory paragraph, a description of one theory, an evaluation of it, a description of a second theory, an evaluation of it, and a concluding paragraph). *Goal-setting* involves evaluating the relevance of information which is available (an example might be deciding whether to include a lengthy description of a particular study or a summary of that study's main findings). These three sub-processes are clearly both interactive and dependent on each other. For example, without being able to generate

information, it is unlikely that a goal can be met, and when a goal has been set, this will influence what new information is generated and how it is organised (Glover and Bruning, 1987).

According to Hayes and Flower, skilled and unskilled writers differ in their abilities to plan a written product in terms of the types of goals they set, how they generate ideas and how well these ideas are organised. Box 15.2 summarises some of the major findings that have been obtained in these respects.

Box 15.2   Some individual differences in planning

Setting goals: Skilled writers set themselves the goal of communicating meaning. Skilled writers also produce more goals and sub-goals than unskilled writers (Hayes and Flower, 1986). The goal of unskilled and immature writers is 'associative writing' or putting down everything in memory that is relevant to a task (Scardamalia and Bereiter, 1987) or avoiding making errors (Birnbaum, 1982).

Generating ideas: Skilled writers can think of many ideas relating to the task they are writing about (Raphael and Kirschner, 1985). This is not necessarily because unskilled writers run out of ideas, but because they have no 'internal cues' to keep the ideas going (Scardamalia et al., 1982).

Organisation: Organisation is important in communicating meaning. Skilled writers plan the meaning they are going to communicate, whereas unskilled writers focus their planning on the mechanics (Geisler et al., 1985). Skilled writers use *cohesive ties*, that is, linguistic devices for linking one idea to the next (Halliday and Hasan, 1976). Unskilled writers have difficulty in writing cohesively and, in particular, assume that the reader knows what is being referred to even if the referent has never been specified (King and Rentel, 1981). Coherent ties enable the organisation of sentences. *Coherent structures* enable an *entire* piece of writing to fit together in an organised way (McCutchen and Perfetti, 1982) as shown in Figure 15.4.

Translating

Typically, the plan constructed during the planning process is much shorter than the final product (Hayes

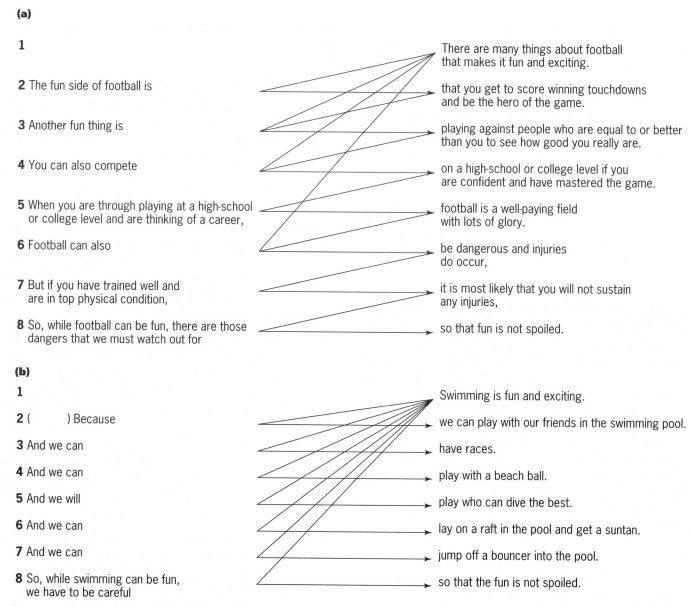

Figure 15.4   In McCutchen and Perfetti's study, students were asked to write an essay beginning with the sentence 'There are so many things about x (where x was a topic chosen by the student) that make it fun and exciting'. The essay was required to end 'So while x can be fun, there are dangers that we must watch out for so that the fun is not spoiled'. In (a), the essay is highly coherent and many of the sentences relate back to both the previous sentences and the chosen topic. In (b), the essay is less coherent because each sentence relates back to the topic sentence only.

and Flower, 1986). Translating (or *sentence generation*) is the process of transforming the writing plan into the actual writing of phrases, either written on paper or stored on computer disc. The starting point for translating is the first part of the writer's plan (such as a definition of the topic in question), which is then transformed into phrases or a sentence. The completion of a sentence is often followed by self-questioning about the next part of the writing plan and how this should be expressed. After the next phrase or sentence has been written, the plan is returned to and, following self-questioning, the process continues in cyclical fashion until the task has been completed.

As Gagné (1985) has noted, translating can stretch working memory to its limits, because the writer is trying to keep many things active in memory at once. Unskilled writers need to read what they have just written in order to maintain cohesion. Skilled writers do not depend on this. This may be because skilled writers have cohesive plans (see Box 15.2) or because more working memory is available to 'hold' what has just been written. More working memory may be available because skilled writers spell and punctuate automatically. In unskilled writers, the need to constantly check spelling and sentence construction results in the representation of what has just been written being lost. An ingenious study of the difference between skilled and unskilled writers in maintaining cohesion during writing is shown in Box 15.3.

Box 15.3   Atwell's (1981) study of cohesion during translating

Skilled and unskilled writers were asked to write an essay on a personal topic. For the first half of the writing session, the writers were able to see what they had written. However, for the second half they used *inkless pens*. Their writing was recorded by means of carbon paper, but since the pens contained no ink, the writers could not see what they had written. Atwell found that writing 'blind' caused a loss of cohesion in the unskilled writers but had little effect on the skilled writers. To maintain cohesion, then, unskilled writers need to read what they have written.

As most students and textbook writers will know, 'getting going' and 'keeping going' are barriers to translating. This *writer's block* has a number of causes, one of which is the need for more knowledge about the task (a problem which has a straightforward solution). Another cause is the application of *rigid rules*. One rigid rule might be to stick to the original writing plan. However, if the plan is inadequate, the writing process is bound to grind to a halt (Eysenck and Keane, 1995).

Similarly, following certain rules that one has been told to apply may also produce writer's block. Examples of such rules include 'always grab the reader's attention immediately', 'begin with a humorous but relevant comment' and 'make at least five evaluative points'. When a task does not lend itself to rules such as these, it is hardly surprising that writer's block occurs (Rose, 1980). Much more effective are rules which facilitate writing and are not stated in absolute terms, such as '*try*

to produce evaluative points in your essay' (Gagné, 1985).

Reviewing

The final process in Hayes and Flower's model involves evaluating what has been written to determine how well it meets the goals that have been set. Clearly, the writer's knowledge of writing, especially its mechanical aspects, is an important part of the revision process (and hence reviewing interacts with planning). Those parts which are considered unsatisfactory are then improved in quality by *reading* and *editing*. Reading involves being sensitive to ideas from the plan that have been omitted, possible superfluous information and mechanical errors (such as spelling mistakes). In editing, the writer rewrites material, moves it from one place to another and changes writing (hence reviewing also interacts with translating).

The evidence suggests that skilled writers are more likely to recognise and overcome coherence and structure-related problems when they review the material than are unskilled writers. They are also more likely to make meaning-related revisions. As a result, skilled writers tend to spend *longer* revising material (Hayes et al., 1985). The evidence also suggests that unskilled writers focus on mechanical errors rather than errors in meaning (Bridwell, 1980) and that they tend not to make revisions which alter the entire structure of what has been written (Faigley and Witte, 1981).

As Figure 15.3 illustrates, Hayes and Flower's model proposes that the component skills of planning, translating and reviewing are guided by the *rhetorical problem*, the *text* that has been produced so far and the writer's *long-term memory*. The rhetorical problem is the writer's interpretation of the task and the achievement of the goals that have been set. If the written text does not match the goals that have been established, then revision is likely to occur. If, however, the match is a close one then not much revision will be undertaken.

Some practical applications of Hayes and Flower's model

As well as identifying the cognitive processes involved in writing, several practical applications derive from

Hayes and Flower's model. Box 15.4 summarises the most important of these.

Box 15.4   Some practical applications deriving from Hayes and Flower's model of the writing process

Setting goals: Effective writing is more likely if clear goals are established. This can be achieved by writing a summary of ideas against which the final product can be compared in order to assess the extent to which the goals have been met.

Outlining for planning: Given that outlining improves the quality of writing and aids in reviewing the final product, writers should outline what is to be written before writing takes place. Outlining also helps the revision process.

Generating ideas: Since skilled writers can think of many ideas related to a particular task, writers should be encouraged to generate ideas.

Communicating meaning: Writers should be encouraged to plan the meaning of what is to be communicated rather than concentrate on the mechanics (although the mechanics of writing are, of course, important).

Revision: For skilled writers, revision is an important part of the writing process. Revision is particularly useful if a goal has been set and an outline developed, since the criteria set may then be checked (see above).

Correcting and rewriting: Feedback about writing can improve performance if the writer re-submits a piece of work since this focuses attention on feedback given about the writing and provides practice in writing correctly.

Peer-editing: Revision can also be aided by having colleagues edit the final product for both coherence and mechanics, and by editing the work of colleagues.

Of course, the success of the processes outlined above depends on other factors, such as *resources*, the provision of extensive practice in writing (e.g. regular essay setting) and the encouragement of writing.

(adapted from Applebee (1984) and Glover and Bruning (1987))

Evaluating Hayes and Flower's model

As the writers of this book are only too painfully aware, writing does not proceed smoothly from planning to translating to reviewing. For example, a brief period of pre-planning may be followed by a writing phase in which the skills of planning, translating and reviewing are employed. Indeed, reviewing may occur *before* writing begins (as when a potential idea is modified) and *during* writing (as when evaluation of a point that has been made occurs) as well as at the end of writing. Indeed, some researchers dispute whether the three processes identified by Hayes and Flower can ever be completely separated from one another.

Eysenck and Keane (1995) have also criticised the model because of its reliance on *protocol analysis* (or *verbal protocols*) as a way of obtaining data. In protocol analysis, the writer verbalises his or her thoughts as writing takes place. However, this method provides information only about those processes of which there is conscious awareness. Eysenck and Keane argue that there is probably little or no conscious awareness of many (or even most) of the processes involved in writing and that 'there is an urgent need to develop ways of investigating these processes'. Notwithstanding these cautions, there is general agreement that Hayes and Flower's model has helped our understanding of the writing process.

Conclusions

Both reading and writing are complex skills (although skills we tend to take for granted). This chapter has reviewed some of the research concerned with understanding the processes involved in reading and writing. Although much data have been accumulated and several theories advanced to explain them, the complete understanding of the processes involved in reading and writing is still some distance away.

SUMMARY

- Reading is an overlearned skill that makes it almost impossible to ignore a written word, as demonstrated by the 'Stroop effect'. The complementary cognitive skill of writing is the production and organisation of connected discourse which, like reading, is invariably meaningful.
- Research into reading began in the 1870s with the invention of the **tachistoscope** and Javal's discovery of **saccadic eye movements**: the eye makes a series of start-stop jumps (**saccades**) and the intervals during which the eyes are at rest are called **fixations**.
- The study of eye movements during the silent reading of words is generally accepted as the best currently available method for investigating reading. Each saccade takes a few milliseconds, during which the eye is essentially 'blind', and covers between seven and nine characters on a line.
- The most important information is processed during fixations, which last about 250 milliseconds, comprising over 90 per cent of total reading time. Maximal **perceptual span** or 'effective field of view' is three to four letters to the left of the fixation and about 15 to the right (for left-to-right languages).
- While most eye movements are forward towards new words, some **regressions** occur, especially in poor readers.
- Whether **phonological mediation** is necessary is one of the oldest questions in reading research. Some support comes from the inner-voice experience and the finding that we can use phonological mediation for reading unfamiliar words. However, this does not necessarily mean that it is the basis of all reading.
- Some studies suggest that not all the letters of a word need to be identified for the whole word to be recognised, but theories of word recognition assume that letter recognition plays some part in word identification.
- Word identification appears to be an automatic process, which involves not just recognition of letters but also **spelling/orthographic regularities**, a word's **shape** and **familiarity**, and, for unskilled readers or poorly presented text, the **context**.
- Different models of word identification all share the assumption that some form of word representation must be activated for identification to occur.
- According to the **logogen model of word recognition**, each word a person knows has a representation (logogen) in long-term memory. A logogen's **resting level of activity** can be increased by stimulus events such as hearing or seeing the word; when this exceeds the threshold, the word is recognised. High-frequency words either have a lower threshold or their meaning can be checked more quickly after firing.
- The **cohort model** claims that words are recognised letter by letter in a left-right manner. Word recognition occurs by eliminating alternative word candidates (cohorts), starting with all words that do not have the first letter in the word and working through the letters until only one word remains.
- According to the **interactive-activation model**, there are three types of recognition unit: the first detects the various features of letters, the second detects the letter represented by that combination of features, the third detects all words that have the recognised letter in a particular position. When the word units which have all of the letters making up a particular word and which appear in a particular position have been activated, integration occurs and the word is recognised.
- While there is some experimental support for all three models, this does not favour one more than the others. Also, much of the evidence derives from studies in which one word is read at a time, via a tachistoscope or computer screen, rather than reading continuous text at the reader's own pace.
- Models of word recognition tell us little about the **comprehension** of written language. Reading involves drawing **inferences** to aid our understanding and activation of appropriate knowledge and expectations to 'fill in the gaps'.
- According to Just and Carpenter's model of reading, after a word's physical features have been extracted, the reader assigns preliminary meaning to the word, which is then integrated with what has previously been read. The meaning of the whole sentence is then assimilated.
- Both long-term memory and working memory contribute to reading, but the main cognitive processes involved occur in the latter. Not only do our schemata affect the way we read, but our existing knowledge is modified by the new content, making reading a dynamic process.
- Just and Carpenter's **immediacy assumption** reflects the limited capacity of working memory, although the assumption seems more doubtful in

view of what is known about readers' **backward eye movements** and **fixations**. Individual differences in working-memory capacity influence how well language is comprehended.

- One measure of working memory is **reading span**, which is correlated with the ability to comprehend written material. Also, people with large reading spans read difficult text faster than those with small reading spans.

- Differences in comprehension ability cannot all be explained in terms of working-memory capacity, as is emphasised by Just and Carpenter's model to the exclusion of more specific processes, limiting its explanatory power. It also says little about eye movements, unlike Rayner and Pollatsek's **interactive model**, which says little about other processes, such as drawing inferences.

- According to Harris and Sipey, learning to read begins with 'reading readiness', which has been defined broadly as comprising a large group of visual skills, auditory factors and 'general co-ordination', and more narrowly in terms of **critical pre-reading skills**.

- According to Marsh et al., there are four stages in learning to read found in children taught in British and American schools, namely **glance and guess, sophisticated guessing, simple grapheme-phoneme correspondence** and **skilled reading**. These have been re-described by Frith as three skills: **logographic skills, alphabetic skills** and **orthographic skills**.

- The **phonics method** of teaching reading emphasises 'symbol-sound' relationships, while the **whole-word method** encourages the recognition of words by sight. On balance, the evidence seems to favour phonic methods.

- The evolution of **written language** is a relatively recent phenomenon in human history, originating from **pictorial writing**, followed by **logography** (such as Egyptian hieroglyphics), **logo-syllabic** and **syllabic writing**, which culminated in **alphabetic writing**.

- Hayes and Flower's **information-processing model** stresses the role of working memory in which **planning, translating** and **reviewing** take place.

- **Planning** involves setting goals and organising ideas on information from the **task environment** and **long-term memory**. Knowledge about writing in general, the particular form that needs to be presented for a given task, the intended audience and specific knowledge about the task can all influence the quality of planning.

- The plan is also influenced by three interactive and interdependent sub-processes: **generating, organising** and **goal-setting**.

- According to Hayes and Flower, skilled writers set themselves the goal of communicating meaning and produce more goals and sub-goals, while unskilled/immature writers produce 'associative writing' and try to avoid errors. Skilled writers also have 'internal cues' to help them generate many ideas and plan the meaning of what they are going to write, using **cohesive ties** and **coherent structures**.

- **Translating/sentence generation** involves transforming the (shorter) writing plan into the (longer) actual writing onto paper or computer disk. There is a continuous process of writing followed by referral back to the plan until the task is completed. Translating can stretch working memory to its limits, especially in the case of unskilled writers. The cohesion of skilled writers is demonstrated by Atwell's **inkless pens** experiment.

- **Writer's block** has a number of causes, including the need for more knowledge about the task and the application of **rigid rules**.

- **Reviewing/revision** involves evaluating what has been written in terms of the goals set. There is interaction between revision and planning, and improvements are made based on **reading** and **editing**. Skilled writers are more likely to make meaning-related revisions, while unskilled writers focus on mechanical errors.

- The component skills of planning, translating and revision are guided by the **rhetorical problem**, the **text** produced so far and the writer's **long-term memory**.

- Hayes and Flower's model implies several practical applications, including **setting goals, outlining for planning, generating ideas, communicating meaning, revision, correcting and rewriting** and **peer-editing**.

- Writing does not proceed from planning to translating to reviewing, as predicted by the model, and some researchers dispute whether the three processes can ever be completely separated from each other. The model has also been criticised for its reliance on **protocol analysis/verbal protocols**, which can only tap processes of which the writer is consciously aware.

16

PROBLEM-SOLVING AND DECISION-MAKING

Introduction and overview

The basic cognitive processes we have considered in the previous chapters of this book are all aspects of 'thought'. However, there is more to thinking than perception, attention, memory and language. Two closely related aspects of thinking which have long been of interest to cognitive psychologists are problem-solving and decision-making. Our aim in this chapter is to consider what psychological research has told us about the processes involved in solving problems and making decisions.

The nature of problems

STAGES IN PROBLEM-SOLVING

A problem is a situation in which there is a discrepancy between a present state and some goal state, with no obvious way in which the discrepancy can be reduced. Problem-solving is an attempt to reduce the discrepancy and achieve the goal state. Bourne et al. (1979) have proposed that problem-solving progresses through a series of logical stages. These are *defining or representing the problem, generating possible solutions* and *evaluating possible solutions*. Some researchers have argued for the existence of an *incubation stage* (in which no attempt is made to solve the problem, but attention is given to other matters) occurring between the generating and evaluating stages. Others (e.g. Wallas, 1926) suggest that incubation typically occurs after preparation.

REPRESENTING AND DEFINING PROBLEMS

The way in which problems can be represented (such as in verbal, visual or mathematical form), their form of presentation and our ability to 'weed out' unimportant information can all influence our understanding of a problem (Duncker, 1945; Simon and Hayes, 1976). Problems which are ill defined are much more difficult to solve than those which are well defined, and problems which are complex are much more difficult to solve than those which are simple (Matlin, 1989).

Once we understand a problem, we can then *generate possible solutions*. In some cases, finding a solution is straightforward, and simply a case of retrieving information from long-term memory. On other occasions, certain tendencies and biases operate which, as we will see later on in this chapter, lead us to overlook potential solutions and so we 'get stuck' on a problem. This is why generating lots of possible solutions can be useful in some contexts.

Once possible solutions have been generated, they can then be *evaluated*. As with generating solutions, the evaluation of solutions is sometimes straightforward, especially when the problem is clearly defined or represented. With unclear or poorly defined problems, though, the solutions that have been generated are typically difficult to evaluate. It is also worth noting that the various stages in problem-solving do not necessarily occur in a fixed order, and we may find ourselves moving between stages or going all the way back to the defining or representing stage.

TYPES OF PROBLEMS

Garnham (1988) distinguishes between two broad classes of problem, *adversary* and *non-adversary*. Adversary problems are those in which two or more people compete for success, as in chess and noughts-and-crosses. In non-adversary problems, other people are involved only as problem setters for the problem solver.

Problem-solving: from behaviourism to information-processing

According to behaviourist psychologists, problem-solving is essentially a matter of *trial-and-error* and *accidental success* (e.g. Thorndike, 1911). Behaviourists argued that as acquired habits are learned, so problem-solving (which can essentially be seen as a chain of stimulus-response associations) improves. Whilst trial-and-error can be an effective approach to the solution of some problems, the behaviourist approach was challenged by *Gestalt psychologists*. As we saw in Chapter 1, Gestalt psychologists proposed that we impose structure and order on things we perceive according to the laws of proximity, closure, similarity and so on.

The Gestalt approach to problem-solving was to look at how we impose *structure* on a problem by understanding how its elements are related to one another. Thus, rather than being 'senseless drill and arbitrary associations' (as Katona (1940) argued was the case with the behaviourist approach), problem-solving is held to occur through *meaningful apprehension of relations*.

Gestalt psychologists distinguished between *reproductive thinking* and *productive thinking* (Maier, 1931). In reproductive thinking, past solutions are applied to new problems. Whilst past experience can lead to success, it can also, as we will see later on in this chapter, hinder problem-solving. In productive thinking, problems are solved by the principle of *reorganisation*, or solving a problem by perceiving new relationships among its elements (see Katona (1940) above).

Consider, for example, the problem of trying to arrange six matchsticks into four equilateral triangles with each side equal to one stick. If you try to arrange the matchsticks by pushing them around on a table, the problem cannot be solved. Through reorganisation, though, and realisation that the matchsticks do not *have* to be arranged in two dimensions, the problem can be solved (as shown in Figure 16.4 at the end of this chapter). The principle of reorganisation is similar to what Wolfgang Köhler (1925) called *insight* in his studies of problem-solving in chimpanzees. Köhler's work is described in Box 16.1.

Box 16.1   Köhler's study of problem-solving in chimpanzees

Köhler suspended an out-of-reach bunch of bananas from the ceiling of the cage of a chimpanzee called Sultan. In the cage were a number of items that could be used to reach the bananas (such as sticks of different lengths), although none of these items on its own was sufficient. Eventually, Sultan solved the problem by placing empty boxes beneath the bananas and then climbing on the boxes.

In another experiment, Köhler allowed Sultan to see a box being placed in the corridor leading to his cage. Sultan was then taken to his cage where, again, bananas were suspended from the ceiling. However, there were no boxes in the cage. Sultan's first strategy was to remove a long bolt from the open cage's door. Quite suddenly, though, he stopped, ran down the corridor, and returned with the box which was again used to retrieve the bananas.

In Köhler's view, Sultan's behaviour was a result of sudden perceptual reorganisation. Köhler called this *insight*, and argued that it was different from trial-and-error learning. Later experiments showed that Sultan's perceptual reorganisation was maintained as a plan of action. So, when the bananas were placed outside the cage, Sultan still built a number of boxes. As we mentioned earlier on, experience can sometimes be an obstacle to problem-solving!

Whilst the Gestalt approach is acknowledged as making a significant contribution to our understanding of the processes involved in solving certain types of problem, Gestalt psychologists did not develop a theory that applies to all aspects of problem-solving. Additionally, whilst the concepts of 'insight' and 'restructuring' are attractive because they are easily understood, especially when accompanied by perceptual demonstrations, they are radically understated as theoretical constructs (Eysenck and Keane, 1995). Thus, it is very unclear under what conditions they will occur and exactly what insight involves.

Information-processing approaches analyse cognitive processes in terms of a series of separate stages. In the case of problem-solving, the separate stages are those we mentioned earlier, that is, representing the problem, generating possible solutions and evaluating those solutions. We have already identified some of the factors that influence our understanding of a problem. In the following section, we will look in detail at the way in which we generate possible solutions.

Generating possible solutions: algorithms and heuristics

ALGORITHMS

An *algorithm* is a systematic exploration of every possible solution until the correct one is found. For example, to solve the anagram YABB, we could list *all* the possible combinations of letters, checking each time to see if the result is a word. Thus, we might generate BBAY (non-word), BYAB (non-word) and so on, until we eventually arrive at BABY. Algorithms *guarantee* a solution to a problem, and are effective when the number of possible solutions is small (as in the above case). However, when the number of possible solutions is large, algorithms are, unless we are fortunate enough to find the solution early, *time consuming*.

HEURISTICS

An alternative to an algorithm is what Newell et al. (1958) term a *heuristic*. Heuristics are 'rules of thumb' which, whilst not guaranteeing a solution to a problem, can result in solutions being reached more quickly. These 'fuzzy' procedures are based on intuition, past experience and any other information relevant to the problem. In the case of solving anagrams, for example, a heuristic approach would involve looking for letter combinations that are and are not permitted in the English language. So BB is not a permitted combination of letters at the beginning of a word and so this would immediately exclude BBAY as a solution to the anagram used in the example above. Although it is unlikely to be the case with four-letter anagrams, heuristic devices applied to anagrams of five or more letters might not be successful, and we might miss a solution based on a lack of intuition, past experience and other relevant factors.

Amongst several heuristic devices are *analogies* and *means-end analysis* (Newell and Simon, 1972). Analogies involve the recognition that a particular problem is similar to one which has been encountered

in the past. In means-end analysis (or *working backwards*), the search for a solution begins at the goal (or end) and works backwards to the original state (the means being the steps that must be taken to get from the present state – the problem – to the goal of solving the problem. A simple illustration of the application of means-end analysis is shown in Box 16.2.

> **Box 16.2   An illustration of means-end analysis**
>
> In one version of the game of 'Nim', 15 matchsticks are placed in front of two players. Each player is allowed to remove at least one matchstick but not more than five on each turn. Players take turns in removing matchsticks until one takes the last matchstick and so wins the game. In order to win, then, a player must reach his or her turn with one to five matchsticks left. By working backwards, we can see that if an opponent is left with six or 12 matchsticks, then it doesn't matter what he or she does because we will always win. The optimum strategy in this game is therefore to remove enough matchsticks so as to leave the opponent with six or 12 matchsticks.

Because it is often not possible to achieve the main goal all in one step, working backwards can involve breaking down the main goal into a series of *sub-goals* or *sub-problems*, each of which has to be solved before the main goal can be reached. This process is known as *problem-reduction representation*. As each of the sub-problems is solved, so the distance between the original state and the goal state lessens (Newell and Simon, 1972). A good example of the forward-looking nature of working backwards (!) is the 'hobbit and orcs' problem (Thomas, 1974). In this, the goal is to get three hobbits and three orcs across a river in a boat that can carry a maximum of two creatures at a time. Additionally, in order to take the boat back across the river, at least one hobbit or one orc must be on it. Moreover, the orcs must never outnumber the hobbits on either side of the river (the reason being that the orcs will eat the hobbits if this is the case).

If we leave aside the main goal of getting everybody across the river, we might begin, as shown in Figure 16.1, by sending two orcs across. Since there is no constraint on the same orc going back to the other side of the river, we might have one make a return trip, pick up another orc, send one orc back, and then allow two

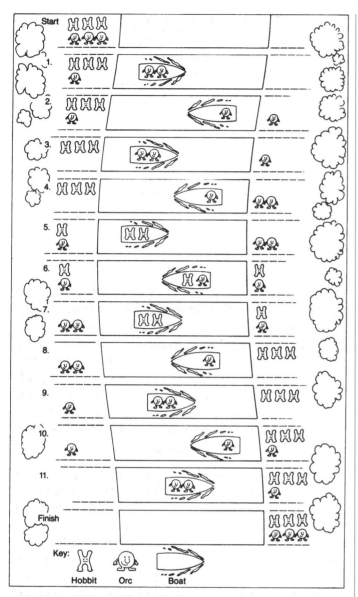

Figure 16.1   The 'Hobbits and Orcs' problem (from *Psychology: An Introduction* 6/E. by Morris, © 1988. Reprinted by permission of Prentice-Hall, Inc., Upper Saddle River, NJ.).

however, cannot hold this amount of information in a limited-capacity working memory. Also, in working backwards we sometimes have to move *further away* from the goal in order to achieve it. One reason why the 'hobbits and orcs' problem is so difficult is that at one point (shown as Step 6 in Figure 16.1), it becomes necessary to take a hobbit *and* an orc *back* to the side they started from, which apparently increases the distance from the final goal (Greene, 1987).

Evaluating potential solutions to a problem is the final stage in problem-solving. In cases where the problem and goal have been stated precisely, as in the case of the 'hobbits and orcs' problem, evaluation is a relatively simple process. With poorly defined problems, evaluating potential solutions is much more difficult.

Problems in solving problems

Earlier on (see page 183), we mentioned that certain tendencies and biases can operate to hinder our ability to solve particular problems. Two circumstances in which past experience hinders rather than helps to solve problems were identified by Gestalt psychologists. These are *mental set* (or *rigidity*) and *functional fixedness*. A third obstacle to problem-solving is called the *confirmation bias*.

MENTAL SET

This term refers to our tendency to continue using a previously successful strategy to solve new problems, even when more efficient strategies exist. In a series of classic experiments, Luchins (1942) and Luchins and Luchins (1959) asked people to imagine they had three different containers each of a different size. The task was to use the containers to obtain exactly a particular amount of liquid. Once this problem had been solved, participants had to imagine they had another three different containers and again try to obtain exactly a particular amount of liquid. A number of these problems, as shown in Table 16.1 were used.

The first five problems shown in Table 16.1 can be solved using the formula B–2C–A (that is, fill container B, pour its contents into container C twice and then pour what remains in container B into container A to leave the desired amount in container B). Whilst

hobbits to cross the river (see Steps 1–5 in Figure 16.1). By working on this particular sub-goal, we can eventually get all the hobbits and orcs across to the other side and, as shown in Figure 16.1, the problem can be solved in 11 moves.

Unfortunately, measuring the progress we are making in this problem is difficult. Computers can be programmed to work out a sequence of all possible moves and then plot the quickest path to a solution (using what is called a *check-every-move algorithm*). People,

Table 16.1 The water container problems used by Luchins and Luchins (1959)

Problem No.	Containers with capacity in fluid ounces			Obtain exactly these amounts of water
	Container A	Container B	Container C	
1	21	127	3	100
2	14	163	25	99
3	18	43	10	5
4	9	42	6	21
5	20	59	4	31
6	23	49	3	20
7	10	36	7	3

Source: Luchins and Luchins (1959)

the sixth problem in Table 16.1 can be solved using the formula B–2C–A, there is a more direct solution, namely A–C. The seventh problem *cannot* be solved using the formula B–2C–A, but can be solved using the formula A–C.

Luchins and Luchins found that once people discovered a solution to the first problem, they continued to use it even when (in the case of the sixth problem) it was less efficient or (in the case of the seventh problem) did not apply. In Gestalt terms, mental set produces reproductive thinking when a problem calls for productive thinking (Scheerer, 1963).

FUNCTIONAL FIXEDNESS

Functional fixedness (or 'fixity') is a type of mental set in which we fail to see that an object may have functions (or uses) other than its normal ones. In Duncker's (1945) classic demonstration of functional fixedness, participants were given a box of drawing pins and a candle and instructed to find a way of attaching the candle to a wall so it would stay upright and burn properly.

Whilst participants devised a number of inelegant solutions to the problem, they did not use a more elegant solution, namely to empty the box, pin it to the wall and place the candle in it. Interestingly, though, when people are shown an *empty* box and the drawing pins are scattered on a table, the box is much more likely to be used as a holder for the candle (Glucksberg and Weisberg, 1966).

CONFIRMATION BIAS

A third barrier to solving problems is our tendency to search for information that confirms our ideas and simultaneously overlook contradictory information that disconfirms our beliefs. Wason (1960) called this the confirmation bias, and demonstrated it in a number of studies. In one, participants were given the three-number sequence 2–4–6 and asked to discover the rule that Wason had in his head which applied to the sequence. Participants were allowed to generate their own three-number sequences and ask Wason if each conformed to the rule that applied to 2–4–6.

Wason's rule was actually a very simple one, namely 'any three ascending numbers'. However, Wason found that nearly 80 per cent of participants failed to discover the rule, despite being extremely confident that they had. Most participants formed a wrong idea about the rule (such as 'counting in twos') and then searched only for confirming evidence (such as 1–3–5 or 42–44–46) which also conformed to Wason's rule. What participants did not do was look for evidence that would *disconfirm* their hypotheses about the rule. Thus, 4–6–9 would disconfirm the counting-in-twos rule, but since it conforms to the rule Wason had in his head, it would have allowed thinking to shift.

Decision-making

Decision-making is a special case of problem-solving in which we already know the possible solutions (or choices). Some of the decisions we have to make are relatively trivial, such as deciding whether to watch *Match of the Day* on BBC or a film on the other side. Others are much more important, such as a married couple deciding whether or not to have children (see

Figure 16.2   One of life's major decisions: to have children or not? Harry Enfield as 'Kevin the Teenager' would probably swing the balance heavily towards not having children.

Figure 16.2), or a student deciding which university to study at. In decision-making, then, we are faced with various alternative choices from which one must be selected and the others rejected.

Compensatory and non-compensatory models of decision-making

COMPENSATORY MODELS

If we were completely logical in our decision-making, we would evaluate how all of the desirable potential outcomes of a particular decision might *compensate* for the undesirable potential outcomes. According to the *additive compensatory model*, we start the decision-making process by listing common features of various alternatives and assigning arbitrary weights that reflect their value to us. The weights are then added up to arrive at a separate score for each alternative, as shown in Table 16.2. Provided that the criteria have been properly weighted and each criterion has been correctly rated,

the alternative with the highest score is the most rational choice given the available information.

Another compensatory model is the *utility-probability model*, which proposes that important decisions are made by weighting the desirability of each potential outcome according to its *utility* and *probability*. Utility refers to the value that is placed on potential positive or negative outcomes. Probability is the likelihood that the choice will actually produce the potential outcome. Table 16.3 illustrates how this model can be applied.

NON-COMPENSATORY MODELS

Rather than using compensatory models, the evidence suggests that we actually use various, and less precise, non-compensatory models. In these, not all features of each alternative may be considered and features do not compensate for each other. At least four such models may be identified. These are described in Box 16.3.

Box 16.3   Some non-compensatory decision making models

Elimination by aspects: According to Tversky (1972), when faced with complex decisions we eliminate various options if they do not meet particular criteria, irrespective of their quality on other criteria. This model assumes that we begin with a maximum criterion and use it to test the various options. If, after applying this criterion, more than one alternative remains, the second most important criterion is used. The procedure continues until just one option remains. This is the option that is chosen.

Maximax strategy: This involves comparing the various options according to their best features and then selecting the option which has the strongest best feature.

Minimax strategy: In this, the weakest feature of each option is considered, and the option whose weakest feature is most highly rated is selected.

Conjunctive strategy: This involves setting a 'minimum' acceptable value on each option. Any option which does not meet or exceed the minimum acceptable value as the criteria are considered from most important to least important is discarded. The chosen option is that which does meet or exceed the minimum acceptable value on each criterion.

To show how these various models can be applied, assume that you have to make a choice between five cars, each of which is competitively priced. Using the criteria of mechanical reliability, comfort, noise, resale and crash protection, choose a number of cars and then give each car a value from 1 to 10. The decisions you should reach are shown at the end of this chapter.

Table 16.2   Compensatory decision table for the purchase of a new car

	Price (weight = 4)	Petrol mileage (weight = 8)	Service record (weight = 10)	Weighted total
Car 1	5 (20)	2 (16)	1 (10)	(46)
Car 2	1 (4)	4 (32)	4 (40)	(76)
Ratings:	5 = Excellent 1 = Poor			

Note: Three criteria (price, petrol mileage and service record) have each been assigned a weighting from 1 to 10. Each car is then rated from 1 to 5 on each of the three criteria. The ratings are multiplied by the weights, and a weighted total calculated for each. The car with the highest weighted total is the one that should be selected.
Source: Adapted from Morris (1988).

Table 16.3   Using the utility-probability model for the decision about whether to get married whilst still at college

Potential outcome	Utility (on a scale of −10 to +10)	Probability (0 to 1.0)	Expected utility (utility × probability)
Choice: Get married			
Happy	+10	.7	+7
Good study habits	+5	.8	+4
Ample alone time (personal space needs)	+6	.2	+1.2
Financial difficulties	−8	.8	−6.4
Friendships limited	−4	.7	−2.8
Lowered motivation to stay trim	−3	.4	−1.2
			+1.8
Choice: Do not get married			
Happy	+10	.2	+2
Good study habits	+5	.3	+1.5
Ample alone time (personal space needs)	+6	.9	+5.4
Financial difficulties	−8	.1	−.8
Friendships limited	−4	.1	−.4
Lowered motivation to stay trim	−3	0	0
			+7.7

Note: Each potential outcome is assigned a utility value (which may be positive or negative) and a probability value indicating the likelihood that the potential outcome will occur. Expected utilities are calculated by multiplying utility and probability. The total expected utility is the sum of the expected utilities. In this example, the decision not to get married has the greatest expected utility and so should be the decision made
Source: taken from Crooks and Stein (1991).

Heuristics in decision-making

Clearly, important decisions should be approached in a systematic fashion. However, it is not always easy to make rational decisions even in important matters because of the absence of information about the various alternatives. Moreover, with all the decisions we have to make in the course of a given day, there is not time to engage in the rational processes we described in the previous section. As a result, we often rely on heuristics, the useful 'rules of thumb' we described earlier. Amos Tversky and Daniel Kahneman (1973) have conducted extensive research into heuristics and decision-making. Two heuristics they have identified are the *availability heuristic* and the *representativeness heuristic*.

AVAILABILITY HEURISTIC

Sometimes, decisions must be made on the basis of whatever information is most readily available in long-term memory. This availability heuristic is based on the assumption that the probability of an event is directly related to the frequency with which it has occurred in the past, and that events occurring more frequently are usually easier to remember than less common events.

For example, if you are asked whether the letter 'K' appears more often as the first letter of words or as the third letter, you would probably guess that 'K' appears more often as the first letter. In fact, 'K' is three times more likely to appear as the third letter, but it is much easier to retrieve words beginning with 'K' than those which have 'K' as their third letter. Because words beginning with 'K' come to mind more easily, we presume that they are more commonplace (Hastie and Park, 1986).

The availability heuristic also plays a role in our tendency to overestimate our chances of being a victim of a violent crime or a plane crash (Tyler and Cook, 1984). This is because the extensive media coverage of these actually very rare events brings vivid examples of them to mind very readily indeed.

REPRESENTATIVENESS HEURISTIC

In a study conducted by Tversky and Kahneman (1973), participants were given the following information about a person called 'Steve':

> 'Steve is very shy and withdrawn, invariably helpful, but with little interest in people, or in the world of reality. A meek and tidy soul, he has a need for order and structure, and a passion for detail'.

The participants were then asked to decide how likely it was that Steve was involved in one of a number of occupations including musician, pilot, physician, salesman and librarian. Tversky and Kahneman found that most people judged the likelihood of Steve's involvement in terms of how well they represented particular prototypes or preconceived notions about people. In Steve's case, most participants guessed he was a librarian, presumably because his personality characteristics matched certain stereotypes about librarians.

Whenever we judge the likelihood of something by intuitively comparing it with our preconceived ideas of a few characteristics that we believe represent a category, we are using the representative heuristic. As another example, consider the following possible outcomes of tossing a coin six times: HHHHHH, TTTHHH and HTTHTH. Most people believe the first outcome to be the least likely of the three and the third outcome to be the most likely. In fact, the probability of the three sequences is *identical*. Our assumption that coin tossing produces a random sequence of heads and tails leads us to decide that the third pattern is the most likely. Indeed, if people observe five consecutive heads and are asked to estimate the probability of the next toss being a head, they tend to suggest that a tail is the more likely outcome, even though the probability of either is actually 0.5. This tendency is termed the *gambler's fallacy*.

The representativeness heuristic can also cause us to overlook important information about *base rates*, that is, the relative frequency of different objects/events in the world. For example, Tversky and Kahneman (1973) asked students to decide whether a student who could be described as 'neat and tidy', 'dull and mechanical' and 'a poor writer' was a computer-science student or a humanities student. Over 95 per cent of participants decided the student studied computing. Even after they were told that over 80 per cent of students at their school were studying humanities, their estimates remained virtually unchanged. So, even when we know the relative frequency of two things, we tend to ignore this information and base a decision on how well something matches our stereotype, that is, how representative it is.

Whilst heuristics are useful in both problem-solving and decision-making, they can, as we have seen, sometimes be misleading. Some other influences on our decision-making are described in Box 16.4.

Box 16.4   Some other influences on decision-making

Belief perseverance

This refers to the tendency to cling to a belief even in the face of contrary evidence (Lord et al., 1979). The bias can be overcome by *considering the opposite*. However, some false beliefs are difficult to remove even when information exists which clearly discredits the belief. For example, even with evidence indicating that another country is not hostile, that country continues to be seen as hostile and ambiguous actions by it are seen as signifying hostility (Jervis, cited in Goleman, 1985).

Entrapment

When we make costly investments in something (such as a relationship) that goes wrong, we may come to feel that we have no choice but to continue because withdrawal cannot justify the costs that have already been incurred (Brockner and Rubin, 1985). For example, industrial disputes often continue beyond the stage where either side can hope to achieve any gains (Baron, 1989).

Over-confidence

This is the tendency to overestimate the accuracy of our current knowledge. Even when we are totally confident about something, we err about 15 per cent of the time (Lichenstein and Fischoff, 1980). Over-confidence can occur because it is generally easier for us to remember successful decisions or judgements than unsuccessful ones. So, using the availability heuristic, we overestimate our success at particular tasks. Over-confidence can be overcome by providing feedback about the accuracy of decisions and judgements, and in several other ways, such as having a 'humbling experience' (Fischoff, 1982).

Loss aversion and costs against losses

Typically, we tend to reject riskier, though potentially more rewarding, decisions in favour of a certain gain *unless* taking a risk is a way to avoid loss (Tversky and Kahneman, 1986). We also tend to see losses as being more acceptable if we label them as 'costs' rather than 'losses' (although the evaluation of a cost depends on the context: Kahneman and Tversky, 1984).

Expectations

Expectations can affect both our perception of the world (see Chapter 2, page 22) and what is done with the information that is perceived. For example, the shooting down of an ascending Iranian airliner by an American warship occurred as a result of initial, but later corrected, information from a computer that the plane was a descending F14 fighter jet. The expectation of an attack led the ship's captain to pay more attention to his crew's reports of an emergency than to the new computer information (Wade and Tavris, 1993).

Hindsight

The term *hindsight bias* refers to our tendency to overestimate the probability that something would have happened after it has happened, as if we knew all along that it would have happened (Hawkins and Hastie, 1990).

Framing

When the same issue is presented (or *framed*) in two different but equivalent ways, we tend to make different judgements about it. For example, Levin and Gaeth (1988) showed that people respond more positively to ground beef if it is described as '75 per cent lean' rather than '25 per cent fat'. Also, medical treatments are seen as being more successful if framed as having a '50 per cent success rate' rather than a '50 per cent failure rate'.

A brief note on computers, problem-solving and decision-making

At the heart of the information-processing approach lies the *computer analogy*, that is, the view that human cognition can be understood by comparing it with the functioning of digital computers. Newell et al.'s (1958)

General Problem Solver (GPS) was an ambitious attempt to simulate the entire range of problem-solving and was the first computational model of a psychological phenomenon. The GPS was based on *verbal protocols* (see Chapter 15, page 180) given by people as they attempted to solve particular problems, and employed the working-backwards heuristic we discussed earlier (see page 185).

Tests of the GPS conducted by, for example, Atwood and Polson (1976) involved giving it and a person the same problem and comparing the performance of both in terms of the number and types of steps gone through and the solution arrived at. The results of such tests indicated that the GPS and people do use similar strategies for solving particular problems, although we should note that measuring the 'goodness of fit' between verbal protocols (which are themselves suspect: see page 180) and the 'traces' of a computer program is difficult (Garnham, 1988; Hampson and Morris, 1996).

Recent research has looked at computer simulations of adversary problems (especially chess: see, for example, Boden (1987) and Garnham (1991)) where substantial *domain-specific knowledge* is required. Studies of experts and novices have, as we saw in Chapter 9, revealed a number of important differences between them (see Figure 16.3). These differences do not necessarily occur because experts are faster thinkers, have better memories or are cleverer than non-experts (Hampson and Morris, 1996). Indeed, and as we saw in Chapter 9 (see page 89), in the case of chess, de Groot (1966) has shown that expert chess players are much better than novices at remembering board positions *only* when the pieces are arranged as they might possibly appear in a game (which allows the pattern of the pieces to be 'chunked'). When the pieces are arranged randomly, experts and novices do not differ in their ability to remember board positions.

Thus, the gain from being an expert would seem to be that it places less strain on working memory. As Greene (1987) has put it, since problem-solving strategies depend on knowledge which is already available, 'the more you know, the less you have to think' (see also Chapter 6 and the distinction between controlled and automatic processing).

EXPERT SYSTEMS

Expert systems (ESs or *intelligent knowledge-based systems*) are computer programs that apply knowledge in a specific area, enabling a computer to function as effec-

Figure 16.3 Chess experts are only able to remember the position of chess pieces when they are positioned as they might be during a game. If the pieces are placed randomly, the experts are no better than anyone else at memorising their positions.

tively as a human expert. Amongst several expert systems which have been devised are MYCIN (Shortliffe, 1976) which helps doctors diagnose and treat infectious diseases and PROSPECTOR (Feigenbaum and McCorduck, 1983) which helps geologists explore for minerals. All of these ESs obtain their 'knowledge' from human experts. However, experts cannot always formulate explicitly the knowledge they use in solving particular problems, nor can they say how they combine different items of information to reach a decision about a particular case. As a result, the writing of ESs is both difficult and time consuming.

Whilst ESs have been shown to be useful (PROSPECTOR, for example, helped to find a deposit of molybdenum worth $100 million at a site ignored by human experts), they are much less flexible than their human counterparts (Boden, 1987). In Boden's view:

'In almost every case, their 'explanations' are merely recapitulations of the previous firing of if-then rules ... for they still have no higher-level representations of the knowledge domain, their own problem-solving activity or the knowledge of their human user'.

Whether ESs can be provided with causal reasoning, so that they can arrive at a conclusion *and* explain the reason for it, is currently the focus of much research interest. A detailed discussion of ESs and the scope of *artificial intelligence* can be found in Gross (1996).

Naturalistic decision-making

Unlike traditional research into decision-making which typically studies the decisions made by naïve participants in laboratory experiments, Naturalistic Decision-Making (NDM) has emerged as a paradigm shift in applied decision-making research (Skriver, 1996). According to Skriver, researchers in NDM argue that only by studying experienced people can they gain insight into the way decision-makers utilise both their domain knowledge and contextual information, and how the contextual factors affect decision-making processes.

Amongst areas attracting the attention of NDM researchers are military command and control, fire-fighting incident command, offshore installation emergency response and medical decision-making (e.g. Heller et al., 1992). The ways in which real decision-makers arrive at difficult, dynamic decisions in environments that are often ill-structured and changing is NDM's major concern. Look at the 'disastrous decisions' briefly described in Box 16.5. Should NDM be a research priority?

Box 16.5   Some 'disastrous decisions'

- In 1902, Mount Pelée erupted on the Caribbean island of Martinique. Despite numerous warning signs that it was about to erupt, the authorities decided to do nothing. Indeed, the Governor decided to post troops to prevent an exodus by the inhabitants of the city of St Pierre. Over 26,000 people died in the blast, and all but two of the 18 ships in the City's harbour were sunk.

- In 1974, a DC10 crashed shortly after leaving Orly Airport, killing 345 people. The plane's cargo door had not been secured properly by a baggage handler. The authorities had earlier decided not to provide adequate instructions in appropriate languages on how to check and lock the door. The baggage handler's error occurred because he did not understand the language the instructions were written in.

- In Riyadh in 1980, the 301 passengers and crew of a Lockheed Tristar died of asphyxiation because the aircraft's captain decided not to evacuate the smoke-filled plane.

- In 1989, the port engine of a Boeing 737 caught fire. The pilot turned off the perfectly good starboard engine and the plane crashed at Kegworth.

(adapted from Dixon, 1994)

Conclusions

Psychological research has revealed much about the cognitive processes that underlie successful and unsuccessful attempts at problem-solving and decision-making. Whilst we might think that our approaches to problem-solving and decision-making are always rational and free from bias, the evidence suggests that this is not the case, and that a number of factors exert an influence on the solutions we arrive at and the decisions we make.

Figure 16.4   Solution to the problem presented on page 184.

SOLUTION TO THE DECISION-MAKING EXERCISE PRESENTED IN BOX 16.3

With the *elimination by aspects strategy*, you should find that if you apply a value (such as six or less) to the first criterion you identified, some of the cars will be eliminated and your chosen car is that which meets or exceeds the minimum acceptable value on each criterion.

With the *maximax strategy*, you should find that the car you rated as having the highest value on the criterion you selected as being most important is your chosen car.

With the *minimax strategy*, the car you rated most highly on the least important criterion should be your chosen car.

Finally, with the *conjunctive strategy*, you should find that the car which reaches or exceeds the minimum acceptable value on every criterion is the car that is selected.

SUMMARY

- Problem-solving is the attempt to reduce the discrepancy between a present state and some goal state so as to achieve the goal state. According to Bourne et al.'s **information-processing approach**, this progresses through a series of logical stages: **defining/representing the problem**, **generating possible solutions** and **evaluating possible solutions**. Others have suggested that an **incubation stage** occurs between stages two and three.

- Problems that are ill defined and complex are more difficult to solve than well-defined, simple ones. Once we understand a problem, we can generate possible solutions, which sometimes might simply involve retrieving information from long-term memory. 'Getting stuck' may be the result of the operation of certain biases/tendencies.

- The evaluation of solutions can be straightforward, especially with well-defined problems. This and the other stages in problem-solving may not occur in a fixed order: we may move between stages or return to the defining/representing stage.

- Garnham distinguishes between **adversary problems** (such as chess and noughts-and-crosses) and **non-adversary problems** (where other people set problems for the problem-solver).

- **Behaviourist** psychologists, such as Thorndike, see problem-solving in terms of **trial-and-error** and **accidental success**. It is essentially a chain of stimulus-response associations which is learned and so can be improved.

- This was challenged by the **Gestalt** psychologists who looked at how we impose **structure** on a problem through **meaningful apprehension of relations**. Maier distinguished between **reproductive** and **productive thinking**, the latter involving **reorganisation**, in which a problem is solved by perceiving new relationships among its elements. This is similar to what Köhler called **insight** based on problem-solving in chimpanzees such as Sultan.

- The Gestalt approach does not seem to apply to all aspects of problem-solving, and, while the concepts of 'insight' and 'restructuring' are easy to understand, they are much more difficult to pin down and define.

- **Algorithms** and **heuristics** represent two ways of **generating possible solutions** to a problem. An algorithm is a systematic exploration of every possible solution, thus **guaranteeing** that one is found. This is very **time consuming**, and hence ineffective, when the number of possible solutions is large; an alternative approach is what Newell et al. called a heuristic ('rule of thumb').

- While heuristics do not guarantee a solution, they can help produce solutions more quickly. They are based on intuition, past experience and any other relevant information. Examples include **analogies** and **means-end analysis**.

- Means-end analysis involves **working backwards** from the goal or end (the solution to the problem) to the original state (the problem); the means are the steps required to get from one to the other. The main goal may sometimes have to be broken down into a series of **sub-goals/sub-problems** through a process of **problem-reduction representation**, as in the 'hobbit and orcs' problem.

- While a computer can be programmed with a **check-every-move algorithm**, human working memory is unable to hold this amount of information. Also, we sometimes have to move **further away** from the goal in order to achieve it. **Evaluating** potential solutions is relatively easy in the 'hobbits and orcs' problem, since the problem and goal are well defined.

- Gestalt psychologists identified **mental set/rigidity** and **functional fixedness/fixity** as two ways in which past experience can hinder problem-solving. Mental set was demonstrated in Luchins' experiments in which participants had to imagine different-sized containers in order to obtain a particular amount of liquid. Once people discovered a solution to the first problem, they continued using it with subsequent problems (reproductive thinking) even when this was less efficient or did not actually apply (i.e. when productive thinking was needed).

- Functional fixedness is a type of mental set in which we fail to see that an object may have functions or uses other than its normal ones. This was demonstrated in Duncker's box of drawing pins and candle experiment.

- **Confirmation bias** represents a third barrier to problem-solving, as demonstrated by Wason's studies in which participants had to discover the rule generating a three-number sequence. They tended to seek confirming evidence, rather than **disconfirming** evidence, when testing their hypotheses about the rule.

- **Decision-making** is a special case of problem-solving in which we already know the possible solutions or choices. According to a **compensatory model**, we evaluate how all of the desirable potential outcomes of a particular decision might **compensate** for the undesirable ones.

- According to the **additive compensatory model**, we list common features of various alternatives, then assign arbitrary weights that reflect their value to us. The weights are then added up to produce a separate score for each alternative; the one with the highest score is the most rational choice given the available information.

- According to the **utility-probability model**, we weigh the desirability of each potential outcome in terms of the value of potential positive or negative outcomes (**utility**) and the likelihood that the choice will actually produce the potential outcome (**probability**).

- **Non-compensatory models** are less precise but more commonly used approaches, in which not all features of each alternative are considered, and features do not compensate for each other. Some examples are **elimination by aspects**, **maximax strategy**, **minimax strategy** and **conjunctive strategy**.

- Rational decisions cannot always be made because of the absence of information and time to do so. So we often resort to what Tversky and Kahneman call the **availability** and **representativeness heuristics**.

- The **availability heuristic** assumes that the probability of an event is directly related to its past frequency: more frequent events are easier to retrieve from long-term memory. This explains why we tend to overestimate our chances of being the victim of a violent crime or a plane crash.

- The **representativeness heuristic** involves judging the likelihood of something by intuitively comparing it with our preconceived ideas of a few characteristics that we believe represent a category (e.g. a particular occupational group). One form this can take is the **gambler's fallacy**. This heuristic can also mislead us as to **base rates**.

- Other influences on decision-making include **belief perseverance** (which can be overcome by **considering the opposite**), **entrapment**, **over-confidence** (which can be overcome through feedback and a 'humbling experience'), **loss aversion and costs against losses**, **expectations**, **hindsight bias** and **framing**.

- Central to the information-processing approach is the **computer analogy**. Newell et al.'s **General Problem Solver (GPS)** attempted to simulate the entire range of problem-solving and was the first computational model of a psychological phenomenon. The GPS was based on **verbal protocols** using means-end analysis.

- When the GPS and a person are given the same problem to solve, they tend to use similar strategies, although it is difficult to measure the 'goodness of fit' between verbal protocols and the 'traces' of a computer program. Recent research has looked at computer simulations of adversary problems (especially chess), which involve substantial **domain-specific knowledge**.

- Compared with non-experts, experts are not necessarily faster, cleverer thinkers, with better memories. In the case of chess, de Groot showed that experts are only better at remembering board positions that could appear in an actual game, as opposed to random positions. Expertise seems to reduce the strain on working memory by enabling the expert to draw on knowledge already available.

- **Expert systems (ESs)** or **intelligent knowledge-based systems** are computer programs that apply knowledge in a specific area (such as medical diagnosis), enabling a computer to function as effectively as a human expert. However, human experts are not always able to make explicit the knowledge they use in solving particular problems or making particular decisions. This makes writing ESs difficult and time consuming.

- ESs are much less flexible than human experts, lacking higher-level representations of the knowledge domain or their own problem-solving activity. This is why, although capable of arriving at a solution, ESs are currently unable to explain how they reached it.

- **Naturalistic Decision Making (NDM)** is a new paradigm in applied decision-making research: only by studying experienced people can researchers gain insight into how decision-makers use both their domain knowledge and contextual information, and how the contextual factors affect decision-making processes.

- NDM's major concern is with how real decision-makers reach difficult, dynamic decisions in often ill-structured and changing environments, such as military command and control, firefighting incident command and medical decision-making. Such research may help to prevent 'disastrous decisions.

17

THE RELATIONSHIP BETWEEN LANGUAGE AND THOUGHT

Introduction and overview

The experience of knowing what we want to say but being unable to 'put it into words' is but one of several examples which indicate that thinking can take place without language (Weiskrantz, 1988). However, the exact relationship between language and thought has been the subject of much debate amongst philosophers and psychologists. For some, thought is dependent on, or caused by, language. Others believe that language is dependent on, and reflects, thought or an individual's level of cognitive development. Yet others maintain that thought and language are initially quite separate activities which come together and interact at a certain point in development.

Our aim in this chapter is to review the evidence relating to each of these major theoretical perspectives concerning the relationship between language and thought. We begin, though, by briefly examining probably the oldest (and least likely to be true) theory of the language-thought relationship, which argues that language and thought are one and the same.

Language and thought are one and the same

J.B. WATSON'S 'PERIPHERALIST' APPROACH

The earliest psychological theory of the relationship between language and thought was advanced by the behaviourist psychologist J.B. Watson (1913). In Watson's view, thought processes are really no more than the sensations produced by tiny movements of the speech organs which are too small to produce audible sounds. Put another way, Watson saw thought as being no more than talking to oneself very quietly. Watson's rejection of 'mind' (a result of his behaviourist perspective) resulted in him having to deny the existence of mentalistic concepts such as 'thought', and hence his reduction of it to 'silent speech'.

Watson's theory is known as *peripheralism* because it sees 'thinking' occurring peripherally in the voice box rather than centrally in the brain. As the philosopher Feigel (cited in Eysenck, 1993) humorously remarked, 'Watson made up his windpipe that he had no mind'. Research has shown that movements of the larynx do occur when 'thought' is taking place. However, such a finding only indicates that such movements may *accompany* thinking and does not show that the movements *are* thoughts or that such movements are *necessary* for thinking to occur.

In one study, Smith et al. (1947) attempted to test Watson's theory by injecting a person (actually Smith himself) with *curare*, a drug that causes total paralysis of the skeletal muscles without consciousness being lost. As well as the muscles of the articulating organs, those of the respiratory system are also paralysed (and this is the method by which curare kills). As a result, Smith had to be kept breathing artificially.

Later, when the effects of the drug had worn off, Smith was able to report on the thoughts and perceptions he had during his paralysis (and you might like to read the original report to discover what these were). Additionally, Furth (1966) has shown that people who are born deaf and mute, and who do not learn sign language, are also capable of thinking in much the same way as hearing and speaking people. For Watson, deaf and mute individuals would be incapable of thought because of the absence of movement in the articulating organs.

Thought is dependent on, or caused by, language

A large number of theorists have taken the view that thought is dependent on, and reflects, language. Bruner (1983), for example, has argued that language is essential if thought and knowledge are not to be limited to what can be learned through our actions (which Bruner calls the *enactive mode of representation*) or images (the *iconic mode of representation*). If what Bruner terms the *symbolic mode of representation* (that is, going beyond the immediate context) is to develop, then language is crucial.

More recently, *social constructionists* (e.g. Gergen, 1973) have argued that our ways of understanding the world derive from other people – past and present – rather than from objective reality. According to social constructionists, we are born into a world where the conceptual frameworks and categories used by people in our culture already exist. Indeed, these frameworks and categories are an essential part of our culture since they provide meaning, a way of structuring our experience of both ourselves and the world of other people.

This view has much in common with the so-called 'strong' version of the linguistic relativity hypothesis, which is the most extensively researched of the theories arguing that thought is dependent on, or caused by, language. It is to the linguistic relativity hypothesis that we now turn.

The linguistic relativity hypothesis

'The limits of my language mean the limits of my world,' wrote the philosopher Wittgenstein (1921). By this, Wittgenstein meant that people can only think about and understand the world through language, and that if a language did not possess certain ideas or concepts, then they could not exist for speakers of that language. The view that language determines *how* we think about objects or events or even determines *what* we think (our ideas, thoughts and perceptions themselves) can be traced back to the writings of Edward Sapir (1929), a linguist and anthropologist, and

Benjamin Lee Whorf (1956), a fire insurance inspector, linguist and student of Sapir.

As a result of their shared beliefs about the relationship between language and thought, their perspective is often termed the *Sapir-Whorf linguistic relativity hypothesis*, although it is sometimes referred to as the *Whorfian hypothesis* in acknowledgement of the greater contribution made by Whorf. For Whorf (1956):

'We dissect nature along the lines laid down by our native languages. The categories and types that we isolate from the world of phenomena we do not find there because they stare every observer in the face; on the contrary, the world is presented in a kaleidoscopic flux of impressions that has to be organised by our minds – and this means largely by the linguistic systems in our minds. We cut nature up, organise it into concepts and ascribe significance as we do, largely because we are parties to an agreement to organise it this way – an agreement that holds throughout our speech community and is codified in patterns of our language'.

According to Whorf's *linguistic determinism*, then, language determines our concepts, and we can only think through the use of concepts. So, acquiring a language involves acquiring a 'world view' (or *Weltanschauung*) of how we 'cut nature up' (it does not come 'ready sliced'). People who speak different languages have different world views and they 'cut nature up' differently (hence linguistic 'relativity') (see Figure 17.1).

Consider, for example, the Inuit Eskimos. Whorf claimed that these people have over 20 words for snow (including words for 'fluffy snow', 'drifting snow' and 'packed snow') whereas Standard Average European languages (such as English) have only one. Similarly, the Hanuxoo people of the Philippines use 92 words for 'rice' depending on whether it is husked or unhusked and its mode of preparation. The Shona people (Zimbabwe) have only three words for colour, and the Dani (New Guinea) just two. 'Mola' is used for bright, warm hues, whereas 'mili' is used for dark, cold hues. The Hopi Indians (whose language Whorf studied for several years) have two words for flying objects, one of which applies to birds and the other applies to anything else that travels through the air (Rathus, 1990).

As well as a language's vocabulary determining how and what an individual thinks and perceives, Whorf

People who speak in sound bites, think in sound bites too

Figure 17.1   At least as far as British politicians are concerned, the relationship between language and thought is (in the eyes of the media) a clear-cut one!

also saw its *grammar* as playing a determinant role. In the Hopi language, for example, no distinction is made between past, present and future which, compared with English, makes it a 'timeless language'. In European languages, 'time' is treated as an *objective* entity, and there is a clear demarcation between past, present and future. Although the Hopi language recognises duration (that is, how long an event lasts), Hopis do not, unlike speakers of European languages, talk about an objective period of time (such as 'ten days'). Rather, they talk about time only as it appears *subjectively* to the observer. For example, rather than saying 'I stayed for ten days', Hopis say 'I stayed until the tenth day' or 'I left on the sixth day'.

Also, the Hopi language does not use tenses for its verbs, and there are no grammatical forms which refer directly to time. Instead, different verb endings are used according to *how certain* the speaker is about an event (such as whether the event has been directly experienced or just heard about). Different voice inflections are used to express whether the speaker is reporting an event, expecting an event or making a generalisation about events. The Hopi language also differs in terms of its use of nouns and verbs. In English, nouns denote objects and events, and verbs denote actions. In the Hopi language, 'lightning', for example, is a verb, since events of necessarily brief duration must be verbs. As a result, a Hopi would say 'it lightninged'.

TESTING THE LINGUISTIC RELATIVITY HYPOTHESIS (LRH)

According to Miller and McNeill (1969), it is possible to distinguish between *three* different versions of the LRH, all of which are consistent with the theory but vary in terms of the *strength* of claim they make. The *strong* version claims that *language determines thought*. The *weak* version claims that *language affects perception*, and the *weakest* version claims that *language influences memory* such that information which is more easily described in a particular language will be better remembered than information which is more difficult to describe. One test of the strong version of the LRH is that conducted by Carroll and Casagrande (1958). The study is described in Box 17.1.

> **Box 17.1   Carroll and Casagrande's (1958) test of the 'strong' version of the linguistic relativity hypothesis**
>
> Carroll and Casagrande compared Navaho Indian children who either spoke only Navaho (Navaho-Navaho) or spoke English and Navaho (English-Navaho) with American children of European descent who spoke only English. The children were tested on the development of *form* or *shape recognition*. The Navaho language stresses the importance of form, such that verbs of 'handling' involve different words depending on what is being handled. For example, long and flexible objects (such as string) have one word form, whereas long and rigid objects (such as sticks) have another.
>
> Research has shown that American children of European descent develop object recognition in the following order: 1) size, 2) colour and 3) form

or shape. If, as the strong version of the LRH claims, language influences cognitive development, then the developmental sequence of the Navaho children should differ from the American children of European descent, and their form or shape recognition abilities should be better than that of the American children of European descent. This is what Carroll and Casagrande found. However, they also found that the English-Navaho group showed form recognition *later* than the American children of European descent.

The strong version of the LRH is supported by the superior performance of the Navaho-Navaho children, but not by the poorest performance of the English-Navaho children. Carroll and Casagrande attributed the poor performance of the English-Navaho children to their experience of shape classification at nursery school, which made them an atypical sample. If this attribution is accepted, then the data *are* consistent with the strong version of the LRH. If the attribution is suspect, the strong version of the LRH is more difficult to accept.

Attempts at testing the 'weak' and 'weakest' versions of the LRH have typically involved the perception and memory of *colour*. Since language users such as, for example, the Jalé (New Guinea) only have terms for the colours black and white, whilst those of the Ibibio culture (Nigeria) have terms for black, white, red and green, tests of colour perception and memory should be more difficult for the Jalé than the Ibibio. Since the Ibibio word for green encompasses the English for green, blue and yellow, the Ibibio should find colour perception and memory tasks more difficult than English speakers.

Early tests appeared to lend support to the two diluted versions of the LRH. For example, Brown and Lenneberg (1954) found that Zuni Indians, who have a single word to describe yellows and oranges, did make more mistakes than English speakers in recognising these colours. However, Brown and Lenneberg's findings (and those of other researchers using a similar methodology) were challenged by Berlin and Kay (1969). Berlin and Kay found that whilst cultures may differ in the number of basic colour terms they use, all cultures draw their basic (or *focal*) terms from only 11 colours. These are: black, white, red, green, yellow, blue, brown, purple, pink, orange and grey. Moreover, Berlin and Kay found that the colour terms emerge in a particular sequence in the history of languages, as shown in Figure 17.2.

So, for cultures which have only two colours, these will always be black and white, whereas in cultures which have three colours, these will always be black, white and red (Newstead, 1995). As Newstead has observed:

'This, then, gives a rather different perspective on the use of colour terms. It had been assumed that verbal labels were chosen more or less arbitrarily, and that those chosen influenced the way in which colour was perceived. Berlin and Kay's findings suggest that there are certain focal colours which will always be labelled if colour terms are used at all. This suggests an alternative explanation for Brown and Lenneberg's findings: that the colours which participants in their study had found easier to learn were the focal colours and these were easy to remember not because they had verbal labels but because they were the most basic colours'.

One study which supports Berlin and Kay's findings and the alternative explanation for Brown and Lenneberg's is described in Box 17.2.

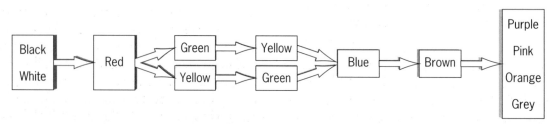

Figure 17.2   The sequence in which focal colours emerge (Berlin and Kay, 1969).

Box 17.2 Heider and Oliver's (1972) study of colour naming

As we have noted (see page 198), the Dani have only two words for colours, whereas native English speakers have words for 11 basic colours. Heider and Oliver (1972) gave both Dani and English-speaking participants a coloured chip which they were allowed to look at for five seconds. After a 30-second delay, participants were asked to pick out a chip of the same colour among a set of 40 different coloured chips. On the weakest version of the LRH, the Dani's colour vocabulary should have influenced their memory for colours, and on the weak version the Dani should have had difficulty in discriminating similar colours of a slightly different hue that they had labelled with the same name.

The results showed that whilst the Dani-speaking and English-speaking participants made many mistakes, there were no significant differences between them in terms of the rate at which they confused similar colours, in spite of the differences between the languages in terms of their colour vocabularies. Moreover, in other research, Heider was able to show that both Dani and English speakers were better able to recognise focal colours than non-focal colours, and that the Dani found it much easier to learn labels for focal colours than non-focal colours.

On the basis of her research, Heider concluded that:

'far from being a domain well suited to the study of the effects of language on thought, the colour-space would seem a prime example of the influence of underlying perceptual-cognitive factors on the formation and reference of linguistic categories'.

By this, Heider means that her data are better explained in terms of *physiological factors* underlying colour vision rather than linguistic factors. Thus, people are sensitive to focal colours because the human visual system processes reality in a certain way (Lakoff, 1987).

Indeed, there is evidence to suggest that focal colours can be discriminated *before* any verbal labels for them have been learned. Bornstein (1988), for example, has argued that the way in which pre-verbal infants categorise the visible spectrum is similar to that of adults, in that categorisation occurs on the basis of the relatively discrete hues of blue, green, yellow and red.

An evaluation of the linguistic relativity hypothesis

According to Sapir and Whorf, the differences between language speakers determine differences in how the world is perceived, thought about and remembered, and the world *is* different depending on what language we speak (or what language we 'think in'). The linguistic relativity hypothesis has, however, been challenged. For example, Berry et al. (1992) and Jackendoff (1993) have argued that Whorf's evidence was anecdotal rather than empirical, and that he exaggerated the differences between Hopi and other languages. Moreover, far from having 'over 20' words for 'snow', it actually turns out that the Inuit Eskimos have relatively few such words (Newstead, 1995).

Even if the criticisms about vocabulary and grammar are ignored, Whorf did not actually *show* that the Inuit Eskimos *perceive* more varieties of snow than English speakers or that the Hopi Indians cannot discriminate between past, present and future in the way that English speakers do. Greene (1975) has argued that if we conduct a Whorfian analysis of English from the perspective of a Hopi Indian, it is unlikely that a Hopi would really believe that we hold the 'primitive' beliefs that cars are female (as in 'she's a fine motor') or that 'a car', 'a hard bargain' and 'a golf ball' are all things that can be 'driven'. This is because we distinguish between the grammar of a language and our perceptual experience. The fact that Hopi can be translated into English (and vice versa) implies that there is a universally shared knowledge of the world which is independent of the particular language in which it is expressed.

What Whorf also appears to have overlooked is *why* Inuit Eskimos have more than one name for snow. One possible answer to this is that the more significant an experience or environmental feature is for us, the larger the number of ways in which it can be expressed (you might remember the British Rail official who, on being asked why trains were not running, caused much of the country mirth with his reply that it was 'the wrong kind of snow'). So, instead of language determining our perceptions, our perceptions (which reflect what is important for us) might be influencing our language. As Solso (1995) has put it:

'The development of specific language codes ... is dependent on cultural needs; the learning of these codes by members of a language group also involves the learning of significant values of the culture, some of which must be related to survival'.

Solso's view is supported by the fact that English-speaking skiers *do* learn to discriminate between varied snow conditions and *invent* a vocabulary to describe these differences. Such terms include 'sticky snow', 'powder', 'corn' and 'boilerplate' (or ice) (Crooks and Stein, 1991).

It is now widely accepted that Whorf overestimated the importance of language differences. As Berry et al. (1992) have observed:

'language as an instrument for thinking has many cross-culturally variant properties. As humans, we may not all be sharing the same thoughts, but our respective languages do not seem to predestine us to different kinds of thinking'.

What language may do, though, is to affect the ease with which information is processed. Newstead (1995), for example, describes research conducted by Hunt and Agnoli (1991) which supports this view. The English word 'seven' has two syllables whereas the French word for 'seven' ('sept') has only one. The English word 'eleven' has three syllables whereas the French word 'onze' has one. Hunt and Agnoli argue that when a name is shorter, information is processed more quickly, and so French speakers would have an advantage over English speakers when performing mental arithmetic involving these numbers, at least in processing terms: the task itself might not be soluble to the person attempting it, depending on their mathematical ability!

The linguistic relativity hypothesis, social class and race

BASIL BERNSTEIN AND SOCIAL-CLASS DIFFERENCES IN LANGUAGE AND THOUGHT

Bernstein, a sociologist, was interested in the role of language as a social (rather than individual) phenome-non, especially in terms of its relation to cultural deprivation. Bernstein showed that whilst there were generally no discrepancies between the verbal and non-verbal intelligence test performance of boys from public schools, boys from lower working-class homes often showed great discrepancies in their performance, with non-verbal performance sometimes being as much as 26 points better than verbal performance. On the basis of a number of investigations, Bernstein argued that working- and middle-class children speak two different kinds (or *codes*) of language which he termed *restricted code* (used by the working class) and *elaborated code* (used by the middle class).

Because Bernstein saw the relationship between potential and actual intelligence as being mediated through language, he argued that the lack of an elaborated code would prevent working-class children from developing their full intellectual potential. Bernstein believed that the different language codes underlay the whole pattern of relationships (to objects and people) experienced by members of different classes, as well as the patterns of learning which their children bring with them to school. Table 17.1 illustrates some of the main characteristics of the two codes, whilst Box 17.3 shows some examples of the sorts of interactions displaying restricted and elaborated code use.

Box 17.3   Restricted and elaborated code language use

The following are examples of imaginary conversations on a bus between a mother and child.

Example 1 (Restricted code)

MOTHER:	Hold on tight.
CHILD:	Why?
MOTHER:	Hold on tight.
CHILD:	Why?
MOTHER:	You'll fall.
CHILD:	Why?
MOTHER:	I told you to hold on tight, didn't I?

Example 2 (Elaborated code)

MOTHER:	Hold on tight.
CHILD:	Why?
MOTHER:	If you don't, you'll be thrown forward and you'll fall.
CHILD:	Why?

Table 17.1   Characteristics of restricted and elaborated codes (Bernstein, 1961)

Restricted code	Elaborated code
1 Grammatically crude, repetitive, rigid, limited use of adjectives and adverbs, uses more pronouns than nouns. Sentences often short, grammatically simple and incomplete.	**1** Grammatically more complex, flexible. Uses a range of subordinate clauses, conjunctions, prepositions, adjectives, adverbs. More nouns than pronouns. Sentences longer and more complex.
2 Context-bound, i.e. the meaning not made explicit but assumes listener's familiarity with the situation being described, e.g. 'He gave me it'; listener cannot be expected to know what 'he' or 'it' refers to.	**2** Context-independent, i.e. the meaning is made explicit, e.g. 'John gave me this book'.
3 'I' rarely used, and much of the meaning conveyed non-verbally.	**3** 'I' often used, making clear the speaker's intentions, as well as emphasising the precise description of experiences and feelings.
4 Frequent use of uninformative but emotionally reinforcing phrases such as 'you know', 'don't I'.	**4** Relatively little use of these reinforcing phrases.
5 Tends to stress the present, the here-and-now.	**5** Tends to stress past and future, rather than the present.
6 Doesn't allow expression of abstract or hypothetical thought.	**6** Allows expression of abstract or hypothetical thought.

Source: Gross (1996)

MOTHER: Because if the bus suddenly stops, you'll jerk forward onto the seat in front.
CHILD: Why?
MOTHER: Now, darling, hold on tightly and don't make such a fuss.

In example 1, the words are being used more as signals than symbols, with very little attempt to explain or reason on the mother's part. This contrasts sharply with the way in which language is used in the Example 2.

(after Stones, 1971)

Bernstein's views have been supported by some research. For example, Hess and Shipman (1965) showed that social-class differences did seem to influence children's intellectual development. In particular, they noted that there was a lack of *meaning* in the mother-child communication system for low-status families, that is, language was used much less to convey meaning (to describe, explain, express and so on) and much more to give orders and commands to the child. A discussion of the implications that Bernstein's theory has for education can be found in Gross (1996).

In Hess and Shipman's view, 'the meaning of deprivation is a deprivation of meaning'. Such a view implies that it is impossible for *upward social mobility* to occur. Yet the evidence disputes this, and it seems clear that the use of two basic types of code oversimplifies things. A much more helpful way of thinking about language codes would be to see 'restricted' and 'elaborated' codes as being two ends of a continuum. We should also note that the terms 'restricted' and 'elaborated' imply a value judgement of middle-class speech as being in some way superior in that it is closer to 'Standard' or 'the Queen's' English than working-class speech. The lack of objectivity makes this judgement very difficult to defend.

BLACK ENGLISH

A version of English spoken by segments of the American Black community is called 'Black English'. The difference between Standard and Black English has been illustrated in a number of studies (see Labov, 1973). For example, when asked to repeat the sentence 'I asked him if he did it, and he said he didn't do it', one five-year-old girl repeated the sentence like this: 'I asks him if he did it, and he says he didn't did it, but I knows he did'. Bernstein argued that Black English is a restricted code and that this makes the thinking of Black English speakers less logical than that of their white elaborated-code counterparts.

One of the major differences between Black and Standard English is in terms of its use of verbs (Rebok, 1987). In particular, Black English speakers often omit the present tense copula (the verb 'to be'). So, 'he be gone' indicates Standard English 'he has been gone for a long time' and 'he gone' signifies that 'he has gone right now'. Bereiter and Engelman (1966) have pointed out that Black English is often termed *sub-standard* and regarded as illogical rather than *non-standard*. According to Labov (1970), Black English is just one dialect of English and speakers of both dialects are expressing the same ideas and understand each other equally well.

Whilst the grammatical rules of Black English differ from those of Standard English, Black English does have consistent rules which allow for the expression of thoughts that are as complex as those permitted by Standard English (Labov, 1973). Several other languages, such as Russian and Arabic, also omit the present-tense verb 'to be' and yet we do not call them 'illogical'. All this would suggest that Black dialects are considered sub-standard as a matter of convention or prejudice and not because they are poorer vehicles for expressing meaning and thinking logically. However, because the structure of Black English does differ in important ways from Standard English, and since intelligence tests are written in Standard English, Black English speakers have clearly a linguistic handicap (as, indeed, do white working-class children).

Labov's research also showed that the social situation can be a powerful determinant of verbal behaviour. A young boy called Leon was shown a toy by a white interviewer and asked to tell him everything he could about it. Leon said very little and was silent for much of the time. His behaviour continued in this way even when a black interviewer took over. However, when Leon sat on the floor and shared a packet of crisps with his best friend and with the same black interviewer introducing topics in a local black dialect, Leon became a lively conversationalist. Had an assessment been made of him based on his behaviour with the white or black interviewers on their own, Leon would have been labelled 'non-verbal' or 'linguistically retarded'.

Quite possibly, black children are *bilingual*. In their home environment, the school playground and their neighbourhoods, they speak the accepted vernacular. In the classroom, however, they must adopt Standard English with which they are unfamiliar. The Standard English register may only apply when children talk to people in authority, and because of their unfamiliarity with it, their sentences are short, their grammar simple and their intonation strange. Once out of school, however, their natural register is easy, fluent, creative and often gifted. So, whilst Black English is certainly *non-standard*, it is another language which has its own grammar which is certainly not sub-standard. Box 17.4 highlights some of the recent issues surrounding *ebonics*.

Box 17.4   'Ebonics': an ongoing debate

Ebonics is a fusion of the words 'ebony' and 'phonics' and was coined in 1975 as an alternative to the term 'Black English'. In 1996, Ebonics was officially recognised by the Oakland public school board in California, and schools were ordered to teach 28,000 black children in their own 'tongue'. The board claimed that Ebonics was a separate language, genetically rooted in the West-African and Niger-Congo language system, rather than a dialect of Standard American English (Hiscock, 1996; Whittell, 1996).

In early 1997, the school board edited its statement so that the word 'genetically' referred to linguists' use of the word for the roots of a language rather than to a gene pool. They also indicated that it was not the intent to teach in Ebonics, but rather to have teachers use the vernacular to understand their children (Zinberg, 1997). Both conservatives and liberals in America claim that the decision to require Ebonics to be taught would be 'political correctness run amok' (Cornwell, 1997). Educationalists, such as Zinberg, disagree. In her view, many students are:

'bewildered, then angered and finally alienated from the schools where their language and self-esteem are belittled by a seemingly insensitive system'.

Language is dependent on, and reflects, thought

According to Jean Piaget, language takes on a form or structure that, at least to a degree, reflects a developing child's understanding of his or her world. Piaget argued that children begin life with some understanding of the world and try to find linguistic ways of expressing their knowledge. As language develops, so it 'maps' onto previously acquired cognitive structures, and so language is dependent upon thought (Piaget and Inhelder, 1969).

One cognitive principle identified by Piaget is that of *object permanence*, that is, the realisation that objects continue to exist even when they cannot be seen (see, for example, McIlveen and Gross, 1997). According to Piaget's theory, a child should begin talking about objects that are not present in its immediate surroundings only after object permanence had developed (see Chapter 12, page 145 and Chapter 13, page 157). Data consistent with this theory have been obtained in a number of studies.

For example, Corrigan (1978) showed that children were able to talk about absent objects only after they had demonstrated an advanced level on a test of object permanence. Similarly, Sinclair-de-Zwart (1969) found that children who had the ability to conserve liquid quantity (that is, to recognise that different-shaped containers can hold the same amount of liquid) understood the meaning of phrases and words such as 'as much as', 'bigger' and 'more', whereas children who could not conserve did not improve their performance of the correct use of these words after having been given linguistic training.

In Piaget's view, children can be 'taught' a language but they will not be able to understand the words they have been taught until they have mastered certain intellectual skills during the process of cognitive growth. So, language can exist without thought, but only in the sense that a parrot can 'speak' a language. Thought, then, is a necessary forerunner to language if language is to be used properly.

The view that thought *structures* language has been challenged from a number of quarters. For example, a case study reported by Luria and Yudovich (1971) suggests that, contrary to Piaget's claims, language does play a central role in cognitive development. As Box 17.5 shows, it is much more reasonable to conclude that language *reflects*, to an extent, our understanding of the world in which we live.

Box 17.5   Luria and Yudovich's (1971) study

Luria and Yudovich studied two five-year-old twin boys whose home environment was unstimulating. The boys played almost exclusively together and had only a very primitive level of speech development. They received little encouragement to speak from adults and they made little progress towards the symbolic use of words. Essentially, their speech was *synpraxic*, that is, it was a primitive form of speech in which words cannot be detached from the action or object they denote.

The twins hardly ever used speech to describe objects or events or to help them plan their actions. They could not understand other people's speech, and their own speech represented a private system of communication which was a kind of signalling rather than symbolic system. Although the twins never played with other children and played with each other in a primitive and monotonous way, they were, in most other ways, normal.

After being separated, one twin was given special remedial treatment for his language deficiency but the other was not. The twin given special treatment did make more rapid progress and, ten months later, was ahead of his brother. However, both made progress, and their synpraxic speech died away. For Luria and Yudovich:

'The whole structure of the mental life of both twins was simultaneously and sharply changed. Once they acquired an objective language system, (they) were able to formulate the aims of their activity verbally, and after only three months we observed the beginnings of meaningful play'.

Thought and language are initially separate activities which interact at a certain point of development

According to Vygotsky, language and thought begin as separate and independent activities. In the early stages of life, thinking occurs without language (and primarily involves the use of images) and language occurs without thought (as when babies cry or make other sounds to express feelings, attract attention or fulfil some other social aim). Around the age of two, however, *pre-linguistic thought* and *pre-intellectual language*:

'meet and join to initiate a new kind of behaviour (in which) thought becomes verbal and speech rational' (Vygotsky, 1962).

The interaction between thought and language is shown in Figure 17.3.

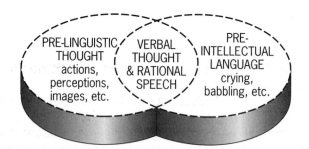

Figure 17.3   A diagrammatic representation of Vygotsky's views on the relationship between language and thought.

Vygotsky believed that between the ages of two and seven, language performs two functions. One of these is an *internal* function which enables internal thought to be monitored and directed. The second is an *external* function which enables the results of thinking to be communicated to others. However, children cannot yet distinguish between the two functions and, as a result, their speech is *egocentric*. Thus, they talk out loud about their plans and actions and can neither think privately nor communicate publicly to others. Instead, they are caught somewhere between the two and cannot distinguish between 'speech for self' (or what Piaget calls *autistic speech*) and 'speech for others' (termed *socialised speech* by Piaget).

Around the age of seven (which is when children typically enter Piaget's *concrete operational* stage of intellectual development: see McIlveen and Gross, 1997), Vygotsky believed that overt language begins to be restricted to the purposes of communication whilst the thought function of language becomes internalised as internal speech or verbal thought. Piaget saw egocentric speech as a kind of 'running commentary' on the child's behaviour and that around the age of seven it was replaced by socialised (or communicative) speech.

Vygotsky, however, showed that when six- or seven-year-olds are trying to solve a problem and a mishap occurs which requires them to revise their thinking (such as a pencil breaking), they often *revert* to overt verbalisation. Adults often do the same in similar situations, especially when they believe that no one can hear them. For example, we will often re-trace our steps out loud (such as 'Now, I know I didn't have it when I went in the room, so what did I do before that?'). On the basis of his findings, Vygotsky felt that the function of egocentric speech was similar to that of inner speech in that it does not merely accompany the child's activity but:

'serves mental orientation, conscious understanding; it helps in overcoming difficulties, it is speech for oneself, intimately and usefully connected with the child's thinking. In the end it becomes inner speech (*see Figure 17.4*).

Eventually, Piaget accepted Vygotsky's view concerning the function and fate of inner speech. Both inner speech and egocentric speech differ from speech for others in that they do not have to satisfy grammatical conventions. Thus, both are abbreviated, incomplete and concerned more with the essential meaning rather than how it is expressed. For Vygotsky, inner speech is a 'dynamic, shifting and unstable thing which "flutters" between word and thought'.

We should note that overt speech can sometimes resemble inner speech in its abbreviated nature long after egocentric speech has been replaced. For example, people who know each other well may talk in an abbreviated form that would not be used with strangers. Understanding occurs because the more familiar we are with others and the more shared experiences we have in common, the less explicit our speech has to be. 'Beer?', for example, asked with a rising inflection and in a particular context, would be interpreted as 'Would you like another beer?' in a way similar to that which adults

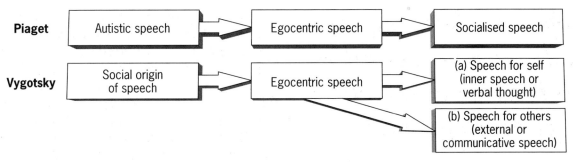

Figure 17.4   The differences between Piaget and Vygotsky with respect to egocentric speech.

use to interpret the holophrastic speech of young children (though 'Beer?' is, we accept, unlikely to be a holophrase used by many children!). In Bernstein's terms, we use restricted code language when we are talking to familiar others in familiar surroundings whose view of the world we assume to be similar to ours.

Conclusions

Whilst there are many examples which indicate that thought can occur without language, the exact relationship between language and thought remains to be determined. Several theoretical perspectives have been advanced, all of which can claim some degree of support from the experimental literature.

SUMMARY

- Philosophical and psychological theories of the relationship between language and thought range from the view that thought is dependent on or caused by language to the view that language reflects thought or an individual's level of cognitive development. Others see them as initially quite separate, but coming to interact later in development.

- According to Watson's **peripheralism**, thought processes are no more than the sensations produced by tiny movements of the speech organs which are too small to produce audible sounds. This represented a behaviourist reduction of 'thought' to 'silent speech'.

- The movements of the larynx that accompany thinking may not be necessary for thinking to occur and do not show that the movements **are** thoughts. Smith et al.'s experimental test of Watson's theory using **curare** showed that thinking can occur despite complete paralysis. Similarly, people born deaf and mute are also capable of thinking, contrary to the predictions of Watson's theory.

- Bruner argues that language is essential for thought and knowledge to progress beyond the enactive and **iconic modes of representation** to the **symbolic mode**.

- **Social constructionists** claim that our ways of understanding the world derive from other people rather than from objective reality. Conceptual frameworks and categories provide meaning within a culture, a way of structuring our experience of ourselves and the world.

- According to the **Sapir-Whorf linguistic relativity hypothesis/Whorfian hypothesis**, language determines **how** we think about objects and events and even **what** we think. Whorf's **linguistic determinism** maintains that we can only think through the use of concepts, and acquiring a language involves acquiring a 'world view': different languages 'cut nature up' differently (linguistic 'relativity').

- Whorf cited the Inuit Eskimos, who have more than 20 words for snow, compared with a single word in Standard Average European languages, such as English. Similarly, the Hanuxoo people use 92 words for 'rice'. Conversely, the Shona people have only three words for colour, and the Dani just two.

- A language's **grammar** also helps to determine a

world view, as in the Hopi Indians' 'timeless language' which, unlike European languages that treat time as an **objective** entity, talks about time only as it appears **subjectively** to the observer. Verbs do not have tenses and there is no distinction made between nouns and verbs as there is in English.

- Miller and McNeill distinguish between the **'strong'** version of the linguistic relativity hypothesis (LRH) (**language determines thought**), the **'weak'** version (**language affects perception**) and the **'weakest'** version (**language influences memory**).
- One test of the strong version is the study by Carroll and Casagrande which compared the development of **form/shape** recognition in Navaho-Navaho, English-Navaho and American (English only) children.
- The 'weak' and 'weakest' versions have been tested typically through perception and memory of **colour**. The fewer colour words there are in a language, the more difficult native speakers will find tests of colour perception and memory, such that the Jalé (who only distinguish black and white) will perform more poorly than those who speak Ibibio (who distinguish black, white, red and green). Both groups will do more poorly than English speakers.
- Early tests seemed to support these two versions, such as Brown and Lenneberg's study of Zuni speakers. However, according to Berlin and Kay, while cultures may differ in the number of basic colour terms they use, all cultures draw their basic or **focal** terms from only 11 colours, which emerge in a particular sequence in the history of languages: black/white, red, green/yellow, blue, brown, purple/pink/orange/grey.
- Supportive of Berlin and Kay's findings are those from Heider and Oliver's study which compared Dani-speaking and English-speaking participants' rate of confusion of similar colours. In other research, Heider found that the Dani learnt labels for focal colours much more easily than for non-focal colours.
- Heider argues that her data are better explained in terms of **physiological factors** underlying colour vision than linguistic factors. This interpretation is supported by Bornstein's study of colour perception in pre-verbal infants.
- Critics have argued that Whorf's evidence was anecdotal rather than empirical, that he exaggerated the differences between Hopi and other languages, and that the Inuit Eskimos actually have relatively few words for snow. Moreover, he did not actually **show** that they **perceive** more varieties of snow or that the Hopi Indians cannot discriminate between past, present and future.

- We distinguish between a language's grammar and our perceptual experience, and translation between languages implies a universally shared knowledge of the world which is independent of any particular language.
- If Inuit Eskimos have many words for snow, this may reflect the importance of snow to their survival. This suggests that our perceptions might be influencing our language (the reverse of the LRH).
- It is widely accepted that Whorf overestimated the importance of language differences and that different languages do not predestine us to different kinds of thinking. However, language does affect how easily information is processed.
- As a sociologist, Bernstein was interested in language as a social phenomenon. He showed that, unlike boys from public schools, those from lower working-class homes often showed large discrepancies in their performance on verbal and non-verbal intelligence tests, with their non-verbal scores being far higher.
- Bernstein argued that working-class children speak a **restricted code** and middle-class children an **elaborated code**. The restricted code is grammatically crude and repetitive, is context-bound, often conveys meaning non-verbally, uses uninformative phrases such as 'you know', stresses the present and does not allow expression of abstract or hypothetical thought. The elaborated code has the opposite characteristics.
- For Bernstein, the relationship between actual and potential intelligence is mediated through language, so working-class children are prevented from developing their full intellectual potential. Language codes underlie the patterns of learning that children bring with them to school.
- Support for Bernstein comes from Hess and Shipman's study, which showed a lack of **meaning** in mother-child communication for low-status families. However, the implication that **upward social mobility** is impossible is simply false and identifying two basic types of code is a great over-simplification. Also, the terms 'restricted' and 'elaborated' imply a value judgement.
- A number of studies have illustrated the difference between Standard and **Black English**, which Bernstein sees as a restricted code. A major difference between Black and Standard English is the former's omission of the present tense of the verb 'to be', which contributes to it being dubbed **sub-standard**, rather than **non-standard**. But

several other languages also do this without being called 'illogical'.

- According to Labov, Black English is one dialect of English with its own grammatical rules which allows the expression of complex thoughts. It is considered sub-standard as a matter of prejudice, but the fact that intelligence tests are written in Standard English puts Black English speakers at a real disadvantage.

- Labov's research involving Leon showed that the social situation, in particular the status of the tester, can be a powerful influence on verbal behaviour and hence of subsequent assessments of a child's linguistic abilities. Black children may be **bilingual**, using the accepted register at home and with their peers fluently and creatively, but adopting the unfamiliar Standard English in the classroom.

- **Ebonics** is an alternative term for Black English and was officially recognised by the Oakland public school board in California in 1996 as a separate language and not a dialect of Standard (American) English. The decision to require Ebonics to be taught in schools has caused much controversy among both politicians and educationalists.

- According to Piaget, language 'maps' onto previously acquired cognitive structures, so that language is dependent on thought. One example is **object permanence**.

- Similarly, children who cannot yet conserve will not benefit from linguistic training on the use of conservation-related terms, as shown by Sinclair-de-Zwart. Words can only be understood if certain intellectual skills have already been mastered, i.e. thought **structures** language.

- Luria and Yudovich's study of the twin boys whose speech was **synpraxic** suggests that language does play a crucial role in cognitive development, contrary to Piaget's claims. Once they acquired an objective language system, they could begin to play in a meaningful way, and the whole structure of their mental life changed.

- According to Vygotsky, language and thought are initially separate and independent activities. At around age two, **pre-linguistic thought** (mainly images) and **pre-intellectual language** (such as crying) begin to interact to form verbal thought and rational speech.

- Between the ages of two and seven, language performs both an **internal** ('speech for itself') and **external** ('speech for others') function. Piaget called these **autistic** and **socialised speech** respectively. The child's failure to distinguish between them results in **egocentric speech**, which largely disappears at around age seven, when the child enters the **concrete operational stage**.

- For Vygotsky, the disappearance of egocentric speech indicates the separation of the two functions, while for Piaget it is simply replaced by socialised or communicative speech. While Piaget saw egocentric speech as a mere accompaniment to a child's activity, Vygotsky saw its function as similar to that of inner speech, which is what it eventually becomes.

REFERENCES

ABERNATHY, E.M. (1940) The effect of changed environmental conditions upon the results of college examinations. *Journal of Psychology*, 10, 293–301.

ABRAMS, D. & MANSTEAD, A.S.R. (1981) A test of theories of social facilitation using a musical task. *British Journal of Social Psychology*, 20, 271–278.

ADAMS, J.A. (1976) Issues for a closed-loop theory of motor learning. In G.E. STELMACH (Ed.) *Motor Control: Issues and Trends*. London: Academic Press.

ADAMS, R.J. (1987) Visual acuity from birth to five months as measured by habituation: A comparison to forced-choice preferential looking. *Infant Behaviour and Development*, 10, 239–244.

ADAMS, R.J. & MAURER, D. (1984) Detection of contrast by the new-born and two-month-old infant. *Infant Behaviour and Development*, 7, 415–422.

AITCHISON, J. (1983) *The Articulate Mammal*. London: Hutchinson.

AITCHISON, J. (1996) Wugs, woggles and whatsits. *The Independent Section Two*, 28 February, 8.

ALBA, J.W. & HASHER, L. (1983) Is memory schematic? *Psychological Bulletin*, 93, 203–231.

ALLPORT, D.A. (1980) Attention and performance. In G. CLAXTON (Ed.) *Cognitive Psychology: New Directions*. London: Routledge & Kegan Paul.

ALLPORT, D.A. (1989) Visual attention. In M. POSNER (Ed.) *Foundations of Cognitive Science*. Cambridge, MA: MIT Press.

ALLPORT, D.A. (1993) Attention and control. Have we been asking the wrong questions? A critical review of twenty-five years. In D.E. MEYER & S.M. KORNBLUM (Eds) *Attention and Performance* (Vol. XIV). London: MIT Press.

ALLPORT, D.A., ANTONIS, B. & REYNOLDS, P. (1972) On the division of attention: A disproof of the single-channel hypothesis. *Quarterly Journal of Experimental Psychology*, 24, 225–235.

ALLPORT, G.W. (1955) *Becoming – Basic Considerations for a Psychology of Personality*. New Haven, CT: Yale University Press.

ALLPORT, G.W. & PETTIGREW, T.F. (1957) Cultural influences on the perception of movement: The trapezoidal illusion among Zulus. *Journal of Abnormal and Social Psychology*, 55, 104–113.

ALLPORT, G.W. & POSTMAN, L. (1947) *The Psychology of Rumour*. New York: Holt, Rinehart & Winston.

ANDERSON, J.R. (1983) *The Architecture of Cognition* (2nd edition). Cambridge, MA: Harvard University Press.

ANDERSON, J.R. (1995a) *Learning and Memory: An Integrated Approach*. Chichester: Wiley.

ANDERSON, J.R. (1995b) *Cognitive Psychology and its Implications*. New York: W.H. Freeman & Company.

ANNIS, R.C. & FROST, B. (1973) Human visual ecology and orientation anisotropies in acuity. *Science*, 182, 729–731.

APPLEBEE, A.N. (1984) Writing and reasoning. *Review of Educational Research*, 54, 577–596.

ASLIN, R.N., PISONI, D.B. & JUSCZYK, P.W. (1983) Auditory development and speech perception in infancy. In P.H. MUSSEN (Ed.) *Handbook of Child Psychology* (4th edition). New York: Wiley.

ATKINSON, R.C. (1975) Mnemonotechnics in second-language learning. *American Psychologist*, 30, 821–828.

ATKINSON, R.C. & SHIFFRIN, R.M. (1968) Human memory: A proposed system and its control processes. In K.W. SPENCE & J.T. SPENCE (Eds) *The Psychology of Learning and Motivation*, Volume 2. London: Academic Press.

ATKINSON, R.C. & SHIFFRIN, R.M. (1971) The control of short-term memory. *Scientific American*, 224, 82–90.

ATTNEAVE, F. (1954) Some informational aspects of visual perception. *Psychological Review*, 61, 183–193.

ATWELL, M. (1981) The evolution of text: The inter-relationship of reading and writing in the composing process. Paper presented at the Annual Meeting of the National Council of Teachers of English, Boston, MA.

ATWOOD, M.E. & POLSON, P.G. (1976) A process model for water-jug problems. *Cognitive Psychology*, 8, 191–216.

BADDELEY, A.D. (1966) The influence of acoustic and semantic similarity on long-term memory for word sequences. *Quarterly Journal of Experimental Psychology*, 18, 302–309.

BADDELEY, A.D. (1968) Closure and response bias in short-term memory for form. *British Journal of Psychology*, 59, 139–145.

BADDELEY, A.D. (1976) *The Psychology of Memory*. New York: Basic Books.

BADDELEY, A.D. (1981) The concept of working

memory: A view of its current state and probable future development. *Cognition*, 10, 17–23.

BADDELEY, A.D. (1986) *Working Memory*. Oxford: Oxford University Press.

BADDELEY, A.D. (1990) *Human Memory*. Hove: Erlbaum.

BADDELEY, A.D. (1995) Memory. In C.C. FRENCH & A.M. COLMAN (Eds) *Cognitive Psychology*. London: Longman.

BADDELEY, A.D. & HITCH, G. (1974) Working memory. In G.H. BOWER (Ed.) *Recent Advances in Learning and Motivation*, Volume 8. New York: Academic Press.

BADDELEY, A.D. & SCOTT, D. (1971) Short-term forgetting in the absence of proactive inhibition. *Quarterly Journal of Experimental Psychology*, 23, 275–283.

BADDELEY, A.D., THOMSON, N. & BUCHANAN, M. (1975) Word length and the structure of short-term memory. *Journal of Verbal Learning and Verbal Behaviour*, 14, 575–589.

BAHRICK, H.P. (1984) Semantic memory content in permastore: Fifty years of memory for Spanish learned in school. *Journal of Experimental Psychology: General*, 113, 1–29.

BAHRICK, H.P. & HALL, L.K. (1991) Lifetime maintenance of high-school mathematics content. *Journal of Experimental Psychology: General*, 120, 20–33.

BAHRICK, L.E., WALKER, A.S. & NEISSER, U. (1981) Selective looking by infants. *Cognitive Psychology*, 13, 377–390.

BANAJI, M.R. & CROWDER, R.G. (1989) The bankruptcy of everyday memory. *American Psychologist*, 44, 1185–1193.

BANDURA, A. (1977) *Social Learning Theory*. Englewood Cliffs, NJ: General Learning Press.

BARON, R.A. (1989) *Psychology: The Essential Science*. London: Allyn & Bacon.

BARRETT, M.D. (1986) Early semantic representations and early word usage. In S.A. KUCZAJ & M.D. BARRETT (Eds) *The Development of Word Meaning*. New York: Springer Verlag.

BARRETT, M.D. (1989) Early language development. In A. SLATER & G. BREMNER (Eds) *Infant Development*. Hove: Erlbaum.

BARTLETT, F.C. (1932) *Remembering*. Cambridge: Cambridge University Press.

BEACH, R. & BRIDWELL, L.S. (1984) *New Directions in Composition Research*. New York: Guildford.

BEE, H. & MITCHELL, S.K. (1980) *The Developing Person: A Lifespan Approach*. New York: Harper & Row.

BEKERIAN, D.A. & BOWERS, J.M. (1983) Eye-witness testimony: Were we misled? *Journal of Experimental Psychology: Learning, Memory and Cognition*, 9, 139–145.

BELEZZA, F.S. (1981) Mnemonic devices: Classification, characteristics and criteria. *Review of Educational Research*, 51, 247–275.

BEREITER, C. & ENGELMAN, S. (1966) *Teaching Disadvantaged Children in The Pre-School*. Englewood Cliffs, NJ: Prentice-Hall.

BERKO, J. (1958) The child's learning of English morphology. *Word*, 14, 150–177.

BERLIN, B. & KAY, P. (1969) *Basic Colour Terms: Their Universality and Evolution*. Berkeley, CA: University of California Press.

BERNSTEIN, B. (1961) Social class and linguistic development: A theory of Social Learning. In A.H. HALSEY, J. FLOYD & C.A. ANDERSON (Eds) *Education, Economy and Society*. London: Collier-Macmillan Ltd.

BERNSTEIN, E. (1987) Response to Terrace. *American Psychologist*, 42, 272–273.

BERRY, J.W., POORTINGA, Y.H., SEGALL, M.H. & DASEN, P.R. (1992) *Cross-cultural Psychology: Research and Applications*. New York: Cambridge University Press.

BIEDERMAN, I. (1987) Recognition-by-components: A theory of human image understanding. *Psychological Review*, 94, 115–147.

BIEDERMAN, I., COOPER, E.E., MAHDEVAN, R.S. & FOX, P.W. (1992) Unexceptional spatial memory in an exceptional mnemonist. *Journal of Experimental Psychology: Learning, Memory and Cognition*, 18, 654–657.

BIRNBAUM, J.C. (1982) The reading and composing behaviours of selected fourth- and seventh-grade students. *Research in the Teaching of English*, 16, 241–260.

BLAKEMORE, C. (1988) *The Mind Machine*. London: BBC Publications.

BLAKEMORE, C. & COOPER, G.F. (1970) Development of the brain depends on the visual environment. *Nature*, 228, 477–478.

BODEN, M. (1987) *Artificial Language and Natural Man* (2nd edition). Cambridge, MA: Harvard University Press.

BORNSTEIN, M.H. (1976) Infants are trichromats. *Journal of Experimental Child Psychology*, 19, 401–419.

BORNSTEIN, M.H. (1988) Perceptual development across the life-cycle. In M.H. BORNSTEIN & M.E. LAMB (Eds) *Perceptual, Cognitive and Linguistic Development*. Hove: Erlbaum.

BOURNE, L.E., DOMINOWSKI, R.L. & LOFTUS, E.F. (1979) *Cognitive Processes*. Englewood Cliffs, NJ: Prentice-Hall.

BOUSFIELD, W.A. (1953) The occurrence of clustering in the recall of randomly arranged associates. *Journal of General Psychology*, 49, 229–240.

BOWER, G.H. (1972) Mental imagery and associative

learning. In L. GREGG (Ed.) *Cognition in Learning and Memory.* New York: Wiley.

BOWER, G.H. (1973) How to . . . uh . . . remember! *Psychology Today*, October, 63–70.

BOWER, G.H. (1981) Mood and memory. *American Psychologist*, 36, 129–148.

BOWER, G.H., BLACK, J.B. & TURNER, T.J. (1979) Scripts in memory for text. *Cognitive Psychology*, 11, 177–220.

BOWER, G.H. & CLARK, M.C. (1969) Narrative stories as mediators for serial learning. *Psychonomic Science*, 14, 181–182.

BOWER, G.H., CLARK, M.C., LESGOLD, A. & WINSENZ, D. (1969) Hierarchical retrieval schemes in recall of categorised word lists. *Journal of Verbal Learning and Verbal Behaviour*, 8, 323–343.

BOWER, G.H. & HILGARD, E.R. (1981) *Theories of Learning.* Englewood Cliffs, NJ: Prentice Hall.

BOWER, G.H. & MAYER, J. (1985) Failure to replicate mood-dependent retrieval. *Bulletin of the Psychonomic Society*, 23, 39–42.

BOWER, G.H. & SPRINGSTON, F. (1970) Pauses as recoding points in letter series. *Journal of Experimental Psychology*, 83, 421–430.

BOWER, T.G.R. (1966) The visual world of infants. *Scientific American*, 215, 80–92.

BOWER, T.G.R. (1971) The object in the world of the infant. *Scientific American*, 225, 38–47.

BOWER, T.G.R. (1979) *Human Development.* San Francisco: W.H. Freeman.

BOWER, T.G.R., BROUGHTON, J.M. & MOORE, M.K. (1970) Infant responses to approaching objects: An indicator of response to distal variables. *Perception and Psychophysics*, 9, 193–196.

BRANSFORD, D.J. (1979) *Human Cognition: Learning, Understanding and Remembering.* Belmont, CA: Wadsworth.

BRANSFORD, J.D., FRANKS, J.J., MORRIS, C.D. & STEIN, B.S. (1979) Some general constraints on learning and memory research. In L.S. CERMAK & F.I.M. CRAIK (Eds) *Levels of Processing in Human Memory.* Hillsdale, NJ: Erlbaum.

BRANSFORD, J.D. & JOHNSON, M.K. (1972) Contextual prerequisites for understanding: Some investigations of comprehension and recall. *Journal of Verbal Learning and Verbal Behaviour*, 11, 717–726.

BRIDWELL, L.S. (1980) Revising strategies in twelfth-grade students' transactional writing. *Research in the Teaching of English*, 14, 197–222.

BRIGHAM, J.C. & MALPASS, R.S. (1985) The role of experience and contact in the recognition of faces of own- and other-race persons. *Journal of Social Issues*, 41, 139–155.

BRITISH PSYCHOLOGICAL SOCIETY (1995) *Recovered Memories: The Report of the Working Party of the British Psychological Society.* Leicester: British Psychological Society.

BROADBENT, D.E. (1954) The role of auditory localisation and attention in memory span. *Journal of Experimental Psychology*, 47, 191–196.

BROADBENT, D.E. (1958) *Perception and Communication.* Oxford: Pergamon.

BROADBENT, D.E. (1982) Task combination and selective intake of information. *Acta Psychologica*, 50, 253–290.

BROADBENT, D.E., COOPER, P.J. & BROADBENT, M.H.P. (1978) A comparison of hierarchical and matrix retrieval schemes in recall. *Journal of Experimental Psychology: Human Learning and Memory*, 4, 486–497.

BROCKNER, J. & RUBIN, Z. (1985) *Entrapment in Escalating Conflict.* New York: Springer-Verlag.

BRODBECK, A. & IRWIN, O. (1946) The speech behaviour of infants without families. *Child Development*, 17, 145–146.

BROWN, J.A. (1958) Some tests of the decay theory of immediate memory. *Quarterly Journal of Experimental Psychology*, 10, 12–21.

BROWN, R. (1965) *Social Psychology.* New York: Free Press.

BROWN, R. (1970) The first sentences of child and chimpanzee. In R. BROWN (Ed.) *Psycholinguistics.* New York: Free Press.

BROWN, R. (1973) *A First Language: The Early Stages.* Cambridge, MA: Harvard University Press.

BROWN, R., CAZDEN, C.B. & BELLUGI, U. (1969) The child's grammar from one to three. In J.P. HILL (Ed.) *Minnesota Symposium on Child Psychology*, Volume 2. Minneapolis: University of Minnesota Press.

BROWN, R. & KULIK, J. (1977) Flashbulb memories. *Cognition*, 5, 73–99.

BROWN, R. & KULIK, J. (1982) Flashbulb memories. In U. NEISSER (Ed.) *Memory Observed.* San Francisco: Freeman.

BROWN, R. & LENNEBERG, E.H. (1954) A study in language and cognition. *Journal of Abnormal and Clinical Psychology*, 49, 454–462.

BROWN, R. & McNEILL, D. (1966) The 'tip-of-the-tongue' phenomenon. *Journal of Verbal Learning and Verbal Behaviour*, 5, 325–337.

BRUCE, V. & GREEN, P.R. (1990) *Visual Perception* (2nd edition). Hove: Erlbaum.

BRUNER, J.S. (1957) On perceptual readiness. *Psychological Review*, 64, 123–152.

BRUNER, J.S. (1975) The ontogenesis of speech acts. *Journal of Child Language*, 2, 1–21.

BRUNER, J.S. (1978) Acquiring the uses of language. *Canadian Journal of Psychology*, 32, 204–218.

BRUNER, J.S. (1983) *Child's Talk: Learning to Use Language*. Oxford: Oxford University Press.

BRUNER, J.S., BUSIEK, R.D. & MINTURN, A.L. (1952) Assimilation in the immediate reproduction of visually perceived figures. *Journal of Experimental Psychology*, 44, 151–155.

BRUNER, J.S. & POSTMAN, L. (1949) On the perception of incongruity. *Journal of Personality*, 18, 206–223.

BRUNSWICK, E. (1956) *Perception and the Representative Design of Psychological Experiments*. Berkeley, CA: University of California Press.

BUSHNELL, I.W.R. & SAI, F. (1987) *Neonatal Recognition of the Mother's Face*. University of Glasgow Report No. 87/1.

BUTLER, S.R., MARCH, H.W., SHEPPARD, M.J. & SHEPPARD, J.L. (1985) Seven-year longitudinal study in the early prediction of reading achievement. *Journal of Educational Psychology*, 77, 349–361.

CALVIN, W.H. (1994) The emergence of language. *Scientific American*, October, 79–85.

CAMPOS, J.J., LANGER, A. & KROWITZ, A. (1970) Cardiac responses on the visual cliff in pre-locomotor human infants. *Science*, 170, 196–197.

CARLSON, N.R. (1987) *Discovering Psychology*. London: Allyn & Bacon.

CARROLL, D.W. (1986) *Psychology of Language*. Monterey, CA: Brooks/Cole Publishing Co.

CARROLL, J.B. & CASAGRANDE, J.B. (1958) The function of language classifications in behaviour. In E.E. MACCOBY, T.M. NEWCOMBE & E.L. HARTLEY (Eds) *Readings in Social Psychology* (3rd edition). New York: Holt, Rinehart & Winston.

CHALL, J. (1967) *Learning to Read: The Great Debate*. New York: McGraw Hill.

CHALL, J. (1983) *Stages of Reading Development*. New York: McGraw Hill.

CHANDLER, C. (1989) Specific retroactive interference in modified recognition tests: Evidence for an unknown cause of interference. *Journal of Experimental Psychology: Learning, Memory and Cognition*, 15, 256–265.

CHERRY, E.C. (1953) Some experiments on the recognition of speech with one and two ears. *Journal of the Acoustical Society of America*, 25, 975–979.

CHERRY, E.C. & TAYLOR, W.K. (1954) Some further experiments on the recognition of speech with one and two ears. *Journal of the Acoustical Society of America*, 26, 554–559.

CHOMSKY, N. (1957) *Syntactic Structures*. The Hague: Mouton.

CHOMSKY, N. (1965) *Aspects of the Theory of Syntax*. Cambridge, MA: MIT Press.

CHOMSKY, N. (1968) *Language and Mind*. New York: Harcourt Brace Jovanovich.

CHOMSKY, N. (1979) *Language and Responsibility*. Sussex: Harvester Press.

CLARK, M.S., MILLBERG, S. & ERBER, R. (1987) Arousal and state dependent memory: Evidence and some implications for understanding social judgements and social behaviour. In K. FIEDLER & J.P. FORGAS (Eds) *Affect, Cognition and Social Behaviour*. Toronto: Hogrefe.

CLIFFORD, B. (1980) Recent developments in memory. In J. RADFORD & E. GOVIER (Eds) *A Textbook of Psychology*. London: Sheldon.

CLIFFORD, B. (1991) Memory. In J. RADFORD & E. GOVIER (Eds) *A Textbook of Psychology* (2nd edition). London: Routledge.

COHEN, G. (1990) Memory. In I. ROTH (Ed.) *Introduction to Psychology*, Volume 2. Milton Keynes: Open University Press.

COHEN, G. (1993) Everyday memory and memory systems: The experimental approach. In G. COHEN, G. KISS & M. LEVOI (Eds) *Memory: Current Issues* (2nd edition). Buckingham: Open University Press.

COLEGROVE, F.W. (1899) Individual memories. *American Journal of Psychology*, 10, 228–255.

COLLINS, A.M. & LOFTUS, E.F. (1975) A spreading-activation theory of semantic processing. *Psychological Review*, 82, 407–428.

COLLINS, A.M. & QUILLIAN, M.R. (1969) Retrieval time for semantic memory. *Journal of Verbal Learning and Verbal Behaviour*, 8, 240–247.

COLLINS, A.M. & QUILLIAN, M.R. (1972) How to make a language user. In E. TULVING & W. DONALDSON (Eds) *Organisation of Memory*. New York: Academic Press.

COLLIS, G.M. & SCHAFFER, H.R. (1975) Synchronization of visual attention in mother-infant pairs. *Journal of Child Psychology and Psychiatry*, 16, 315–320.

COLTHEART, M. (1979) When can children learn to read and what should they be taught? In T.G. WALLER & G.E. McKINNON (Eds) *Reading Research: Advances in Theory and Practice* (Volume 1). New York: Academic Press.

CONRAD, C. (1972) Cognitive economy in semantic memory. *Journal of Experimental Psychology*, 92, 148–154.

CONRAD, R. (1964) Acoustic confusion in immediate memory. *British Journal of Psychology*, 55, 75–84.

CONWAY, M.A., ANDERSON, S.J., LARSEN, S.F., DONNELLY, C.M., McDANIEL, M.A., McCLELLAND, A.G.R. & RAWLES, R.E. (1994). The formation of flashbulb memories. *Memory and Cognition*, 22, 326–343.

COREN, S. & GIRGUS, J.S. (1978) *Seeing is Deceiving: The Psychology of Visual Illusions*. Hillsdale, NJ: Erlbaum.

CORNWELL, T. (1997) Board tones down Ebonics policy. *The Times Educational Supplement*, 31 January, 14.

CORRIGAN, R. (1978) Language development as related to stage-6 object permanence development. *Journal of Child Language*, 5, 173–189.

CORTEEN, R.S. & WOOD, B. (1972) Autonomic responses to shock-associated words in an unattended channel. *Journal of Experimental Psychology*, 94, 308–313.

COSKY, M.J. (1976) The role of letter recognition in word recognition. *Memory and Cognition*, 4, 207–214.

COWAN, N. (1984) On short and long auditory stores. *Psychological Bulletin*, 96, 341–370.

CRAIK, F.I.M. & LOCKHART, R. (1972) Levels of processing. *Journal of Verbal Learning and Verbal Behaviour*, 11, 671–684.

CRAIK, F.I.M. & TULVING, E. (1975) Depth of processing and retention of words in episodic memory. *Journal of Experimental Psychology: General*, 104, 268–294.

CRAIK, F.I.M. & WATKINS, M.J. (1973) The role of rehearsal in short-term memory. *Journal of Verbal Learning and Verbal Behaviour*, 12, 599–607.

CRIDER, A.B., GOETHALS, G.R., KAVANAUGH, R.D. & SOLOMON, P.R. (1989) *Psychology* (3rd edition). London: Scott, Foresman and Company.

CROMER, R.F. (1974) The development of language and cognition: The cognition hypothesis. In B.M. FOSS (Ed.) *New Perspectives in Child Development*. Harmondsworth: Penguin.

CROOKS, R.L. & STEIN, J. (1991) *Psychology: Science, Behaviour and Life*. New York: Harcourt Brace Jovanovich.

CURTISS, S. (1977) *Genie: A Psycholinguistic Study of a Modern-Day 'Wild Child'*. London: Academic Press.

DALE, P.S. (1976) *Language Development: Structure and Function* (2nd edition). New York: Holt, Rinehart and Winston.

DARWIN, C.J., TURVEY, M.T. & CROWDER, R.G. (1972) An auditory analogue of the Sperling partial report procedure: Evidence for brief auditory storage. *Cognitive Psychology*, 3, 225–267.

de GROOT, A.D. (1966) Perception and memory versus thought: Some old ideas and recent findings. In B. KLEINMUNTZ (Ed.) *Problem-Solving: Research, Method and Theory*. New York: Wiley.

DELBOEUF, J.L.R. (1892) Sur une nouvelle illusion d'optique. *Bulletin de L'Academie Royale de Belgique*, 24, 545–558.

DELK, J.L. & FILLENBAUM, S. (1965) Differences in perceived colour as a function of characteristic colour. *American Journal of Psychology*, 78, 290–293.

DEREGOWSKI, J. (1972) Pictorial perception and culture. *Scientific American*, 227, 82–88.

DEUTSCH, J.A. & DEUTSCH, D. (1963) Attention: Some theoretical considerations. *Psychological Review*, 70, 80–90.

DEUTSCH, J.A. & DEUTSCH, D. (1967) Comments on 'Selective attention: Perception or response?' *Quarterly Journal of Experimental Psychology*, 19, 362–363.

de VILLIERS, P.A. & de VILLIERS, J.G. (1979) *Early Language*. Cambridge, MA: Harvard University Press.

DEVLIN REPORT (1976) Report to the Secretary of State for the Home Development of the Departmental Committee on Evidence of Identification in Criminal Cases. London: HMSO.

DIXON, N.F. (1994) Disastrous decisions. *The Psychologist*, 7, 303–307.

DODWELL, P.C. (1995) Fundamental processes in vision. In R.L. GREGORY & A.M. COLMAN (Eds) *Sensation and Perception*. London: Longman.

DRIVER, J. (1996) Attention and segmentation. *The Psychologist*, 9, 119–123.

DRIVER, J. & MATTINGLEY, J.B. (1995) Normal and pathological selective attention in humans. *Current Opinion in Neurobiology*, 5, 191–197.

DUNCAN, H.F., GOURLAY, N. & HUDSON, W. (1973) *A Study of Pictorial Perception among Bantu and White Primary-school Children in South Africa*. Johannesburg: Witwatersrand University Press.

DUNCAN, J. & HUMPHREYS, G.W. (1992) Beyond the search surface: Visual search and attentional engagement. *Journal of Experimental Psychology: Human Perception and Performance*, 18, 578–588.

DUNCKER, K. (1945) On problem-solving. *Psychological Monographs*, 58 (Whole No. 270).

DURKIN, K. (1995) *Developmental Social Psychology: From Infancy to Old Age*. Oxford: Blackwell.

EBBINGHAUS, H. (1885) *On Memory*. Leipzig: Duncker.

EHRENFELS, C. von (1890) Über Gestaltqualitäten. *Vierteljahresschrift für wissenschaftliche Philosophie und Soziologie*, 14, 249–292.

EICH, E. & METCALFE, J. (1989) Mood-dependent memory for internal versus external events. *Journal of Experimental Psychology: Learning, Memory and Cognition*, 15, 443–455.

EIMAS, P.D. (1975) Speech perception in early infancy. In L.B. Cohen and P. Salapatek (Eds) *Infant Perception: From Sensation to Cognition*, Volume 2. New York: Academic Press.

ELLIS, A.W. (1993) *Reading, Writing and Dyslexia: A Cognitive Analysis* (2nd edition). Hove: Erlbaum.

ELLIS, A.W. & YOUNG, A.W. (1988) *Human Cognitive Neuropsychology*. Hove: Erlbaum.

EPSTEIN, R., LANZA, R. & SKINNER, B.F. (1980) Symbolic communication between two pigeons. *Science*, 210, 220–221.

ERIKSEN, C.W. (1990) Attentional search of the visual

field. In D. BROGAN (Ed.) *Visual Search*. London: Taylor & Francis.

ERIKSEN, C.W. & YEH, Y.Y. (1987) Allocation of attention in the visual field. *Journal of Experimental Psychology: Human Perception and Performance*, 11, 583–597.

ESTES, W. (1972) An associative basis for coding and organisation in memory. In A. MELTON & E. MARTIN (Eds) *Coding Processes in Human Memory*. Washington, DC: Winston.

EYSENCK, M.W. (1982) *Attention and Arousal: Cognition and Performance*. Berlin: Springer.

EYSENCK, M.W. (1984) *A Handbook of Cognitive Psychology*. London: Lawrence Erlbaum Associates.

EYSENCK, M.W. (1986) Working memory. In G. COHEN, M.W. EYSENCK & M.A. LE VOI (Eds) *Memory: A Cognitive Approach*. Milton Keynes: Open University Press.

EYSENCK, M.W. (1993) *Principles of Cognitive Psychology*. Hove: Erlbaum.

EYSENCK, M.W. (1994) Attention. In C.C. FRENCH & A.M. COLMAN (Eds) *Cognitive Psychology*. London: Longman.

EYSENCK, M.W. (1997) Absent-mindedness. *Psychology Review*, 3, 16–18.

EYSENCK, M.W. & EYSENCK, M.C. (1980) Effects of processing depth, distinctiveness and word frequency on retention. *British Journal of Psychology*, 71, 263–274.

EYSENCK, M.W. & KEANE, M.J. (1995) *Cognitive Psychology: A Student's Handbook* (2nd edition). Hove: Erlbaum.

FAIGLEY, L. & WITTE, S. (1981) Analysing revision. *College Composition and Communication*, 32, 400–414.

FANTZ, R.L. (1961) The origin of form perception. *Scientific American*, 204, 66–72.

FEIGENBAUM, E.A. & McCORDUCK, P. (1983) *The Fifth Generation*. New York: Addison-Wesley.

FIELDS, H. (1991) Depression and pain: A neurobiological model. *Neuropsychiatry, Neuropsychology and Behavioural Neurology*, 4, 83–92.

FISCHER, K.W. & LAZERSON, A. (1984) *Human Development: From Conception through Adolescence*. New York: W.H. Freeman.

FISCHOFF, B. (1982) Debiasing. In D. KAHNEMAN, P. SLOVIC & A. TVERSKY (Eds) *Judgement Under Uncertainty: Heuristics and Biases*. Cambridge: Cambridge University Press.

FLOWER, L.S. & HAYES, J.R. (1983) Plans that guide the composing process. In C.H. FREDERIKSON & J.F. DOMINIC (Eds) *Writing: Process, Development and Communication*. Hillsdale, NJ: Erlbaum.

FLOWERS, J.H., WARNER, J.L. & POLANSKY, M.L. (1979) Response and encoding factors in ignoring irrelevant information. *Memory and Cognition*, 7, 86–94.

FODOR, J.A. & PYLYSHYN, Z.W. (1981) How direct is visual perception? Some reflections on Gibson's 'ecological approach'. *Cognition*, 9, 139–196.

FOUTS, R.S. (1983) Chimpanzee language and elephant tails: A theoretical synthesis. In J. de LUCE & H.T. WILDER (Eds) *Language in Primates: Perspectives and Implications*. New York: Springer-Verlag.

FOUTS, R.S., FOUTS, D.H. & VAN CANTFORT, T.H. (1989) The infant Loulis learns signs from cross-fostered chimpanzees. In R.A. GARDNER, B.T. GARDNER & T.H. VAN CANTFORT (Eds) *Teaching Sign Language to Chimpanzees*. New York: State University of New York Press.

FREDERIKSON, J.R. & KROLL, J.F. (1976) Approaches to the internal lexicon. *Journal of Experimental Psychology: Human Perception and Performance*, 2, 361–379.

FREUD, S. (1901) The psychopathology of everyday life. In J. STRACHEY (Ed.) *The Standard Edition of the Complete Works of Sigmund Freud*, Volume 6. London: Hogarth Press.

FRITH, U. (1985) The usefulness of the concept of unexpected reading failure: Comments on 'Reading retardation revisited'. *British Journal of Developmental Psychology*, 3, 15–17.

FRUZZETTI, A.E., TOLAND, K., TELLER, S.A. & LOFTUS, E.F. (1992) Memory and eyewitness testimony. In M. GRUNEBERG & P.E. MORRIS (Eds) *Aspects of Memory: The Practical Aspects*. London: Routledge.

FURTH, H.G. (1966) *Thinking Without Language*. New York: Free Press.

GABRIELI, J.D.E., COHEN, N.J. & CORKIN, S. (1988) The impaired learning of semantic knowledge following bilateral medial temporal lobe resection. *Brain*, 7, 157–177.

GAGNÉ, E.D. (1985) *The Cognitive Psychology of School Learning*. Boston: Little, Brown and Company.

GARDINER, J.M., CRAIK, F.I.M. & BIRTWISTLE, J. (1972) Retrieval cues and release from proactive inhibition. *Journal of Verbal Learning and Verbal Behaviour*, 11, 778–783.

GARDNER, B.T. (1981) Project Nim: Who taught whom? *Contemporary Psychology*, 26, 381–404.

GARDNER, H. (1985) *The Mind's New Science*. New York: Basic Books.

GARDNER, R.A. & GARDNER, B.T. (1969) Teaching sign language to a chimpanzee. *Science*, 165, 664–672.

GARDNER, R.A. & GARDNER, B.T. (1977) Comparative psychology and language acquisition. In K. SALZINGER & R. DENMARK (Eds) *Psychology: The State of the Art*. New York: Annals of the New York Academy of Science.

GARDNER, R.A. & GARDNER, B.T. (1978) Comparative psychology and language acquisition.

Annals of the New York Academy of Science, 309, 37–76.

GARDNER, R.A. & GARDNER, B.T. (1984) A vocabulary test for chimpanzees (Pan troglodytes). *Journal of Comparative Psychology*, 98, 381–404.

GARNHAM, A. (1988) *Artificial Intelligence: An Introduction.* London: Routledge, Kegan Paul.

GARNHAM, A. (1991) *The Mind in Action.* London: Routledge.

GATHERCOLE, S.E. & BADDELEY, A.D. (1990) Phonological memory deficits in language-disordered children: Is there a causal connection? *Journal of Memory and Language*, 29, 336–360.

GAUKER, C. (1990) How to learn language like a chimpanzee. *Philosophical Psychology*, 3, 31–53.

GEISELMAN, R.E. (1988) Improving eyewitness memory through mental reinstatement of context. In G.M. DAVIES & D.M. THOMSON (Eds) *Memory in Context: Context in Memory.* Chichester: Wiley.

GEISLER, C., KAUFER, D. & HAYES, J.R. (1985) Translating instruction into skill: Learning to write precisely. Paper presented at the Annual Meeting of the American Educational Research Association, Chicago (March).

GELB, I.C. (1952) *A Study of Writing.* Chicago: University of Chicago Press.

GERGEN, K.J. (1973) Social psychology as history. *Journal of Personality and Social Psychology*, 26, 309–320.

GERRARD, N. (1997) Nicaragua's deaf children. *The Observer Review*, 30 March, 5.

GIBSON, E.J., SHAPIRO, F. & YONAS, A. (1968) Confusion matrices of graphic patterns obtained with a latency measure: A program of basic and applied research. *Final Report Project No. 5-1213*, Cornell University.

GIBSON, E.J. & WALK, P.D. (1960) The visual cliff. *Scientific American*, 202, 64–71.

GIBSON, J.J. (1950) *The Perception of the Visual World.* Boston: Houghton Mifflin.

GIBSON, J.J. (1966) *The Senses Considered as Perceptual Systems.* Boston: Houghton Mifflin.

GIBSON, J.J. (1979) *The Ecological Approach to Visual Perception.* Boston: Houghton Mifflin.

GILHOOLY, K. (1996) Working memory and thinking. *The Psychologist*, 9, 82.

GILLING, D. & BRIGHTWELL, R. (1982) *The Human Brain.* London: Orbis Publishing.

GLANZER, M. & CUNITZ, A.R. (1966) Two storage mechanisms in free recall. *Journal of Verbal Learning and Verbal Behaviour*, 5, 928–935.

GLANZER, M. & MEINZER, A. (1967) The effects of intralist activity on free recall. *Journal of Verbal Learning and Verbal Behaviour*, 6, 928–935.

GLEASON, J. (1967) Do children imitate? *Proceedings of the International Conference on Oral Education of the Deaf*, 2, 1441–1448.

GLEITMAN, H. & JONIDES, J. (1978) The effect of set on categorisation in visual search. *Perception and Psychophysics*, 24, 361–368.

GLOVER, J.A. & BRUNING, R.H. (1987) *Educational Psychology: Principles and Applications.* Boston: Little, Brown and Company.

GLUCKSBERG, S. & COWAN, N. (1970) Memory for non-attended auditory material. *Cognitive Psychology*, 1, 149–156.

GLUCKSBERG, S. & WEISBERG, R. (1966) Verbal behaviour and problem-solving: Some effects of labelling upon availability of novel functions. *Journal of Experimental Psychology*, 71, 659–664.

GODDEN, D. & BADDELEY, A.D. (1975) Context-dependent memory in two natural environments: On land and under water. *British Journal of Psychology*, 66, 325–331.

GOLDIN-MEADOW, S. & FELDMAN, H. (1977) The development of a language-like communication without a language model. *Science*, 197, 401–403.

GOLEMAN, D. (1985) Political forces come under new scrutiny of psychology. *The New York Times*, 2 April, C1 and C4.

GOMBRICH, E.H. (1960) *Art and Illusion.* London: Phaidon.

GORDON, I.E. (1989) *Theories of Visual Perception.* Chichester: Wiley.

GOSWAMI, U. (1993) Orthographic analogies and reading development. *The Psychologist*, 6, 312–316.

GOVIER, E. (1980) Attention. In J. RADFORD & E. GOVIER (Eds) *A Textbook of Psychology.* London: Sheldon Press.

GRAY, J.A. & WEDDERBURN, A.A. (1960) Grouping strategies with simultaneous stimuli. *Quarterly Journal of Experimental Psychology*, 12, 180–184.

GREENE, J. (1975) *Thinking and Language.* London: Methuen.

GREENE, J. (1987) *Memory, Thinking and Language.* London: Methuen.

GREENE, J. (1990) Perception. In I. ROTH (Ed.) *Introduction to Psychology* (Volume 2). Milton Keynes: Open University Press.

GREENFIELD, P.M. & SMITH, J.H. (1976) *The Structure of Communication in Early Language Development.* New York: Academic Press.

GREGOR, A.J. & McPHERSON, D. (1965) A study of susceptibility to geometric illusions among cultural outgroups of Australian aborigines. *Psychologia Africana*, 11, 490–499.

GREGORY, R.L. (1966) *Eye and Brain.* London: Weidenfeld & Nicolson.

GREGORY, R.L. (1970) *The Intelligent Eye.* London: Weidenfeld & Nicolson.

GREGORY, R.L. (1972) Visual illusions. In B.M. FOSS (Ed.) *New Horizons in Psychology 1*. Harmondsworth: Penguin.

GREGORY, R.L. (1973) *Eye and Brain* (2nd edition). New York: World Universities Library.

GREGORY, R.L. (1980) Perceptions as hypotheses. *Philosophical Transactions of the Royal Society of London, Series B*, 290, 181–197.

GREGORY, R.L. (1983) Visual illusions. In J. MILLER (Ed.) *States of Mind*. London: BBC Productions.

GREGORY, R.L. (1996) Twenty-five years after 'The Intelligent Eye'. *The Psychologist*, 9, 452–455.

GREGORY, R.L. & WALLACE, J. (1963) *Recovery from Early Blindness*. Cambridge: Heffer.

GROEGER, J. (1994) The working-memory man: An interview with Professor Alan Baddeley. *The Psychologist*, 7, 58–59.

GROSS, R.D. (1994) *Key Studies in Psychology* (2nd edition). London: Hodder and Stoughton.

GROSS, R.D. (1996) *Psychology: The Science of Mind and Behaviour* (3rd edition). London: Hodder and Stoughton.

GRUENDEL, J.M. (1977) Referential overextension in early language development. *Child Development*, 48, 1567–1576.

GRUNEBERG, M. (1992) *Linkword Language System: Greek*. London: Corgi Books.

GUERIN, B.J. (1993) *Social Facilitation*. Cambridge: Cambridge University Press.

GUNTER, B., CLIFFORD, B. & BERRY, C. (1980) Release from proactive interference with television news items: Evidence for encoding dimensions within televised news. *Journal of Experimental Psychology: Human Learning and Memory*, 6, 216–223.

GUSTAFSON, G. & HARRIS, K. (1990) Women's responses to young infants' cries. *Developmental Psychology*, 26, 144–152.

GWIAZDA, J., BRILL, S., MOHINDRA, I. & HELD, R. (1980) Preferential looking acuity in infants from two to 58 weeks of age. *American Journal of Optometry and Physiological Optics*, 57, 428–432.

HABER, R.N. (1969) Eidetic images. *Scientific American*, 220, 36–44.

HABER, R.N. (1980) Eidetic images are not just imaginary. *Psychology Today*, November, 72–82.

HALLIDAY, M.A.K. & HASAN, R. (1976) *Cohesion in English*. London: Longman.

HALLIGAN, P.W. (1995) Drawing attention to neglect: The contribution of line bisection. *The Psychologist*, 8, 257–264.

HAMPSON, P.J. (1989) Aspects of attention and cognitive science. *The Irish Journal of Psychology*, 10, 261–275.

HAMPSON, P.J. & MORRIS, P.E. (1996) *Understanding Cognition*. Oxford: Blackwell.

HAMPTON, J.A. (1979) Polymorphous concepts in semantic memory. *Journal of Verbal Learning and Verbal Behaviour*, 18, 441–461.

HARRIS, A.J. & SIPEY, E.R. (1983) *Readings on Reading Instruction* (2nd edition). New York: Longman.

HARRIS, M.G. & HUMPHREYS, G.W. (1995) Computational theories of vision. In R.L. GREGORY & A.M. COLMAN (Eds) *Sensation and Perception*. London: Longman.

HARRIS, T.L. & HODGES, R.E. (Eds) (1981) *A Dictionary of Reading and Related Terms*. London: Heinemann Educational.

HART, J., BERNDT, R.S. & CARAMAZZA, A. (1985) Category-specific naming deficit following cerebral infarction. *Nature*, 316, 439–440.

HASSETT, J. & WHITE, K.M. (1989) *Psychology in Perspective* (2nd edition). New York: Harper and Row.

HASTIE, R. & PARK, B. (1986) The relationship between memory and judgement depends on whether the judgement task is memory based or on-line. *Psychological Bulletin*, 93, 258–268.

HAWKINS, S.A. & HASTIE, R. (1990) Hindsight: Biased judgements of past events after the outcomes are known. *Psychological Bulletin*, 107, 311–327.

HAYES, J.R. & FLOWER, L.S. (1980) Identifying the organisation of writing processes. In L.W. GREGG & E.R. STERNBERG (Eds) *Cognitive Processes in Writing*. Hillsdale, NJ: Erlbaum.

HAYES, J.R. & FLOWER, L.S. (1986) Writing research and the writer. *American Psychologist*, 41, 1106–1113.

HAYES, J.R., FLOWER, L.S., SCHRIVER, K., STRATMAN, J. & CAREY, L. (1985) *Cognitive Processes in Revision*. Technical Report No. 12. Pittsburgh, PA: Carnegie Mellon University.

HAYES, K.H. & HAYES, C. (1951) Intellectual development of a house-raised chimpanzee. *Proceedings of the American Philosophical Society*, 95, 105–109.

HAYES, P. (1996) Memory. In M. CARDWELL, L. CLARK & C. MELDRUM (Eds) *Psychology for A Level*. London: HarperCollins.

HEBB, D.O. (1949) *The Organisation of Behaviour*. New York: Wiley.

HEIDER, E. & OLIVER, D. (1972) The structure of the colour space in naming and memory for two languages. *Cognitive Psychology*, 3, 337–354.

HELD, R. & BOSSOM, J. (1961) Neonatal deprivation and adult rearrangement: Complementary techniques for analysing plastic sensory-motor co-ordinations. *Journal of Comparative and Physiological Psychology*, 54, 33–37.

HELD, R. & HEIN, A. (1963) Movement-produced stimulation in the development of visually guided behaviour. *Journal of Comparative and Physiological Psychology*, 56, 607–613.

HELLER, R.F., SALTZSTEIN, H.D. & CASPE, W.B.

(1992) Heuristics in medical and non-medical decision-making. *Quarterly Journal of Experimental Psychology*, 44A, 211–235.

HERMAN, L.M., MORREL-SAMUELS, P. & PACK, A.A. (1990) Bottlenosed dolphin and human recognition of veridical and degraded video displays of an artificial gestural language. *Journal of Experimental Psychology: General*, 119, 215–230.

HERSHENSON, M., MUNSINGER, H. & KESSEN, W. (1965) Preference for shapes of intermediate variability in the newborn human. *Science*, 147, 630–631.

HESS, E.H. (1956) Space perception in the chick. *Scientific American*, July, 71–80.

HESS, R.D. & SHIPMAN, V. (1965) Early experience and the socialisation of cognitive modes in children. *Child Development*, 36, 860–886.

HIGBEE, K.L. (1996) *Your Memory: How it Works and How to Improve it*. New York: Marlowe and Co.

HIGHFIELD, R. (1996) Maths is child's play for monkeys. *The Daily Telegraph*, 21 February, 15.

HIGHFIELD, R. (1997) Forgetfulness opens windows on the mind. *The Daily Telegraph*, 18 July, 3.

HIRST, W., SPELKE, E.S., REAVES, C.C., CAHARACK, G. & NEISSER, U. (1980) Dividing attention without alternation or automaticity. *Journal of Experimental Psychology: General*, 109, 98–117.

HISCOCK, J. (1996) Schools recognise 'Black English'. *The Daily Telegraph*, 21 December, 12.

HOCHBERG, J.E. (1970) Attention, organisation and consciousness. In D.I. MOSTOFSKY (Ed.) *Attention: Contemporary Theory and Analysis*. New York: Appleton Century Crofts.

HOCHBERG, J.E. (1971) Perception. In J.W. KLING & L.A. RIGGS (Eds) *Experimental Psychology*. New York: Holt.

HOCHBERG, J.E. (1978) Art and perception. In E.C. CARTERETTE & H. FRIEDMAN (Eds) *Handbook of Perception*, Volume 10. London: Academic Press.

HOCKETT, C.D. (1960) The origins of speech. *Scientific American*, 203, 88–96.

HOUSTON, J.P., HAMMEN, C., PADILLA, A. & BEE, H. (1991) *Invitation to Psychology* (3rd edition). London: Harcourt Brace Jovanovich.

HUBEL, D.H. & WIESEL, T.N. (1962) Receptive fields, binocular interaction and functional architecture in the cat's visual cortex. *Journal of Physiology*, 160, 106–154.

HUBEL, D.H. & WIESEL, T.N. (1968) Receptive fields and functional architecture of monkey striate cortex. *Journal of Physiology*, 195, 215–243.

HUDSON, W. (1960) Pictorial depth perception in sub-cultural groups in Africa. *Journal of Social Psychology*, 52, 183–208.

HUEY, E.B. (1908) *The Psychology and Pedagogy of Reading*. Cambridge, MA: MIT Press.

HUMPHREYS, G.W. & RIDDOCH, M.J. (1987) *To See but not to See – A Case Study of Visual Agnosia*. London: Erlbaum.

HUMPHREYS, G.W., RIDDOCH, M.J. & QUINLAN, P.T. (1985) Interactive processes in perceptual organisation: Evidence from visual agnosia. In M. POSNER & O.S.M. MARIN (Eds) *Attention and Performance* (Volume XI). Hillsdale, NJ: Erlbaum.

HUNT, E. & AGNOLI, A. (1991) The Whorfian hypothesis: A cognitive psychological perspective. *Psychological Review*, 98, 377–389.

HUNTER, I.M.L. (1957) *Memory, Facts and Fallacies*. Harmondsworth: Penguin.

HYDE, T.S. & JENKINS, J.J. (1973) Recall for words as a function of semantic, graphic and syntactic orienting tasks. *Journal of Verbal Learning and Verbal Behaviour*, 12, 471–480.

IRWIN, F.W. & SEIDENFELD, M.A. (1937) The application of the method of comparison to the problem of memory change. *Journal of Experimental Psychology*, 21, 363–381.

ITTELSON, W.H. (1952) *The Ames Demonstrations in Perception*. Princeton, NJ: Princeton University Press.

JACKENDOFF, R. (1993) *Patterns in the Mind: Language and Human Nature*. Hemel Hempstead: Harvester-Wheatsheaf.

JACOBS, J. (1887) Experiments on 'prehension'. *Mind*, 12, 75–79.

JAHODA, G. (1966) Geometric illusions and the environment: A study in Ghana. *British Journal of Psychology*, 57, 193–199.

JAMES, H. (1958) Guessing, expectancy and autonomous change. *Quarterly Journal of Experimental Psychology*, 10, 107–110.

JAMES, W. (1890) *Principles of Psychology*. New York: Holt.

JENKINS, J.G. & DALLENBACH, K.M. (1924) Oblivescence during sleep and waking. *American Journal of Psychology*, 35, 605–612.

JOHANSSON, G. (1975) Visual motion perception. *Scientific American*, 14, 76–89.

JOHNSON-LAIRD, P.N., HERRMAN, D.J. & CHAFFIN, R. (1984) Only connections: A critique of semantic networks. *Psychological Bulletin*, 96, 292–315.

JOHNSTON, W.A. & DARK, V.J. (1986) Selective attention. *Annual Review of Psychology*, 37, 43–75.

JOHNSTON, W.A. & HEINZ, S.P. (1978) Flexibility and capacity demands of attention. *Journal of Experimental Psychology: General*, 107, 420–435.

JOHNSTON, W.A. & HEINZ, S.P. (1979) Depth of non-target processing in an attention task. *Journal of Experimental Psychology*, 5, 168–175.

JOHNSTON, W.A. & WILSON, J. (1980) Perceptual processing of non-targets in an attention task. *Memory and Cognition*, 8, 372–377.

JONES, W. & ANDERSON, J. (1987) Short- and long-term memory retrieval: A comparison of the effects of information load and relatedness. *Journal of Experimental Psychology: General*, 116, 137–153.

JUOLA, J.F., BOWHUIS, D.G., COOPER, E.E. & WARNER, C.B. (1991) Control of attention around the fovea. *Journal of Experimental Psychology: Human Perception and Performance*, 15, 315–330.

JUST, M.A. & CARPENTER, P.A. (1980) A theory of reading: From eye fixations to comprehension. *Psychological Review*, 87, 329–354.

JUST, M.A. & CARPENTER, P.A. (1984) Eye movements and reading comprehension. In D.E. KIERAS & M.A. JUST (Eds) *New Methods in Reading Comprehension Research*. Hillsdale, NJ: Erlbaum.

JUST, M.A. & CARPENTER, P.A. (1992) A capacity theory of comprehension: Individual differences in working memory. *Psychological Review*, 99, 122–149.

KAHNEMAN, D. (1973) *Attention and Effort*. Englewood Cliffs, NJ: Prentice-Hall.

KAHNEMAN D. & HENIK, A. (1979) Perceptual organisation and attention. In M. KUBOVY & J.R. POMERANTZ (Eds) *Perceptual Organisation*. Hillsdale, NJ: Erlbaum.

KAHNEMAN, D. & TVERSKY, A. (1984) Changing views of attention and automaticity. In R. PARASURAMAN, D.R. DAVIES & J. BEATTY (Eds) *Varieties of Attention*. New York: Academic Press.

KALNINS, I.V. & BRUNER, J.S. (1973) The co-ordination of visual observation and instrumental behaviour in early infancy. *Perception*, 2, 307–314.

KAMINER, H. & LAVIE, P. (1991) Sleep and dreaming in Holocaust survivors: Dramatic decrease in dream recall in well-adjusted survivors. *Journal of Nervous and Mental Diseases*, 179, 664–669.

KANIZSA, A. (1976) Subjective contours. *Scientific American*, 234, 48–52.

KASSAJARJIAN, H.H. (1963) Voting intentions and political perceptions. *Journal of Psychology*, 56, 85–88.

KATONA, G. (1940) *Organising and Memorising*. New York: Columbia University Press.

KAUSHALL, P., ZETIN, M. & SQUIRE, L. (1981) A psychological study of chronic, circumscribed amnesia: Detailed report of a noted case. *Journal of Nervous and Mental Disorders*, 169, 383–389.

KELLOGG, W.N. (1968) Communication and language in the home-raised chimpanzee. *Science*, 162, 423–427.

KELLOGG, W.N. & KELLOGG, L.A. (1933) *The Ape and the Child*. New York: McGraw Hill.

KEPPEL, G. & UNDERWOOD, B.J. (1962) Proactive inhibition in short-term retention of single items. *Journal of Verbal Learning and Verbal Behaviour*, 1, 153–161.

KING, M.L. & RENTEL, V.M. (1981) Research update: Conveying meaning in written texts. *Language Arts*, 58, 721–728.

KLEINER, K.A. (1987) Amplitude and phase spectra as indices of infants' pattern preference. *Infant Behaviour and Development*, 10, 49–59.

KOFFKA, K. (1935) *The Principles of Gestalt Psychology*. New York: Harcourt Brace and World.

KOHLER, I. (1962) Experiments with goggles. *Scientific American*, 206, 67–72.

KÖHLER, W. (1925) *The Mentality of Apes*. New York: Harcourt Brace Jovanovich.

KREBS, D. & BLACKMAN, R. (1988) *Psychology: A First Encounter*. London: Harcourt Brace Jovanovich.

LaBERGE, D. (1983) Spatial extent of attention to letters and words. *Journal of Experimental Psychology: Human Perception and Performance*, 9, 371–379.

LABOV, W. (1970) The logic of non-standard English. In F. WILLIAMS (Ed.) *Language and Poverty*. Chicago: Markham.

LABOV, W. (1973) The boundaries of words and their meanings. In C.J.N. BAILEY & R.W. SHUY (Eds) *New Ways of Analysing Variations in English*. Washington, DC: Georgetown University Press.

LACHMAN, S.J. (1984) Processes in visual misperception: Illusions for highly structured stimulus material. Paper presented at the 92nd annual convention of the American Psychological Association, Toronto, Canada.

LAKOFF, G. (1987) *Women, Fire and Dangerous Things: What Categories Reveal About The Mind*. Chicago: University of Chicago Press.

LAMBERT, W.W., SOLOMON, R.L. & WATSON, P.D. (1949) Reinforcement and extinction as factors in size estimation. *Journal of Experimental Psychology*, 39, 637–641.

LAWSON, E.A. (1966) Decisions concerning the rejected channel. *Journal of Experimental Psychology*, 18, 260–265.

LENNEBERG, E.H. (1967) *Biological Foundations of Language*. New York: Wiley.

LEVIN, I.P. & GAETH, G.J. (1988) How consumers are affected by the framing of attribution information before and after consuming the product. *Journal of Consumer Research*, 15, 374–378.

LEWIN, R. (1991) Look who's talking now. *New Scientist*, 130 (1766), 48–52.

LEY, P. (1988) *Communicating with Patients: Improving Communication, Satisfaction and Compliance*. London: Chapman Hall.

LICHENSTEIN, S. & FISCHOFF, B. (1980) Training for calibration. *Organisational Behaviour and Human Performance*, 26, 149–171.

LIMBER, J. (1977) Language in child and chimp. *American Psychologist*, 32, 280–295.

LINDSAY, P.H. & NORMAN, D.A. (1977) *Human*

Information Processing: An Introduction to Psychology (2nd edition). New York: Academic Press.

LLOYD, P., MAYES, A., MANSTEAD, A.S.R., MEUDELL, P.R. & WAGNER, H.L. (1984) *Introduction to Psychology: An Integrated Approach.* London: Fontana.

LOCKE, J. (1690) *An Essay Concerning Human Understanding.* New York: Mendon (reprinted, 1964).

LOFTUS, G. (1974) Reconstructing memory: The incredible eyewitness. *Psychology Today*, December, 116–119.

LOFTUS, E.F. (1975) Leading questions and the eyewitness report. *Cognitive Psychology*, 1, 560–572.

LOFTUS, E.F. (1979) Reactions to blatantly contradictory information. *Memory and Cognition*, 7, 368–374.

LOFTUS, E.F. (1980) *Memory.* Reading, MA: Addison and Wesley.

LOFTUS, E.F. & LOFTUS, G. (1980) On the permanence of stored information in the human brain. *American Psychologist*, 35, 409–420.

LOFTUS, E.F. & PALMER, J.C. (1974) Reconstruction of automobile destruction: An example of the interaction between language and memory. *Journal of Verbal Learning and Verbal Behaviour*, 13, 585–589.

LOFTUS, E.F. & ZANNI, G. (1975) Eyewitness testimony: The influence of wording on a question. *Bulletin of the Psychonomic Society* 5, 86–88.

LOGAN, G.D. (1988) Toward an instance theory of automatisation. *Psychological Review*, 95, 492–527.

LORD, C.G., ROSS, L. & LEPPER, M.R. (1979) Biased assimilation and attitude polarisation: The effects of prior theories on subsequently considered evidence. *Journal of Personality and Social Psychology*, 37, 2098–2107.

LOVAAS, O. (1987) Behavioural treatment and normal educational and intellectual functioning in young autistic children. *Journal of Consulting and Clinical Psychology*, 55, 3–9.

LUCE, T.S. (1974) Blacks, whites and yellows, they all look alike to me. *Psychology Today*, November, 105–106, 108.

LUCHINS, A.S. (1942) Mechanisation in problem-solving: The effect of Einstellung. *Psychological Monographs*, 54 (Whole No. 248).

LUCHINS, A.S. & LUCHINS, E.H. (1959) *Rigidity of Behaviour.* Eugene, OR: University of Oregon Press.

LURIA, A.R. (1968) *The Mind of a Mnemonist.* New York: Basic Books.

LURIA, A.R. & YUDOVICH, F.I. (1971) *Speech and the Development of Mental Processes in the Child.* Harmondsworth: Penguin.

LYONS, J. (1970) *Chomsky.* London: Fontana.

MACKAY, D.C. & NEWBIGGING, P.L. (1977) The Poggendorf and its variants do arouse the same perceptual processes. *Perception and Psychophysics*, 21, 26–32.

MACKAY, D.G. (1973) Aspects of the theory of

comprehension, memory and attention. *Quarterly Journal of Experimental Psychology*, 25, 22–40.

MacNAMARA, J. (1982) *Names for Things.* Cambridge, MA: Bradford MIT Press.

MAIER, N.R.F. (1931) Reasoning in humans II: The solution of a problem and its appearance in consciousness. *Journal of Comparative Psychology*, 12, 181–194.

MALMSTROM, P. & SILVA, M. (1986) Twin talk: Manifestations of twin status in the speech of toddlers. *Journal of Child Language*, 13, 293–304.

MANDLER, G. (1967) Organisation and memory. In K.W. SPENCE & J.T. SPENCE (Eds) *The Psychology of Learning and Motivation*, Volume 1. New York: Academic Press.

MANSTEAD, A.S.R. & SEMIN, G.R. (1980) Social facilitation effects: Mere enhancement of dominant responses? *British Journal of Social and Clinical Psychology*, 19, 19–36.

MARATSOS, M.P. (1983) Some current issues in the study of the acquisition of grammar. In J.H. FLAVELL & E.M. MARKMAN (Eds) *Cognitive Development*, Volume 3. In P.H. MUSSEN (Ed.) *Handbook of Child Psychology* (4th edition). New York: Wiley.

MARR, D. (1982) *Vision: A Computational Investigation into the Human Representation and Processing of Visual Information.* San Francisco, CA: W.H. Freeman.

MARR, D. & HILDRETH, E. (1980) Theory of edge detection. *Proceedings of the Royal Society of London, Series B*, 207, 187–217.

MARR, D. & NISHIHARA, K.H. (1978) Representation and recognition of the spatial organisation of three-dimensional shapes. *Proceedings of the Royal Society of London, Series B*, 200, 269–294.

MARSH, G., FRIEDMAN, M., WELCH, V. & DESBERG, P. (1981) A cognitive-developmental theory of language acquisition. In G.E. MacKINNON & T.G. WALLER (Eds) *Reading Research: Advances in Theory and Practice.* New York: Academic Press.

MARSLEN-WILSON, W.D. (1984) Function and process in spoken-word recognition: A tutorial review. In H. BOUMA & D.G. BOUWHUIS (Eds) *Attention and Performance X: Control of Language Processes.* Hillsdale, NJ: Erlbaum.

MASSARO, D.W. (1989) *Experimental Psychology: An Information Processing Approach.* New York: Harcourt Brace Jovanovich.

MATLIN, M. (1989) *Cognition* (2nd edition). Fort Worth, TX: Holt, Rinehart & Winston.

McBURNEY, D.H. & COLLINS, V.B. (1984) *Introduction to Sensation and Perception* (2nd edition). Englewood Cliffs, NJ: Prentice-Hall.

McCLELLAND, D.C. & ATKINSON, J.W. (1948) The projective expression of need: I. The effect of different intensities of the hunger drive on perception. *Journal of Psychology*, 25, 205–222.

McCLOSKEY, M. & ZARAGOZA, M. (1985) Misleading information and memory for events: Arguments and evidence against memory impairment hypothesis. *Journal of Experimental Psychology: General*, 114, 3–18.

McCORMICK, L.J. & MAYER, J.D. (1991) *Mood-congruent recall and natural mood*. Poster presented at the annual meeting of the New England Psychological Association, Portland, ME.

McCUTCHEN, D. & PERFETTI, C. (1982) Coherence and connectedness in the development of discourse production. *Text*, 2, 113–139.

McILVEEN, R., LONG, M. & CURTIS, A. (1994) *Talking Points in Psychology*. London: Hodder and Stoughton.

McILVEEN, R. & GROSS, R. (1997) *Developmental Psychology*. London: Hodder and Stoughton.

McLEOD, P., DRIVER, J., DIENES, Z. & CRISP, J. (1991) Filtering by movement in visual search. *Journal of Experimental Psychology: Human Perception and Performance*, 17, 55–64.

McNEILL, D. (1970) *The Acquisition of Language*. New York: Harper & Row.

MEHLER, J. & DUPOUX, E. (1994) *What Infants Know*. Oxford: Blackwell.

MELHUISH, E.C. (1982) Visual attention to mothers' and strangers' faces and facial contrast in one-month-olds. *Developmental Psychology*, 18, 299–333.

MELTZOFF, A.N. & MOORE, M.K. (1992) Early imitation within a functional framework: The importance of person identity, movement and development. *Infant Behaviour and Development*, 15, 479–505.

MESSER, D. (1995) Seeing and pulling faces. *The Psychologist*, 8, 77.

MILLER, G.A. (1956) The magical number seven, plus or minus two: Some limits on our capacity for processing information. *Psychological Review*, 63, 81–97.

MILLER, G.A. (1978) The acquisition of word meaning. *Child Development*, 49, 999–1004.

MILLER, G.A. & McNEILL, D. (1969) Psycholinguistics. In G. LINDZEY & E. ARONSON (Eds) *The Handbook of Social Psychology*, Volume 3. Reading, MA: Addison-Wesley.

MILLER, G.A. & SELFRIDGE, J.A. (1950) Verbal context and the recall of meaningful material. *American Journal of Psychology*, 63, 176–185.

MITCHELL, D.E. & WILKINSON, F. (1974) The effect of early astigmatism on the visual recognition of gratings. *Journal of Psychology*, 243, 739–756.

MOERK, E.L. (1989) The LAD was a lady, and the tasks were ill-defined. *Developmental Review*, 9, 21–57.

MOERK, E.L. & MOERK, C. (1979) Quotations, imitations and generalisations: Factual and methodological analyses. *International Journal of Behavioural Development*, 2, 43–72.

MOFFETT, M. (1990) Dance of the electronic bee. *National Geographic*, 177, 134–140.

MOORE, T. (1996) Crash pilot 'confused by levers on plane'. *The Daily Telegraph*, 10 February, 9.

MORAY, N. (1959) Attention in dichotic listening: Affective cues and the influence of instructions. *Quarterly Journal of Experimental Psychology*, 11, 56–60.

MORGAN, M.J. (1969) Estimates of length in a modified Müller-Lyer figure. *American Journal of Psychology*, 82, 380–384.

MORPHETT, M.V. & WASHBURNE, C. (1931) When should children begin to read? *Elementary School Journal*, 31, 496–503.

MORRIS, C.G. (1988) *Psychology: An Introduction* (6th edition). London: Prentice-Hall.

MORRIS, P.E. (1977) On the importance of acoustic encoding in short-term memory: The error of studying errors. *Bulletin of the British Psychological Society*, 30, 380.

MORRIS, P.E. (1992) Prospective memory: Remembering to do things. In M. GRUNEBERG & P.E. MORRIS (Eds) *Aspects of Memory, Volume 1: The Practical Aspects*. London: Routledge.

MORTON, J. (1964) A preliminary functional model for language behaviour. *International Audiology*, 3, 216–225.

MORTON, J. (1969) Interaction of information in word recognition. *Psychological Review*, 76, 165–178.

MORTON, J. (1970) A functional model for memory. In D.A. NORMAN (Ed.) *Models of Human Memory*. New York: Academic Press.

MORTON, J. (1979) Facilitation in word recognition: Experiments causing change in the logogen model. In P.A. KOLERS, M.E. WROLSTAD & H. BOUMA (Eds) *Processing of Visible Language*. New York: Plenum Press.

MULLER, H.J. & MAXWELL, J. (1994) Perceptual integration of motion and form information: Is the movement filter involved in form discrimination? *Journal of Experimental Psychology: Human Perception and Performance*, 20, 397–420.

MUNDY-CASTLE, A.C. & NELSON, G.K. (1962) A neuropsychological study of the Kuysma forest workers. *Psychologia Africana*, 9, 240–272.

MURDOCK, B.B. (1962) The serial position effect in free recall. *Journal of Experimental Psychology*, 64, 482–488.

MURDOCK, B.B. & WALKER, K.D. (1969) Modality effects in free recall. *Journal of Verbal Learning and Verbal Behaviour*, 8, 665–676.

NAVON, D. (1977) Forest before trees: The precedence of global features in visual perception. *Cognitive Psychology*, 9, 353–383.

NAVON, D. (1984) Resources – A theoretical soup stone? *Psychological Review*, 91, 216–234.

NAVON, D. & GOPHER, D. (1979) On the economy of the human processing system. *Psychological Review*, 86, 214–255.

NECKER, L.A. (1832) Observations on some remarkable phenomena seen in Switzerland, and an optical phenomenon which occurs on viewing of a crystal or geometrical solid. *Philosophical Magazine*, 1, 329–337.

NEISSER, U. (1967) *Cognitive Psychology*. New York: Appleton Century Crofts.

NEISSER, U. (1976) *Cognition and Reality*. San Francisco, CA: W.H. Freeman.

NEISSER, U. (1981) John Dean's memory: A case study. *Cognition*, 9, 1–22.

NEISSER, U. (1982) *Memory Observed*. San Francisco: Freeman.

NEISSER, U. & BECKLEN, R. (1975) Selective looking: Attending to visually specified events. *Cognitive Psychology*, 7, 480–494.

NEISSER, U. & HARSCH, N. (1992) Phantom flashbulbs: False recollections of hearing news about Challenger. In E.O. WINOGRAD & U. NEISSER (Eds) *Affect and Accuracy in Recall: Studies of 'Flashbulb' Memories*. New York: Cambridge University Press.

NELSON, K. (1973) Structure and strategy in learning to talk. *Monographs of the Society for Research in Child Development*, 38, 149.

NEWELL, A. & SIMON, H.A. (1972) *Human Problem-Solving*. Englewood Cliffs, NJ: Prentice-Hall.

NEWELL, A., SHAW, J.C. & SIMON, H.A. (1958) Elements of a theory of human problem-solving. *Psychological Review*, 65, 151–166.

NEWSTEAD, S. (1995) Language and thought: The Whorfian hypothesis. *Psychology Review*, 1, 5–7.

NORMAN, D.A. (1968) Toward a thoery of memory and attention. *Psychological Review*, 75, 522–536.

NORMAN, D.A. (1969) Memory while shadowing. *Quarterly Journal of Experimental Psychology*, 21, 85–93.

NORMAN, D.A. (1976) *Memory and Attention* (2nd edition). Chichester: Wiley.

NORMAN, D.A. (1981) Categorisation of action slips. *Psychological Review*, 88, 1–15.

NORMAN, D.A. & BOBROW, D.G. (1975) On data-limited and resource-limited processes. *Cognitive Psychology*, 7, 44–64.

NORMAN, D.A. & SHALLICE, T. (1986) Attention to action: Willed and automatic control of behaviour. In R.J. DAVIDSON, G.E. SCHWARTZ & D. SHAPIRO (Eds) *The Design of Everyday Things*. New York: Doubleday.

ONO, T., SQUIRE, L.R., RAICHLE, M.E., PERRETT, D.I. & FUKUDA, M. (Eds) (1993) *Brain Mechanisms of Perception and Memory. From Neurone to Behaviour*. New York: Oxford University Press.

PAIVIO, A. (1979) Psychological processes in the comprehension of metaphor. In A. ORTONY (Ed.) *Metaphor and Thought*. New York: Cambridge University Press.

PAIVIO, A. (1986) *Mental Representations: A Dual-Coding Approach*. Oxford: Oxford University Press.

PALMER, S., SCHREIBER, C. & FOX, C. (1991) Remembering the earthquake: 'Flashbulb' memory for experienced versus reproted events. Paper presented at the Annual Meeting of the Psychonomic Society, San Francisco.

PARKIN, A.J. (1987) *Memory and Amnesia: An Introduction*. Oxford: Blackwell.

PARKIN, A.J. (1993) *Memory: Phenomena, Experiment and Theory*. Oxford: Blackwell.

PATTERSON, F.G. (1980) Innovative uses of language by a gorilla: A case study. In K. NELSON (Ed.) *Children's Language*, Volume 2. New York: Gardner Press.

PATTERSON, F.G. & LINDEN, E. (1981) *The Education of Koko*. New York: Holt, Rinehart & Winston.

PATTERSON, F.G., PATTERSON, C.H. & BRENTARI, D.K. (1987) Language in child, chimp and gorilla. *American Psychologist*, 42, 270–273.

PENFIELD, W. (1969) Consciousness, memory and man's conditioned reflexes. In K. PRIBRAM (Ed.) *On the Biology of Learning*. New York: Harcourt, Brace Jovanovich.

PEPPERBERG, I.M. (1990) Cognition in an African grey parrot (Psittacus erithacus): Further evidence for comprehension of categories and labels. *Journal of Comparative Psychology*, 104, 41–52.

PERIANI, D., BRESSI, S., CAPPA, S.F., VALLAR, G., ALBERONI, M., GRASSI, F., CALTAGIRONE, C., CIPLOTTI, L., FRANCESCHI, M., LENIZ, G.L. & FAZIO, F. (1993) Evidence of multiple memory systems in the human brain. *Brain*, 116, 903–919.

PETERSON, L.R. & PETERSON, M.J. (1959) Short-term retention of individual items. *Journal of Experimental Psychology*, 58, 193–198.

PETTITO, L.A. & SEIDENBERG, M.S. (1979) On the evidence for linguistic abilities in signing apes. *Brain and Language*, 8, 162–183.

PIAGET, J. (1952) *The Child's Conception of Number*. London: Routledge & Kegan Paul.

PIAGET, J. & INHELDER, B. (1969) *The Psychology of the Child*. London: Routledge & Kegan Paul.

POGGIO, T. & KOCH, C. (1987) Synapses that compute motion. *Scientific American*, 255, 46–92.

POLLATSEK, A., BOLOZKY, S., WELLS, A.D. & RAYNER, K. (1981) Asymmetries in the perceptual span for Israeli readers. *Brain and Language*, 14, 174–180.

POMERANTZ, J. & GARNER, W.R. (1973) Stimulus configuration in selective attention tasks. *Perception and Psychophysics*, 14, 565–569.

POSNER, M.I. (1980) Orienting of attention. *Quarterly Journal of Experimental Psychology*, 32, 3–25.

POSNER, M.I., NISSEN, M.J. & OGDEN, W.C. (1978) Attended and unattended processing modes: The role of set for spatial location. In H.L. PICK & I.J. SALTZMAN (Eds) *Modes of Perceiving and Processing Information*. Hillsdale, NJ: Erlbaum.

POSNER, M.I., SNYDER, C.R.R. & DAVIDSON, B.J. (1980) Attention and the detection of signals. *Journal of Experimental Psychology: General*, 109, 160–174.

PREMACK, A.J. & PREMACK, D. (1972) Teaching language to an ape. *Scientific American*, 227, 92–99.

PREMACK, D. (1971) Language in chimpanzee? *Science*, 172, 808–822.

RABBIT, P.M.A. (1967) Ignoring irrelevant information. *American Journal of Psychology*, 80, 1–13.

RAMACHANDRON, V.S. & ANSTIS, S.M. (1986) The perception of apparent motion. *Scientific American*, 254, 80–87.

RAPHAEL, T.E. & KIRSCHNER, P. (1985) Improving expository writing ability: Integrating knowledge of information sources and text structures. Paper read to the Annual Meeting of the American Educational Research Association, Chicago (March).

RATHUS, S.A. (1990) *Psychology* (4th edition). New York: Holt, Rinehart & Winston.

RAYNER, K. & POLLATSEK, A. (1989) *The Psychology of Reading*. London: Prentice-Hall.

RAYNER, K. & SERENO, S.C. (1994) Eye movements in reading: Psycholinguistic studies. In M.A. GERNSBACHER (Ed.) *Handbook of Psycholinguistics*. New York: Academic Press.

REASON, J.T. (1979) Actions not as planned: The price of automatisation. In G. UNDERWOOD & R. STEVENS (Eds) *Aspects of Consciousness: Volume 1, Psychological Issues*. London: Academic Press.

REASON, J.T. (1992) Cognitive underspecification: Its variety and consequences. In B.J. BAARS (Ed.) *Experimental Slips and Human Error: Exploring the Architecture of Volition*. New York: Plenum Press.

REASON, J.T. & MYCIELSKA, K. (1982) *Absentmindedness: The Psychology of Mental Lapses and Everyday Errors*. Englewood Cliffs, NJ: Prentice-Hall.

REBER, A.S. (1985) *The Penguin Dictionary of Psychology*. Harmondsworth: Penguin.

REBOK, G. (1987) *Life-Span Cognitive Development*. New York: Holt, Rinehart & Winston.

REDER, L.M. & ANDERSON, J.R. (1980) A comparison of texts and their summaries: Memorial consequences. *Journal of Verbal Learning and Verbal Behaviour*, 19, 121–134.

REEVES, A. & SPERLING, G. (1986) Attention gating in short-term retention of individual verbal items. *Psychological Review*, 93, 180–206.

REICHER, G.M. (1969) Perceptual recognition as a function of meaningfulness of stimulus material. *Journal of Experimental Psychology*, 81, 275–281.

REITMAN, J.S. (1974) Without surreptitious rehearsal, information in short-term memory decays. *Journal of Verbal Learning and Verbal Behaviour*, 13, 365–377.

RHEINGOLD, H.L. (1961) The effect of environmental stimulation upon social and exploratory behaviour in the human infant. In B.M. FOSS (Ed.) *Determinants of Infant Behaviour*, Volume 1. London: Methuen.

RHEINGOLD, H.L., GERWITZ, J.L. & ROSS, H.W. (1959) Social conditioning of vocalisations in the infant. *Journal of Comparative and Physiological Psychology*, 51, 68–73.

RICE, M. (1989) Children's language acquisition. *American Psychologist*, 44, 149–156.

RICHARDSON, J. (1993) The curious case of coins. *The Psychologist*, 6, 360–366.

RIESEN, A.H. (1947) The development of visual perception in man and chimpanzee. *Science*, 106, 107–108.

RIESEN, A.H. (1965) Effects of early deprivation of photic stimulation. In S. OSTER & R. COOK (Eds) *The Biosocial Basis of Mental Retardation*. Baltimore: Johns Hopkins University Press.

RIPS, L.J., SHOBEN, E.H. & SMITH, E.E. (1973) Semantic distance and the verification of semantic relations. *Journal of Verbal Learning and Verbal Behaviour*, 12, 1–20.

RIVERS, W.H.R. (1901) Vision. In A.C. HADDON (Ed.) *Reports of the Cambridge Anthropological Expedition to the Torres Straits*, Volume 2, Part 1. Cambridge: Cambridge University Press.

ROBINSON, J.O. (1972) *The Psychology of Visual Illusions*. London: Hutchinson.

ROCK, I. (1983) *The Logic of Perception*. Cambridge, MA: MIT Press.

ROCK, I. (1984) *Perception*. New York: W.H. Freeman.

ROSE, M. (1980) Rigid rules, inflexible plans and the stifling of language: A cognitivist analysis of writer's block. *College Composition and Communication*, 31, 389–401.

ROSSI, P.J. (1968) Adaptation and negative after-effect to lateral optical displacement in newly hatched chicks. *Science*, 160, 430–432.

ROTH, I. (1986) An introduction to object perception. In I. ROTH & J.P. FRISBY (Eds) *Perception and Representation*. Milton Keynes: Open University Press.

ROTH, I. (1995) Object recognition. In I. ROTH & V. BRUCE (Eds) *Perception and Representation: Current Issues* (2nd edition). Buckingham: Open University Press.

ROY, D.F. (1991) Improving recall by eyewitnesses through the cognitive interview: Practical applications and implications for the police service. *The Psychologist*, 4, 398–400.

RUBIN, D.C. & OLSON, M.J. (1980) Recall of semantic domains. *Memory and Cognition*, 8, 354–366.

RUBIN, E. (1915) *Synsoplevede Figurer*. Kobenhaun: Gyldendalske Boghandel.

RUMBAUGH, D.M. (1977) *Language Learning by a Chimpanzee: The Lana Project*. New York: Academic Press.

RUMBAUGH, D.M. & SAVAGE-RUMBAUGH, E.S. (1978) Chimpanzee language research: Status and potential. *Behaviour Research Methods and Instrumentation*, 10, 119–131.

RUMBAUGH, D.M., von GLASERFELD, E., WARNER, H., PISANI, P. & GILL, T.V. (1974) Lana (chimpanzee) learning language: A progress report. *Brain and Language*, 1, 205–212.

RUMELHART, D.E. (1975) Notes on a schema for stories. In D.G. BOBROW & A. COLLINS (Eds) *Representation and Understanding: Studies in Cognitive Science*. New York: Academic Press.

RUMELHART, D.E. & McCLELLAND, J.L. (1982) An interactive activation model of context effect in letter recognition. Part 2: The contextual enhancement effect and some tests and extensions of the model. *Psychological Review*, 89, 60–94.

RUNDUS, D. & ATKINSON, R.C. (1970) Rehearsal procedures in free recall: A procedure for direct observation. *Journal of Verbal Learning and Verbal Behaviour*, 9, 99–105.

SALAME, P. & BADDELEY, A.D. (1982) Disruption of short-term memory by unattended speech: Implications for the structure of working memory. *Journal of Verbal Learning and Verbal Behaviour*, 21, 150–164.

SALAPATEK, P. (1975) Pattern perception in early infancy. In L.B. COHEN & P. SALAPATEK (Eds) *Infant Perception: From Sensation to Cognition, Volume 1. Basic Visual Processes*. London: Academic Press.

SANDERS, G.S. (1984) Effects of context cues on eyewitness identification responses. *Journal of Applied Social Psychology*, 14, 386–397.

SANFORD, R.N. (1937) The effects of abstinence from food upon imaginal processes. A further experiment. *Journal of Psychology*, 3, 145–159.

SAPIR, E. (1929) The study of linguistics as a science. *Language*, 5, 207–214.

SAVAGE-RUMBAUGH, E.S. (1990) Language as a cause-effect communication system. *Philosophical Psychology*, 3, 55–76.

SAVAGE-RUMBAUGH, E.S., RUMBAUGH, D.M. & BOYSEN, S.L. (1980) Do apes have language? *American Scientist*, 68, 49–61.

SCARDAMALIA, M. & BEREITER, C. (1987) Written composition. In M. WITTROCK (Ed.) *Third Handbook of Research on Testing*. New York: Macmillan.

SCARDAMALIA, M., BEREITER, C. & GOLEMAN, H. (1982) The role of productive factors in writing ability. In M. NYSTRAND (Ed.) *What Writers Know: The Language, Process and Structure of Written Discourse*. New York: Academic Press.

SCHAFFER, H.R. (1989) Early social development. In A. SLATER & G. BREMNER (Eds) *Infant Development*. Hove: Erlbaum.

SCHANK, R.C. (1975) *Conceptual Information Processing*. Amsterdam: North-Holland.

SCHANK, R.C. (1982) *Dynamic Memory*. New York: Cambridge University Press.

SCHANK, R.C. & ABELSON, R.P. (1977) *Scripts, Plans, Goals and Understanding*. Hillsdale, NJ: Erlbaum.

SCHEERER, M. (1963) Problem-solving. *Scientific American*, 208, 118–128.

SCHNEIDER, W. & FISK, A.D. (1982) Degree of consistent training: Improvements in search performance and automatic process development. *Perception and Psychophysics*, 31, 160–168.

SCHNEIDER, W. & SHIFFRIN, R.M. (1977) Controlled and automatic human information processing: I. Detection, search and attention. *Psychological Review*, 84, 1–66.

SCHUMAN, H. & RIEGER, C. (1992) Collective memory and collective memories. In M.A. CONWAY, D.C. RUBIN, H. SPINNLER & W. WAGENAAR (Eds) *Theoretical Perspectives on Autobiographical Memory*. Dordecht: Kluwer Academic Publishers.

SCOLLON, R. (1976) *Conversations With a One-Year-Old*. Honolulu: University of Hawaii Press.

SEGALL, M.H., CAMPBELL, D.T. & HERSKOVITS, M.J. (1963) Cultural differences in the perception of geometrical illusions. *Science*, 139, 769–771.

SELFRIDGE, O.G. (1959) Pandemonium: A paradigm for learning. In *Symposium on the Mechanisation of Thought Processes*. London: HMSO.

SELLEN, A.J. & NORMAN, D.A. (1992) The psychology of slips. In B.J. BAARS (Ed.) *Experimental Slips and Human Error: Exploring the Architecture of Volition*. New York: Plenum Press.

SERPELL, R.S. (1976) *Culture's Influence on Perception*. London: Methuen.

SHAFFER, L.H. (1975) Multiple attention in continuous verbal tasks. In P.M.A. RABBITT & S. DORNIC (Eds) *Attention and Performance* (Volume V). London: Academic Press.

SHALLICE, T. (1967) Paper presented at NATO symposium on short-term memory, Cambridge, England.

SHALLICE, T. & WARRINGTON, E.K. (1970) Independent functioning of verbal memory stores: A neurophysiological study. *Quarterly Journal of Experimental Psychology*, 22, 261–273.

SHIFFRIN, R.M. & SCHNEIDER, W. (1977) Controlled

and automatic human information processing: II. Perceptual learning, automatic attending and a general theory. *Psychological Review*, 84, 127–190.

SHORTLIFFE, E.H. (1976) *Computer-Based Medical Consultations: MYCIN*. New York: American Elsevier.

SHULMAN, H.G. (1970) Encoding and retention of semantic and phonemic information in short-term memory. *Journal of Verbal Learning and Verbal Behaviour*, 9, 499–508.

SIMON, H.A. & HAYES, J.R. (1976) The understanding process: Problem isomorphs. *Cognitive Psychology*, 8, 165–190.

SINCLAIR-de-ZWART, H. (1969) Developmental psycholinguistics. In D. ELKIND & J. FLAVELL (Eds) *Studies in Cognitive Development*. Oxford: Oxford University Press.

SKINNER, B.F. (1957) *Verbal Behaviour*. New York: Appleton-Century-Crofts.

SKINNER, B.F. (1985) Cognitive science and behaviourism. Unpublished manuscript. Harvard University.

SKRIVER, J. (1996) Naturalistic decision-making. *The Psychologist*, 9, 321–322.

SLATER, A. (1989) Visual memory and perception in early infancy. In A. SLATER & G. BREMNER (Eds) *Infant Development*. Hove: Erlbaum.

SLATER, A. (1995) Perceptual development in infancy. *Psychology Review*, 1, 12–16.

SLATER, A. & MORISON, V. (1985) Shape constancy and slant perception at birth. *Perception*, 14, 337–344.

SLOBIN, D.I. (1975) On the nature of talk to children. In E.H. LENNEBERG & E. LENNEBERG (Eds) *Foundations of Language Development*, Volume 1. New York: Academic Press.

SLOBIN, D.I. (1979) *Psycholinguistics* (2nd edition). Glenview, ILL: Scott, Foresman and Company.

SLOBIN, D.I. (1986) *The Cross-Linguistic Study of Language Acquisition*. Hillsdale, NJ: Erlbaum.

SMITH, E.E., SHOBEN, E.J. & RIPS, L.J. (1974) Structure and process in semantic memory: A feature model of semantic decisions. *Psychological Review*, 81, 214–241.

SMITH, E.M., BROWN, H.O., TOMAN, J.E.P. & GOODMAN, L.S. (1947) The lack of cerebral effects of D-tubo-curarine. *Anaesthesiology*, 8, 1–14.

SMITH, M.M., COLLINS, A.F., MORRIS, P.E. & LEVY, P. (1994) *Cognition in Action* (2nd edition). Hove: Erlbaum.

SMITH, P.K. & COWIE, H. (1991) *Understanding Children's Development* (2nd edition). Oxford: Blackwell.

SMITH, S.M. (1979) Remembering in and out of context. *Journal of Experimental Psychology: Human Learning and Memory*, 5, 460–471.

SNOW, C.E. (1977) Mother's speech research: From input to interaction. In C.E. SNOW and C.A. FERGUSON (Eds) *Talking to children: Language input and acquisition*. New York: Cambridge University Press.

SNOW, C.E. (1983) Saying it again: The role of expanded and deferred imitations in language acquisition. In K.E. NELSON (Ed.) *Children's Language*, Volume 4. New York: Gardner Press.

SNOWMAN, J., KREBS, E.V. & LOCKHART, L. (1980) Improving information of recall from prose in high-risk students through Learning Strategy Training. *Journal of Instructional Psychology*, 7, 35–40.

SNYDER, F.W. & PRONKO, N.H. (1952) *Vision with Spatial Inversion*. Wichita, Kansas: University of Wichita Press.

SOLSO, R.L. (1995) *Cognitive Psychology* (4th edition). Boston: Allyn & Bacon.

SPACHE, G.B. (1981) *Diagnosing and Correcting Reading Disabilities*. Boston: Allyn & Bacon.

SPELKE, E.S., HIRST, W.C. & NEISSER, U. (1976) Skills of divided attention. *Cognition*, 4, 215–230.

SPERLING, G. (1960) The information available in brief visual presentation. *Psychological Monographs*, 74 (Whole No. 498).

SPERRY, R.W. (1943) The effect of 180-degree rotation in the retinal field on visuo-motor co-ordination. *Journal of Experimental Zoology*, 92, 263–279.

SQUIRE, L.R. (1987) *Memory and Brain*. Oxford: Oxford University Press.

STEWART, V.M. (1973) Tests of the 'carpentered world' hypothesis by race and environment in America and Africa. *International Journal of Psychology*, 8, 83–94.

STONES, E. (1971) *Educational Psychology*. London: Methuen.

STRATTON, G.M. (1896) Some preliminary experiments on vision. *Psychological Review*, 3, 611–617.

STRATTON, G.M. (1897) Vision without inversion of the retinal image. *Psychological Review*, 4, 341–481.

STROOP, J.R. (1935) Studies of interference in serial verbal reactions. *Journal of Experimental Psychology*, 18, 643–662.

TARTTER, V. (1986) *Language Processes*. New York: Holt, Rinehart & Winston.

TEMPLIN, M.C. (1957) *Certain Language Skills in Children: Their Development and Interrelationships*. Minneapolis: University of Minnesota Press.

TERRACE, H.S. (1979) *Nim*. New York: Knopf.

TERRACE H.S. (1985) In the beginning was the 'name'. *American Psychologist*, 40, 1011–1028.

TERRACE, H.S., PETTITO, I.A., SANDERS, R.J. & BEVER, T.C. (1979) Can an ape create a sentence? *Science*, 206, 891–900.

THOMAS, E.L. & ROBINSON, H.A. (1972) *Improving Reading in Every Class: A Sourcebook for Teachers*. Boston: Allyn & Bacon.

THOMAS, J.C. (1974) An analysis of behaviour in the 'hobbit-orcs' problem. *Cognitive Psychology*, 28, 167–178.

THORNDIKE, E.L. (1911) *Animal Intelligence*. New York: Macmillan.

TIPPER, S.P. & DRIVER, J. (1988) Negative priming between pictures and words: Evidence for semantic analysis of ignored stimuli. *Memory and Cognition*, 16, 64–70.

TITCHENER, E.B. (1903) *Lectures on the Elementary Psychology of Feeling and Attention*. New York: Macmillan.

TIZARD, B., JOSEPH, A., COOPERMAN, O. & TIZARD, J. (1972) Environmental effects on language development: A study of young children in long-stay residential nurseries. *Child Development*, 43, 337–358.

TOON, K., FRAISE, J., McFETRIDGE, M. & ALWIN, N. (1996) Memory or mirage? The False Memory Syndrome debate. *The Psychologist*, 9, 73–77.

TREISMAN, A.M. (1960) Contextual cues in selective listening. *Quarterly Journal of Experimental Psychology*, 12, 242–248.

TREISMAN, A.M. (1964) Verbal cues, language and meaning in selective attention. *American Journal of Psychology*, 77, 206–219.

TREISMAN, A.M. (1988) Features and objects: The fourteenth Bartlett memorial lecture. *Quarterly Journal of Experimental Psychology*, 40A, 201–237.

TREISMAN, A.M. (1991) Search, similarity, and integration of features between and within dimensions. *Journal of Experimental Psychology: Human Perception and Performance*, 17, 652–676.

TREISMAN, A.M. & GEFFEN, G. (1967) Selective attention: Perception or response. *Quarterly Journal of Experimental Psychology*, 19, 1–18.

TREISMAN, A.M. & GELADE, G. (1980) A feature-integration theory of attention. *Cognitive Psychology*, 12, 97–136.

TREISMAN, A.M. & RILEY, J.G.A. (1969) Is selective attention selective perception or selective response?: A further test. *Journal of Experimental Psychology*, 79, 27–34.

TREISMAN, A.M. & SATO, S. (1990) Conjunction search revisited. *Journal of Experimental Psychology: Human Perception and Performance* 16, 459–478.

TREISMAN, A.M. & SCHMIDT, H. (1982) Illusory conjunctions in the perception of objects. *Cognitive Psychology*, 14, 107–141.

TULVING, E. (1968) Theoretical issues in free recall. In T.R. DIXON & D.L. HORTON (Eds) *Verbal Behaviour and General Behaviour Theory*. Englewood Cliffs, NJ: Prentice-Hall.

TULVING, E. (1972) Episodic and semantic memory. In E. TULVING & W. DONALDSON (Eds) *Organisation of Memory*. London: Academic Press.

TULVING, E. (1974) Cue-dependent forgetting. *American Scientist*, 62, 74–82.

TULVING, E. (1985) How many memory systems are there? *American Psychologist*, 40, 395–398.

TULVING, E. & PEARLSTONE, Z. (1966) Availability versus accessibility of information in memory for words. *Journal of Verbal Learning and Verbal Behaviour*, 5, 389–391.

TULVING, E. & THOMSON, D.M. (1973) Encoding specificity and retrieval processes in episodic memory. *Psychological Review*, 80, 352–373.

TURNBULL, C.M. (1961) *The Forest People*. New York: Simon & Schuster.

TVERSKY, A. (1972) Elimination by aspects: A theory of choice. *Psychological Review*, 79, 281–299.

TVERSKY, A. & KAHNEMAN, D. (1973) Judgement under uncertainty: Heuristics and biases. *Science*, 185, 1124–1131.

TVERSKY, A. & KAHNEMAN, D. (1986) Rational choice and the framing of decisions. *Journal of Business*, 59, 5251–5278.

TVERSKY, A. & TUCHIN, M. (1989) A reconciliation of the evidence on eyewitness testimony: Comments on McCloskey and Zaragoza. *Journal of Experimental Psychology: General*, 118, 86–91.

TYLER, T.R. & COOK, F.L. (1984) The mass media and judgement of risk: Distinguishing impact on personal and societal level judgements. *Journal of Personality and Social Psychology*, 47, 693–708.

UNDERWOOD, G. (1974) Moray vs. the rest: The effects of extended shadowing practice. *Quarterly Journal of Experimental Psychology*, 26, 368–372.

VALENTINE, E.R. & WILDING, J.M. (1994) Memory expertise. *The Psychologist*, 7, 405–408.

VERNON, M.D. (1955) The functions of schemata in perceiving. *Psychological Review*, 62, 180–192.

Von FRISCH, K. (1974) Decoding the language of the bee. *Science*, 185, 663–668.

Von SENDEN, M. (1932) *Space and Sight. The Perception of Space and Shape in the Congenitally Blind Before and After Operations* (translated by P. HEATH, 1960). London: Methuen.

Von WRIGHT, J.M., ANDERSON, K. & STENMAN, U. (1975) Generalisation of conditioned GSRs in dichotic listening. In P.M.A. RABBIT & S. DORNIC (Eds) *Attention and Performance*, Volume 1. London: Academic Press.

VOSS, J.F., VESONDER, G.T. & SPILICH, G.J. (1980) Text generation and recall by high-knowledge and low-knowledge individuals. *Journal of Verbal Learning and Verbal Behaviour*, 19, 651–667.

VYGOTSKY, L. (1962) *Thought and Language*. Cambridge, MA: MIT Press (originally published in 1934).

WADE, C. & TAVRIS, C. (1993) *Psychology* (3rd edition). London: HarperCollins.

WALLAS, G. (1926) *The Art of Thought*. London: Cape.

WASON, P.C. (1960) On the failure to eliminate hypotheses in a conceptual task. *Quarterly Journal of Experimental Psychology*, 12, 129–140.

WATSON, J.B. (1913) Psychology as the behaviourist views it. *Psychological Review*, 20, 158–177.

WAUGH, N.C. & NORMAN, D.A. (1965) Primary memory. *Psychological Review*, 72, 89–104.

WEISKRANTZ, L. (1956) Behavioural changes associated with ablation of the amygdaloid complex in monkeys. *Journal of Comparative and Physiological Psychology*, 49, 381–391.

WEISKRANTZ, L. (1988) *Thought Without Language*. Oxford: Oxford University Press.

WELLS, G.L. (1993) What do we know about eyewitness identification? *American Psychologist*, 48, 553–571.

WERTHEIMER, M. (1970) *A Brief History of Psychology*. New York: Holt Rinehart & Winston.

WHITEHURST, G.J. (1982) Language development. In B.B. WOOLMAN (Ed.) *Handbook of Developmental Psychology*. Englewood Cliffs, NJ: Prentice-Hall.

WHITTELL, G. (1996) Black American slang wins place in classroom. *The Times*, 21 December, 11.

WHORF, B.L. (1956) *Language, Thought and Reality*. Cambridge, MA: MIT Press.

WICKENS, C.D. (1972) Characteristics of word encoding. In A. MELTON & E. MARTIN (Eds) *Coding Processes in Human Memory*. Washington, DC: Winston.

WICKENS, C.D. (1992) *Engineering Psychology and Human Performance* (2nd edition). New York: HarperCollins.

WIESEL, T.N. (1982) Post-natal development of the visual cortex and the influence of environment. *Nature*, 229, 583–591.

WILDING, J.M. (1982) *Perception: From Sense to Object*. London: Hutchinson.

WILDING, J.M. & VALENTINE, E.R. (1994) Memory champions. *British Journal of Psychology*, 85, 231–244.

WINGFIELD, A. (1979) *Human Learning and Memory*. New York: Harper & Row.

WITKIN, H.A., DYK, R.B., FATERSON, H.F., GOODENOUGH, D.R. & KARP, S.A. (1962) *Psychological Differentiation*. London: Wiley.

WITTGENSTEIN, L. (1961) *Tractatus Logico-Philosophicus* (translated by D.F. PEARS & B.F. McGUINNESS). London: Routledge & Kegan Paul (originally published in 1921).

WOODRUFF, G., PREMACK, D. & KENNEL, K. (1978) Conservation of liquid quantity by the chimpanzee. *Science*, 202, 991–994.

WOODWORTH, R.S. (1938) *Experimental Psychology*. New York: Holt.

WRIGHT, D.B. (1993) Recall of the Hillsborough disaster over time: Systematic biases of 'flashbulb' memories. *Applied Cognitive Psychology*, 7, 129–138.

WULF, F. (1922) Über die Veränderung von Vorstellungen. *Psychologisch Forschung*, 1, 333–373.

WYMAN, A. (1983) Animal talk: Instinct or intelligence? *Detroit Free Press*, 25 October, 1B, 2B.

YARBUS, A.L. (1967) *Eye Movements and Vision* (translated by B. HAIGH). New York: Plenum.

YERKES, R.M. & LEARNED, B.W. (1925) *Chimpanzee Intelligence and its Vocal Expression*. Baltimore, MD: Williams & Wilkins.

YESAVAGE, J.A. & ROSE, T.L. (1984) Semantic elaboration and the method of loci: A new trip for old learners. *Experimental Aging Research*, 10, 155–160.

YOUNG, C.V. (1971) *The Magic of a Mighty Memory*. West Nyack, NY: Parker Publishing Company.

YUILLE, J.C. & CUTSHALL, J.L. (1986) A case study of eyewitness memory of a crime. *Journal of Applied Psychology*, 71, 291–301.

ZINBERG, D.S. (1997) Ebonics unleashes tongues. *The Times Higher Education Supplement*, 14 February, 14.

INDEX

Page numbers which appear in **bold** refer to definitions and main explanations of principal concepts.

PICTURE CREDITS

The authors and publishers would like to thank the following copyright holders for their permission to reproduce illustrative materials in this book:

American Association for the Advancement of Science for Figure 14.4 (p. 168); **Academic Press Inc.** for Figure 5.4 (p. 61) and Figure 1.11 (p. 14); **BBC Worldwide Ltd** for Figure 16.2 (p. 188); **BFI Stills** for Figure 11.1 (p. 128); **The British Journal of Psychology** for Figure 1.6i (p. 9, bottom); **Colorific** for Figure 14.3 (p. 166); **Corbis-Bettman/UPI** for Figure 16.3 (p. 192) **Cordon Art** for Figure 1.4b (p. 3, right) and 1.8d (p. 11, bottom) M.C. Escher's *Circle Limit IV* and *Relativity* © 1997 Cordon Art – Baarn-Holland. All rights reserved; **Dr. Jon Driver** for Figure 5.6 (p. 64); **Eastern Counties Newspapers Ltd** for Figures 2.6 (p. 25, left); **David Gaskill** for Figure 17.1 (p. 199) © David Gaskill; **Professor Richard L. Gregory** for Figure 2.1 (p. 21, left); **Heldref Publications** for Figure 4.3 (p. 50) from the *Journal of Social Psychology*, 52, 183–208 (1960). Reprinted with permission of the Helen Dwight Reid Educational Foundation. Published by Heldref Publications, 1319, 18th St., N.W., Washington, D.C. 20036-1802. Copyright © 1960; **Kaiser Porcelain Ltd** for Figure 1.4a (p. 3, right); **Life File** for Figure 6.1 (p. 68) © Nicola Sutton and Figure 6.3 (p. 72) © Emma Lee; **The Open University** for the figure in Box 2.3 (p. 28) from Roth, I. and Bruce, V. *Perception and Representation*, 2nd edition (1995); **Prentice Hall** for Figure 16.1 (p. 186); **Private Eye** for Figure 6.4 (p. 75); **Scientific American** for Figure 4.4 (p. 51); **Times Newspapers Ltd** for Figure 13.2 (p. 154) © Peter Brooks/*The Times*, 1996; **Weidenfeld & Nicolson Ltd.** for Figure 1.2 (p. 2, right); **Worth Publishers Inc.** for the figure in Box 1.1 (p. 4, centre, right) from David G. Myers, *Exploring Psychology*, Second Edition, Worth Publishers, New York, 1993. Used with permission.

Every effort has been made to obtain necessary permission with reference to copyright material. The publishers apologise if inadvertently any sources remain unacknowledged and will be glad to make the necessary arrangements at the earliest opportunity.

Index prepared by Frank Merrett, Cheltenham, Gloucs.